LIMERICK CITY LIBRARY

Phone: 407510
Website:
　merickcity.ie/library
　itylib@limerickcity.ie

The Granary,
Michael Street,
Limerick.

ok is issu d s bject to the Rules of this Library.
　rned not later than the last date
　low.

9907

HIGGY

MATCHES, MICROPHONES AND MS

ALASTAIR HIGNELL

BLOOMSBURY

Published in 2011 by Bloomsbury Publishing Plc
50 Bedford Square, London WC1B 3DP
www.bloomsbury.com

First edition 2011
Reprinted 2011

Copyright © 2011 Alastair Hignell

ISBN 978-1-4081-2924-1

Cover photographs © Getty Images and © Shutterstock
Designed by James Watson
Commissioned by Charlotte Atyeo
Edited by Kate Wanwimolruk

This book is produced using paper that is made from wood grown in managed, sustainable forests. It is natural, renewable and recyclable. The logging and manufacturing processes conform to the environmental regulations of the country of origin.

Typeset in Tibere by seagulls.net

Printed and bound in Great Britain by Clays Ltd, St Ives plc

Picture credits: All photographs © Alastair Hignell with the exception of the Picture section pages 4 (bottom), 12 (top), 13 (bottom), 16 (top) © Press As Images; 7 © Getty Images; 14 (bottom), 15 courtesy of Stroud News and 16 (bottom) Charles Green Photography

CONTENTS

PREFACE
14 December 2008, The Echo Arena, Liverpool

One after the other the gleaming limos pull up. One after the other the sports stars emerge, blinking against the lights and step on to the seemingly mile-long purple carpet. Paparazzi and autograph hunters jostle each other behind the barricades. Flashbulbs pop, cheers go up, and TV cameras follow potential winners through the swing doors and on into the bowels of the building. It's the eagerly awaited *BBC Sports Personality of the Year Awards* 2008 in the phenomenal auditorium at the state-of-the-art Echo Arena in Liverpool. The air buzzes as sporting icons, champions and record-breakers chat excitedly with administrators, umpires and commentators. A stentorian voice on the PA system invites them all to take their seats. The atmosphere crackles with tension. An audience of nearly ten thousand waits expectantly, enthralled by the Formula One car suspended from the ceiling and the startlingly steep ramp that descends from an entrance high up on one side of the hall to the centre of the auditorium. Fingers point wonderingly at the glittering array of trophies on plinths at the side of the hall, and the massed ranks of the BBC Concert Orchestra in front of the stage.

Nine million television viewers settle back in their seats as Gary Lineker, Sue Barker and new boy Jake Humphrey get the 55th running of the *BBC Sports Personality of the Year* underway. It had been an Olympic year, and most of the athletes who had helped Britain to a record medal haul are present, dressed up to the nines in their best party frocks and their sharpest suits, only too happy to parade their medals and take the salute of a rapturous audience.

Joe Calzaghe, winner of the award the previous year, marches onto the stage with the trophy. He's a contender for the award yet again, and so too is tennis star Andy Murray (whose absence suggests he won't win this year). The top-ten contenders have been nominated by the BBC and the viewing public invited to vote.

Then, after about 25 minutes, just after the radiantly smiling Paralympics swimmer Ellie Simmonds has received the Young Sports Personality of the Year award, Sue Barker turns to the camera. 'Our next award is presented in honour of our late and much-loved BBC colleague Helen Rollason who died of cancer in 1999... This award is for courage and achievement in the face of adversity, and this year's recipient has those qualities in abundance, as Lawrence Dallaglio now describes...'

The unmistakable, square-jawed former England captain pops up on the many huge overhead screens, showing pictures of the Guinness Premiership final, the acutely memorable day of my last rugby commentary six months previously. 'A few of us rugby players decided to call it a day at the end of last season but, of all of us, there's one man who deserves a global fanfare. He hung up his microphone that day, but he'd already hung up his boots some thirty years ago. And it's fair to say there hasn't been anyone really like him ever since. Alastair Hignell, or "Higgy" as he is fondly known, didn't just play Test rugby for England; he also hit a century against the West Indies. A really gifted sportsman, he was the first man to captain Cambridge University at both rugby and cricket.'

Film footage of my sporting career fills the screens – me commentating, flashbacks of me proudly playing rugby for England as a slim, bearded 23-year-old, with long hair and huge, old-fashioned rugby boots, then a recent clip of me struggling painfully up a staircase to interview players...

'For over a decade his listeners on Radio Five Live would have been completely unaware of the challenges he has faced. He has been battling a virulent form of multiple sclerosis, which simply doesn't give up. Fortunately for us, neither does Higgy. Whenever I came off an international rugby pitch, he always had the right words to say to me – whether we'd won a game, or whether we'd lost a game. It was never about him – it was always about you. Together with his wife, Jeannie, they've worked to help campaign and raise awareness, to fund research so that others suffering from MS may have a better quality of life than Alastair has been able to have so far...'

The screens show me on my trusty mobility scooter applauding at the Stroud half-marathon as exhausted charity runners stagger across the finish line, including my wife Jeannie, with her arms aloft and a dazzling smile...

'I feel very privileged and proud to have retired on the same day as you. You will be sorely missed by all your friends – week in week out. Higgy, I salute you and I'm honoured to be your friend.'

The cameras swing round to where I am sitting alongside my wife Jeannie and our sons Adam and Dan, as the BBC Concert Orchestra starts to play the incredibly moving Robbie Williams ballad, 'Angels'. It's all I can do to fight back the tears of emotion as I haul myself unsteadily to my feet, adjust my stick and pray that my slightly too large, rarely worn, shiny black shoes won't cause me to slip on the walk up to the stage. Ten yards on the flat, then a shallow slope. I'm concentrating on my feet but become aware of an extraordinary noise reverberating all around me. Almost ten thousand people are applauding. My face contorts as I try even harder to keep back the tears. I look up to see Sir Clive Woodward waiting to present me with the trophy, BBC colleagues Ian Robertson and Jill Douglas, Eddie Butler, who was at Cambridge with me, Bill Beaumont my captain in the England side, Matt Dawson, Martin Bayfield and Hugo MacNeill who've worked alongside me in the commentary box, legendary England props Jason Leonard and Gareth Chilcott, former Wales captain Rob Jones and my great friends through the charity connections, Lawrence and Rachel Wood – all of them standing on stage – for me. By then I'm really choked but somehow manage to hold it together just long enough to speak:

'I consider myself deeply honoured to find my name alongside previous winners of this award and that of Helen herself. I have always considered myself a very lucky man to have had not just one career in sport but three – in rugby, cricket and broadcasting. And since my diagnosis with MS I have discovered just how blessed I am in having a wonderful wife, Jeannie, and a fantastic friend, Ian Robertson. My employers at the BBC have been brilliant in helping me to squeeze an extra seven, eight, maybe nine years in the commentary box. It's been a great time and I've had enormous support and encouragement from producer Ed Marriage and the rugby media. But above all I've had the good will and warmth and generosity of the sporting world in particular, and the rugby world in general. And I know this: I really am a very lucky man ... Thank you.'

PART ONE
MS (ANGER)

CHAPTER ONE

EARLY WARNINGS

I should have known there was something seriously wrong when I came within a centimetre of spilling a glass of red wine onto the cream carpet of our living room. I joke now that while my wife Jeannie, whose cry alerted me to the imminent disaster, was more concerned about the carpet, I was more worried about the wine – a particularly enjoyable Chianti, if memory serves. In truth, we were both aghast at what had happened to my right arm.

My shoulder had rotated forwards and inwards, while my wrist had twisted and dropped and my fingers had begun to lose their grip on the glass. I hadn't noticed, or felt a thing.

A few weeks later, my arm let me down again – this time at work. I had just finished reporting on a match at Gloucester for *Sport on Five*. Just after the post-match press conference, I asked Richard Hill, then Gloucester's director of rugby, for an interview for the 'Sports Report' section of the programme. We stepped outside the Portakabin, which in those days served as Kingsholm's media centre, I switched on my minidisc recorder and then watched – in embarrassment more than alarm – as the microphone in my hand began to shake. While one part of my brain was concentrating on asking intelligent questions, another part was screaming silent instructions to my right arm to keep still. As the arm still wouldn't behave, I had to surreptitiously bring my left hand – the one still holding the minidisc recorder – up and forward to grab my right elbow. While I struggled desperately to keep my eyes on my interviewee and my mind on the questions, I was equally desperate that Richard wouldn't notice my discomfort and that the extraordinary stance I had adopted wouldn't cause me to switch off the recorder by accident.

Both these episodes were temporary, and the effects so short-lived that it was tempting to dismiss them as the result of cramp or bad weather. Maybe I had inadvertently adopted a bad posture over a long period of time and the spasms were just instinctive corrections by the arm? Maybe the tremors were caused by delayed reaction to cold weather? At Gloucester, for instance, I had been squashed into an open-air commentary box in the freezing cold for two and a half hours before spending 15 minutes in an overcrowded, overheated press conference and then stepped straight outside again into the icy evening.

But one thing that didn't go away was the alternate tingling and numbness in my right thumb and forefinger. I had originally noticed it after an evening match at Leicester. Initially, I thought it was chilblains; my hands had got painfully cold – I have poor circulation anyway – and then painfully warm as the blood rushed back. That tingling had died down but never really gone away. The right arm felt fuller somehow, more solid than the left arm and certainly less sensitive.

Never having experienced anything like it, I reckoned that was how a trapped nerve would manifest itself; my GP agreed and, in the belief that this was probably the result of an old rugby injury, packed me off to a specialist. He wired up my arm, sent electric current down all the relevant pathways, checked out my left arm, my back and my legs for good measure – and found nothing worth reporting.

The orthopaedic surgeon who examined my right leg made the same point, but much more vehemently. He had performed a hip replacement operation some 15 months previously and rejected outright any suggestion that anything might have gone wrong. He even brandished the X-rays as proof that he'd done an excellent job. And, to be fair, even my untutored eye could see that the replacement looked strong, clean, solid and beautifully positioned with regard to the rest of the leg. So why, a year or so on from the operation, was I finding it as difficult as ever to get around? Why, much more alarmingly, was my foot dragging every time I attempted a long walk? Why was I tripping over myself with increasing regularity? Why, just occasionally, did I fall heavily to the ground?

The alarm bells had rung on a walk round Tickenham in north Somerset. We'd walked the Cotswold Way a decade or so earlier, when our sons Adam and Dan were seven and six respectively, and still counted it as one of our most enjoyable holidays ever. As a result, we planned even more adventurous long walks in the future and kept in practice in the short term, whenever time allowed, by attempting some of the beautiful circular walks in the Bristol and Bath area. The Tickenham walk was only moderately demanding but when it came to a long uphill stretch through the woods towards the end of the ramble, I kept tripping over. I just couldn't get my right foot to lift high enough off the ground to guarantee I kept climbing the slope. The ground always seemed to be there before my foot was ready to tread on it. The harder I tried to lift the foot to clear the path, the more tired I became. The harder I tried to compensate with my left leg, the more I compromised my balance. By the time the walk was over, I was staggering and stumbling all over the place, and both legs ached as if I'd spent a hundred overs in the cricket field on a hot summer's day.

But the surgeon was adamant there was nothing wrong orthopaedically. Perhaps all this was referred pain from my back? I had several sessions with a chiropractor off the Gloucester Road in Bristol before concluding that the answer was no. Perhaps the nerve pathways were somehow blocked? I tried a course of acupuncture at a private clinic on the Downs with the same result. Perhaps I needed to strengthen the relevant muscles through concentrated training? I started swimming 50-plus lengths at the baths in north Bristol of a lunchtime and cycling round the Downs before breakfast. But the swimming did nothing for the foot-drop while the cycling almost did for me altogether. Returning from a five-mile workout one morning, I came to a halt at a T-junction. When I put out my right leg to balance on the ground while waiting for the traffic to pass, it gave way completely. I was catapulted out onto the main road, all tangled up in bike and entirely at the mercy of the oncoming cars. By some minor miracle, the lead car slowed and I escaped with minor damage to my knees and major damage to my pride.

But it was my dignity that was most compromised by another of the rogue symptoms that were eventually to lead to my diagnosis. My bladder became unreliable. The first time I wet myself was in Australia. I'd been sent to Brisbane to commentate on a Wales-Australia Test in 1996, a stopover on the way to New Zealand where Scotland had already embarked on a month-long tour. After the match, I'd had dinner with the travelling Welsh journalists, followed by a few drinks. Walking the few blocks back to my hotel, I'd recognised the familiar warning signs from my bladder but calculated that I would have plenty of time to reach my room. I collected my key, took the lift, walked to my room at the far end of the corridor and discovered not only that the swipe-card key wouldn't work but also that I had lost control of my bladder. Within seconds, what seemed like gallons of urine had soaked my trousers and formed a huge pool on the corridor carpet. My only consolation was that it was so late that nobody else was up and about, but I was so mortified that I didn't want to run the risk of sharing a lift with anyone as I went to get another key. I therefore squelched past the elevators to the very end of the corridor and down the six flights of stairs to reception, waddled over to the desk with as much nonchalance as I could muster, got another key cut, and splashed my way back to my room. The rest of the corridor didn't look too bad but there was such a telltale pool outside the door that, after changing my underpants and trousers, I spread the remaining room towels over the offending puddle and, with the help of the room-issue hairdryer, managed to erase the embarrassing evidence before my neighbours started stirring for breakfast.

I'd still managed to dismiss the incident as a temporary aberration, and I had any number of excuses to hand. I'd been jet-lagged, and maybe a little bit inebriated. I could no longer drink like I used to, and I'd been incredibly unlucky that the key-card wouldn't work. I knew I'd escaped huge embarrassment by the skin of my teeth. I would never let it happen again.

But then, driving home via a short cut across the Downs in late 1998, I suddenly realised that I was not even going to make it to my front door. I had none of those carefully thought through excuses. I wasn't jet-lagged and I had hardly drunk anything all evening and yet, if I didn't get out of the car right there and then, my bladder was going to empty immediately. It was only later I appreciated the irony attached to the location: Ladies' Mile had been so named because in the 19th century it had become a well-known haunt for prostitutes. A hundred or so years on, here was another bloke unbuttoning in haste – for an entirely different reason!

At the time I was consumed with horror. Amateur psychologists will say that it all went back to the days of a painfully insecure seven-year-old at boarding school for the first time, when bed-wetters were subjected to merciless teasing from their peers. Whatever, I was embarrassed even by the thought of incontinence. The thought that I might suffer from it was not only embarrassing; it was also deeply humiliating and absolutely shameful.

The urologists poked tubes into my penis, fed water into me and measured it on the way out, poked and prodded around my nether regions and pronounced that essentially there was nothing wrong with my bladder. All I had to do was pay attention to the warning signs and accept that, as I got older (I was only 43, for God's sake!), I might have to consider drinking halves rather than pints and re-learn a mantra we'd adopted for the kids when they were younger, 'Always go before you go!'

While it was a huge relief, pardon the pun, to discover I was not incontinent, and actually had nothing wrong with my waterworks, I still did not link my experiences in Brisbane and on the Downs to any of the other medical problems that had been causing concern over the last couple of years. Nor did my GP, until I booked another appointment to discuss the onset of severe migraine-like headaches and a sense of utter fatigue. I was knackered and couldn't explain it, and my head hurt too. She immediately referred me for an MRI scan.

The MRI scan gave me a free preview of what it's like to be in a coffin, except that I was fully alive and therefore fully aware of every groan and creak made by the machine in the thirty or so minutes I had to lie absolutely still inside it. It was like being in an old elevator stuck between floors, and a lot less fun. Basically an MRI scanner is a large metal tube surrounded by a giant circular magnet, which produces a picture of the body's internal organs by scanning tiny radio signals emitted from it. The more still you are, the better the picture. Mind you, as I lay on a couch and was slid into the contraption I couldn't help thinking that there were no other options. It was completely claustrophobic.

Still the radiographers were happy enough with the picture I produced, and the neurosurgeon felt it warranted further discussion. A fortnight later I was on my way to Outpatients.

CHAPTER TWO

DIAGNOSIS

Friday 8 January 1999, Neurology Outpatients, Southmead Hospital, Bristol

They speak a different language in the NHS. I had no idea then that 'appointment' meant 'clinic' and that, when they give a time, they always omit the prefix 'from'. While I checked in at the huge desk at the back of the poetically named Outpatients 3 in the expectation that I might see a senior neurological consultant pretty close to the time designated on the letter I presented, the reality was that the named consultant might or might not turn up depending on his commitments, the clinic might or might not start on time, depending on other vague and never specified hospital emergencies, and in any case, four others had also been given the same time and had already checked in. So if I wouldn't mind waiting...

Even though I had never imagined there would be any reason to bring something to read, the first hour flew by. The following day, Saturday, was always the busiest day of my working week and the enforced inactivity of the waiting room gave me a golden opportunity to run a mental checklist over an inevitably complicated weekend.

This one was more unpredictable than most. For a start it was a Tetley's Bitter Cup weekend and, as that competition was still at the interesting stage when giant-killings were a possibility, I was scheduled to cover Sedgeley Park, then as now a modest lower-league outfit, against Wasps, then as now one of the best teams in the land. I was not exactly stepping into the unknown for I'd already traipsed up the M5/M6 during the week to do a feature for *Sport on Five* on Dewi Morris, the ex-Lions and England scrum-half now acting as a sort of consultant for the Manchester-based club. Truth be told, I didn't think I'd need to know too many Sedgeley Park names, while I'd covered Wasps a fair bit in the last few seasons and I had even interviewed that weekend's debutant Fraser Waters when he was a student at Bristol University and I was at HTV. In any case, there was to be no commentary, so instant recognition was not quite so imperative. What was going to make my job so much harder was the lack of facilities at the Sedgeley Park ground. The Beeb had judged it hardly worth installing a temporary ISDN point for me to do the sort of reports that are the staple diet of the *Sport on Five* programme. Instead, I was to keep more of a watching brief, on hand in the unlikely event of an upset, but otherwise expected to use my mobile to add a bit of colour on very few occasions throughout the afternoon.

The mobile was on charge, there was petrol in the car and I'd already compiled and filed my regional radio wrap – a weekly, illustrated preview of all the weekend's big rugby fixtures – which BBC Sport disseminated to the regions every Friday lunchtime. Time to concentrate on domestic arrangements for the weekend. My wife Jeannie was in Atlanta, Georgia, on a company buying trip. She would be away all weekend; responsibility for our two teenage sons, Adam and Dan, rested with me and, providentially, with Jeannie's widowed mum, who lived in the next suburb to our house in Bristol.

I rehearsed the weekend arrangements. Both boys were at school that Friday morning; I would drop them round to their Nana's on the Saturday before heading for Sedgeley Park; Adam, aged 17 and in the Lower Sixth at Bristol Cathedral School, had a hockey match for the school, while Dan, 15, would be spending the afternoon with friends. They would both sleep at our house on Saturday night and would set off from there on Monday morning for another day at school. Sunday would be spent knocking around with their mates, theoretically catching up on schoolwork and coinciding with me when they wanted feeding.

The second hour passed infinitely more slowly. There's only so many out-of-date *Autotraders* a non-petrolhead can skim through before terminal boredom sets in, while the alternatives promised either to get up close and personal with a Hollywood starlet I'd never heard of or up close and personal with a medical condition that was equally unknown and twice as embarrassing.

After establishing that a trip to the nearest newspaper kiosk would mean leaving the building and losing my place in the queue for the consultant, I settled down to people watching. A couple diagonally opposite attracted my attention: he, unkempt and overweight, slumped awkwardly in his seat, she, petite and beautifully turned out, perched on the edge of hers. He had a vacant, almost nonplussed expression on his face, while his gaze seemed fixed somewhere in the middle-distance. Her face was pinched with worry and her eyes never left him. When he hauled himself to his feet and tottered away, leaning heavily on a stick, in the direction of the loo, she thrust out her hand as if to defy all laws of physics and catch him if he fell. After he had moved away, she left her arm extended in a sort of silent prayer that no accident would befall him out of her sight.

Poor things, I thought. How awful for him to be so imprisoned by a condition that every spark of self should appear to have been extinguished, and every simple action should appear so difficult and require such concentration. How awful for her that the presumably once vibrant, probably once agile man she had committed herself to had turned into this shambling wreck with so little apparent awareness of his surroundings and so little control of his body. I would never be like that. We would never be like that.

Not, that Friday morning in January, that there seemed any danger. I was 43, if not quite in the prime of life, then not far from it. I was pretty healthy, eating well, sleeping well and exercising regularly. Sure, I had a few niggles, a few unexplained symptoms but then, who hadn't? Sure, I was waiting to see a consultant in a neurosurgery outpatients' department, but I expected him to give me a simple explanation, a pat on the back, maybe a bit of advice to take things a bit easier and, above all, reassurance that there was nothing wrong with me that couldn't be fixed.

That had always been an easy assumption to make. Growing up in a medical family – my father and one of my brothers were doctors, my mother and sister had been nurses – and never having encountered chronic illness or disability, I never had any reason to doubt the power of medical science. Whenever I had been ill before, the doctors had always come up with a medicine or a treatment that could make me better. This time was going to be no different. And anyway, the symptoms that had triggered the recommendation for an MRI scan had all but disappeared in the intervening few weeks. I still felt tired, but that was because the job was demanding as well as satisfying. And, in all those years of playing two sports at the highest level, of burning the candle at both ends on rugby tours and on the cricket circuit, of partying till dawn as a student, of marking books late into the night while teaching, of taking my turn nappy-changing in the small hours as a new parent, of meeting the needs of a 24-hour radio station, I'd never had a problem with re-charging my batteries. If at times I had lived life at a hundred miles an hour and if occasionally I had hit a wall of exhaustion, I had always been able to pick myself up and, after only a minor readjustment, get straight back in the fast lane. This, I had no doubt, was going to be no different.

The next half-hour was a bit of a blank. As the nurse apparently responsible for escorting patients into the presence of the neurosurgeon marked yet another delay on the whiteboard with my consultant's name on it, I had just worked out precisely why hospitals keep the windows closed and the heat turned up in their waiting rooms – in the hope that patients would fall asleep and forget just how long they had been kept waiting – when my eyelids started to droop...

I awoke to a hand on my shoulder and voice in my ear, 'Mr Hignell, the consultant will see you now.' I followed the nurse out of the waiting room, down a short corridor and into an examining-room with a large desk, a couple of chairs a couch and a tall, slender, academic-looking fifty-something with a ready smile and hair that was slightly too long. If he wasn't wearing a bowtie, he should have been. It turned out that he knew of my rugby past as well as my current calling – which gave us the opportunity to establish an immediate rugby-based familiarity. He asked me to take my shoes and socks off, roll up my trousers and hop on the couch, where he proceeded to tap my knee with a mallet, scratch my foot with a pin, and test my grip with an arm-wrestle. He looked in my eyes, examined my coordination by getting me to alternately touch his finger and my nose, and felt my feet and hands to see if the temperature differed between right and left. At each successive exercise he nodded as if confirming something to himself, before inviting me to put my shoes and socks back on and sit at the chair in front of my desk. He explained the results of my MRI scan which highlighted the presence of some scattered and tiny white pinpricks on the otherwise grey mass of my brain. 'These are scars' he said, 'from some previous damage to the central nervous system. The Latin name for scars is scleroses and, as you can see, there are lots of them. I want to run some more tests but I'm pretty certain you've got multiple sclerosis. How much do you know about MS?'

CHAPTER THREE
DAYS AFTER DIAGNOSIS

What kind of hospital was this? I'd gone in expecting an answer and come out with a question. What kind of a consultant asks you a question and then just bids you goodbye? I'd expected him to give me a diagnosis, an analysis of cause and effect and an action plan both to mend whatever was wrong with me and to prevent its recurrence. Instead of definites, I'd got some probables, a couple of possibles, a definite don't know and an invitation to return for more tests. At least, he'd given me a couple of words to latch on to. Probably.

What did I know of multiple sclerosis? Not a lot, to be honest. Enough to know that it was something to do with the nervous system – or was it the brain? – and that a male cousin and the wife of a college friend had been diagnosed half a dozen years previously. I was – still am – a terrible correspondent, so I didn't know much more than that. I was vaguely aware that my cousin had had the diagnosis and little else, while my friend's wife was 'struggling' – how badly, I had no idea.

The other thing I knew about MS was that I couldn't have it. A friend, an ex-nurse, had said that it usually affected young people – under 40s in her definition – and, as I was by now 43, the chances of my having MS were small. Anyway, I'd looked it up in the only vaguely medical book we had at home – Andrew Lockie's *The Family Guide to Homeopathy* – and discounted it.

Lockie defines MS as 'damage to nerve fibres in the central nervous system caused by inflammation of the fatty tissue (myelin) which sheathes and insulates them'. I couldn't see that applying to me. I just didn't have the imagination or the experience to think beyond the specifics. There was something – some things – wrong with bits of me, but I just couldn't accept that there was something wrong with all of me. I knew what pulled muscles, strained ligaments and broken bones were. I knew how to react to them, how to cope with them. They were site-specific. Damage to a whole system – one I'd only been vaguely aware of, one I'd always taken for granted – was somehow beyond my comprehension.

Nerves? I knew what nerves did. They gave that faintly nauseous feeling before you went out to bat or before you ran out to play an international. They were also exhilarating. They sent the blood racing round your body and they raised the hairs on the back of your neck. They were the pulses of excitement that preceded every big test. They were the chemicals that got the brain whirring at the start of an exam, the triggers that identified players during a commentary and provided the right words to describe them in an instant. I was absolutely convinced that nerves were good and that my nerves were in great shape. Naively, I equated bad nerves with tics and twitches and timidity. And, I prided myself, I had none of those.

Lockie went on to describe the 'first signs, often noticed after a hot bath or exercise, may be tingling, NUMBNESS, or weakness, affecting a hand, foot or one side of the body, DOUBLE VISION, or things suddenly looking misty or blurred' and to declare that these signs disappear after a day or two and, while for some people they never reappear, for others they are 'repeated and lead to some measure of disability, depending on severity and frequency'.

I reasoned myself out of that pretty easily. Sure I'd got the numbness and the tingling, and the weakness affecting a hand, and a foot and, OK, one side of the body but, and these considerations had so much more weight for me than any other argument, I didn't have DOUBLE VISION, things didn't look misty or blurred, I didn't notice things get worse after a hot bath and my symptoms didn't disappear after a day or two. They stayed with me. So there!

A combination of selective amnesia and wilful blindness worked pretty well for the rest of the description. According to *The Family Guide to Homeopathy*, one line of research into the cause of MS 'points to a virus, another to congenital defects in the myelin coating of nerves'. My brain dismissed both ideas as impertinences. How could I, who had always been fit, healthy and brimming over with energy, have had a virus, particularly one I had never noticed? How could I, descendant of a long line of long-living, robust, vital high achievers, have a congenital weakness? And as for the suggestion that 'MS is attributed to inherent weakness of the nervous system, aggravated by trauma, shock, infection, toxic metals or solar radiation', how could that apply to me? How preposterous of Doctor Lockie! How naive of me!

What was I thinking? Did I imagine that by ignoring the words that had just been spoken to me I could get them unsaid? Did I think that I could will myself into a parallel universe from which the last hour could be expunged? Did I seriously believe that if I blocked out the diagnosis it wouldn't apply? Was I seriously convinced that a terrible mistake had been made and that the follow-up tests on Wednesday would show that after all there wasn't really very much wrong with me?

'Yes' was the answer to all those questions. I headed back from Southmead Hospital on autopilot. I phoned the office for any last-minute instructions, made supper for the boys and myself, watched some telly and went to bed. On the Saturday I drove to Sedgeley Park, reported on a predictable Wasps victory, drove home and had a glass of wine before going to bed. The next day I had a lie-in, sorted the boys out, read the papers and meandered down to the Memorial Ground, where Bristol, as expected, were beaten by London Irish. A pasty before the game, a couple of pints with friends after it – the time-honoured and much-cherished rituals reinforced the cocoon of normality. It was only when I'd got back home, and Adam and Dan had been persuaded of the advisability of completing long overdue homework, that I allowed myself to consider – in a hypothetical way, of course, since one part of my brain was still hell-bent on rewriting the history of the last few days – just what was meant by MS.

This time I was scared witless. This time my eyes only saw words like neuropsychiatric disorder, cognitive disability and damage to the brain and spinal cord. My imagination took flight at the thought of an immune system attacking itself and a nervous system failing to send effective signals to different parts of the body. My brain registered that the cause of MS was still unknown and nobody knew how to cure it or even to predict the course it would take. Everywhere I looked I couldn't see past reports that the drugs to treat MS were often poorly tolerated, that alternative therapies were unproven, off-the-wall or bogus, that in the majority of cases the disease was progressive and that the end of that progression was disability.

Disability! The word struck terror into my heart. I don't think I'd ever shied away from it, but I'd never embraced it either. I inhabited a fit, active, sporty, able-bodied world; none of my family was disabled, and none of my friends. I'd known a couple of teachers who got around on wheelchairs and in invalid cars but I hadn't really registered anything else about them. Insomuch as I gave much thought to disabled people, I admired those I'd heard of who overcame the difficulties placed in front of them and philosophically I espoused their rights to be treated the same as the rest of society. But that's about as far as it went. I'd never really imagined that I would ever come face-to-face with disability. I was totally unprepared for the thought that I might become disabled. And especially not for the fact that, if my frantic Internet research was to be believed, it wouldn't be long...

CHAPTER FOUR
'IT'S NOT YOUR MS, IT'S OURS'

It is the best thing anybody's ever said to me, bar none. The speaker was my wife Jeannie, seconds after I had broken the news that I had in all probability contracted a disease that had no known cause, no known cure, a totally unpredictable course and a strong chance of leaving me confined to a wheelchair, and possibly bedridden.

We were sitting at the kitchen table of our house in the Westbury Park suburb of Bristol. Jeannie had returned only moments before from her business trip to Atlanta and, though tired from the flight, was understandably fired up from the whole experience. After a near-sleepless night in the grip of the terror induced by my research into MS, I was hovering somewhere at the opposite end of the emotional spectrum. But I'd done my limited best to make the house look tidy and I'd been out and bought a bunch of flowers for Jeannie. And then I'd hit her with the devastating news of my diagnosis.

And this amazing woman, my wife of 18 years, the mother of our teenage sons, hadn't batted an eyelid, hadn't stopped for a single second to feel sorry for herself and in a single sentence given me the most amazing message. As I had tossed and turned throughout the small hours of the morning, all my nightmares had been centred on myself. In my mind's eye I'd pictured a gradual loss of control over my limbs, my balance, my bladder and my vision: I'd envisaged the disappearance of my memory, my perception and eventually my mind; I'd projected myself onto crutches, into a wheelchair and finally into a nursing home; I'd seen myself surrendering my dignity, my control and my personality to the dreadful and inexorable march of the disease. And in every nightmare I was on my own.

But Jeannie's words pierced the bubble of despair just as it was threatening to take off into the stratosphere. In a single sentence she tamed the wildest of my wild imaginings, restored the perspective that had gone missing overnight, and gave me the strength to face up to whatever it was that the future would throw – not at me, but at us.

Of course neither of us could know what that future might hold. We had no idea how the disease would develop and how it would change us. We couldn't possibly guess at the demands it would make on us, as individuals and as a couple, and on our families, friends and colleagues. We hadn't the faintest idea, that Monday in January 2009, how just about every aspect of our lives would have to be re-shaped to deal with the new reality. Probably just as well. But acknowledging that fact there and then, and resolving, babes-in-the-wood style, to cling together for the duration enabled us to put things in perspective, and make a start.

The first thing we decided was that it was better to assume I had MS, and hope that the follow-up tests would turn out negative, than the opposite. But we also decided that we didn't want to put ourselves through a mind-blowing succession of long-winded explanations – we both come from large close-knit families – about something we didn't yet understand and which might (just possibly, please God!) turn into a false alarm. I was due to return to Frenchay for the night on Wednesday with a lumbar puncture and something called an 'evoked potentials' test preceding a Thursday afternoon appointment with the neurosurgeon. A white lie was needed to explain to the BBC why it would be impossible for me to attend any midweek media briefings. Slightly less subterfuge was needed to prevent Adam and Dan suspecting anything. As teenagers they were completely engrossed in their own lives. As boys, they hadn't really got the hang of empathy, and nor would they for several years to come. As sons, they hadn't had much of a role model. I was very locked-up at the time. Call it introverted, call it repressed, call it private; blame it on boarding school or the self-orientated world of top-class sport, where it was regarded as weakness to show your feelings, whatever. I was pretty buttoned-up, and the boys had every excuse for not noticing what was going on with their dad.

So, when we told them I was going in to hospital for some tests, it barely registered. If they felt that there was something momentous about the appointment, or that there was something to worry about, or that there was an extra tension around the house, they didn't show it, and there was no reason for them to do so.

The thought of that lumbar puncture brings tears to my eyes, even now. In people with multiple sclerosis the number of white cells is up to seven times higher than normal, while the antibodies which should be fighting infection have attacked the myelin surrounding the nerves have proliferated as well. The idea of a lumbar puncture is to get hold of some cerebro-spinal fluid – the fluid that surrounds the brain (cerebrum) and spinal cord – and check for abnormally high numbers of white blood cells and antibodies.

And how! Or should that be ow! A local anaesthetic was needed before a large needle – it was a good job I had my back to the medic and couldn't see just how big – was inserted in the space between two vertebrae and left there for the best part of two minutes. That's what the book says. My horror-filled memory says that the needle was at least ten inches long, twice as thick as normal and was left in my back for half an hour. It also tells me the lumbar puncture gave me the most excruciating headache of my life. Admittedly, I was told to lie still after the injection but I woke up desperate for a pee and took myself off to the toilet. When I got back, wave after wave of agony crashed around my skull for the best part of an hour – and quite took my mind off hospital food.

The evoked potentials test was conducted the next morning at a different hospital. For a clear diagnosis of MS, the doctor has to find evidence that multiple parts of the central nervous system are affected, so, in separate tests, my eyes were stimulated by looking at a test pattern, my hearing was stimulated by listening to a test tone, and the nerves of my arms and legs were stimulated by an electrical pulse before the findings were sent off to the neurosurgeon.

Bedside manner had he none. I admit that, as he – decked out in a bowtie and accompanied by a retinue of fawning acolytes – confirmed my worst fears, I wasn't at my most receptive, or my most appreciative. I acknowledge also that there may not have been a way of dressing it up or playing it down. I sympathise entirely with professionals who from time to time have to be the bearers of bad news. I accept that patients have to play their part in what should, at least in part, be a dialogue. But Jeannie, who was going to be every bit as affected as I was, was equally frustrated. The surgeon's visit left us with feelings of utter futility, hopelessness and isolation – and that can't be right. We had in effect been handed a life sentence with absolutely no possibility of time off for good behaviour. The surgeon's parting platitudes – along the lines of, 'Well, it may not be as bad as you imagine' – were undoubtedly true and well meant, but they were totally unsatisfactory. We wanted information – not just about the disease but also about the treatments available. We wanted guidance – not just on how to deal with MS, but where to go to find out more. We wanted far more encouragement than he was prepared to give.

What we got was a hospital leaflet, an appointment to come back in three months' time and a course of steroids, which, if nothing else, served to show just how much of a mystery MS really is. Steroids have been a standard MS treatment for fifty years and still nobody knows exactly how they help. Some studies have shown that they are effective in speeding up recovery from relapse, while others indicate that they actually make no difference either to the degree of recovery or to the long-term progression of the condition. As far as I was concerned, steroids spelled hyperactivity. I felt as if I was on a dozen cups of coffee a day. I couldn't relax and I couldn't sleep. I couldn't concentrate and I couldn't switch off. I was wired up and ready to explode, and I could feel myself just going through the motions for Radio Five Live. The first Saturday after diagnosis, I remember driving up to the Stoop to cover a match between Harlequins and Northampton and feeling suddenly unable to join in the press-room banter. I covered the match in a preoccupied and perfunctory sort of way and instead of hanging about for a chat – as had been my habit for years – I just got back in the car and drove home.

It is fair to say that, if not in shock, we were in limbo. We didn't know how to BE anymore. We'd been given a label but did not know what it meant. We certainly didn't want to wear it on our foreheads. We were desperate to turn the clock back to BD – before diagnosis – but couldn't. While we knew that life would no longer be the same, we didn't know how it would change, or what control we would have over it.

We sought guidance wherever we could find it. The Church of England had been a central part of both our upbringings, and although we were lapsed churchgoers, both of us felt the need for some sort of spiritual peace. We took ourselves off to Evensong in the magnificent setting of Bristol Cathedral in a bid to acquire it. Whether it worked or not, we came up with a plan. The MS would be our secret. We would tell close family for the time being, but no one else. While we made a pact to make time to discuss the emotional and psychological effects of the disease, as well as its physical presentations, we also resolved not to go public yet. We just weren't ready for that. At least I wasn't.

For a start I didn't feel afflicted. I wasn't even unwell. I'd had a few symptoms that had puzzled me, but if I'd had to assess my state of health, I'd have unhesitatingly said it was good. I was still reasonably fit, still reasonably active and, if I had to, I could run to catch a bus. It's true that I couldn't run round the Downs any more but that was because I'd had a hip replacement two years previously and had some residual soreness on my right side. I was sleeping well and eating well. I was used to working long days and driving across country to report on matches and media briefings. I had no problems with a totally unpredictable shift-pattern.

I could quite easily convince myself that the only difference between this week and last week was that now I had a label. And just as easily, I could convince myself that I didn't have to wear it. After all, it was only words. There wasn't necessarily any substance to them. And if the odds were that actually the diagnosis did mean something, then wasn't I – as an ultra-competitive former professional sportsman – used to challenging the odds and beating them? Hadn't my cousin been diagnosed with MS all those years ago and barely noticed it since? That – and not the devastating strain that afflicted my friend's wife – was the sort of MS I wanted. Perhaps I even felt entitled to it. And perhaps because all through my life I had been successful in so many competitive fields, I felt that I could make medical history and beat an unbeatable disease. Why not?

PART TWO
MATCHES (BOY)

CHAPTER FIVE

A CHIP OFF THE OLD BLOCK
(1955–62)

I hero-worshipped my dad. Big, strong, graceful and good-looking, he excelled at all sports and had represented Great Britain at athletics. Much more importantly, he lived in our house, with his golf clubs and his cricket bag and – objects of awe and wonder for me – his blazer badges and his trophies.

Tony Hignell was born in Kroonstad, South Africa, in July 1928. His mother was a South African doctor and my grandfather was a Gloucestershire-born colonial administrator. The family returned to England when his father, Harry, retired and Tony was sent to board at Denstone College, his dad's old public school in Staffordshire. At Denstone, the strapping six-footer displayed his father's aptitude for cricket and rugby – Harry had played for Bristol at the turn of the century and been invited to trials at Gloucestershire – but it was only when he went up to read medicine at Cambridge – where he played one first-class cricket match for the university – that Tony discovered that he had a talent for throwing the javelin. Before long he was setting national records and earning his England and Great Britain vests. The highlight of his athletic career was the long trip to Auckland in 1950, when he threw the javelin for England in the Empire Games – and finished just outside the medals.

By the time I was born, on 4 September 1955, athletics was on the back burner, though I have vague memories – enhanced by ancient and amateur cine film – of watching him launching his javelin into orbit at an athletics event in Cyprus where he was stationed as a medical officer in the RAF from 1958 to 1960. Those cine films much more often show this blond, tanned giant in his cricket whites setting off to play for one of the teams on the island. I don't know if it was then that I started pestering him to take me along but I do know that until well into my teens, when the opportunity presented itself, that's what I wanted to do; watch my dad play cricket.

And in tagging along, I got to field at pre-match tap-ups, I got to 'wag the tin' (work the scoreboard) and, if I took my own tiny bat along as well, I might get a hit myself during lunch and tea breaks. And, once I had experienced the exhilaration that comes when everything goes right – when the middle of the bat hits the ball at just the right moment for maximum effect and with the sweetest sound propels it away at a scarcely believable speed – I was hooked on cricket.

My mum was a Devon girl, daughter of an Exeter builder's merchant and a Welsh Baptist mother. She met my dad when she was a ward sister at Frenchay Hospital in Bristol and he was a junior doctor. They got married at Alveston, near my dad's family home in Gloucestershire, on 21 January 1954. Patricia Nixon stood only a fraction of an inch over five foot – more than a foot shorter than the man she married – but what she lacked in inches she more than made up for with energy, determination, persistence, devotion and sheer hard work. 'There's no such word as can't' was not just a motto, but also the code she lived by. In marriage she channelled all the drive, the enthusiasm and the compassion that had propelled her through the ranks of nursing into the Herculean task of motherhood. She bore five children in six years, changed living quarters almost as often and, with extraordinary efficiency, patience and energy, made each one both a home and a hub, a launch pad and a resting-place, the centre of activity and the eye of the storm.

And with the extraordinary – and, from this distance, inhuman – demands made on officers' wives in Cold War Britain, we had a lot of homes. In the early years particularly, my dad was posted to a different airbase every few months. So, while my oldest brother Robert was born in Bristol, I was born in Cambridge and my sister Cathy first saw the light of day in Retford, Nottinghamshire. Our two younger brothers, Stephen (born 1958) and Ben (1960), were at least born in the same place (RAF Akrotiri in Cyprus) but that was probably the longest the family ever stayed in one place.

In Cyprus at least Mum had help – not just from the climate, which encouraged her to turn demanding toddlers outside at every available opportunity, but also from the next-door neighbours. Keith de Belder was a doctor with a permanent commission in the RAF – like my dad. Liz de Belder had been a nurse – like my mum. They, too, loved children and ended up with five sons and a daughter. The four eldest – Matthew, Simon, Guy and Mark – were my playmates and then my mates from those earliest Cyprus pre-school days right through to the end of my formal education.

Matthew, Simon and Guy were older than me, while Mark was a few months younger. We spent the sun-drenched late 1950s in and out of each others' houses and gardens, playing cricket, football, marbles and cowboys and indians, trooping down to the beach in giant estate cars overflowing with picnic baskets, rugs, inflatable mattresses, beach-balls, towels and children. We raced eagerly to hospital to greet a new arrival and marched much more soberly and, unrecognisably scrubbed and crammed into uncomfortable Sunday best, to church for the christenings that followed.

From earliest times then, I was knocking around with older boys and devoting all my energies to be like them, to be accepted by them, to be as good as them at games, and ultimately to be better than them at the things we did together.

My parents had long ago reached the conclusion that the only way to achieve any sort of stability in the face of constant RAF upheavals was to send their children to boarding school. My dad, like his father before him, had gone to Denstone College in Staffordshire and then on to Cambridge. If his children could follow suit he'd be more than happy.

The de Belders had also come to a similar conclusion about the RAF and, influenced no doubt by my dad's Denstone tales, were keen to start their eldest two, Matthew and Simon, at the preparatory school, Smallwood Manor, near Uttoxeter. Being older, they would fit into the lower part of the school while Rob – who would be eight at the start of the academic year – would be the right age for the intake class. That left a thorny question for my parents: what to do about not yet seven-year-old Alastair?

They had just received notice of another posting, which would have involved yet another change of school. If, as planned, I was to go on to Smallwood at eight, I would by that time have started four consecutive school years at different schools. They were confident that, academically, I could hold my own with elder boys but in order for me to be accepted a year early they would need a favour from Smallwood's headmaster.

CHAPTER SIX
A BOY DRIVEN (1962–69)

WPC Davies was a huge man with a barrel chest and tree-trunk thighs. Only seven years earlier he had scattered Springbok defenders across the high veld as a centre on the Lions tour of South Africa. Now he swung a mighty leg and thumped a little leather rugby ball high into the Staffordshire air. It seemed to take an impossibly long time to come down and, when I had caught it, the kicker seemed an impossibly long way away. But I booted the ball back with all the strength my tiny six-year-old frame could muster and thought no more about it. Legend has it that this was my entrance test. As I caught the ball, Phil Davies made up his mind to accept me at the school. When I kicked it back, he started thinking scholarships. The event – or any version of it – doesn't register in my memory, but then it wouldn't. As long as I could remember I had pestered my dad – and, to be honest, any ambulant adult – to catch, pass, kick, throw, hit or return any ball (or anything that looked like a ball). Of course, if one of my dad's friends had kicked a ball in my direction, I would have returned it. It would never have crossed my mind that this was some sort of test.

There began my love affair with rugby. Whether he recognised it as a cunning psychological ploy or not, WPC Davies refused to allow me to play rugby that first year. He was more likely swayed by my physique, or lack of it. According to a school report I at one time measured 4 foot 2 inches while weighing a scarcely believable 4 stone 2 pounds. On games afternoons, therefore, I had to play football with the rest of the first year and, no matter how many goals I scored, and no matter how many tantrums I threw, I was not going to be allowed to play rugby.

That didn't stop me joining the pick-up games on a Sunday and it only fanned the flames of a burning desire to represent the school at its only winter sport. In those days Smallwood didn't mess with football or hockey. From September to Easter rugby was the only sport that mattered.

When I was finally allowed to play organised rugby, I took to the game like a duck to water, first as a tiny and determined try-hungry wing, then as a fly-half who still scored tries but also kicked conversions, took touch kicks and bossed everybody else around. I also practised every spare minute before and after every games lesson and continued to play some sort of rugby every Sunday. When age-group teams were announced there was never any doubt that I would be in them, while promotion to the first XV was guaranteed as soon as I became big enough.

Cricket, though, had no such sensibilities. I was picked for the under-11s at seven, the second XI at eight and spent five years in the first XI. In the classroom, I proved a quick learner with an excellent memory. I was also a hard worker and, looking back, ridiculously competitive. I just had to be top of the form, to have my name announced last at those archaic and verging on barbaric end-of-term assemblies when not just your position in class but also your marks were read out to the entire school. I was desperate to be first.

Whatever the reasoning behind it, I was repeatedly bumped up the school; at eight I was in a class with the third years, two years later I was competing academically with 12- and 13-year-olds preparing for their leaving exams. I spent two years in that form and another two in the sixth form where the goal was a scholarship to public school.

With the benefit of hindsight, I'm not sure this constant promotion did much for my emotional development. When you live cheek by competitive jowl in a same-sex institution, you learn quickly to hide your weaknesses, guard your privacy and internalise your hurt. You live alongside your mates but you construct a protective shell to prevent them entering in.

While this brittle armour reinforced my basic shyness, further moves towards socialisation were thwarted by life at home. We had moved by this time from RAF Colerne in Wiltshire, where of necessity the other children you could play with would nearly always also come from boarding schools, to my father's family home at Alveston in Gloucestershire, which, standing in its own grounds on the edge of a relatively small village, was isolated. The weather didn't help; we spent the coldest winter on record, 1963, in a huge, draughty, corrugated-roofed icebox of a house in which, when the pipes were frozen or the coalman didn't deliver, we could quite easily be snowed in.

So, when the chance of another overseas posting came along, my father grabbed it with both hands. This was the summer of 1965, and we were heading off on a three-year secondment to the Royal Rhodesian Air Force. By careful planning Dad managed to arrange it so that our journey out to RAF Thornhill – at Gwelo (now Gweru), halfway between the capital Salisbury (Harare) and Bulawayo – should start at the beginning of the summer holidays and that his embarkation leave should finish at their end.

The journey out was a logistical masterpiece. We travelled by plane, with stopovers at Aden, Mogadishu (for fuel) and Nairobi before landing at Salisbury where we also spent a couple of days before driving down to Gwelo. As well as five children aged between four and eleven, my parents had no less than 19 pieces of luggage to account for. Once again their powers of persuasion and their communication of enjoyment turned a potential nightmare into a thrilling adventure. Rob and I were given responsibility for a certain number of cases each and, faced with a challenge, embraced it. We also knew that Smallwood was going to arrange a prize for the best holiday project so we zealously hoarded anything with a map or a logo on it (including those tiny little salt and pepper thimbles dished out by airlines) and we took photos of anything that moved.

The holiday itself was magical. No sooner had we moved into officers' quarters at Thornhill than we set off again on our own mini-safari. Over the next few weeks we took in Bulawayo, the Matopos Hills, Cecil Rhodes' grave, the ancient city of Zimbabwe, the Wankie Game Reserve and the Victoria Falls. We saw lions and giraffes, springboks and monkeys, kudu and wildebeest, hippos and rhinos. We crammed a year's worth of sightseeing into little more than a month and carried a suitcase-load of souvenirs back to Smallwood with us.

The one thing my dad didn't plan on, however, was Ian Smith's announcement of UDI for Rhodesia and the subsequent expulsion of all seconded British Forces' personnel. In October 1965, he was ordered to leave Rhodesia. By the start of December, via a road trip through the southern third of Africa and a cruise ship voyage from Cape Town he was back in the UK. By the start of the Christmas holidays he had another overseas posting. This one was much closer to home, at RAF Rheindahlen in Germany.

Competition and companionship was provided by other forces' children – Michael Foale, destined to be the first British man into space, lived round the corner – but mainly by the de Belders. In previous holidays, while Keith was posted to Ghana, they had spent time with us at Alveston. Now they were up the road from us, at RAF Hospital Wegberg, and there was rarely a problem getting someone to play with. Even when I couldn't rustle up opposition, sport dominated my days. I discovered that the library had any number of sports books, and hoovered up anything by Neville Cardus, EW Swanton, RC Robertson-Glasgow, JBG Thomas and CLR James. I read of the exploits of the great Yorkshire cricketers of the 1930s and the Surrey stars of the 1950s. I loved the accounts of the MCC tours to Australia and the West Indies and I lapped up the stories of Hobbs and Hammond, Grace and May, Miller and Lindwall, the three 'Ws', Prince Ranjitsinhji and the Nawab of Pataudi. I dreamed I could one day emulate my heroes.

And when I wasn't reading and dreaming, I was practising. There was a patch of grass in front of a wall next to our house. Against this wall I spent countless hours tapping and trapping and shooting a football. In front of it I placed a slip catching 'net' and spent even longer setting myself even more difficult catching challenges. I would go out to play by myself and come back hours later covered in mud. My mum would just sigh, and crank up the washing machine.

The only setback of any sort was an ankle injury I picked up on the last day of a school skiing trip. Although this was nothing compared to the broken leg that Guy de Belder had suffered earlier in the holiday, it was still worrying enough for us to consult Guy's dad, orthopaedic surgeon Keith, on our return.

'An extra centre of ossification on the medial malleolus' was the phrase that stuck in my mind as a result of his investigations. Basically, it transpired that I had been born with an extra spur of bone on each ankle. This prevented the ankle functioning to maximum efficiency and left me rather like a car without shock absorbers. One solution was to open me up, remove the offending spurs and then effectively 'retrain' the feet to operate without them. This would entail a couple of operations, lengthy time in hospital and about a year of sporting inactivity, but would probably – but not definitely – be better in the long run.

We went for option two; do nothing. Keith could see that the innate weakness in the ankle had had no effect whatsoever. I was the fastest runner in my age group at school, punched above my weight at rugby and cricket and lived the same turbo-charged, sports-driven, energetic life as his sons. He could see that a year on the sidelines at this stage of my life – just as new sporting horizons were opening up – would be hideously cruel in the short term, and not necessarily kind in the long term. Dad and I wholeheartedly agreed.

Hindsight is a wonderful thing. We were not to know at the time that I would pick up six ankle injuries in seven years of top-class rugby, that ankle problems would force my retirement from rugby at the age of 24 and contribute to my retirement from professional cricket at the age of 28. Even so, I'm not sure I'd have changed a thing.

And as maths teacher John Shouksmith encouraged me to dream my dreams in cricket, so new headmaster David Ives encouraged me to broaden my horizons in rugby. At age 13, I went on my first rugby tour. Long before such trips of any sort became the norm for schools with any aspirations, he decided to take Smallwood on a rugby tour of Brittany, with the youth hostel at St Brieuc as a base, and fixtures at St Brieuc, Vannes and Lorient. With no idea of what to expect, and with no sports travel firm to guide him, he had booked a coach and crossed his fingers...

The results were irrelevant – though I think we beat St Brieuc and Vannes and lost to Lorient. The experiences off the field were priceless. We got to speak French – taking it in turns to go to the shops and buy lunch for 25. We got to see something of France – the Bayeux Tapestry, the Landing Beaches and the monastery at Mont St Michel. And, as all rugby tourists do, we got to laugh, joke, interact and bond in a common purpose that every few days demanded teamwork, courage and skill. We also – we may have been 13 but we knew all about touring tradition – managed a few beers, bought in the supermarket by our biggest forward and downed greedily and guiltily in the local park.

David Ives also decided to keep me at Smallwood for an extra scholarship year. Undoubtedly good for my brother Rob, in that it allowed him to go on to Denstone unencumbered by a younger sibling, and undoubtedly good for Smallwood rugby, it was also pretty good for my cricket. I had achieved one dream of scoring a century the previous year, a week after Guy de Belder became the first Smallwood batsman in living memory to achieve the feat. Now, in my final year I had captained confidently and scored freely until it all came together in a match against Brocksford Hall. I scored 200 not out, from a total of 241 for two declared, with 10 sixes and 25 fours, in 93 minutes. The innings earned me a first ever mention in a national publication, *The Cricketer*. It also earned me a photo in the school magazine that showed just how shy I was. Several days later after the event, I had to get kitted up in my cricket whites, pads and gloves, and stand leaning on my bat in front of a scoreboard recording the famous score. While the photographer was getting ready a large fly settled on my lip. He obviously didn't notice it. I was too timid to draw his attention to it, with the result that the most striking thing about the photo of the greatest achievement in the first 13 years of my life is what looks like a large zit.

That double-century was the zenith of my cricketing career at Smallwood but I still had time to sign off in style – against the school I would be joining. A Denstone under-14 XI bore the brunt of my last innings for Smallwood; 100 not out in 38 minutes. I was ready to move on.

CHAPTER SEVEN

BOY IN A MAN'S WORLD
(1969–72)

Ken Ryder made me smile. Literally. He was a young, stocky, cocky enthusiastic English teacher who, in casting for *Hamlet* (Denstone never did anything other than Shakespeare), decided that the parts of Rosencrantz and Guildenstern should be played by Mark de Belder and myself and that the desired comedic effect could only be achieved if the two fawning courtiers spent the entire play grinning obsequiously at Hamlet and performing their every movement in absolute synchronisation. Mark and I had a blast, constantly changing our movements – a nose scratch here, a cough there, now folding our arms, now crossing our legs – to see if the other could keep up, and all the time smiling great big Cheshire cheese smiles that stayed with us, with me certainly, from then on. I don't know whether it was Ken's intention but I swiftly realised how much easier it was to smile than to scowl, and I'm still appreciating the benefits. Smile at people and they smile back. They feel better and so do you. It's not the answer to everything but it's certainly a step in the right direction.

Phil Smith made me laugh. A lot. He was a big jovial man with a great sense of humour, and the ability to see the best in everyone. He was witty, he was clever, he was the head of history at Denstone and the master in charge of cricket. He set high standards, both in the classroom and on the sports field, but he never let things get out of perspective. He enjoyed life and he appreciated people. He loved cricket, the people who played it, the values it represented and the spirit it engendered. And he had the priceless ability to communicate both the responsibility and the joy of sport. He also ran the Denstone Wanderers cricket team. This was an invitation team made up of masters, old boys and current pupils which not only had an impressive home fixture list – most Sundays throughout the summer term they hosted matches on Denstone's main square – but also undertook an annual tour to the West Country where at their peak they played as many as 15 matches in the same number of days. The

Wanderers played competitive cricket to a high standard, but they also played it for fun. Thanks to Phil Smith and my dad, who also turned out a few times, I received the best possible introduction to men's cricket.

I'd already chucked a coin down a well in Devon one summer holiday, wishing myself a career in cricket, and all my efforts were still directed towards that goal. An early century for the under-14s led to swift promotion to the school first XI, where I continued to score runs. Even so, I was amazed – largely because I had never heard of it – to be selected for the GHG Doggart Public Schools Under-16s XI for a match against an England Schools representative team at the ESCA Festival in Liverpool.

I had, of course, read about Hubert Doggart as a member of the famous Cambridge University sides of the 1950s who, alongside JG Dewes and DS Shepherd, had played for Test cricket for England while still at university. He was to go on to be President of the MCC but he was now a headmaster – at King's Bruton – and he wanted me to play in a side that also included Peter Roebuck of Millfield and Vic Marks of Blundell's. The game ended in a draw. As a non-bowling No. 6 in a two-day game, I was never likely to get too much to do and so it proved. But it gave me a chance to measure up against the best cricketers in my age group in the country, and I was in no way dispirited by the comparison.

My dad drove me to Liverpool. Just as uncomplainingly he had flogged across country from Staffordshire back to Lincolnshire on a frozen Sunday in May to deliver me to the County Colts trial and just as selflessly he delivered me to all the matches played that summer holidays by the Lincolnshire under-19s (star player Phil Neale, soon to become a professional footballer with Lincoln City and a county cricketer with Worcestershire).

I was also encouraged to look beyond the school team in rugby. Several small forests must have been chopped down to provide the paper with which the Rugby Football Schools Union deluged its members. Denstone's master in charge of rugby – former Oxford Blue Ralph Green – always pinned up the circulars he thought relevant, and in October 1971 one of them caught my eye. It was an invitation from the Cambridgeshire Schools' Union for all those wanting to play representative rugby in the forthcoming holidays to get in touch.

My dad had just been posted to the RAF hospital in Ely and we'd already made contact with the Cambridgeshire Colts' cricket selectors. If age-group rugby could be half as much fun as age-group cricket, I was all for it. I did get into the team that Christmas holiday as outside-half, although I can't remember whether we won or lost any matches. Of much more far-reaching consequence was the fact that several of my teammates were pupils at the Perse School in Cambridge. They had to spend most of their school rugby careers withstanding a barrage of requests, demands, orders, blandishments and bribes to turn out for the Old Perseans. As that was an 'open' club, they saw no reason why I shouldn't spend a bit of time in the firing line as well.

Captain of the Old Perseans Rugby Club was a man called Phil Harvey. An estate agent in Cambridge in the daytime and an England hooker in his dreams, Phil expended extraordinary amounts of energy on the Old Perseans Rugby Club. As well as captaining the side, he also took it on himself to organise recruitment, fixtures, referees, tours, pitches and post-match entertainment.

I was a willing victim. Would I like to play some rugby in the Easter holidays? Yes. Would I be available for a match for the Old Persean second team in Cambridge this Saturday? Yes. Could my dad get me to the Perse School playing fields for a 2.30 kick-off? (Glance at Dad.) Yes. Could he referee the match?

To be honest, this last question wasn't actually asked – then. A quarter of an hour before kick-off it was discovered that while we had a full team of 15, the opposition could only rustle up 12. Some bright spark suggested that we could have a 14-a-side match if we loaned them one player, and the referee turned out on their team as well. If that was a logical solution – after all he had brought his boots – so was the next brainwave – to ask one of the spectators to referee instead of the appointed official. Unfortunately, there was only one spectator. My dad had not only recently had an operation for his varicose veins and he'd turned up in sports jacket, slacks and brown Hush Puppies. Still, necessity is the mother of invention and all that, and we played a full 80 minutes – or thereabouts. My first game of adult rugby was 14-a-side, played on a back pitch and refereed by a man in brown Hush Puppies perched on a shooting stick. It was a cracking match as well, ultra-clean and scrupulously honest, with players often calling their own side back for a scoring-pass or a knock-on. What innocence, what fun!

By the end of those Easter holidays I had graduated to the Old Perseans first XV and been selected for the Old Perseans' Easter tour to Brighton in Sussex. I had had to travel separately – from the Public Schools' Fives Championships at Whitgift School in Surrey – and I wasn't too perturbed to be the only Old Persean at the ground half an hour before kick-off. The guys were never too good at timekeeping and they were all coming down on the same coach from Cambridge, so why worry? Concerns about having gone to the wrong ground or having got the wrong time were dispelled by their arrival at ten minutes to kick-off, though I was a little embarrassed at how the rest of the team declared themselves quite so happy – in an over-emotional, un-English and slightly maudlin way – to see me. The fact they had already consumed the tour supply of 240 cans of beer on the way down to Brighton may have had something to do with it – but I was too naive at the time to even guess it. Nor to understand that the way we started the match – exuberantly, extravagantly, full of daring – was going to last all of ten minutes before the agony of trying to run around with a gutful of beer took over.

Not surprisingly we lost the match, with the *Cambridge Evening News* report – obviously phoned in by Phil – making the excuse that the players were 'obviously suffering from the effects of a long coach journey'. I wasn't. I had a blinder: making breaks, kicking goals, pulling off tackles, and as we trooped off was gratified to have that acknowledged by my teammates.

'Tour tradition,' says one, 'before we change we always buy a pint for the man of the match' – which was handed to me – 'and invite him to drink it'. I raised it to my lips. 'In one.' I was pretty dehydrated so it was easy to comply. 'Tour tradition number two relates to the top scorer of the day'. Another pint was passed to me. I think I twigged then, or it may have been on tour tradition number five or six, relating to tackles made or yards carried, that the criteria didn't matter. This was my induction as a rugby tourist. I can't say whether I passed or failed. All I know is that as the team checked into a hotel later on that evening, intent only on dumping their bags before a night on the town, I was intent only on going to bed. With the result that while the next morning's hearty English breakfast represented sustenance to me, it had quite the opposite effect on teammates who by kick-off for the next match were in scarcely better state. Which meant that, at the end of the game, there was only one candidate to comply with tour traditions ... and it happened the next day as well. Was I really that naive?

At the start of the next vacation I was playing adult cricket as well, for Ely. Just as it pays to be suspicious of any hotel called Splendid, so was Ely's ground a misnomer. Paradise (or as it came from the lips of our captain, 'Pair o'doice') could not by any stretch of the word be described as heavenly. The outfield was rutted, the square was worn and the pitches were of variable quality and uneven bounce. But it was in walking distance from our house in the RAF hospital married quarters and it was home – or, at least in a summer holidays of almost daily cricket for anybody who would have me, it was one of many homes. I scored loads of runs for Ely, and for the Public Schools (in a match against England Schools at Beckenham), Denstone Wanderers, Cambridgeshire Colts, the National Association of Young Cricketers and a touring youth team called the Robins. According to a rough and ready calculation made in a local newspaper I topped 3,000 runs in all forms of cricket that golden summer. I was closing in fast on a career in professional cricket.

Even so, there was never any question of my missing out on university, especially as my fallback option, teaching, required at the very minimum a degree. I was keen to follow my dad – and my grandfather and my Uncle Steve – to Cambridge, and even though Denstone only put forward a handful of Oxbridge candidates every year, my teachers were confident I had the academic ability to meet the first requirements – A grades at A-level – as long as I didn't get too distracted by other things.

CHAPTER EIGHT

DOUBLE INTERNATIONAL
(1972–73)

Circumstances conspired against them. Ralph Green put up another circular from the Rugby Football Schools Union and, emboldened by my success with Cambridgeshire the previous Christmas, I aimed at selection for the Eastern Counties. The trial took place before the end of term but that didn't stop an extraordinary schoolmaster by the name of Percy Morgan, accompanied by his wife Freda and a thermos of coffee, from driving his ancient Humber from Essex to Denstone on a Sunday to watch me perform poorly in a lacklustre win over the Old Denstonians. His report to the Easter Counties selectors who stayed at home that day suggested they hadn't missed much.

That would have been that but for Phil Harvey. He had persuaded a lad called Chris Heron to play at outside half for the Old Perseans. Chris played brilliantly for the OPs and sailed through the Eastern Counties Schools trial; there was no question of my filling the No. 10 shirt for either team. So Phil asked me to play scrum-half for the Old Perseans and I combined so well with Chris in a couple of early Christmas holiday games that when the Eastern Counties Schools scrum-half got injured, Percy was persuaded to take the same gamble.

Eastern Counties Schools won the matches in which I appeared during those Christmas holidays – they always played in a quadrangular competition against Kent, Surrey and Middlesex – and when London Schools, a team made up of players from those four teams, triumphed over the South West in the annual match at the Lensbury Club in Roehampton, I was invited to play for the South East in matches against the Midlands and the North. After the final England Schools trial at Bisham Abbey I was picked, alongside future Grand Slam winner John Scott, then a lock, and Gosforth full-back Brian Patrick, both of whom had already faced the All Blacks touring team, to play for England Schools.

There was no such thing as a schools' international championship in the early 1970s. Ireland may have had a mature and flourishing schools' set-up but

England wouldn't play them. Wales had a different interpretation of what was meant by the phrase 'under-19', which meant that while some of the England Schools team were eligible to face the Welsh in Cardiff they were ruled out of the fixtures either side – against Scotland and France.

We beat a Scotland side, containing future Scottish international and British Lion John Rutherford at outside-half, 27-9 at Galashiels. Rutherford was described in the times as showing 'touches of genuine class' while I made 'huge contribution in service, break and plunder', which was to yield a 14-point haul including a try and a drop goal. Nothing, however, worked particularly well against Wales at the Arms Park. England had changed the team considerably to take advantage of the extended age-range but the older players did not prove to be better and we lost 14-10 to a Welsh team containing future Cambridge friend Alun Lewis at scrum-half, future Welsh international Dai Richards at outside-half and Jeremy Charles, nephew of Welsh football legend John, on the flank.

The selectors made even more changes for our third and final international of the season – against France at Headingley – and one of those was to make me captain. I'd like to say that I was positively Churchillian in restoring morale to a badly dispirited group of players – but I can't. Nevertheless the Wales defeat was shrugged off as if it had never happened, we played some pretty good rugby, I scored one of five tries (according to the *Daily Telegraph* my 'flair and acceleration always threatened', while *The Times* wrote of a 'match-winning combination with the back-row') and we ran out winners, by a record margin of 28-0.

The match took place at the start of the Easter holidays and nothing now stood in the way of a good solid bout of A-level revision except for the Public Schools Fives Tournament at Whitgift in Surrey, a pre-season debut for the Cambridgeshire Minor Counties cricket team in a friendly against Essex at Chelmsford, and a few matches for the Old Perseans.

All I can remember about the Fives Championship (played in a black-walled chamber the size of a squash court with a hard white leather ball and, instead of a racket, a padded glove on either hand) was a quarter-final defeat by Vic Marks. All I can remember about the cricket match was the extreme cold, and the sledging from Essex keeper Neil Smith and his slips as they queried what the callow, nervous and obviously out-of-touch schoolboy was doing, batting so high up the order in such company.

I was an unorthodox batsman. I was blessed with a good eye and a natural sense of timing, but my instinct was either to play everything off the back foot, as late as possible, or, if I got on to the front foot, to aim to hit the ball over fielders rather than past them. This was obviously a risky tactic. In defence my bat was not always as straight as it ought to be, and all the coaches I had come into contact with – including former England batsman Jack Ikin who had recently been brought in to assist at Denstone – had been dissuaded from recommending a major overhaul by the weight of runs I was making.

33

I continued to score heavily in my final year of school cricket and repeated mentions in the *Daily Telegraph*'s regular round-up obviously sent the right message to the right people. I was invited to play for the Rest against the South in the Public Schools trial at Eastbourne. The pick of the players from this match would play against the England Schools Cricket Association and the best from that match had every chance of featuring in a three-Test series against the touring Indian Schools.

A second-innings hundred at Eastbourne set me up for a summer of high-profile cricket, which in turn was to excite the interest of several first-class counties. Initially, though, it led to a place in an England Schools team of extraordinary batting ability. Nigel Briers, who had already played first-class cricket for Leicestershire, was the captain and he opened with either Gehan Mendis (Sussex and Lancashire) or future Somerset player Phil Slocombe. A future Somerset captain Chris Tavaré, who also played for Kent and England, was at No. 3 while my fives opponent, future Oxford University captain and England spinner Vic Marks, batted one place lower. I was No. 5, while yet another future England cricketer and county captain Paul Parker was at No. 6.

Vic hadn't yet turned to twirling nor had Nigel developed the right-arm medium pace with which he has been subsequently credited, so this was a team bereft of all-rounders. Wicketkeeper Tim Rukin batted at No. 7, which left four bowlers, two of them off-spinners Mark Allbrook (Cambridge University and Nottinghamshire) and Paul Tipton (Lancashire), to share the duties. Steve Perryman (destined for a long career with Warwickshire and Worcestershire) was on the civilian side of military medium, while the final slot was shared over the three Test matches between three different bowlers.

Somehow we won the first Test at Hove (with Allbrook taking seven for 20 in the first innings to make the Indians follow on) and won again at Bradford (after an astonishing self-induced second innings collapse by India and a composed 89 from Tavaré) before drawing at Edgbaston to clinch the series. Even more remarkably I ended up top scorer. After scoring 9 and 14 not out at Hove, I hit a fifty at Bradford before becoming the first batsman to score a hundred in the series, at Edgbaston. Chris Tavaré followed suit in the second innings, but I had a big not out to keep my place at the top of the averages. With several more big scores for Cambridgeshire Colts, including 184 not out against Norfolk at Lakenham, I ended up being named as the Cricket Society's Most Promising Player of the Season (future England captain Chris Cowdrey picked up the Under-16 award, while Paul Parker was named the best young fielder) at a posh London dinner in November.

By that time I had applied to Cambridge (Oxford, Bristol, Durham and York were the other names on my UCCA form, though only Durham ever bothered to reply) and opted for Emmanuel as my college of choice. Denstone had no contacts at the university and I chose Emmanuel simply because it could boast cricketers Majid Khan and Bill Snowden, and rugby players Gerald Davies and Bob Wilkinson, so I reasoned it must look favourably on aspiring sportsmen.

The interview at Emmanuel didn't go too well. I was dressed in my only suit (the relaxation in school rules allowed us to choose colours other than grey and to my shame I have to own up to the fact that what I chose was brown and crimplene) and experienced an early flare of optimism as I noticed that the admissions tutor was wearing the same tie (London Schools Rugby). That was quickly extinguished as he excused himself from the formal interview, which was to be conducted by three History dons.

'I see you played both rugby and cricket for England Schools last year?' said one. I thought he was being sympathetic, so launched into an answer laced with just the right amount of modesty and humility, about being lucky, taught by excellent coaches, in the right place at the right time, etc.

'Which one are you going to give up?' was the unexpectedly brutal follow-up. I stumbled through an answer explaining how with good time management, self-discipline etc, it was possible not only to shine at sport but also in the classroom.

'We'll be the judges of that', said the third don. 'I see you only got one A and two B-grades at A-level, including one in the subject you're planning to read in this college. So I'll ask again, are you going to give up your rugby or your cricket?'

I bumbled my way to a conclusion that if something had to go it would be rugby, but that if I organised myself and my time efficiently enough, it might not come to that.

'And if your history is good enough,' rejoined the first inquisitor. 'I see one of your special studies at A-level was the Thirty Years War. Tell us about it.'

I had no idea whether they wanted a learned discourse or a glib but clever one-liner, I had no idea whether they wrote textbooks on the subject or had only the vaguest general knowledge. I knew how to write about academic subjects, but not talk about them – and that became painfully obvious as I stuttered and muttered through a series of incoherent ramblings that evoked not the slightest flicker of a response from the stony-faced trio opposite. I can't remember how the interview ended or how I got the train back to Denstone, but when the letter of rejection arrived the day after Boxing Day I was hardly surprised. However, I wasn't despondent because on Christmas Eve I had received another letter from Cambridge. Under the clearing system, whereby candidates rejected by their first-choice college are put into a pool based on the subject they want to study, I had been offered – and had accepted – a place at Fitzwilliam.

By this time, I'd chosen to play county cricket for Gloucestershire. My prolific summer had prompted enquiries from Leicestershire, Lancashire, Warwickshire and Essex. All were prepared to pay more but because my dad had played for Gloucestershire and I could live cheaply at my grandmother's house in Alveston, the latter were already favourites even before they got me tickets for the Gillette Cup final – in which Gloucestershire picked up their first trophy since the days of WG Grace – by beating Sussex.

A visit to the County Ground in Bristol the following week clinched my decision. The pavilion was at its shabbiest. Secretary Graham Parker's office was reached by wading through an outer office whose every surface was covered with old scorecards, membership forms, telephones, telephone books, ashtrays, stewards' armbands, umpires' coats, typewriters – some of them working – and assorted cricket paraphernalia. The dressing rooms had obviously changed little since Wally Hammond's heyday in the 1930s, while the showers with their huge intricate wrought iron roses would have been cutting-edge technology to WG Grace. The floor of the Hammond Room, where Graham invited Dad and me to join the players for tea – they were in the middle of a three-day fixture with Glamorgan – was partly covered with frayed green lino. The rest was discoloured and splintered floorboard.

Concentration on builder's tea and curling sandwiches was disturbed by the sight of a strange red-coloured figure dodging between the kids' cricket matches on the outfield, bounding up the steps as if chased by the dogs of war and stuffing two sandwiches and a custard slice into his mouth at the same time as taking a slurp of tea and greeting every player on both sides. This, I was informed, was Gloucestershire reserve wicketkeeper Andy Brassington, and his skin was only red because of all the rust that had fallen from the workings of the scoreboard that young cricketers not on first-team duties had to operate.

The chance to work a scoreboard again was not the reason I put pen to paper that evening, but Brassy was the personification of the friendliness, the enthusiasm and the love of cricket that permeated the club. As well as meeting Andy, I got to exchange words that afternoon with captain Tony Brown as well as Mike Procter, youngsters David Graveney, Jimmy Foat and Andy Stovold, and veterans Arthur Milton and John Mortimore. The welcome from them all was warm and genuine. These were to be my teammates for the next decade, and these scruffy surroundings were to be my cricketing home.

By Christmas I had finished my last term at Denstone and lined up a job as an assistant teacher at Tockington preparatory school near Bristol. I had spent my last school term as scrum-half and captain, by the end of which I had been named as skipper of the London Schools side to take on the touring Australian Schools at Twickenham. This was the first of the trail-blazing outfits from Down Under. Their immediate successors, the 1977-78 vintage of the three Ella brothers and 15 future Wallabies, were to dazzle the world with their unbeaten rampage around the British Isles, but this lot – whose star players included future internationals Ken Wright and Phil Crowe – suffered little by comparison. The only game they lost was their final tour match against England Schools at Twickenham at the end of January. I was captain of England that day, and goal-kicker. Not for the last time in my international career at Twickenham, I missed an important kick at goal in the second half, only for us to be awarded a controversial and ultimately decisive penalty try when one Australian forward knocked the ball on inside the dead-ball area and another impeded England's chasing players. We spent the rest of the match defending desperately but held on for a 15-9 win. The match was also my first ever appearance on the BBC's *Rugby Special*. In those far-off, pre-Sky days, the Beeb were the only broadcasting show in town and they had a regular slot at 7.20 on a Saturday evening on BBC2. I'd just taken my boots off when I was asked, as winning captain, to step back into the tunnel to be interviewed by Nigel Starmer-Smith. This led to another first – exposure to what, down the years, has come to be dubbed 'the media wait'. This occurs when everything and everybody – camera, sound, lights, interviewer and interviewee – are in place but for no very obvious reason, nothing can happen, and when it does somebody demands a re-take. After standing on a cold floor in stockinged feet for the best part of 20 minutes, my feet were like blocks of ice, but at least I had appeared on the telly and at least my last schoolboy international and my first appearance at Twickenham had ended on a winning note.

The post-match banquet was both the occasion for my first after-dinner speech – I've still got the menu card on which I adapted a John Wayne line about 'injuns' to come up with the line that the only beaten Australian is 'one who's behind when the final whistle is blown' – and an illustration of two contrasting attitudes to rugby. One RFSU committeeman on top table recommended that, as I was now teaching in the Bristol area, I should join the Clifton club for a 'bit of rugger and a lot of fun'; while another suggested that I should join Bristol where it would be tough, hard and competitive just to get into the Colts team.

PART THREE
MS (DENIAL)

CHAPTER NINE
'DEAR BOB'

Head of Sport, BBC Radio Five Live
April 2000

Dear Bob

I apologise for not being able to break this news face to face. Possibly it's better, anyway, that I notify you in writing. I would welcome the chance of a chat at some point. For now, though... I have multiple sclerosis.

The original diagnosis was made last January. I am confident that I have demonstrated through two Five/Six Nations tournaments and a World Cup that it has not affected my ability to do my job. Why therefore am I telling you at all?

1. It has put a huge strain on my wife, my family and myself to be evasive.

2. It has been unfair to the orthopaedic surgeon responsible for replacing my hip two and a half years ago to blame my walking difficulties on him.

3. There are different types of MS. In the benign form, the symptoms that led to the diagnosis can disappear, sometimes for good. In other forms, the relapsing-remitting symptoms can be relatively mild. Most of my worst symptoms were connected with my right leg. As it was such a coincidence that this had been the leg that had just had a new hip put in, I was hoping these symptoms had something to do with the operation. To that end, I have been back to the consultant, seen a back specialist, a pain specialist, an osteopath and a podiatrist. A return visit to the neurologist last week, however, confirmed that MS is the cause of my not being able to walk any distance without feeling discomfort. It is also the cause of a loss of feeling in my right arm, some unsteadiness and, from time to time, extreme fatigue. So far, I am anxious to repeat, this has not affected the performance of my job, or my enthusiasm for it.

4. I have to tell the DVLA and my car insurance company. If people outside my family and close friends have to know, I feel it is only fair that you should be the first to be informed.

I don't know what all this means. MS, apart from being a condition that has no known cause and no known cure, is wildly unpredictable and completely atypical. It's impossible to say how it will affect me next week, never mind next year or for the last fifteen and a half years of my working life. I am hopeful that I will be able to surmount any difficulties it poses. I may need to ask the BBC for some help. Certainly, I could do with your understanding and support.

I thought it important that you should be the first, in a work context, to know that I have MS. It is no longer a secret. Please feel free to tell whomever you feel should know. I am sending a copy of this e-mail to Gordon, and I am hoping to speak to Robbo. Ed is on holiday.

Sorry to drop this on you.

All the best

Higgy

My attempt to make medical history had hit the buffers. For 16 months I had poured all my energies into pretending that I didn't have multiple sclerosis. I had gone to huge lengths to disguise the physical symptoms, I had driven myself to the point of exhaustion in an attempt to counter their effects and I had plumbed the depths of despair and frustration as the disease marched on. If I was a general, I was winning a few battles but losing the war.

In sporting terms, I was a non-league club in the third round of the FA Cup. If I played the game of my life and my opponent had an off day, I might just be able to nick a draw and live to fight another day. If he had a shocker, I might just get a result. In either case I would have to repeat the experience again and again with never enough time between fixtures and no chance of changing an ever-dwindling squad. My letter to Bob Shennan, Head of Sport at Radio Five Live, was an acknowledgement that I couldn't keep a secret. It was by no stretch of the imagination an acknowledgement of defeat.

CHAPTER TEN
SO WHAT!

I have never interviewed a single sportsman before a match who did not think he could win. I was no exception when I first faced up to the fact that I had multiple sclerosis. Whatever the books said about MS being implacable as well as incurable, unpredictable as well as inexplicable, I was going to beat it. Even though it was probably as debilitating as it was progressive, I was going to rely on the well-honed competitive instincts of a top-class sporting career and put it in its place. I was going to channel all the anger I felt when confronted with the diagnosis, I was going to bend all the intelligence that I had been born with and I was going to direct the full force of my energy into dominating the disease. It may have ruined other lives. It was barely going to affect mine.

That's what I resolved in January 1999, and for the next year and a bit I set about making it happen. I resumed fitness training immediately. It's fair to say that throughout my playing career I had always regarded exercise as a means to an end. For me, the most important thing about sport, by a distance, was the event itself. There was no substitute for playing – at the highest level and against the best opposition that you could manage – and nothing could really replicate it or truly prepare you for it. It was important from a team point of view to rehearse the various set plays and it was important from an individual point of view to refine your technique and practise your skills. Fitness training was a means to the end of making those easier to repeat. Gym work, by the same token, was an aid to success, and not, by any stretch of my imagination, an integral part of it.

But, with my playing days long behind me, and a job that in any case entailed working at a time when I could be playing, it was to the gym that I headed. I became a member at the Horfield Leisure Centre in Bristol, completed a supervised induction course and embarked on a regime of two or three weight-training circuits a week. And, fuelled by the shock of my diagnosis and anger at its unfairness, I pushed myself to the limit. I couldn't run properly – my right hip was still giving me problems following its replacement 18 months or so previously – but I could pound the pedals on the exercise bike, sweat buckets on the step machine, and really hammer into the rowing machine.

I lost a stone in weight. I changed shape, became leaner in the face and around the middle. I glowed as the endorphins coursed around my body. But I also wiped myself out. Whenever I'd finished a session, I'd collapse. I would dismount from the bike after some furious pedalling – and end up in a heap on the floor. I would struggle to get dressed after exercise, struggle to lift my kitbag and only just have the strength to steer the car home. I would fall asleep as soon as I got home, and have next to no energy for doing anything else.

I read that swimming – in terms of the ratio between time and energy expended on it – yielded the best results for overall fitness and was, moreover, kinder to the joints. I took myself off to the Bristol North Swimming Baths on Gloucester Road, invested in a pair of goggles, and ploughed up and down for at least an hour at a time. There was no other word to describe it but boring. I invented all sorts of counting and multiplication games, I calculated the distance I had done and estimated the speed I was travelling, I counted up and I counted down in English, French, German and Italian, but I couldn't make the time pass any quicker or more enjoyably. And, at the end of my session, which I always finished off with a couple of sprinted lengths, I was so exhausted that it was a real effort to haul myself out of the pool, while getting dressed again was a real endurance test.

I pushed myself to the limit when we went out walking in the countryside round Bristol, something that we regularly did as a family. But I found that my legs, despite, or possibly because of, all the other extra training I was doing, got very heavy very quickly, and at times – and against my best efforts – started to drag.

This was the only external sign of my MS – or so I fondly hoped. I was starting to limp quite noticeably after sitting in the car on long drives, or in a cramped commentary box. I wasn't getting around the stadiums as well or as nimbly as I had, I was stumbling quite often and tripping up with a frequency that I felt, in my hypersensitive state, was both noticeable and embarrassing. I was quite shameless in blaming the orthopaedic surgeon for a faulty hip replacement and quite relieved when friends and colleagues swallowed the lies. I convinced myself that they couldn't tell that anything else was wrong. As well as training harder than I'd ever done, I was working harder as well. I volunteered for everything, covered more matches, attended more media briefings, produced more features, wrote more articles and drove more miles than at any time before or since. In 1999, World Cup year, the quiet months of summer were eaten up by training-camps and warm-up internationals. With the tournament taking place in Britain and France, every team and every match was just about accessible from home – provided I set off early enough and didn't mind what time I got back. And when I was in Bristol, I was doing my best to support Jeannie as she started up a new business venture, a ceramic decoration café called 'Make Your Mark', whose operational headquarters for the whole of the autumn of 1999 was our dining room. I volunteered for everything I could, did everything that was asked of me, and I was knackered. But Jeannie was the only one who was allowed to see it.

This imposed a huge mental strain on us both. We were both desperate to tell the truth to our friends, to give a proper explanation for my exhaustion, my clumsiness and my lethargy on days off, but I was scared that it would change their attitude towards me. I felt they would start to pity me, and I couldn't bear that. I wanted them to hang on to the illusion that I was strong, capable and forceful. I was terrified that if they saw me as weak, dependent and unsure, they would start to feel sorry for me, and the dynamics of our relationship would be altered – and not for the better.

It also imposed a huge strain on our sons. When we had told Adam and Dan that I had MS, they had reacted quietly – too quietly for our comfort. In the days and months that followed it often seemed that the news hadn't registered at all. In our naive way, we had hoped that we could charge on with our lives pretending to the rest of the world that nothing had happened while expecting that our sons would not only continue with the charade in public but mutate from self-obsessed teenagers to caring young adults – in an instant.

They had their own issues to deal with. Adam, in particular, was still raging against the world and still unsure of his place in it. Now, whether as an unconscious reaction to the news that his dad had an incurable and debilitating disease or not, he began to miss lessons. He would take the bus down to school, make sure that he was seen at about the time of morning assembly and then go off skateboarding. That the spot favoured by most of the skateboarders was just a stone's throw from the school, and that any teacher nipping out for lunch or an a shopping errand was bound to pass within yards of it, didn't seem to have occurred to Adam. Or maybe it had, and he wanted to provoke a showdown. Whatever, it didn't take long for the Bristol Cathedral School's extremely able headmaster Kevin Riley to get in touch and it didn't take long for all of us to conclude that there was little to be gained from forcing Adam to stay at school against his will.

Jeannie and I were already at the end of our tether with Adam when the MS was diagnosed. As a result of it, we had nothing left to fight his demand to leave school. We argued that he had actually chosen to do his A-levels at the Cathedral School, we pointed out that a starring role in the school play showed how much he was rated by the teachers, and we dangled the carrot of the school hockey tour to India for which he had already been selected. But he was determined, and we had other battles to fight. He left home that summer, a few months short of his 18th birthday.

Adam's departure emphasised the strain of trying to keep the MS secret. Life was difficult enough without having to pretend. I had always disliked sham and pretence in others and I now hated it in myself. And as time went on and I still hadn't slipped into the black hole of permanent disability, the reasons why it had seemed imperative to hide my MS from the world seemed more and more unimportant. The reasons why I should disclose it were spelled out in bold type – as far as the DVLA was concerned. 'Failure to notify the DVLA is a criminal offence and is punishable by a fine of up to £1,000'. Given the thousands of miles I was driving every year, the risk wasn't worth taking, especially if it would have knock-on effects if I needed to make an insurance claim. And if the DVLA had to be told, it seemed stupid not to tell my employers. Hence the letter to Bob Shennan.

But I was still petrified that friends and colleagues would start to pity me. I was worried stiff that they would make allowances and excuses for me. I was desperate that they shouldn't try to make things easier for me, or spare me the more difficult tasks. Above all I didn't want people making decisions for me, or treating me any differently just because I had MS. That was the central thrust of my letter; I was desperate to convince Bob that I had done my job as well as it could be done even though I had MS, and I was desperate for him to believe that going public about my condition would make no difference whatsoever to the way I worked.

So what was the point of going public? It was partly to do with the distaste for subterfuge. I would feel better about myself if I wasn't always trying to conceal something. It was also a need to be reassured that some of my worst fears had not been realised. It was a grudging acceptance of the fact that I had got an incurable disease. And it was the permission I needed to stop fighting it head-on. By naming it, I wasn't exactly shaming it but I was giving myself access to other ways of dealing with it. By joining the ranks of people with MS, I could gain access to all their coping mechanisms: the drugs, the therapies, the benefits and the support systems.

But I was still thinking in terms of winners and losers. I may have lost the battle to keep my MS a secret but I hadn't lost the battle against MS itself. I had simply acknowledged its existence and recognised that it was going to be a handicap. But I wasn't giving in. I still wanted to do my job and be a parent and partner to the best of my ability. I wanted to be a valued and valuable member of society. I was still going to be a winner. I was going to be a walking embodiment of the phrase: 'I've got MS, So what?'

PART FOUR
MATCHES (MAN)

CHAPTER ELEVEN
GOING FIRST-CLASS

When I joined Bristol in 1974, it was the best team in the country. To prove it, we won the *Sunday Telegraph* Pennant, which in those far-off strictly amateur days was the equivalent of the Premiership. Not that there was anything like a play-off, a final at Twickenham or even a league programme. In a hundred years or so of club rugby, fixture-lists had developed in a haphazard fashion, dictated more by tradition and proximity than by playing strength. The top English clubs didn't always play each other and, if they did, not always on a home-and-away basis and not always with their best players. Bristol's fixture-list was heavily skewed towards Wales – with matches against Cardiff, Swansea and Newport over an eight-day period in early September, Llanelli between Christmas and New Year, and games against Pontypool, Aberavon and the South Wales Police. Matches against Saracens and Wasps tended to be arranged when Bristol's top players were on county duty. Basically though, Bristol played anybody and everybody in a season that regularly crammed in upwards of fifty fixtures between the start of September and the end of April.

And won most of them. Even so, the 1973–74 season hadn't been noticeably more successful than normal when one bright spark announced that a win over Rosslyn Park was the thirtieth of the season and another one discovered that most of them had been against English opposition. All we had to do to be crowned champions of England was to win two of three home matches against Northampton, Leicester and Coventry. I was in the team by then – as scrum-half and goal-kicker – as we landed the title with a game to spare.

I owed my place in the team to the miners' strike. Restrictions on the use of electricity in the spring of 1974 meant that Wednesday night fixtures had to be cancelled or played in the afternoon. One Wednesday in March, while Pontypool exercised its right to stage the Pontypool Park fixture against Bristol just after lunch, a number of Bristol players exercised their right to stay at work rather than face the 'Viet-Gwent'. Several others succumbed to 'Welsh flu' – a mysterious malady that tended to strike Englishmen on their way to matches in the Principality in the 1970s. Regular scrum-half Alan Pearn, a goal-kicking Devonian with more than 1,300 points for the club, couldn't get time off from his teaching duties and, at 18 and a half, I was picked to make my debut as scrum-half against the team with the fiercest pack in the country. My abiding memory is of Wales hooker Bobby Windsor rampaging round the front of the line-out and equally uncompromising fellow international Terry Cobner bearing down from the tail, both intent on burying the baby-faced Englishman in the letter G shirt. I must have done something right, for the *Evening Post* named me man of the match and I kept my place for the rest of the season.

Pre-season training at Gloucestershire County Cricket Club officially began in the first week of April. The best that could be said about it was that it was limited – by philosophy as much as by facilities. Even in 1974, a significant and far from silent minority remained unconvinced by arguments in favour of any physical training whatsoever. Cricket was too complicated, they would argue – the match-days both too long and too tightly packed together, the action within them too stop-start – for any sort of training regime to replicate it or to prepare for it. Fast bowlers – the real workhorses of the game – followed the Fred Trueman dictum that the only way to get fit for bowling was to bowl lots of overs. Batsmen and spinners believed that as success was all in the mind, it didn't matter too much what shape your body was in, while fielding, despite the advent of the 40-over Sunday League, was incidental to the main action.

There were just two indoor nets at the County Ground in Bristol – with wooden floorboards, cracked lino and bowling run-ups of less than five yards – while the rarely protected outdoor nets had to last the whole season, and the square was sacrosanct. If it rained in April, which it nearly always did, training consisted of no more than a couple of laps round a sodden outfield, a perfunctory bat and bowl in the indoor nets and lunch at home. To be fair to Gloucestershire captain Tony Brown, he did try to move us into the modern sporting era. In those quaint days, when sponsors were far from ubiquitous and tracksuits were rarely worn by cricketers and not considered as leisure-wear, he very proudly announced a deal he had done with sportswear firm Bukta, whereby we would each get one free tracksuit. It would be important for team unity, he stressed, if we all wore the tracksuit at the same time, and of course it would acknowledge the generosity of the sponsors. When he came to unveil our new training-strip, however, it was unclear who was doing whom a favour. With red, green, cream, brown and blue jostling for prominence on the club flag, Gloucestershire has more official colours than any other county. The new tracksuit – shapeless yellow top, on which the letters GCCC had been embroidered in flowery script, and baggy black bottoms – featured none of these colours, with the whole ensemble suggesting not so much end of line but a line that could surely never have seen the light of day.

Still we did wear them for the pre-season photo shoot, and we did wear them for daily laps of the outfield, which, not altogether surprisingly, were met with wildly differing levels of enthusiasm. Tony Brown would set a captain's example by chugging off in front. Fit young pups Jimmy Foat, Andy Brassington, PE student Andy Stovold and myself would gambol around trying to slow down to the captain's pace. A gap would open up to the two Devonians – David Shepherd, leaning backwards to balance a girth made even larger by a winter's indolence, and Jack Davey, leaning forwards because he only ever bowled into the wind. Still further back would be Zaheer Abbas and Sadiq Mohammad, whose ingenious solution to the British climate – wearing pyjamas under cricket whites under new tracksuit – did wonders for his circulation but nothing at all for his mobility. One of the senior statesmen, inveterate smoker Ron Nicholls, would be at the back, delayed by the need to extract every last gasp from his latest fag, while another, Arthur Milton, who allegedly only ever wasted effort at the bookies, would be heading directly towards the finish, reasoning that there was no point going the long way round the boundary because he could see where we were heading!

That first season, I was paid the grand total of £800 for six months' work – which was not only the minimum wage for uncapped professionals but also, as I was constantly reminded, the maximum I could hope for. Gloucestershire – like other counties wholly reliant on handouts from the Test and County Cricket Board (TCCB) – were almost completely unable to attract either sponsors or crowds, and had been losing money hand over fist since the early 1960s. They'd sold off part of the ground for £30,000 in 1967 but relief was only temporary. They posted a record loss of £26,158 at the end of that 1974 season when, according to Graham Parker in his book *Gloucestershire Road*, the club was insolvent.

A hand-to-mouth existence demanded unusual sacrifices. As junior pros we had to help the groundstaff: painting the sightscreen and the picket fence, moving essential equipment to the out-grounds and manning the new scoreboard that had been built in the close season under the direction of county coach Graham Wiltshire. There was one major problem with Wilt's grand design. During the run-through the day before Gloucestershire's first Benson and Hedges match against Hampshire, we noticed that while we could work the numbers very well from the inside of the box, the absence of any other holes in the board meant we couldn't see out. Wilt briefly toyed with the idea of a walkie-talkie link up to the scorer's room in the main pavilion so that Bert Avery could instruct us how and when to advance the totals. Bert objected on the grounds that he already had too much to do keeping the scorebook in his exemplary copperplate. We objected on the grounds that being cooped up in a hot, dark, airless room for two hours at a time deprived us of the chance of watching any cricket, and that we were expected to operate a scoreboard we couldn't see by a complicated sort of remote control, which was bound to end in tears.

Wilt's first solution was to cut holes so we could see out. Unfortunately, as he didn't cut them big enough for us to poke our heads out and look back at the numbers we had been changing, we had no way of checking that they had slotted correctly into place. Even more unfortunately, this problem wasn't spotted till the morning of the match when several of the dozen or so spectators who had braved the cold got to enjoy an interactive experience, shouting instructions up at us to move this number on a bit, that number back a bit, while at the same time watching the cricket, keeping their own score, unwrapping their sandwiches and pouring coffee from their thermos flasks. When the noise got too distracting for those not involved, Wilt nipped down to an antique shop on Gloucester Road and came back with four long mirrors which, when painstakingly positioned on hard-back chairs on the gangway in front of the scoreboard, enabled us to see a back-to-front reflection of the numbers we had just changed. The system worked perfectly until the first drunk of the season lurched out of the Jessop Tavern and staggered straight into the carefully sited apparatus. It needed the 'Dicko Tweak'. John Dixon, a madcap fast-bowler from Bath who had joined the county on the same day as me, was deployed to warn spectators from straying too close to the mirrors.

'Prepare to meet your doom!' he would growl as more than one intoxicate looked vainly about for the source of the warning. 'Oh, the evils of strong liquor!' Dicko would declaim. 'Renounce your wicked ways! It is never too late!' he would roar out in a big bass voice from the depths of the scoreboard, while the poor unfortunate would be rooted to the spot, gazing panic-stricken in every direction until we could suppress the laughter no longer.

The rugby season was still going strong in April, but nobody at Gloucestershire seemed too bothered that their new signing was bunking off from time to time. The geographical proximity of the County Ground and Bristol's Memorial Stadium was crucial. On one occasion, I was able to savour – from my vantage point inside the scoreboard – an astonishing century by Barry Richards of Hampshire before heading the half-mile or so up the Gloucester Road to play for Bristol against the South Wales Police. We lost by a point as three of my goal-kicks, including a potentially match-winning, last-minute conversion, bounced off the woodwork, but I still got back in time to work the board for the last hour or so of Gloucestershire's despairing run-chase.

Whether the cricket was to blame or not, my goal-kicking went to pot in those last few weeks of the rugby season; apart from the South Wales Police setback, I only managed to convert one of the six tries against Leicester while Bristol's final match of the season – against Coventry – was the first of many to highlight my inconsistency in front of goal. 'Unhappy finale for Hignell' ran the *Bristol Evening Post* headline, before the copy went on to explain how my success rate of one from seven was in no small way responsible for a 13-7 defeat.

I was attracting the wrong kind of headlines on the cricket pitch as well, though these were not of my own making. The spelling mistake (as in the *RAF*

Times' 'Bignell (115 no) wrecks victory hopes'– a century on my first appearance in Gloucestershire colours, against the RAF Association) I could cope with. A ruling that I was ineligible to play in the County Championship was an awful lot harder to bear. The problem was the one-off pre-season friendly I had played the previous April for Cambridgeshire against Essex. The Minor County had reckoned they might be able to use me during the summer holidays and had registered me accordingly. TCCB rules stated that once registered by one county, minor or major, a cricketer could only join another the following year as a special registration. Gloucestershire hadn't spotted Rule 3: subsection B (1a), which further restricted an individual county to seven special registrations in five years. I was Gloucestershire's eighth. Even though the TCCB's own rules allowed it to use its discretion if (a) it is in the best interests of county cricket as a whole and (b) that it is in the best interests of the cricketer concerned, it chose not to. I suppose I should have been flattered. As it was plainly in my best interests to be registered for Gloucestershire, I can only conclude that the suits at Lord's were panic-stricken at the thought of the damage a small, shy public schoolboy might do to the fabric of a sport that had survived and flourished for the best part of a century.

The ban was lifted in mid-July, but only after two appeals from Gloucestershire had been turned down and not before the registration rules had themselves been re-written. But I don't recall burning either with a sense of injustice, or with frustration. I was disappointed not to be picked for the one game I could play in, for to make my debut for Gloucestershire against Cambridge University just as my dad had done in 1947 appealed to my sense of history, but I had plenty of cricket – for the second XI, the under-25s, England Young Cricketers (for whom I scored 133 against the West Indies at Arundel), the Whitbread Wanderers and other invitation teams as well as my local club side, Thornbury, to keep me busy.

My Gloucestershire debut, when it did come, was against Surrey at the Oval. In the first innings, I patted my first ball, an intentionally gentle full-toss from Robin Jackman, past mid-on for two. The second I spooned to cover and was caught. In the second innings, which required collusion from the Surrey captain and our own Tony Brown to leave us with a run-chase of 217 in 165 minutes. I survived a couple of bouncers from Jackman and hoicked Pat Pocock out of the ground for six before, attempting a repeat, being bowled by the off-spinner for 25. However, thanks to an unbeaten 98 from Mike Procter, my first match as a professional cricketer ended in victory.

My second match provided an introduction to the harsh realities of the county circuit. It started well enough. John Dixon, brought in to bolster a bowling line-up that lacked the injured Procter, had Neil Abberley brilliantly caught by Tony Brown in the first over. As he received our congratulations Dicko was heard to promise 'I'll go through them now'. When the innings had to close after a hundred overs, Warwickshire were 465 for 1! Rohan Kanhai and

John Jameson had both smacked massive, unbeaten double-centuries and we were so shell-shocked we never recovered.

The rest of my truncated first season was also spent on a sharp learning curve. The averages didn't lie: 14 innings, 161 runs, highest score 27, average 12.38, while David Green's club history merely noted that Hignell 'played eight games without making any impact except with his fielding'. Still, I had arrived, and I could head off to Cambridge University not just as undergraduate, but as county cricketer as well.

CHAPTER TWELVE

RUGBY BLUE (1974–75)

My grandfather went to Cambridge, my father went to Cambridge and my uncle went to Cambridge. I was born there and had lived near the city for three years. I thought I knew what to expect. But Cambridge didn't live up to my expectations. It exceeded them – by approximately a million miles.

Cambridge flooded my senses; spiritually – the grandeur and permanence of the place, the history and tradition round every corner; aesthetically – the soaring, sweeping buildings, the beauty of the Backs, the college quadrangles; intellectually – some of the finest minds in the world lived in the city and something was bound to rub off; and socially – it was home, too, to some amazing people from all walks of life, all races, creeds and cultures. There was the joy of being alive, and young, and fit and healthy. And there was the sport.

Cambridge University was a power in the land at both my chosen sports. Matches played by the cricket team against the counties had always been deemed first-class and as recently as the 1950s, undergraduate students had been selected for England. The rugby Varsity Match at Twickenham was a fixed point in the rugby calendar that attracted both television coverage and huge crowds. Even warm-up matches attracted the national media – as I discovered on my debut, against St Mary's Hospital.

That both *The Times* and the *Daily Telegraph* should each send a top reporter to produce 300 or so words on a one-sided contest between two sets of students may seem bizarre now, but at the time it was considered entirely normal. The university had built up a reputation as a hothouse of rugby talent, and it had also built up an impressive fixture-list. Because there were no leagues, a club could play against whomever it chose and Cambridge, with its fast, firm Grange Road pitch and its reputation for callow forwards and adventurous backs, was always an attractive option. And because rugby was strictly amateur, a lighter, younger, less experienced university side could nearly always provide a good match for a top club team because it was fitter, faster, better-drilled and, born of the necessity of having to make do with only 20 per cent possession at times, more inventive. A good contest for the clubs meant good copy for the press, for whom the December Varsity Match at Twickenham was, in the absence of autumn internationals, the pre-Christmas focal point. By watching the top teams against Oxford and Cambridge, they could not only build a narrative towards that fixture but could get a feel for which players and which clubs they would need to be watching as the international season approached. What's more, because there were no floodlights at Grange Road, Cambridge always kicked off early and copy deadlines could be comfortably met. All in all, a trip to Cambridge in the 1970s was an attractive option for rugby writers and, by extension, for national selectors.

And in 1974, we had plenty to interest them, especially behind the scrum. Half-backs Alan Wordsworth and Richard Harding would go on to play for England, while centre Peter Warfield already had. One wing Mike O'Callaghan was an All Black, while the other, Gordon Wood, was one of the best finishers not to get a cap. The other centre, Jim Moyes, was to play for England Under-23s and win half a dozen caps for Canada. All they needed was a full-back. I'd never played there in my life. It was too good an opportunity to miss.

Our coach, Ian Robertson, had a unique, exhilarating and audacious vision of rugby and a way of delivering it that would have gone down like a lead balloon at any other club in the country, but which pressed all the right buttons for us.

'You', he would say, addressing all of us, 'are, by virtue of the fact that you are studying at Cambridge, in the top one per cent of the brightest people in the country.' 'They', whoever the opposition were that day, 'are not only older and slower than you, they are THICKER! All you have to do is to go out and make them look as stupid as they really are!'

'You', he had by now turned his attention to the forwards, 'are DONKEYS. All you have to do is to work very hard and get the backs some ball. They don't mind how you do it, or even how little you come up with, but you must give them some ball to play with.' Robbo's knowledge of forward play by now exhausted, he would send the 'donkeys' off to work with Murray Meikle, a no-nonsense New Zealander who had once turned out for the Junior All Blacks.

And then Ian would devote the rest of his coaching session to the backs, challenging us to come up with new moves, reminding us that, as our attacking opportunities would inevitably be limited, we had to turn most of them into tries, inspiring us to trust in ourselves and each other and, if it was on, to run the ball from anywhere and everywhere.

In Alan Wordsworth, Ian had the ideal man to turn his vision into reality. Alan may have only been 11 stone when dripping wet, but he was the most talented outside-half I ever played with or against – a list that included Phil Bennett, Ollie Campbell and Tony Ward. He was deceptively quick, could kick the ball miles off either foot, and had the most sublime array of handling skills. But what was unique about Alan was that, even when lined up alongside some pretty bright blokes, his thought processes seemed much faster than anybody else's, and his time on the ball seemed seconds longer. He had the cheek of a street-urchin and the nerve of a gambler and, at the slightest sign from him, the rest of us were only too happy to swarm on to the attack.

'Cambridge set the blood tingling' was the headline after a 16-all draw with Cardiff. 'Awesome Cambridge' and 'Slick Cambridge' described our win over London Scottish, while victories over Richmond and Blackheath, a draw with Northampton and the narrowest of defeats to Leicester and a Steele-Bodger's Invitation XV containing ten internationals made us favourites for the Varsity Match.

Cambridge's success also earned me some flattering reviews. 'Cambridge owe it to Hignell's flair' was a *Daily Telegraph* headline that found its way into the family scrapbook, as did a *Rugby World* magazine profile entitled 'Alastair Hignell – complete footballer', and a *Sunday Express* piece which, apart from likening my appearance to a ' young Viking', reported my belief that I saw full-back as a temporary position, and that my real future lay at scrum-half. I didn't tell this to reporter John Reed, but I had calculated that the bonus of a Blue (only awarded if you actually play in the Varsity Match) would more than compensate for a few matches out of position, and that once I was established in the Varsity set-up, it would be easier to return to my rightful role.

First, though, was the Varsity Match itself. I swiftly discovered that the whole occasion was shrouded in tradition. Once the team had been announced at a 'Black Velvet' cocktail party at St John's, the chosen XV had to report to a gentleman's outfitters to be measured up not just for the distinctive Light Blue blazer, which you would never dream of wearing before the day of the match, but also the jersey, the socks (you could only wear the light blue at Twickenham, and had to wear college socks in other matches) and the accesories. These included a special edition of the club tie, a Blues' scarf (only to be worn after you'd played), a Blues' bowtie and cummerbund (for the post-match ball) and a cricket sweater (optional). All of which you had to pay for – and willingly did so.

Then there was the Port and Nuts. The whole team was invited to the Master's Lodge at Selwyn College where club president and celebrated historian Owen Chadwick was in residence – and took our places round a vast oak dining-table. As the port was passed and the nuts were cracked, we were invited to join in a toast proposed by 1920s Blue and Wales international, Windsor Lewis. 'GDBO' he would solemnly intone, adding 'God Damn Bloody Oxford' for those who didn't know. 'GDBO' we would reverentially repeat, far too much in awe of the tradition to succumb to the giggles.

Up to 1974, Varsity Match crowds had been dwindling in line with playing-standards but the autumn form shown by both teams – Oxford had picked up some useful wins as well – bucked the trend of previous years and boosted the 1974 attendance to well over 30,000. Cambridge were favourites but Oxford refused to follow the script. Although Peter Warfield and I scored tries to establish a healthy lead, the Dark Blues' outside-half, Nigel Quinnen, kept kicking his goals. His fifth penalty reduced our lead to one point, which was 16-15 with 19 minutes to go. It also set up a desperate finale in which I missed a penalty, Oxford snatched at a drop-goal attempt and Quinnen shaved the underside of the crossbar from 45 metres out. The only break referee Ken Pattinson gave Cambridge in the second-half was to blow for full-time a minute early.

My first Varsity Match had ended in victory and a 12-point haul earned me a fair share of the headlines. It also earned me selection for Gloucestershire – at outside-half. The county already had a prolific goal-kicking full-back (Peter 'the Boot' Butler) and they already had a scrum-half in Richard Harding, but they'd lost confidence in their usual fly-halves. The selectors were well aware that I hadn't worn the No. 10 shirt since I was in the lower sixth at Denstone, and they also knew that I wouldn't be returning from Cambridge University's three-match tour to Italy until the eve of the county championship quarter-final. They obviously reckoned Richard and I could sling a few passes round the Colosseum, practise our calls at the Sistine Chapel, and fine-tune our understanding among the pigeons in St Mark's Square.

But they hadn't reckoned on Richard getting injured, and Cambridge hadn't reckoned on most of the tour party joining him on the sidelines. By the time we got to Brescia for our third match in five days, we only had 15 fit players – and only then by playing a flanker on the wing, a hooker in the back row and pressing Ian Robertson into service at outside-half. Robbo was not only lame – from the knee injury that had curtailed his playing-career with Scotland – but he was also blind. The milk-bottle glasses he habitually wore were totally inappropriate for a game of rugby, and when the trip started there had been no need to pack his contact lenses. As his scrum-half, I soon realised that there was no point in trying to pass the ball in front of him – he just wouldn't see it. Instead I hurled it at him and hoped that his hands would react quickly enough to hold on to it. Miraculously they did (there is absolutely no truth in the rumour that my passes were so slow that his centres had time to shout instructions to him about their height, velocity and trajectory) and nearly as miraculously we scored three tries to nil to win 14-6.

The return flight was delayed, so I didn't get to bed till well after midnight on the eve of my rugby debut for Gloucestershire in which, after four matches in seven days as a scrum-half, I was going to represent the defending champions in a must-win quarter-final, in a position in which I hadn't played a single minute of senior rugby. Moreover, I was going to do it in partnership with a man I had never met before, a team I'd never trained with, in a combination that contained only three players from Bristol, the other 12 coming from arch-rivals Gloucester.

To be honest, though, I hadn't given it much thought. My optimism may now seem naive and unthinking but in my defence I had no reason to doubt. I still saw myself as a cricketer filling in time before the new season. I had an affinity for rugby and, slightly to my surprise, I had enjoyed nothing but success – as a scrum-half at Bristol and as a full-back at Cambridge. Why shouldn't things go well as an outside-half for Gloucestershire?

They nearly went horribly wrong. The Gloucester players didn't seem to like playing at the Memorial Ground, and the Memorial Ground fans were upset at the omission of Bristol's England and Lions hooker John Pullin from the Gloucestershire line-up. They became even more annoyed as Hertfordshire played well and Gloucestershire made mistake after mistake. When Gloucester prop Mike Burton, sent off halfway through the second half for a second act of skulduggery, made a theatrical bow in their direction, they were incandescent. In the end, it took a last-minute penalty from Peter Butler to win a thoroughly unsatisfactory match. Although, according to *The Times*, I 'began with a most versatile flourish,' I felt the *Express* was more accurate in reporting that I was out of my depth. The flirtation with fly-half – and full-back for that matter – was over and I could get back to life at scrum-half. Or so I thought.

The groundwork had already been done. I'd been appointed secretary of Cambridge University rugby, which meant that not only did I have to attend committee meetings and write the teams out in flawless longhand every week – complete with full initials and school and college details for every player – but I also got to sit on selection. Richard Harding was not available after Christmas, while Alun Lewis was firmly ensconced in the Bedford team with whom he was to win the John Player National Knockout Cup that year. The only thing that threatened a clear run for me in the No. 9 shirt was a murderous fixture-list that required a deliberately reduced-strength team to travel to both Moseley and Gloucester – clubs that had contested the first-ever knockout final three years previously and still possessed the two toughest forward packs in the country.

Moseley had the current England half-backs Martin Cooper and Jan Webster and the press, increasingly despondent as England contrived to lose their first three matches in the Five Nations, became increasingly strident in championing the cause of the Cambridge pairing of Wordsworth and Hignell. Flattered though we were by these articles and by suggestions that we should be in the squad for that summer's England tour to Australia, our only rugby focus was Cambridge University's Easter tour to Japan. A combined Oxford and Cambridge side had blazed a rugby trail to the Land of the Rising Sun back in the 1950s, but few sides had visited since then. Oxford were co-invitees this time as well but, because of a mix-up over paperwork, they couldn't travel, so Cambridge – with all the senior players restored – were going it alone on a four-match tour at the end of April.

Japan was astonishing, exhilarating and exotic. We flew there on Aeroflot, the Russian state airline notorious for the size of its air stewardesses and the inedibility of its food. That though was the only part of the trip that was economy class. The Japanese Rugby Football Union, surfing on the tireless enthusiasm of President 'Shiggy' Kono, had arranged sponsorship, newspaper coverage and boundless hospitality. We were billeted for the first few days with expat businessmen and their families and in the course of the next fortnight we were proudly shown the beauties of this amazing country – the temples in Tokyo, the Imperial Palaces, the gardens in Kyoto, the bullet train, Mount Fuji, Osaka, Nagoya...

We were also introduced to some peculiar Japanese customs. For some reason – maybe because I was the youngest – I was nominated to take part in the saké-drinking ceremony. My host proffered what looked like a highly decorated egg-cup, poured a measure of what looked like tepid washing-up water into it and indicated that I had to bow, sip, gulp and then down the liquid in one before handing it back. Then it would be my turn to pour. He nodded, bowed, sipped, gulped, swallowed and poured again. Then I did. Then he did. Then it was my turn again... I bowed and nodded and smiled and poured... Before long my smile was fixed, my eyes were glazed and my lips were numb. I wasn't going to back down and neither was my host, and even if I knew the words, I wasn't sure I could enunciate the question. How exactly did the ceremony end?

The earthquake was rather less well choreographed. The night before our final match – against an All-Japan XV at the Olympic Stadium in Tokyo – the hotel began to shake. The geologists in the party had already warned us not to try the lifts. Now they reminded us that the recommended course of action was to stand in an open doorway until long after the last tremor. That way, they said we would be safer, though by what margin, given that we were already 24 floors up, they declined to say.

That final match was the only game we lost, going down 16-13 to a late penalty in a violent encounter which saw two of our players carried off after having their heads split open, and a third playing the last twenty minutes with a broken arm. Sometime on the tour I received a message informing me that I had been picked to go on the England tour to Australia the following month. My first question was 'Who is the other scrum-half?' The second was 'How long have I got after I get back before the cricket Varsity Match at Lord's?' I already had an answer to the third, 'How was I going to get time off from my exams?'

It appeared that history's unmissable exams – Parts One and Two of the Tripos – were sat in the second and third year of the degree course. The first year exams could be postponed and I would meet the residential requirements – to gain a degree, apparently, an undergraduate must spend a set number of nights in college – by staying on at the end of my three years to do a Postgraduate Certificate in Education.

After fitting in a couple of nets with the university cricketers and a squad weekend with the England Under-23s, I popped down to Burton's to be measured up for an England blazer and flannels. For the third time in five months I was off on a rugby tour. And, three months short of my twentieth birthday, I was going to play for England.

CHAPTER THIRTEEN

BATTLE OF BALLYMORE
(SUMMER 1975)

On the day that England announced their tour party for Australia, a Welsh legend likened me to the greatest scrum-half the game has ever seen, and the England selectors picked me as a full-back. Bleddyn Williams (Cardiff, Wales, the Lions), revered in the Principality as 'the Prince of Centres', wrote that 'while it would be asking too much of England to produce a Gareth Edwards out of the hat,' the England selectors 'should use their vision to pick a man with the basic credentials'. For his money that was 'Alastair Hignell, who is built on the same lines as Edwards, is aggressive and not short of speed'.

The England selectors had other ideas. They'd already selected 28 players in a Five Nations campaign that had only avoided a whitewash with a 7-6 win over Scotland in the last match; now, even though England had never won a series in Australia, they left 15 full internationals at home, and set off for the land of Oz with 12 uncapped players in a tour squad of 25.

I'm not complaining; I was one of them. The other full-back, Gloucester's Peter Butler, was also untried at Test level while the four half-backs chosen for the trip had one cap between them and one of the flankers, Steve Callum of Upper Clapton, had only ever played four first-class matches – for Eastern Counties.

It's hardly surprising that we didn't know what hit us either on the field or off it. Firstly, prop Steve Finnane lived up to his nickname as 'the phantom puncher of Sydney' and laid out three Englishmen in the first week. Then our own prop Phil Blakeway, accompanied by a close-up of his bulging biceps and a headline about his brief spell as a heavyweight boxer, succumbed to a tabloid set-up and threw oil on the flames of an already brutal tour by claiming that whatever happened in the rugby, 'England wouldn't lose the fight!'

England may have had a heavyweight boxer in the party, but we also had both the President and Vice President of the RFU who, and I quote from the Test match programme, are 'past-masters at the fine old English art of extending hospitality. What is more, they are adept at following their countrymen's sinister drinking custom – an allusion that the erudite may appreciate!'

The manager of the tour was chairman of selectors Alec Lewis, while the coach was John Burgess, a short, stocky Lancastrian with a penchant for planting great big smacking kisses on the foreheads of his forwards. He also had an unbridled passion for rugby and such love of his country that his team-talks swiftly degenerated into table thumping, mouth-frothing chauvinistic rants. At one point in a three-and-a-half-minute tirade – and I know because I counted them – he managed to use the f-word 27 times, while there were nine c-words and several bloodies. The gist, of course, was that we had to tear into the f-ing Australians from the outset, fight fire with f-ing fire, get our f-ing retaliation in first, etc, etc.

To say the policy backfired is an understatement. It's also fair to say that we weren't helped by the RFU's decision to send us on tour without either a physio or a doctor, for by the time England had lost the first Test – as well as two of the four warm-up games – a whopping 20 per cent of the party that left England less than three weeks earlier had been sent home injured, while another 20 per cent were walking wounded.

I was one of them. Right at the end of my first appearance for England – a 65-3 thrashing of Western Australia in Perth – I went over on my right ankle. Three days later I had still not been able to train, nor had I gone for an X-ray. While the selectors were hoping I'd be able to play on the Saturday against New South Wales, I was just hoping to be able to walk without pain. As far as physiotherapy was concerned, I was graciously allowed to avail myself of the services of the Australian Institute of Sports Medicine on the other side of Sydney, but only if I got there myself. That meant an hour-long taxi ride in each direction and no clear indication as to who was going to pick up the tab. Until it was confirmed that the RFU were going to stump up, I took two buses.

I was rushed back into the midweek side four days before the first Test and kicked my first points in an England shirt – the conversion of a try by left-wing, and future Labour MP, Derek Wyatt – in a single-point defeat at the hands of the New South Wales Country XV. I was not 100 per cent fit but England had by that stage run out of bodies. Although the *Guardian* described me as 'encouragingly aggressive', I wasn't ready to play in the first Test that Saturday. That didn't stop England sticking me on the bench but as a team was only allowed to use two replacements – no matter how many players were actually injured – the selectors thought the gamble worthwhile. As it happened, Tony Neary and Neil Bennett were injured early on, and I could play no part in a 16-9 defeat.

It wasn't difficult for England to develop a siege mentality. Off the pitch we were being labelled as whingeing Poms. On it we were being bullied as well as beaten. But if the rest of the squad was retreating into a bunker, I was playing a 'get out of jail' card. The midweek match against Queensland had been a personal triumph. I had landed a penalty and three conversions in a morale-boosting 29-3 win. More importantly, according to *The Times*, I 'tackled like a lion, kicked well at goal, was swift and incisive in attack'. As a result, at the age of just 19 years and 270 days, I was selected to play for England against Australia in the second Test at Brisbane on 31 May 1975.

The omens were not auspicious. I had less than 20 games under my belt as a full-back, and was coming into a patched-up side already one-down in a two-match series, with an Australian referee smarting from some pointed – and gleefully reported – criticism from the English coach, and Australian opposition whipped up to boiling-point by their own tub-thumper David Brockhoff.

With Brockhoff breathing fire in the Australian dressing room – no doubt reminding his team, in between the head-banging, the fist-pumping and the obscenities, that they hadn't won a series at home since beating the Springboks in 1965 – the match that was to be dubbed the 'Battle of Ballymore' got off to a predictable start. From kick-off, the first ruck started with the whole of the Australian pack tap-dancing on the head of England prop Barry Nelmes and the whole of the England pack wading in to exact retribution. The ball went into touch and the players eventually responded to referee Bob Burnett's whistle, while Bill Beaumont trudged off the field for stitches to a head-wound. When England hooker John Pullin threw the ball in, it sailed over the waiting line-out bobbled forlornly in the middle of the pitch as both sets of forwards piled into each other. A penalty to England was reversed when the referee spotted England prop Mike Burton landing a head-butt on the Australian hooker. While he sensed that the whistle had blown, Burton also knew that he might never get a better chance to get revenge on a player who had been one of our dirtiest opponents in the warm-up matches.

'He had to have it' was an excuse accepted by all his teammates, especially as the resulting kick at goal sailed wide. Not quite so excusable was Burton's next act, a spectacularly posthumous late tackle on the Australian right wing following up his own kick-ahead less than a minute later. Mr Burnett didn't hesitate. Mike Burton became the first Englishman ever to be sent off in an international. My England debut was less than two minutes old.

Inevitably the incident has become enshrined in myth, legend and after-dinner story. On being told that he was being sent off for the late tackle, Burton is alleged to have made a plea for mitigation: 'Late tackle, ref? I got there as soon as I could!' And Beaumont, returning to the field with his head bandaged to discover that he would spend 78 minutes of his second-ever international appearance in the front-row, is alleged to have remarked, on being told of the reason for Burton's dismissal, and looking at a clock which now read two minutes past three, 'He couldn't have been that bloody late, could he?'

The Battle of Ballymore – almost incidentally, won 30-21 by Australia – has gone down as one of the dirtiest matches in rugby history. Commentators have always cited it as a benchmark of the game's violent past. For me, though, it was and will always remain, the highpoint of my rugby career simply because it was the first time I had worn the white shirt with the red rose in an international match. From the moment the team was announced, through pre-match training, the telegrams at the team hotel, the extraordinary sense of togetherness in those fire-breathing team meetings, the almost dream-like experience of the bus journey to the stadium and the walk through the crowds to the dressing rooms, the slightly hysterical laughter at mildly funny comments, the hyperactive checking of boots and studs and mouth guard, the unbearable loneliness out on the field for the first time, the incredible frustration of trying to stand still for the anthems while every nerve in my body was screaming for the action to begin, the hairs standing on the back of my neck as 'God Save the Queen' rang out, the knowledge that out of all the hundreds of thousands of rugby players in the country, I and 14 others were going to represent England on the biggest stage... I savoured every moment then and I luxuriate in the memory even now.

The disappointment of defeat, the disgust at the violence and the shame of being associated with such a notorious game in rugby history would dwindle over time. The label of England rugby player would stay with me for ever. Which is more than can be said for the shirt I wore that day, and which I refused to swap on the final whistle just in case there might not be another. Thieves rifled some of the England kitbags, which had been dumped in the team-bus while we attended the reception, and my jersey was one of the things they swiped. The great Andy Ripley – who had enlivened the rather dull proceedings by temporarily 'swapping' blazers with Australia's reserve hooker Chris Carberry, who was a good 14 inches shorter – sensed my upset and gave me an Australian jersey from the match, a big-hearted gesture that meant a huge amount to me.

The days that followed included a rather pointless match against a Queensland country XV in Townsville. I was on the bench but didn't get on the pitch and I think we won. To suggest that there was a carefree, end-of-term feeling about the match would be an understatement; we were so disinterested that shortly after half-time I was sent out to get ice creams for the replacements!

The whole point of our being in Australia was to play a Test series against the Wallabies. We'd done that, and been beaten. Once it was over, all we wanted to do was go home. All I wanted to do was get back to playing cricket. There was still a month to go till the Varsity Match at Lord's.

CHAPTER FOURTEEN

CRICKET BLUE (SUMMER 1975)

The tour to Australia officially ended at Heathrow on Thursday, 5 June 1975. I got back to an England that was unseasonably cold – snow had stopped play at a County Championship match in Derbyshire that week – to a Fitzwilliam College that was unusually quiet – university exams were still in full swing – and a message from Gloucestershire. Could I play in a John Player League match against Middlesex in Bristol on Sunday? While they appreciated that I might be suffering from jet-lag and hadn't held a bat in anger for over a month, needs must. The financial meltdown of the previous winter had left them with just 14 professionals on the staff. One of them was me, and although we had an agreement that I would only be available when the university season was over, a run of injuries had left them short.

Of course I agreed. Although there was still a month to go till the Varsity Match, and I'd only missed two first-class fixtures with Cambridge, the chances were they had decided on their Lord's line-up. If I was to be surplus to requirements at Cambridge, the sooner I got back to Gloucestershire the better. I bashed a couple of boundaries from memory as Gloucestershire lost a low-scoring contest and rushed back to Cambridge to find out where I stood from skipper Chris Aworth.

My first chance to speak to him came on the morning of the university's match against Lancashire. I arrived to find the dressing room in a mild state of panic. All-rounder Dave Russell had a back-strain and all the likely reserves were still sitting their exams. The match against Lancashire was due to start at 11.30. I was in the right place at the right time. I was batting by lunch; by tea I had made my maiden first-class half-century – caught Shuttleworth, bowled Hughes 64. I hit 44 in the second innings as well, and another half-century in the university's next fixture, a non-first-class match against the MCC, to clinch a place in the 12-man squad for the short tour that traditionally preceded the Varsity Match.

The fixture was enjoying a mini-renaissance. Oxford had one current Test player, Imran Khan of Pakistan, while two future England players, Chris Tavaré and Vic Marks, were freshers. Their arrival at the same time as Somerset's Peter Roebuck and I went up to Cambridge helped foster the belief that the fixture was about to enter another golden era. Almost half of the 22 players who took the field at Lord's had county experience, but it was two unknown bowlers who hit the headlines on the first day. Ed Jackson turned in a magical spell for Cambridge to wreck the Oxford innings, only for Dave Fursdon, batting at No. 9, to score his maiden first-class century for the Dark Blues. That left Cambridge with an awkward hour before stumps and Imran Khan, racing in like a sleek and lethal panther, soon reduced us to 20 for three. Which is where I came in.

This was by far the fastest and bounciest wicket I had encountered in my life. The tracks at Fenner's, and indeed in Gloucestershire, were usually slow and low and the best advice for any batsman at the beginning of an innings was 'when in doubt, lunge forward'. This strategy was entirely useless against Imran at Lord's that Saturday evening. Batsmen – with the exception of Mike Brearley who had a home-made fibreglass temple-protector – wouldn't have dreamt of wearing helmets and there was no limitation on the number of short-pitched balls a bowler could deliver in an over. I was therefore immediately subjected to a ferocious barrage from Imran, which had me ducking and bobbing and weaving and hopping just to survive. One delivery pinged me on the left ear as I tried to get out of the way and shot off in the direction of the fine-leg boundary. 'Catch it,' demanded the future international statesman. Wicketkeeper Paul Fisher, good enough to play county cricket for Essex and Worcestershire, leapt vainly to his left, just failing to get a gauntlet on the ball as it raced towards to pavilion boundary. I set off towards the bowler's end, rubbing my throbbing ear and hoping that fine leg would cut the ball off, and I could have a respite from the Imran onslaught. Peter Roebuck, just as concerned to continue watching from a safe distance, sprinted towards me, shouting 'Push him! Come back for two!' The ball was travelling too fast for the fielder and thudded into the wall just next to the pavilion steps. Umpire John Langridge signalled four, even though I was still rubbing my head. I pointed to my ear, which was by now swollen and purple-red and clear proof that I couldn't possibly have hit the ball with my bat. He called me over. 'The way it's going, son,' he said, 'you're not going to be out here too long. You may as well take all the runs you can get!'

But I survived till stumps largely by adopting a technique that was as ugly as it was effective, as graceless as it was calculated. Whenever Imran dropped the ball short – the frequency increasing with the length of time I stayed at the wicket – I got out of the way. If I could get underneath the ball, I did. More often than not, I found the ball rearing towards my throat and I could only hurl myself backwards to land in an undignified heap on my backside with my feet up in the air. But at least I kept my eye on the ball – which you can tell from a magnificent photo that was taken that day and deemed so ripe for comedy that it was broadcast to ten million or so viewers on Esther Rantzen's *That's Life* show on the same evening.

There was even a reasonably happy ending to the story. Peter Roebuck – a man bright enough to graduate with a first-class degree in law – explained his plan for our survival next morning. 'You look after Imran,' he said, 'and I'll take Vic Marks.' The strategy worked. He scored a magnificent 158, I hit 60 and we put on 161 in 140 minutes to earn a first-innings lead. I played on to be bowled by Marks in the first innings, while Imran took his revenge second time around when I was caught behind for just two. With Roebuck being trapped lbw by Marks for 33, our attempt to get 206 in 143 minutes to win the match was stymied early; the Varsity Match was drawn for the 14th time in 16 years.

As soon as I got back to Gloucestershire, I was thrust straight into the first-team. One of my early matches was yet another nail-biting Gillette Cup semi-final at Old Trafford. Back in 1971 the same fixture had ended at 8.45 p.m. with Lancashire left-arm spinner David Hughes hitting 24 in an over to snatch an unlikely win for the home team. Now, four years later, 22,000 spectators had crammed into Old Trafford desperate to see a repeat. Gloucestershire notched up a thoroughly reasonable total – for those days – of 236 all out, thanks to a century from Sadiq Mohammad and no thanks to me. I went in at No. 7 and apparently throughout my long walk to the crease TV viewers were given a lyrical description of my England rugby debut by Peter West, who'd covered the tour for the *Daily Telegraph*, followed by an encomium on my fighting spirit, natural games-playing ability and big-match temperament. The semi-final was perfectly poised. Sadiq's brilliance had set us up for a big total but Lancashire had got Zaheer out for nought and Mike Procter for just 13. We'd slumped from 126 for three and, when I went in, had just lost two wickets for one run. England fast bowler Peter Lever raced in, blond hair flying, roared on by a raucous crowd, and sent down a frighteningly rapid delivery that raced through my hurried defensive shot and rapped me on the thigh. Twenty thousand voices screamed their 'Owzats' and umpire Bill Alley raised his finger. In the biggest match of my cricket career to date, I was out first ball. There was no referral system to vindicate my belief that the ball would have bounced well over the top of the stumps and there was no fairytale ending either. Lancashire, thanks this time to some lusty hitting from off-spinner Jack Simmons, got home with three balls to spare. Gloucestershire were mortified.

But that extraordinary team for which I already loved playing were never down for long. Just as his valiant 45 had led the tail-end resistance that afternoon, David Shepherd – who was to become a world-renowned umpire and who sadly died of cancer while this book was being written – led the singing in the bar that night and I chipped in with my 'I'm a Little Teapot' party-piece. And then we turned to other things. The season was so crowded in the 1970s that there was little choice but to get back in the saddle, or in our case back in our cars, and flog up and down the motorways of England in a relentless sequence of back-to-back encounters.

One of those took us to Eastbourne and another extraordinary finish. Sussex, captained by new England skipper Tony Greig, had had much the better of a three-day match. The wicket, baked by the extraordinary weather we were enjoying that summer, was perfect for batting. Even though he could call on England's best fast bowler John Snow, Greig doubted that Sussex would be able to bowl Gloucestershire out on the last afternoon. Equally, he didn't want to risk losing – especially as Sussex had made all the running in the game so far. Accordingly, he delayed a declaration until mid-afternoon on the third day, and resigned himself to the fact that Gloucestershire would bat out for a draw and the game could be called off half an hour early, with no hope of a result. He was so relaxed about it that he gave his wicketkeeper, who was suffering from a migraine, permission to go home, asked opening batsman Mark Faber to take the gloves and settled down to watch both sides go through the motions.

Which is what happened till tea when Gloucestershire, having been set 303 to win in three hours, were chugging along at under three runs an over. The crowd in their deckchairs thought we were heading for a draw. Sussex, in between checking their maps to see where they had to go next and calculating whether they had enough petrol to get there, were resigned to a draw. And we junior pros in the Gloucestershire were convinced we were batting out time until someone – probably the arch-optimist David Shepherd or maybe the arch-competitor Mike Procter – suggested, over the jam tarts and fish paste sandwiches, that maybe we could win. Sussex never saw it coming and neither did the crowd. Suddenly Gloucestershire shifted up a gear and started smashing boundaries and snatching quick singles. Even though Sussex stemmed the flow with a couple of wickets, Gloucestershire kept on throwing the bat. The score mounted, the required run-rate came down and Tony Greig, until then genial, affable and almost avuncular, became almost apoplectic with rage. 'You f-ing cheat!' he screamed at Jim Foat – the man who had sensationally run him out in the Gillette Cup final a couple of years before – and stopped in mid-delivery to try to prove that Foaty was backing up too far.

'You bearded c-!' he roared at me, as Jim and I ran for everything, even at one point stealing a bye as the deputy wicketkeeper fumbled the ball. Poor Mark Faber fell to pieces in the face of his captain's wrath, which finally reached boiling point as I hoicked John Snow over square leg in the penultimate over of the match to ensure the most unlikely of victories.

I shall never forget the bemusement in Faber's voice as we returned to the pavilion. 'I say, twelfthers,' he drawled in the cut-glass, Eton-educated drawl of a grandson of Harold Macmillan, 'could you bring my drink onto the verandah? I don't think one should venture inside the pavilion with the captain in SUCH a mood!'

I managed to get up Geoffrey Boycott's nose that season as well. I was at the crease for the final over of a John Player League match at Scarborough. Gloucestershire needed 32 off the last six balls to win, and were still on course after four of them. I had smashed three sixes and a two off Graham Stevenson and his captain was frothing at the mouth, running up to his bowler after each delivery, frantically changing the field and alternately demanding Stevenson bowl it wide of off-stump, in the block-hole, short of a length, full toss...

'Cap-tin', said 'Moonbeam' – as he was fondly known – with a rather resigned look on his face,' I can only bawl wun ball at a fooking time!'

He got me out with the last ball of the match, having saved it with a dot-ball the delivery before. The match, like my cricket season as a whole, ended within touching distance of glory but also in anti-climax. Not that, as I celebrated my twentieth birthday, I had too much time to ponder the might-have-beens. I had to get back to Cambridge to sit some exams and the new rugby season had already started.

CHAPTER FIFTEEN

FIVE NATIONS (1975–76)

September is a crazy month. The cricket season hasn't quite finished – and may in fact be reaching its climax – while the rugby season, with its inevitable fanfare of extra fixtures, has only just begun. In September 1975, I was ending the cricket season as an integral part of Gloucestershire's middle order and starting the rugby season as England's full-back and a resident Blue at Cambridge.

I was also due to take some exams, with the threat of being kicked out of college if I failed. I should have taken my first-year history exams at the end of May but had been playing for England in Australia instead. In return for Fitzwilliam College allowing me to go on the tour, I had agreed to take my Prelims, as they were called, before the start of the next academic year. I'd imagined I'd have both the time and the self-discipline to do the necessary revision, but two and a half months in the Gloucestershire first-team had compromised my good intentions. Now I was sitting alone at a desk in the Fitzwilliam College library, with the invigilator, genial Director of Studies Leslie Wayper, looking up occasionally from the weighty tome he was reading to check that I was getting something down.

I completed all the necessary papers – and scraped a pass – but Doctor Wayper and his colleagues clearly felt that, given the demands made on my time as a member of the university rugby and cricket teams, I might be in need of guidance when it came to my studies.

'Tell me,' he said, as we had an exam debrief in his study, 'How much time are you actually spending on history per week?' I did some rapid calculations in my head, working out what he'd believe, what he'd accept and what I could get away with. I'd made it a rule during term-time to get down to the history library for 9 o'clock every morning, whether I had a lecture or not. I'd made it a point of honour not to leave until the last minute, allowing me just enough time to cycle back to college, grab some lunch in the cafeteria and get off to training, and

I prided myself that I had the self-discipline to buckle down to reading when it was required and produce essays reasonably on time. I got to the figure I actually spent at my studies – and doubled it.

'About 40 hours Doctor Wayper,' I replied, worried that maybe he'd think that a bit on the high side. 'Oh dear,' he said. 'I think at a university like Cambridge, we expect a little more of our undergraduates. That's the minimum amount of reading you should be doing each week. The lectures, essays and tutorials should, of course, be extra.'

I promised to reform.

My good intentions lasted less than a week as I fractured a metatarsal in the second minute of the opening match of the season. Because of the cricket and the exams I had missed what in those days passed for pre-season training and had only had time for a brief run through with the team before the game. That may seem ridiculously risky by today's standards but back in the 1970s hardly an eyebrow was raised. Rugby wasn't as myopic as cricket, where in some quarters there was genuinely a belief that the only way to get fit for a sport was through playing it, but it was still light years away from today's 'gym bunny' generation. In any case, I reasoned, I was young, naturally fit, I'd just spent the summer playing professional sport and our opponents, Cambridge City, were not expected to offer much more than token resistance. What could go wrong?

Quite a lot, actually. The first time I touched the ball in open play I fell awkwardly in a tackle and the pain in my foot was so instant and so agonising that I knew something serious had happened. X-rays showed that I had broken a bone. Best estimates reckoned it would take six weeks to heal, with non-weight bearing rest the only immediate recommendation.

Easily said, next to impossible to achieve, especially in the light of my recent discussions with Dr Wayper. I didn't feel that I could start my new more study-oriented regime by lying on my bed and missing lectures. And, as secretary of the rugby club, my duties included regular liaisons with the programme printers on the other side of town. I had to be able to get about, no matter how painful it was. I felt I had no other choice but to keep going to lectures and keep putting in the hours at the Seeley History Library, and no other option but to attend nearly all the training sessions and certainly all the matches played by Cambridge University.

Even though the club captain and fellow England international Peter Warfield was also on the long-term injured list, Cambridge never missed a beat. Alun Lewis, a scrum-half with an extraordinary powerful pass, an unbreakable self-confidence and an unrivalled sense of the possible, was outstanding as playmaker-in-chief for the Light Blues and tormentor-in-chief of the opposition. Wordsworth was back at his inventive best, Wood and O'Callaghan were running in tries for fun, and scintillating, high-scoring victories against knockout champions Bedford, perennial powerhouses Leicester and West Country heavyweights Gloucester were no more than Cambridge deserved.

By the time I was fit again, the Light Blues were in red-hot form. We pulverised Oxford in the Varsity Match – and the scrapbook kept by my dad bulged accordingly. 'Hot-shot Hignell hits the jackpot' trumpeted the *Express*, 'Hignell steps in' roared the *Mail*, while the *Cambridge Evening Post* proclaimed 'Hignell's kicking destroys the Dark Blues' in recognition of my 19 points – the most ever scored by any player in the history of the fixture. Actually, I missed as many penalties as the five I landed, and it took a typically cheeky display from Alun Lewis, whose drop goal and try added the final insults, to ensure that our coach Ian Robertson, who had backed us to win by 20 points, could set off on his honeymoon safe in the knowledge that his bookmaker was paying for it.

The final England trial at Twickenham that year was another personal triumph, though I was probably the only player who thought so. The *Sunday Express* was distinctly underwhelmed: 'full-back Alastair Hignell landed nine goals for England, fly-half Alan Old six for The Rest and referee Alan Welsby blew his whistle to distraction', in a match that gave 'no Welshman or Scotsman present much to worry about'.

But they could wait, for it was Australians who were the immediate concern – especially for the suits at Twickenham. As far as the RFU hierarchy was concerned, Mike Burton had been forgiven and the Battle of Ballymore should be forgotten. 'Let's wipe the slate clean – and start afresh,' pleaded President Tarn Bainbridge in a message aimed at both sets of players. Viv Jenkins, writing in the match programme, closed his article with the hope that, irrespective of the outcome, 'the game of rugby itself would not be sullied'.

It wasn't sullied, but it wasn't enhanced either. England won 23-6, but we needed a burst of three tries in six minutes halfway through the second half to silence the jeers of a crowd that had been growing more and more impatient with our error-strewn performance. I kicked 11 points – three penalties and a conversion – and tackled well, but I made a hash of several kicks to touch. Still, as the newspaper reports insisted, a win is a win and England victories were so rare in those days that the selectors had little hesitation in naming an unchanged team for the match against Wales a fortnight later.

My third appearance in an England jersey was also my first in the Five Nations Championship and this experience, far more than the back-to-back showdowns with the Wallabies, brought home to me just what international rugby was all about. Because the opposition were Wales, the build-up was feverish. The press speculation had begun as soon as the final whistle sounded on our victory over the Wallabies, and not much of it was complimentary to England. Both teams might have beaten Australia by similar scores but rugby fans were left in no doubt that while we were lucky, Wales were clinical. The difference between us, in the words of the *Sunday Express*, was the difference between beer and champagne.

I could never sleep much before an international and the nervous tension before that 1976 encounter with Wales would have made relaxation impossible in any case. The Petersham Hotel in Richmond is very dignified, refined and so well situated that the view from its dining room window has been immortalised in a Turner painting. But it was next to impossible to get some quiet downtime before the showdown with Wales.

And in those innocent and amateur days, few players had any understanding of diet. We had only the vaguest idea of what to eat and when. Our food choices were governed by superstition and custom rather than science. Bristol back-row Dave Rollitt, for instance, favoured a raw egg in sherry, while the rest of the pack seemed to believe in the virtues of pre-match red meat. I had read that fish was good for the brain and we backs tended to opt for that.

We must have had a police motorcycle escort for the Australia game as well, but the first time I was aware of it was for this match. For a start, the outriders had to keep slowing down as we fought our way through the traffic past the parked cars and across the torrent of spectators heading for the stadium. All of these seemed to be dressed in red, and all of them seemed to be waving leeks, sporting daffodils and singing.

Twickenham was transformed by their presence. Billy Williams's cabbage patch is now a state-of-the-art, hi-tech, fully enclosed rugby stadium, complete with hotel, fitness suite, hospitality boxes and all the trappings of modern sport. Then, it had a large green wooden stand on each side of the ground and the South Stand, recently demolished to make way for the final piece of the wrap-around stadium, hadn't even been built. Twickenham in the 1970s had a ramshackle slightly worn-out feel to it and the crowds reflected their surroundings. Respectful and restrained, they were neither excitable nor particularly passionate. And in the days before 'Swing Low, Sweet Chariot' they didn't even have a song to sing.

Wales' supporters, to be fair, didn't yet have 'Delilah' – but that was no loss. The great wooden stands at Twickenham provided a cathedral-like atmosphere for them to belt out 'Guide Me O Thou Great Redeemer', 'Land of My Fathers', 'Calon Lan' and 'Sospan Fach' with religious fervour and ensured that when England took to the field just before kick-off, we ran into a wall of sound.

This was the first time I had ever experienced this phenomenon at close quarters and to say that I wasn't quite prepared for it is an understatement. I had, along with the rest of the team, filed in through the players' entrance, dumped my kitbag in the changing room and, still dressed in blazer and tie, gone straight out onto the pitch to get a feel for the playing surface and the weather conditions. But that was about an hour and a half before kick-off when only a handful of spectators had actually claimed their places. There were only a few more when we came out, this time in playing kit, for a team photo. For the rest of the time, bizarre as it may seem now, we stayed inside. With all that huge open space to run about on outside, we stretched and twisted in a confined space. Instead of striding out across the soft green turf, we ran up and down on a hard, shiny surface. Instead of acclimatising to the outside temperature we worked up a sweat in a hot, fetid, claustrophobic centrally heated atmosphere. Instead of getting used to the noise of a 67,000 crowd, we went through our pre-match routine in near silence punctuated only occasionally by a few words from the coach and, in the last minute or so before kick-off, a few hearty and often expletive-filled exhortations from the captain. And then we stepped out...

Wales blew England away at Twickenham in 1976 and my opposite number, JPR Williams, hogged the headlines. On the day he won a record 34th cap for a Welsh full-back, he scored two tries – one in each half – 'showed superlative courage and skill', 'gave one of the displays of his life' and ended up being touted as the next prime minister by one euphoric reporter. While Williams was 'wonderful', scrum-half Gareth Edwards, scorer of Wales' third try, was masterful, and the whole Welsh team was so much better organised than England. Edwards's try came from a set-piece mix up between No. 8 Andy Ripley and scrum-half Mike Lampkowski, while both JPR's efforts stemmed from communication breakdown in our defence. The video doesn't make good watching. He crunched through my tackle for the first and left me waving pathetically in mid-air for the second. The press, though, were astute enough to report that I'd been left for dead by a skilful sidestep and I was more than happy to take their word for it – especially as I had a damaged shoulder. I was also pretty pleased with three penalties – all from upwards of 40 yards – while the general verdict on the team's performance was that it had been gutsy in defence, if a little one-dimensional in attack. There was no disgrace in losing to Wales, and there was plenty to build on for our next game.

I had picked up my injury midway through the first half of the match. I had just put in a long diagonal kick to take play deep into the Welsh half and, as I watched it spiralling through the air and then kicking on after the first bounce to cross the touchline, I allowed myself a little moment of satisfaction at a skill well executed. Suddenly, I was hit by a ton of bricks in the shape of Ray Gravell. 'Gravs' was big, burly and uncompromising, the inspiration for the hand-made banners proclaiming 'Gravell Eats Soft Centres' and the originator of the advice 'Get your first tackle in early – even if it's late'. He was also an ultra-passionate Welsh nationalist who was reputed to get so wound up before internationals that he would be physically sick in the dressing room.

There was not a single trace of vomit on his bushy beard. I was in a unique position to verify that as, several seconds after clattering into me, he levered himself to his feet – making sure that he pushed me further into the Twickenham turf as he did so. Now looming over me, he offered to haul me to my feet – by yanking still harder on my damaged right arm.

'Fuck off!' I screamed, loudly enough for a couple of teammates to square up to Gravell, and loudly enough to attract the attention of referee George Domercq. He blew his whistle a couple of times to keep the antagonists apart and then, standing between Gravs and me, asked in his best franglais: 'Expliquez please... What eez going on?'

'Just trying to help an opponent get back on his feet, sir,' said Gravs in that lovely singsong voice. 'You all right, butt?' he asked me, the sincerity oozing from every fibre of his being.

I chipped in with my best A-level French, 'Plaquage en retard, monsieur. Absolument impardonnable!' pointing an accusing finger at Gravell. 'Penalité, au moins!'

Monsieur Domercq was not impressed by this advice, and he was reluctant to believe that anything untoward had happened.

'Enfin,' he said. 'I did not see 'zis, but, whatever 'as 'appened, must not 'appen again. I am warning you,' he said to Gravell, 'Do not do zis again!'

'Right you are, sir.' Gravell was still at his most ingratiating in case Domercq changed his mind. Then he took a meaningful look at my right arm, which now hung limply by my side. 'Don't worry, ref, I think I got 'im right the first time!'

I was lucky that it was England's turn to sit out the next round of championship matches. By the time of our next match, against Scotland in Edinburgh on the third weekend of February, the muscles around my collarbone had repaired, and I had proved my fitness by emerging unscathed from Cambridge University's fixture with Trinity College, Dublin. It was late February, and incredibly cold. Murrayfield was more exposed to the elements than any other Five Nations stadium, with the wind capable of howling in around the giant clock at the southern end, and across the terraced mound on which Scotland's hard-core supporters stood. In view of the fact that both teams were due to be presented to the Queen before the match, the England players had made the not unreasonable request that we be allowed to wear our tracksuits until the last possible moment.

This sent the committee into paroxysms of anguish. The zealous guardians of the amateur ethos had for some time been concerned at what they saw as the slow insidious creep of commercialism into their treasured sport. They were so worried that we might not be buying our own boots that they had barred Adidas representative, former Leicester player Robin Money, from the team hotel before the match against Wales – with eye-opening consequences for me.

'Come on, Higgy,' said my room-mate Peter Squires, as I lounged on the bed reading a book and killing time. 'We're going for a walk.'

'But I don't want a walk.'

'Believe me, you do – and believe me, you also want to take your kitbag with you.'

And who should we find in the hotel car park, just out of sight of the main bedrooms, with a big smile on his face and his car-boot already open? Robin Money, of course. And, surprise, surprise, he had the style of boots I preferred, in my size. If I'd like to try them in a match sometime?

For some members of the RFU the next stop from leniency over boot sponsors was Armageddon, or professionalism, which in their eyes amounted to pretty much the same thing. A stand had to be made, and a line had to be drawn. So, no, the England team would not be permitted to take the field in their tracksuits. The reason; the tracksuits had a tiny little Adidas trefoil on the chest, and three bright white lines running down the legs and arms. As each player was to be presented in turn to the Queen, he was bound to be photographed. Her Majesty would unthinkingly be adding cachet to a deal with Adidas that, according to the backwoodsmen on the committee, already contravened the spirit if not the letter of the law on amateurism. Unthinkable.

Some of the team may have been busting for a showdown with the administrators; the rest of us were just concerned with preventing hypothermia. We were united in insisting that we keep our tracksuits on until just before kick-off. The stalemate was only averted when Don Rutherford, the former England player who, as Technical Administrator was one of very few salaried staff at Twickenham, came up with alternative tracksuit tops. These were mainly white, tennis-style blouson jackets, which had been worn – and returned – by the England squad that had toured the Far East in 1972. Crucially, they were unsullied by a logo, untainted by a maker's name. We grudgingly accepted that we would wear these, but no tracksuit trousers.

'Lowest of the low... ' Deep in the bowels of Murrayfield, England captain Tony Neary was in full flow, whipping up his team, clad in their flimsy tennis jackets and hanging on his every word, for the expected opening onslaught from Scotland. 'Lowest of the f-ing low... that's how the press are describing us... that's how the other teams think of us... well, look around this dressing room, look each other in the eye...'

'What's that?' Neary's warm Lancashire tones had given way to the slightly querulous, unmistakably cut-glass tones of RFU secretary Bob Weighill. He was pointing at the black attaché-style case lying on the ground next to our physio Don Gatherer.

'Oh that,' said Don. 'That's my new medical case... it's brilliant... it's got a place for everything, strapping, cold sprays, tape, padding, disinfectant... it's even got elastic loops to hold my scissors... '

'Well, it'll have to stay in the dressing room.' Air Commodore Weighill was used to command and his tone brooked no argument. 'It's got the word Adidas plastered all over it, and we can't have that. Leave it behind.'

'But I need it, the team needs it... ' Gatherer had been several hundred ranks lower than Weighill in the RAF and trained never to answer back to a superior officer, but in this case his ability to do a job was being called into question and he somehow managed to break the habits of a lifetime.

'Put the stuff in another bag, man.' Weighill was imperious and we were due out on the pitch very soon. We turned back to Neary.

'Lowest of the f-ing low...'

'Just a minute, captain.' Weighill was weighing in once more. 'Just checking you're up to speed on the protocol. Don't forget it's not mam as in pram, but marm as in farm... and "Your Majesty" when you are first introduced... So, how are you going to introduce your team?'

Neary hardly batted an eyelid.

'That's easy,' he said, 'I'm going to say "Good afternoon, Your Majesty, can I introduce you to the lowest of the f-ing low... ma'am?"'

The team-talk never really got going after that, especially when Don Rutherford appeared to remind each one of us to be absolutely certain to hand our tracksuit tops back to him before kick-off. What on earth was he on about? How, in the few short seconds between anthems and kick-off, with our minds focused solely on playing for our country, would we have the time or the inclination to steal the RFU's property? And even if we did have the time and the inclination how, in the full view of 70,000 fans in the ground, and countless millions more on television, would we have the opportunity?

The game was a bit of a disaster too, as once again England flattered to deceive. The horror-show began when Derek Wyatt, on early as a replacement for David Duckham, hoisted a speculative cross kick which not only caught the rest of the England team unawares but bounced so kindly for Scotland that it created what amounted to a five-man overlap. The Scots swept 70 yards upfield, inter-passing among themselves till scrum-half Allan Lawson was able to touch down under the posts. That try, of course, became a collector's item, not just for Scots who could savour it as the turning point of the match, but also for rugby fans the world over. Lawson was the son-in-law of Bill McLaren, who passed away in January 2010, at the age of 86. The legendary commentator's masterly description of the try masked the intense joy he was feeling both as a proud Scot and as a relative of the scorer and will serve for ever as a testimony to the sheer professionalism and expertise of the 'Voice of Rugby'.

As a human being, Bill was from the very top drawer. Warm and generous, caring and humorous, he seemed to possess boundless energy as well as an infectious enthusiasm for life in general, and for rugby in particular, with extra special places in his huge heart for his wife Bette, for his home town Hawick and his beloved Scotland. I knew him first as a voice, whose informed passion and whose magical, lyrical turns of phrase lit up the winter afternoons of my youth. Then as an observer, patrolling the touchlines at England run-outs, snatching a few cheery words with each and every player, doling out 'Hawick balls' from a tin with the words 'Take one of these, son, it'll put a yard on your pace'. As an inspiration to a young commentator just starting out in the business, he was wise with his advice, generous with his time and supportive with his encouragement. As a colleague – in particular during the 1999 Rugby World Cup – he was great fun to be with and a privilege to work alongside. The sport of rugby is so much poorer without him.

Lawson scored another try before the end of a match that had turned into a nightmare. For the second time in two matches, England had done everything right for most of the game only to chuck it away in a few moments of madness, or carelessness, or both. And we weren't any better against Ireland. Up at half-time, 9-0, we lost 13-12 and were, in the words of the *Daily Telegraph*'s John Mason, reduced to 'bumbling, fumbling inefficiency' by the end. Our confidence was so low that, four points behind with a minute left to play, we opted for a kick at goal rather than attempting to score the try that might have levelled the scores.

I escaped some of the worst criticism, largely because I had left the field just before half-time with a torn hamstring. Up to that point I had done some good things, including a try-saving tackle on Ireland wing Tom Grace and a burst into the line in attack that created a bit of havoc in the Irish defence. But in the process, I felt a sudden, sharp stabbing pain in my right hamstring which, the longer I stayed on the field, only got worse. I watched England unravel from a seat in the stand, with an icepack strapped to the back of my thigh.

It was only a fortnight till England were due to play France in the final match of the championship and I had little chance of being fit for that. Which was probably just as well from a personal point of view, with France running in six tries in a 30-9 hammering and England ending up with the wooden spoon for only the second time in history. My first full season as an England player had ended in a Five Nations whitewash. I hadn't blazed an unforgettable trail across the tournament, but I hadn't been a damp squib either. I'd kicked a few goals in the only match that I'd had the responsibility, I'd fielded just about everything kicked at me, made one or two line breaks, and put in a few crucial tackles. Just as importantly, I hadn't missed any and hadn't let anyone down. I'd not been the worst player in a poor team, but I'd not been one of the best either. As the brickbats rained down on England – summed up in one John Mason paragraph as 'poor judgment, plain ham-handedness, indifferent application of basic skills, not of international standard' – I was by and large excused. In my favour was my youth – I was still only 20 – and the continuing uncertainty as to my best position.

But while the media in best straw-clutching mode were using the last few months of the season to campaign for my return to scrum-half, I was not interested in hypothetical arguments. Yes, I believed that scrum-half was my best position, but no, I wasn't going to turn England down if they asked me to play at full-back. Yes, I would be happy to play wherever I was asked but no, I didn't fancy going too far afield to further my rugby career. Yes, I was deeply honoured, thrilled and proud to play for England but no, rugby wasn't my number one sport. I was a cricketer, and my ambition to get to the top at that sport hadn't changed a bit. And I was so determined to polish up my skills as a batsman that I'd already asked Cambridge to push me up the order. When the new season started, I was going to open the batting.

CHAPTER SIXTEEN

FLANNELLED FOOL, MUDDIED OAF (SUMMER 1976)

AJ Hignell c Breakwell b Botham 33. It was just one of 1,172 career wickets for the future knight, hardly worth a footnote in any biography. The match – Cambridge University against Somerset on a miserable midweek in late April 1976 – had little or no tradition, needle or resonance. The statisticians will log it as just another game. Even those who played in it will be hard-pressed to remember the details. Although Cambridge University still enjoyed first-class status, the counties tended to treat the fixtures as elongated nets, giving out-of-form batsmen a chance to play themselves back into nick, and statistically-minded batsmen a chance to fill their boots. Inexperienced bowlers could fine-tune their actions while any county pro worth his salt would expect to take wickets against university opposition. A bowler shouldn't get too carried away when he got an undergraduate out.

But here was the young Botham, bellowing like an angry bull and waving me theatrically towards the dressing room, while his colleagues tried to keep a straight face. The handful of spectators who had gathered at Fenner's that damp Wednesday morning were rather bewildered. The Cambridge University innings was not yet four overs old, and one of those had been a maiden, bowled by Tom Cartwright and watched carefully by the Light Blues' wicketkeeper/batsman Steve Coverdale. He had not yet troubled the scorers while I had faced 13 deliveries, bashed eight of them for four, and then holed out to a rather red-faced Botham. My first-ever innings as an opening batsman had come and rather quickly gone.

It was a brave decision of Cambridge University captain Tim Murrills to pick me, let alone allow me to open the batting. To say that I hadn't quite got my head round the requirements of the job was an understatement. I was clear in my mind that in order to further my ambitions to play cricket for England I had to iron out a few faults in my technique, learn to build an innings and take more responsibility as a front-line batsman. I was clear that the best way to achieve that was through opening the innings. I was clear also that going in at the top of the order for Cambridge during the first part of the season would give me absolutely the right credentials to cement a place in the Gloucestershire middle order at the sharp end of the season.

The theory was simple. Putting it into practice was far from straightforward. The hamstring injury I had suffered against Ireland may have cost me a cap against France but I was as right as rain by April. That was the month the England rugby chose to focus on the Under-23s – inviting some 60 players to a long and gruelling weekend at Bisham Abbey – and asked me, as a full cap, to set an example by attending. It was also the month when the university rugby team went on an Easter tour to France; where as a scratch combination with Oxford University we took on top French team Lourdes, before playing two more matches on our own. Travel was by coach, budget aeroplane and train, while accommodation had been arranged at an agricultural college in the Limousin. Primitive, basic, exhausting and exhilarating, this was rugby touring as it should be. We had a whale of a time off the field, played some outrageous rugby on it, survived brutal assaults from opposition players, shrugged off bizarre decisions from biased referees and somehow dragged our weary bodies to three victories in four days. We got back very late on a Tuesday evening. Less than 12 hours later, I was facing Beefy.

AJ Hignell c Denness b Rowe 101. My maiden first-class century could just as easily been part of the first 'pair' of my career. After edging a catch to the wicket-keeper in the first innings, I was rapped on the pads by the first ball I faced from Norman Graham in the second. I had no chance. The umpire was Ray Julian, his reputation as the 'smiling assassin' based as much on the way that his face contorted into a grin every time he gave a player out as on the suspicion that, as a bowler in his former life as a professional cricketer with Leicestershire, he had a deep-rooted antipathy towards batsmen. But nobody appealed. Ray Julian's grin froze on his face and while his finger stayed in his pocket, he spent the rest of the afternoon reminding me, every time I got to the non-striker's end, that I was 'f-ing lucky'.

And I continued to ride my luck for the rest of the Cambridge season, never reaching three figures again but chipping in with the odd half-century and several scores in the 20s, 30s and 40s. By the time we embarked on our traditional pre-Varsity Match tour, I'd scored over 400 first-class runs and I was averaging nearly 40.

Our last pre-Lord's away fixture was against Nottinghamshire at Trent Bridge where, from a public phone box just inside the main gate, I learned my examination results in Part One of the History Tripos. Results were always pinned up on a noticeboard outside the University's Senate House. The only way I had of finding out how I'd fared in exams which were essential to my continued existence at Cambridge was to pile up a stack of ten pence coins, dial the call-box in the porter's lodge at my girlfriend's college and hope that she was near enough to answer it.

'You jammy bastard' were the first words she uttered and, to be truthful, the only ones that mattered. It appeared that she'd scanned the Third Class awards category, panicked when she couldn't find my name among those whom the examiners deemed to have only just done enough to pass, and been utterly astonished to find it nestling among the 'Honours, Second Class'.

I tried hard not to be hurt by her surprise. I had neither the intellect nor the burning desire to aim for a First and a 2:1 would have required study-time that, because of all my extramural sporting commitments, I just did not have. But I'd been lucky that the history papers were nearly always scheduled for the last few days of the exam period – giving me a precious cricket-free week to blitz the revision – and I'd prepared well by carefully studying past papers to work out which were the most likely topics to be examined. I'd banked on exam-technique and a good memory, and played the percentages. A 2:2 would do – very nicely.

We lost the Varsity Match at Lord's by ten wickets. Oxford in 1976 were without future Pakistan captain Imran Khan but their future England players Vic Marks, the captain, and Chris Tavaré got them out of trouble on the morning of the first day and their stand of 149, combined with the pace of David Gurr – a tall, lanky fast bowler who was to sign with Somerset, be tipped for England honours, 'lose' his action and drop out of the game all in the space of about three seasons – effectively settled the match as a contest. I was yorked by Gurr on the first evening, while Peter Roebuck was dismissed in a similar fashion next morning for 0 as Cambridge, despite 37 from our own future England batsman Paul Parker, were shot out for 116. Roebuck and I both made amends in the second innings but both got out before the close of the second day, my two-and-a-half-hour 57 ending with a lapse of concentration and a catch at short leg in the very last over. We made them bat again but they won the match comfortably, with seven overs to spare.

The early finish gave us more time for the traditional ritual of choosing our captain for the following season. Peter Roebuck, fresh from a First in Part One of his law degree, was not only our brightest but also our best player, and for both those reasons I had proposed him as skipper at the end of the 1975 Varsity Match, when he'd also scored a stunning century. He'd lost out that time to Tim Murrills. Now, a year later, there was no opposition – but he didn't want the job. Peter's priority was gaining a First – a charge that could never be levelled at me. Even though I was also entering my Finals year, I was only too happy to have my name put forward for the captaincy – and delighted to be given the job.

When I got back to Gloucestershire I found myself living on the set of *Men Behaving Badly*. If the hit TV series had been in need of a template, the house I shared with Jimmy Foat, Julian Shackleton and John Childs would have provided it. The day after the Varsity Match I arrived in Bristol to find a kitchen sink overflowing with unwashed crockery, while every surface was littered with dirty coffee cups, overflowing ashtrays, empty beer cans and milk bottles that had not yet been rinsed. There was spilt sugar on the side and spilt cornflakes in the cupboard. The floor was grimy and the kitchen bin was overflowing with takeaway containers. This was to be my home for the rest of the season.

My guess that the kitty system had broken down was confirmed in separate conversations with my new housemates. The reason that there were wax crayon markings on one of the coffee-jars was that 'Shack' was convinced that the others were helping themselves to something he'd bought with his own money. 'Foaty' had hidden his teabags for the same reason, but was prepared to let me help myself until I got settled – as long as I didn't reveal the whereabouts of his stash. I was advised by each of them that if I had a favourite breakfast cereal I was to keep it in my room. More worrying by far was the revelation that nobody was prepared to take responsibility for buying toilet-paper, 'Foaty' arguing that if he needed to 'go', he 'went' at the County Ground during the day, or at the pub during the evening.

The pub was the Robin Hood's Retreat – now a gastro pub on the Gloucester Road, but then a very basic sort of boozer. The establishment was owned by Tom Hennessy, an Irish-Catholic cricket fanatic who served on the committee at Gloucestershire, and it provided the social centre for the county players and a fair few supporters. Shep (David Shepherd) was a regular, Proc (Mike Procter) was a frequent visitor, and the youngsters on the staff used it as a base from which they would set off on an evening out and to which they would return, as often as not, for an after-hours nightcap. It was basic, it was scruffy, it was rough and ready, but the Retreat exuded warmth, friendliness and welcome. To young cricketers struggling to make ends meet on uncapped player's wages – in 1976 still pegged at around £1,000 for the season – and far away from the comforts of home – Foaty's family home was in the Midlands, Shack's in Hampshire while 'Charlie' Childs came from Devon and my father was serving in Holland – it was our base.

The Robin Hood's Retreat didn't serve food but it was handily placed for all the Indian and Chinese takeaways, fish and chip shops and burger bars on the Gloucester Road. If we weren't on the road with the first-team – when on the strength of not very generous expenses we could stretch to a Berni Inn – we ate almost exclusively at these establishments. And we didn't know any better. Diet was a four-letter word to professional cricketers in the 1970s. We ate what we fancied, when we fancied, and drank by the same criteria. What was important was what happened between start of play – as late as 11.30 a.m. in those far-off days – and the close of play seven hours later. As bowlers, batsmen and fielders, we all counted deliveries. No one I knew counted calories. There was nothing scientific about our intake of food or drink and if anybody had suggested there should be, we'd have regarded it as the greatest attack on our personal freedom, and the greatest slight on our sense of personal responsibility. Away from the cricket ground we were free to eat and drink what, when and where we wanted. At it, we ate whatever was put in front of us – or we went without.

Not that there was any danger of wasting away. The County Ground at Bristol did a mean bacon sandwich for those who'd skipped breakfast at home, while there was always a tray of biscuits to go with the pot of tea that was served in the dressing room just before start of play, and a tray of cakes to go with the pot of tea that was served mid-afternoon. Lunch may have been only 40 minutes long, but there were still three courses to be crammed in – it was not uncommon to be fed pâté de maison and toast, steak and chips with onion rings and peas and Black Forest gateau to follow, before coffee was served. At stumps, there might be some sandwiches left over but the far more important ritual was the close-of-play drink. It was an established custom on the county circuit that, wherever you were playing, a complimentary drink would be provided by the host county the moment play was over. It was a key function of the twelfth man to compile a list of his teammates' requirements during the day, and fetch 13 drinks – one for the scorer as well – from the bar just before the end of proceedings. These were usually in pint glasses and quite often alcoholic. Shep, for instance, was a real ale devotee, and invariably requested a glass of the 'local wallop', while Mike Procter always ordered lager and Zaheer, surprisingly considering he was a Muslim, used to opt for a pint of Guinness. When we'd showered, there'd be drinks at the bar with the opposition, and sometimes in the marquee with the sponsors as well; before, if we were away from home, the search for an evening meal and a nightcap or three in the team hotel. When put on the spot, we might have acknowledged that we were putting too much of the wrong stuff into bodies that we weren't doing much to look after, but we wouldn't give much house room to the idea of abstention. After all, weren't we regularly playing with and against world-class cricketers who quite clearly had long ago ceased to regard the body as a temple?

In the summer of 1976 there was no bigger glutton than Zaheer Abbas. His appetite was for runs and it was all but insatiable. In first-class cricket alone the Pakistani Test player scored 2,554 runs – more than anyone else in the country, with nine centuries and two double-centuries at an average of just over 75. Tall, thin and bespectacled, Z had a high back-lift, an extravagant twirl of the bat in the pick-up, and a savage whip-like follow-through that sent the ball racing away from the bat at a speed completely improbable from a man of such slender frame. What's more he sent it almost unerringly to places where the fielders weren't.

In an incredible summer, rare failures stood out like sore thumbs. He was out for 1 in the Gillette Cup quarter-final at Old Trafford where Gloucestershire once again came a cropper, but even that was more than he managed against the West Indies at the end of August. Z's duck at Bristol paved the way for my finest hour as a Gloucestershire cricketer.

In 1976 England's new captain Tony Greig had famously promised to make the West Indies 'grovel' – and then seen his team hammered 3-0 in the Test series. In the fifth Test, English humiliation could hardly have been more abject. Viv Richards scored a magnificent 291 in the first innings, while Holding took 14 wickets in the match. England turned to nine different bowlers in the first innings and couldn't take a wicket in the second when the West Indies couldn't be bothered to enforce the follow-on. A few days later they arrived in Bristol.

Holding, Roberts and Daniel were magnificent. A mesmerising combination of grace, power, athleticism, co-ordination and aggression, they unleashed delivery after delivery of unrelenting accuracy and intimidating pace – in the nets. The bowling attack that actually took the field against Gloucestershire contained only Vanburn Holder from the Test team, backed up by all-rounders Bernard Julien of Kent and Collis King of Glamorgan, with Rephick Jumadeen and Albert Padmore to bowl spin. Even without the superstars, they had us on the ropes at 9 for two, with Sadiq dismissed for three and Zaheer without scoring. And that's where I came in, to bat for four-and-a-half hours, hit 13 fours and score 119 – my first century for Gloucestershire and my highest first-class score to date.

It wasn't anywhere near the best innings I had played but, in that it helped ward off a mini-crisis for the team and allowed me time to build an innings over a protracted period against high-class opposition, it was certainly the most important. If there had been any doubts about my ability to survive and thrive as a batsman in first-class cricket, there were none now. I had proved to myself that I had both the talent and the tenacity to get to the top in cricket. I could shrug off the criticisms of my batting style ('he would not win prizes at a *concours d'elegance*') and I didn't mind being damned by faint praise ('he ought not to do badly, for he is a natural athlete and a tryer'). This was proof positive that I had arrived as a cricketer.

As well as scoring valuable runs for Gloucestershire, I was also taking catches. I spent most of our time in the field 'under the bat' – at short square leg for the quicker bowlers and at silly point or gully for the slow men. Knees bent, hands touching the ground, helmetless and unencumbered by shin pads, I would crouch down before delivery ready to throw myself forward and under the bat at the slightest hint of a tentative defensive prod or backwards and flat whenever the bat was raised with attacking intent. So accurate were our bowlers that I rarely needed to take evasive action and even if I did take a blow, I would play the rugby hard-man and refuse to show the pain. As a result I picked up 16 catches in half a season, including four in one innings in the defeat of Hampshire.

The cuttings tell me I top scored each time Gloucestershire batted in that game, and that when I reached 65 against Somerset in the penultimate match, I had passed 1,000 runs for the season for the first time. I'd scored 691 runs for Gloucestershire at an average of 36.36 to finish third, behind Zaheer and Sadiq, in the county averages. As I celebrated my 21st birthday with a pint or three at the Robin Hood, I could look back with some pride on my first full season. But I didn't. There was no time in my life for introspection or retrospection. I bade my fond farewells to the *Men Behaving Badly* set – after undertaking to tidy up the kitchen, I found no less than 94 milk bottles in need of cleaning, sterilising and returning to the dairy – snatched a quick holiday with my parents in Holland, and returned to Cambridge.

CHAPTER SEVENTEEN
DEGREE OF BALANCE (1976–77)

The Cambridge rugby squad of 1976 was even stronger than it had been the previous record-breaking year. Angus Stewart's success as stand-in skipper had been rewarded by a unanimous vote of confidence by the players, and he was now installed officially as captain. He was one of four Blues remaining in a pack that was to be transformed by the arrival of a fresh-faced teenager from Monmouth School. The jungle drums had already told us how Eddie Butler had forced his way into the Pontypool pack, then the most efficient and most feared in the country. Anticipation was therefore huge for the traditional freshman's trial. And Eddie didn't disappoint. Tall, powerful and athletic, he soon showed that he had all the right physical attributes. But it was when he put boot on bodies that we knew for sure. All the senior players watching that October afternoon suddenly felt safer. We sensed immediately that no pack with Eddie in it was going to roll over and surrender. In the matches to come, both literally and metaphorically, we would pack a punch.

As expected, Cambridge won a fifth consecutive Varsity Match but nowhere near as comfortably as we'd hoped or was predicted. On a wet, windy day, we were perhaps over-ambitious while Oxford, led by South African international Dugald McDonald, harried us into too many unforced errors. Still, we won convincingly enough, 15-0, and, in converting the only try and landing three penalties from four attempts, I entered the record-books as the leading scorer in the fixture. One sad statto took the opportunity to point out that, including trials and internationals as well as Varsity Matches, I had notched up a 'phenomenal' 85 points in big matches at Twickenham in just two years. Paying tribute to my 'nonchalant class and fierce competitiveness' he inferred that the England's national stadium was obviously my lucky ground, little realising how hideously ironic those words would turn out to be before the season was out.

England's new selectors, meanwhile, were intent on root and branch reform for the national team following the previous season's whitewash. Of the side that lost England's last match, in France in March, only five were selected for the senior team in the final trial ten months later. I was picked at scrum-half for a Possibles team that beat the Probables 6-0, but was so ill at ease in my old position that the experiment was quickly shelved. I still managed to get injured in the Sunday squad session, 'popping' an inter-costal rib cartilage so painfully that it would have ruled me out of the Cambridge tour to Italy – if we could have contacted a replacement. Instead, I returned from a brief Christmas break with my parents in Holland to face a tough question: would I rather mooch around cold and closed-up Cambridge, dividing my time between empty libraries and painful physio appointments, or would I like to take up the spare ticket to Italy and go on tour as touch-judge? It didn't take long to answer.

Our first fixture brought us into contact with two England coaches. Dick Greenwood, father of Will, and Brian Ashton were both playing for L'Algida, a club which played its home matches at the future national stadium, Stadio Flaminio, and was linked to the local ice-cream manufacturer. Nevertheless the Light Blues won easily and, in the tradition of touring teams past, present and future, settled down to socialise with the locals. The L'Algida players undertook to take us to their usual city-centre bar and we undertook to teach them 'Fizz Buzz', a drinking game in which the word Fizz must be substituted for any number divisible by five and the word Buzz takes the place of a seven and reverses the direction of the counting in the group. Simple enough in English, played slowly, when sober. Vastly more complicated at pace, in Italian and under the influence. Played by English speakers who are unfamiliar with Italian, and Italians who are unfamiliar with the rules, it was absolutely hilarious.

Especially when a short, expensively leather-jacketed Italian shouldered Eddie Butler aside just as the giant Welshman was working out whether the number that followed trente quattro was a Fizz or a Buzz or both. Unfortunately one of the L'Algida players was so keen to show off his bilingual skills that he rendered a full and graphic translation of Eddie's involuntary Anglo-Saxon response. The little man in the leather jacket hurled himself at Eddie, and suddenly seemed intent on what Bill McLaren might have termed an 'argy-bargy'. The speed at which the landlord and his bar-staff stepped in before a blow could be landed and manhandled the Italian lads from the bar suggested that they'd had trouble with this gang before. The emphasis with which the landlord pulled down the metal shutter after them suggested that he didn't want them back, while we had to put up with a lock-in. Every cloud and all that... where were we... trente quattro? Crash! The metal shutter buckled under a blow from a heavy object and was then wrenched upwards. Little leather jacket hurled into the room; arms ready to belt Eddie with an ugly-looking car-jack. He was grabbed in mid-strike and so were his mates. The landlord, though, had had enough. While the gang of hooligans was being hurled out into the freezing January for the second time in under 15 minutes, he was dialling the polizia. And just so nobody would even think of sidling out before the boys in blue arrived he flourished a revolver and laid it menacingly on the cash desk. Our first instinct – to hide Eddie – was easier said than done. But the tables in the back bar seemed big enough, and there Eddie crouched for the next hour or so. As a fellow Fitzwilliam undergraduate, I felt it was only my duty to keep him company. How Robbo also got under the table as well, has puzzled us ever since...

We therefore weren't able to witness what happened next. As the polizia arrived, Dick Greenwood stepped forward to explain that as an Englishman who lived in Rome and spoke fluent Italian, and someone who'd seen the whole incident from start to finish, he'd be only too happy to provide a truthful and unbiased account.

'Fine,' said the policeman, 'if you would just step outside for a moment... ' Whereupon Dick was immediately arrested, bundled into the back of a Black Maria and stuck in a prison cell for three days.

And we weren't to know that during those three days Brian Ashton had spent several fruitless hours searching for his friend's whereabouts and, on discovering them, had immediately gone to the L'Algida club president to demand he do something. When the president just shrugged his shoulders and murmured soothing words about the Italian justice system, Brian had apparently declared that if the president wouldn't go to the police and kick up a fuss, he would.

'Not a good idea, Brian,' said the president, 'If you make a fuss, they will deport you.'

'Ye gods,' said Brian. 'This is supposed to be a civilised European country, not some third world banana republic. How could they possibly do that?'

'That's simple,' said the president. 'You see, when I arranged for you to come over and play for us, I forgot to organise a work permit.'

By this time we were up in L'Aquila ready to play the second of our tour fixtures. L'Aquila, of course, has recently hit the headlines for the appalling earthquake that devastated the town in 2009. Back in 1977 it was home to arguably the best rugby club in Italy, and definitely the one with the best home record. For the last three years, or so we were told, Italian teams had come and gone to L'Aquila and so had a handful of teams including Cardiff. None of them had dared to come away with a win.

That sort of talk didn't particularly put us off, though a first inspection of the stadium, with its moat, high wire fences to keep the spectators from the playing area and sunken tunnel which ensured that when the players first stepped onto the pitch they were at least 20 yards from the fans, should have alerted us to a potentially volatile atmosphere. The L'Aquila fans had long ago decided that they had the right to a say in any decisions made by match officials. Which made the stance taken by the referee that day even more courageous. He actually awarded Cambridge a few penalties, admittedly in the first few minutes when he calculated they couldn't influence the result too much and admittedly near the halfway line where he calculated they couldn't be turned into points. Unfortunately for him, Cambridge had a brilliant goal-kicker, Nick Greensmith, whose unerring accuracy sent the ball over the crossbar and between the posts several times in the opening minutes. The agitation of the fans increased as Cambridge scored a couple of breakaway tries. As time ticked away and the Light Blues continued to hold out, the crowd seemed set on scaling the fences to get at the referee and, for all I knew, the visiting touch-judge. The ref made sure he blew his final whistle when play was as close to the tunnel as possible, and I made sure that I beat him off the field, just as the L'Aquila fans fought their way on to it.

The dressing rooms had to be barricaded against the angry mob whose frenzied chants of 'Stronzo! Stronzo!' could be translated as 'Shit-house! Shit-house!' and were directed at the referee who, far from acceding to their requests for an immediate meeting, was insistent on changing in our dressing room. The crowd still hadn't dispersed by the time we were ready to board our coach and we felt the only humane thing to do was to smuggle the referee out with us. We therefore stuffed all our dirty, smelly kit into sports-bags and stowed the referee in the kit-basket. The more observant fans might have thought it odd that we chose to stow the kit-basket in the main body of the coach rather than the boot, but we would have got away with it if the referee hadn't decided to leave his hiding-place before the coach was safely away from the stadium. On spying their prey, the crowd immediately surrounded the coach and, when he refused their invitation to come out for a chat, threatened to tip him out of it by rocking it from side to side. The driver was by now as scared as the rest of us and, abandoning all concerns for pedestrian safety, slammed his foot on the accelerator and his hand on the horn, and barrelled his way on to the main road.

There followed one of the great nights of my rugby touring career. One of the L'Aquila players, a former Rosslyn Park back-rower called Paddy Costello, had a bar in town, and one of our players, Paul Parker, had a guitar. His party piece was a South African ditty entitled 'Ach Daddy, pleeease (won't you take us down to Durban'). We followed that with more songs, more drinking and tall rugby tales. We then shared a meal, and sang and drank some more in beautiful surroundings into the early hours. It was wonderful.

And, as far as I was concerned, the feel-good factor was prolonged well into January 1977 – on just about every front. At a meeting of the rugby Varsity Match squad I was elected captain – the first person in history to be chosen to skipper both rugby and cricket teams. I received a letter from the secretary of the BIRUT (British and Irish Rugby Union Tours) committee sounding out my availability for the Lions tour to New Zealand that summer. The medics gave my rib injury the all-clear. And, despite my absence from the final trial, England picked me for the opening Five Nations match against Scotland at Twickenham.

The result was sweet revenge for the previous season's Murrayfield humiliation. The new selectors must have believed that all their Christmases had come at once as not only did we record the biggest Calcutta Cup victory since 1871, and not only did the four tries in our 26-6 win double the entire tally for the previous season, but two of them were scored by debutants – Charles Kent in the centre and Malcolm Young at scrum-half – and a third was touched down by new captain Roger Uttley.

My contribution was not so resounding. Despite landing two touchline conversions and two penalties, I hit a post with one of my kicks at goal and missed entirely with four more. If I'd kicked all my goals, England would have won by 40 points but, after the 1976 whitewash, any victory was sweet indeed, and no one was getting carried away.

Especially as our next fixture was against Ireland in Dublin. England hadn't won an away match in the championship for six years and hadn't beaten Ireland anywhere in the same period. The Troubles cast a heavy pall over Anglo-Irish relations – it was still only five years since Wales and Scotland had cancelled their championship visits because of security concerns and only four since John Pullin's team had earned England a standing ovation just for turning up. And the Irish were taking no chances for our visit. Security guards were everywhere and throughout our stay a uniformed policeman was stationed on our corridor at the Shelburne Hotel in Dublin's city centre.

Despite all the precautions, nobody seemed to mind us taking a stroll around St Stephen's Green on the morning of the match nor to object when some of us chose to walk to the ground on Lansdowne Road – some 15 minutes away. That way I got to experience for the first time just what makes Dublin so special on match-day; the noise, the colour, the banter, the passion, the good humour, the excitement, all mixed with the nerves churning away in my stomach created an indelible impression. Since then, I've been lucky enough to play or work at all of the world's great rugby stadiums but none of them has supplanted Lansdowne Road in my affection. As a place to work, particularly for a disabled journalist, the old stadium ended up right at the bottom of my list. However, as a place to play, back in 1977, it was magic.

A 4-0 victory – tries were only worth four points in the 1970s – meant that England found themselves in a surreal position at the halfway stage of the 1977 Five Nations tournament. The previous year's wooden spoonists were now top of the table, played two, won two and still on course for a Grand Slam and a Triple Crown. All we needed to do was beat France at Twickenham and Wales in Cardiff – we weren't exactly favourites to do either.

But we could and should have beaten France. And the reason we didn't was that I missed five kicks out of six, two of them in the last ten minutes, and England lost the match 4-3. After it, I sat on a hard wooden bench in the England changing room and stared at the floor for 20 minutes. I couldn't look my teammates in the eye. I didn't respond as several of them patted me on the shoulder and attempted to offer some words of consolation. I had let them down. I had let England down. I re-lived each of those failed kicks in my head. I went through the preparation ritual over and over again and each time I asked myself the same questions. Should I have dug a deeper mound before placing the ball, or a shallower one? Should I have taken more time over each kick or less? Was it the placement of the non-kicking foot that was the problem, or the follow-through? Why didn't I read the wind better? Why had I kept on believing in my ability to land the crucial penalty, despite the evidence to the contrary? Why didn't I hand over the kicking duties to someone else?

The answer to that last question was simple. There was no one else. England's other goal-kicker was Malcolm Young. The Gosforth scrum-half was well on his way to a 500-point season for his club but he'd left the field injured at half-time. His replacement, Steve Smith, was emphatically not a goal-kicker. Nor did anybody else put up their hand. And why should they have done so? Twickenham, as several of the papers had pointed out, was a lucky ground for me. Over my last nine matches at the stadium, I had been averaging ten points a game. It had taken me a while to find my range, landing my one successful penalty in the 58th minute of the match, but there was no reason to suppose that once I'd found it in a wind that was variously described as twisting, swirling and angry I wouldn't keep it.

I didn't, and I also dropped a garryowen, which led indirectly to the French try. Not a great day at the office, to put it bluntly. But by the evening, after the cross-town coach ride, cocktails and dickie-bow dinner at the Hilton, I had regained some sense of perspective. I had tackled well, made one or two breaks and had not let the missed kicks affect the rest of my game. I felt I deserved another chance and I felt confident that when the selectors examined the video, they would agree.

And sure enough, when the team to face Wales at the Arms Park was announced, my name was at the top of the list. Never had I been more grateful for the quaintly illogical tradition of naming the team with the backs first from 15 down to 9, and then the forwards, numbering them upwards from 1 to 8. Never had I been so grateful for the loyalty shown to me by the selectors. They, it seemed, were unperturbed by the killer statistic that I had apparently only been successful with two kicks out of 17 in the three championship matches so far. Seen through a 21st-century prism, such a return is mind-boggling. I'm pretty sure that Alastair Hignell the journalist would deem it totally unacceptable, and demand that Alastair Hignell the player should never again come within a million miles of the job as England's goal-kicker.

But the selectors were keen to emphasise that this was already England's most successful season for some time and keen to take some credit for the continuity of their selection. Their predecessors may have chopped and changed – 37 players in six games in 1975, 28 in five matches the following season – but England's byword in 1977 was to be stability. England would only be using 17 players in the entire championship.

And we were well on course to land the Triple Crown – until well into the second-half against Wales in Cardiff. I landed two penalties in the first ten minutes to put England 6-0 up. My third success, from five attempts, established a 9-7 lead with a quarter of the match to go. But Steve Fenwick nailed a second long-range penalty and JPR Williams extended his extraordinary run against England by scoring the decisive try. We lost the match 14-9, my consolation being a return to kicking form, a *Sunday Times* write-up as 'easily the outstanding player on his side' and widespread media acclamation as a near-cert for the Lions tour.

But the Lions were due to leave the UK before my Finals were due to start. I was hoping that a precedent had been set in 1971 when Gerald Davies was allowed to fly out late to New Zealand after sitting his Cambridge exams, but the Lions themselves were not keen on a repeat. Any player making the trip, they decreed, had to be available for its entirety. And the university authorities were equally adamant; the gist of their reply to my request for special dispensation was that no student had ever sat his or her Finals anywhere or at any time other than in a place and at a time previously ordained by the university. In other words, no. Oh well, I was still the university cricket captain...

They say the best days of your life are spent at university. That spring, of March 1977, I would have found it impossible to disagree. Fit, healthy, happy, surrounded by friends, living in a beautiful place with enough money in my pocket, stretched mentally and physically by the twin challenges of study and sport, I was only vaguely aware of just how privileged I was. I was having a whale of a time, even if the nearest I was going to get to the Lions was a confidential letter inviting me to stand by as a reserve. This time. I'd only be 24 when the next Lions tour started and by then I'd never have to sit another exam. In the meantime, there was a degree to acquire and a cricket career to develop.

CHAPTER EIGHTEEN
GLORIOUS GLOSTERS (SUMMER 1977)

One of the duties of the captain of Cambridge University Cricket Club in the 1970s was to attend the annual meeting of the first-class captains at Lord's. Hobnobbing with the likes of Mike Brearley, Keith Fletcher, Ray Illingworth and Geoff Boycott was all very well, but I wouldn't have dared to make a noise as they discussed things like bonus points, limited overs matches, over rates and fines. None of those applied to Cambridge and it was transparently obvious that while my presence at the get-together was tolerated, it was entirely irrelevant.

Mind you, I did think Geoff might at least have recognised me when he brought his Yorkshire team to play at Fenner's in late April, especially as, in addition to rubbing shoulders on allegedly equal terms at Lord's, I had also played against the Tykes for Gloucestershire on at least two occasions and had rather memorably given him last-over palpitations in a Sunday League match a couple of seasons previously.

'Morning, Alex,' he greeted me as I welcomed him to a damp and windswept Cambridge.

'Come on, Alex. Let's get this toss over with,' he demanded as 11 o'clock approached.

'We'll bowl, Alex,' he announced with some satisfaction after calling correctly.

'Played, Alex' was his grudging appreciation of the 70 I scored out of the university's 164 all out.

I collared him over a close of play drink on each of the first two evenings.

'My name is Alastair, Geoff. That's what everyone calls me. Or Higgy.'

'Hard luck, Alex,' he offered me his hand at the end of the match, after a calamitous second-innings collapse by Cambridge had gifted his side an innings victory. 'Tha' needs someone to get hold o' this lot.'

'Cheerio, Alex,' he said, as he carried his cricket gear to his car, turning only to stare in complete incomprehension as I wished him bon voyage.

'Mind how you go, Gordon!'

In truth, a batting collapse was a rarity for Cambridge that year. The team was chock full of strokemakers. Wicketkeeper/batsman Steve Coverdale was in his fourth year in the side; Peter Roebuck and I were in line for our third Blues; while future England star Paul Parker was in his second year. Freshmen included Matthew Fosh of Essex, Nigel Popplewell of Somerset and Ian Greig, brother of the England captain. In fact so full of runs were we that in the match against Glamorgan I had the dizzy luxury of declaring with a first-innings lead and theoretically two chances of winning the match. In hitting a career-best 149, including the fastest hundred of the season, I'd seen Cambridge to a slight lead by teatime on the second day. I could have let Cambridge bat on for a massive lead but I was pretty certain that, however much time that left us, we didn't have the firepower to take ten second innings wickets, especially if all Glamorgan had to do was bat for a draw. I gambled therefore that if I gave Glamorgan a chance to get back into the match, they might, once they had knocked off the deficit, respond by setting Cambridge a reasonable target to win it. We could have had a third day with both sides attempting to secure victory. We didn't. My desire to become the first Cambridge captain to record a victory over first-class opposition for several years was matched by Alan Jones's horror that Glamorgan might go down in the record-books for all the wrong reasons. He batted for 218 minutes for 115 runs and Glamorgan refused even to set a token declaration. What's the Welsh for turgid?

Still, if victory continued to elude me as captain, the runs continued to flow for me as a batsman. I followed my ton against Glamorgan with an even more rapid 95 against Essex and a Gold Award as man of the match in the Benson and Hedges Cup against Kent. The national newspapers began to write me up as a potential England player. Well, some of them. Well, one of them. The *Sunday Express* posed the question in a headline: 'Could Hignell Become A Test Batsman Too?' And while astute enough to note that I was no Peter May, the ineffably smooth and graceful strokeplayer of the 1950s, reckoned instead that I could be a Colin Milburn, the heavyweight belter of the 1960s. I may have been winning no marks for poise or elegance but I was earning plenty for aggression and confidence with one innings being described as 'splendidly uncomplicated, of the type that too few contemporary batsmen dare to attempt'. In truth, I was in what is now described as 'the zone'. Batting was remarkably uncomplicated. If I received a delivery I liked the look of, I belted it as hard as I could, no matter who was the bowler. I had a terrific eye, a reasonable technique and an unfazed confidence.

But we didn't win the match that mattered – the Varsity Match – largely because, despite two declarations on my part (preceded by a fifty in each innings), we didn't have the necessary bowling resources to dismiss Oxford twice. Once Oxford decided to give up the run-chase, we just couldn't dislodge their tail-enders. The match ended in a draw but also with a vote of confidence for me.

My teammates wanted me to stay on as captain. I was going to enter my fourth and final year at Cambridge as captain of both cricket and rugby. Even more importantly I was going into it as a fully-fledged graduate. With a 2:2 in my Finals, I was now a BA (Cantab.).

As far as Gloucestershire were concerned, however, I was a cup-tied inconvenience. For, while I'd been sauntering disconsolately round the Parks after making just two and nine for the Combined Universities against the Australians Mike Procter had been delivering one of the most devastating bowling spells ever seen in one-day cricket. In the Benson and Hedges semi-final at Southampton, he had removed four top-order Hampshire batsmen, including batting legends Barry Richards and Gordon Greenidge, in the space of five deliveries. Gloucestershire had crept home by seven runs and were on their way to Lord's. Without me. Because I had played for the Combined Universities in the zonal rounds, I was ineligible for Gloucestershire in the knockout stages. I could play in all the championship and John Player matches either side of the big game, but I was surplus to requirements for the final itself. I wasn't even allowed to be twelfth man.

The Benson and Hedges final, in which Brian Brain took three wickets for nine runs in seven overs as Gloucestershire thrashed Kent by 64 runs, brought home to us that when everything clicked we were actually unstoppable. With Procter back to his fastest and most penetrating, Brain was the other half of the most effective opening attack in the country. There was simply no respite for opposing batsmen. Procter was all power and explosive energy, spearing the ball into the batsman off the wrong foot from approximately wide mid-off. Brain, all sinew and rapier-like intensity, could get in so close to the stumps that he came at the batsman from the leg-side of middle. Both delivered the ball at 90 plus miles an hour and, in 1977 at least, could bowl for ever. Andy Stovold, as he also proved in that final, could produce match-turning innings, and so, of course, could Zaheer, Sadiq and Procter. Left-armers John Childs and David Graveney exploited the inevitable inroads made by Brain and Procter; while the latter's high, flighted off-spin and Sadiq's theatrical leg-breaks gave us a multi-faceted attack. The rest of us could chip in as and when the situation demanded. Gloucestershire hadn't won the County Championship for a hundred years but, almost as if a switch had been flicked, we suddenly believed that we could do so again.

Or did we? Really? Deep down? As July rolled into August, the victories were mounting up and all the luck seemed to be going our way. We were winning crucial tosses, taking fluke catches, getting the benefit of the fifty-fifty decisions. Even the weather, which had earlier caused two matches to be abandoned without a ball being bowled, now seemed to stay dry when we wanted it to and close in when we needed it to. With David Shepherd as senior pro, it was hardly surprising that we became obsessively superstitious. Shep already had us lifting our feet off the ground whenever the score was on 'Nelson' (111 – one arm, one leg, one eye) or any multiple of it. If we could take the fifth opposition wicket when the score was on 123 (123 for 5 – get it?) he would act as if he'd just won the lottery. For Shep, superstition was a way of life. From black cats to hearses, from ladders to cracks in pavements, he could see an omen in everything. To ward off bad luck and to ensure good luck he had a ritual for everything, from putting his kit on in a certain order, to always sitting in the same seat, changing at the same peg, eating the same food for lunch, ordering the same drink for close of play.

With the wins piling up and the rub of the green consistently going our way, Shep could only conclude that we must be doing something right, and that, whatever it was, we must keep on doing it. What did we do on the night before our last win? Oh yes, we had a few drinks together as a team. Better do that again, then. Who was driving and who were his passengers when we had such a good day in the field? Better stick to the same arrangements. Did some of the team not have time to shave before we piled up a stack of runs? Better not use the razor on batting days.

This all turned into a moustache-growing competition. As Jimmy Foat and David Graveney compared stubble and speculated on which of them could grow the better 'tache, Mike Procter – a man who had never been known to shirk a challenge – decided that the whole team should take part. With one exception. Me. I already had a full bushy beard and was therefore ideally equipped to judge their efforts. As I explained to the media, I would be awarding marks both for luxuriance and artistic impression and severely penalising any attempts at sabotage or the use of hair dye, make-up pencils or cigarette ash. And, as I explained to the players at the end-of-season party, there was only one winner. While John Childs had been awarded a booby prize for a pathetic effort that hardly darkened his cherubic baby face, and Zaheer had earned a special mention for a moustache that was in parts, improbably ginger, the winner by a street was Shep. He'd managed to join up sideburns and moustache in a thoroughly convincing impersonation of a Victorian butcher.

As Gloucestershire were surging up the table, I was in prime form. After scoring over 500 runs for Cambridge in the first-half of the season, I'd contributed important runs – often batting at No. 4 – and taken valuable catches at key moments. I'd hit a one-day best of 85 not out as we'd failed by a whisker to beat Gillette Cup holders Northamptonshire and, as the season's climax approached, I was feeling on top of my game. Gloucestershire had timed their run perfectly, going to the top of the table at the start of the last round of matches. From 21 matches we had 216 points with Middlesex and Kent locked together on 211. With thunderstorms forecast, the weather could still play a part as we took on Hampshire at Bristol, Middlesex lined up against Lancashire at Blackpool and Kent played Warwickshire at Edgbaston. But as far as we were concerned the maths was simple; victory would guarantee us the title.

We may have had home advantage but we didn't have a great success rate at Bristol, where the wicket was slow, low, even-paced and bland. There was normally not enough pace in it for fast bowlers, Procter and Brain, not enough turn in it for our left-arm spinners Childs and Graveney, and too much clay in it for it to disintegrate. We needed to take 20 wickets to win the match and we knew we would have our work cut out. With rain forecast, our first priority, after winning the toss, was to get runs quickly.

And it was nearly all over before it had begun. We were 28 for three when I went in to bat and 28 for four when I came back. But Mike Procter rescued us with an extraordinary innings of 115 and then took six for 37 in 25 overs to leave us only six runs behind on first innings. And as if that wasn't enough, he smashed 57 in the second innings as well after we found ourselves once more staring down the barrel at 12 for two.

This time at least, I made a contribution: after stands of 101 with Zaheer and 81 with Procter, I was 67 not out when bad light and the promised thunderstorm brought play to an early end. We knew that both Kent and Middlesex were on top in their matches and we knew we had to score runs quickly on the third morning to give ourselves a chance of forcing victory. Perhaps we pushed on a bit too hard – I was caught at slip for 92 and our total of 276 all out left Hampshire the not unreasonable task 271 to win at a run a minute. Crucially for us, though, it meant we had four and a half hours to bowl them out.

'Higgy, I've always wanted to ask you what you think of deep-sea fishing in Cornwall.' Graham Wiltshire, our certifiably eccentric county coach, put his arm round my shoulder and asked the question in an earnest whisper just as we were taking the field. I slowed down as my brain desperately searched for the response that might help him get back to his own planet. I only just caught the back end of the PA announcement '... has been awarded his county cap'. As I stepped on the field I realised that my teammates had formed a semi-circle just inside the boundary, Mike Procter was holding out a navy blue cap embroidered with the Gloucestershire crest, the crowd was cheering and a photographer was stepping forward to record the event for posterity.

I was gobsmacked. Of course I had set my sights on a cap. It was an accolade that counties bestowed on senior players as an indication that they valued them as key members of the team, established players from whom they expected to get at least another ten years' service. But I still hadn't played a full season for Gloucestershire and wasn't going to be able to till the summer of 1979. Although my latest innings had seen me to 1,000 runs for the second consecutive season and although I knew that my batting adaptability and my fielding had made me an automatic choice when available, I had only just turned 22 and by no stretch of the imagination classed myself as an old pro. I was a youngster with plenty still to learn. In my mind I hadn't arrived at all. I was still on the journey. It was an understatement to say that when the announcement was made I hadn't the faintest idea of what was afoot. I was stunned to be awarded my cap, and incredibly grateful. Now, in order to make the day complete, we had to win the match.

Of course, we made a complete hash of it. Hampshire blazed away from the start. Already assured of a mid-table finish, they had no intention of letting their last match of the season peter out into a draw. They were either going to win it by playing positive aggressive cricket, or they were going to perish in the attempt. Which would have been music to our ears – if we had held our chances. But Brian Brain dropped a fairly straightforward chance at mid-off from a miscued Gordon Greenidge drive, while substitute Julian Shackleton missed a much more difficult catch off David Turner at short extra cover. Otherwise all their miscued shots fell between or over fielders and they raced to victory by six wickets with over an hour to spare. One of the largest post-war crowds seen at the County Ground was reduced to stunned silence. The champagne that had been put on ice to celebrate a first County Championship win in 100 years was opened anyway. It might have been fizzy mouthwash for all we cared as, grins fixed, eyes staring, we stood on the pavilion balcony and ruefully saluted our loyal fans. We were gutted. They were gutted. There could not have been a more cruel way to end a season.

We weren't to know that it was to be the best County Championship season Gloucestershire were to enjoy for some time. As I write this some 33 years later, Gloucestershire have still not lifted the trophy. And I wasn't to know either that I'd just enjoyed the longest injury-free period of my sporting career. Sport had a few more cruel twists in store.

CHAPTER NINETEEN
TEACHING A LESSON (1977–78)

'Let's face it, Alastair. If you have to rely on your voice you'll never get very far.' John Lello, Head of History in the postgraduate education faculty at the University of Cambridge, had just sat in on a lesson I had delivered to the fourth form at the Leys School. He wasn't to know that I would earn a living through broadcasting for the best part of a quarter of a century.

Nor was I. As a schoolboy I had set my sights on becoming a teacher and, even though I now had a degree, a county cap for cricket and a regular place in the England rugby team, nothing much had changed. Neither of the two sports constituted a full-time career – rugby was still rigidly amateur while cricket, despite the recent Kerry Packer-inspired revolution, was still a seasonal and poorly paid occupation. If I wanted to pursue either sport at the highest level when I left university, I would have to have another string to my bow. If I wanted to pursue both, and as summer turned to autumn in 1977 I could see no reason why I shouldn't, I reckoned that schoolteaching, with its inbuilt long holidays, was my best option.

I'd already been offered a job at Bristol Cathedral School for when I left university. I was to teach for two terms each year, leaving the summer free to play for Gloucestershire, and although I would be involved in rugby coaching, I would be allowed to play for Bristol – and England – when required. It was a day school so I could easily get to twice-weekly evening training with Bristol, and it was sited right in the middle of the city so I could get there easily from the home that my parents – in preparation for my dad's retirement from the RAF – had just bought in the city. Perfect.

But if my long-term future looked settled, short-term prospects were dire. Two minutes into my second match as the elected captain of Cambridge University, and for the second time in three seasons, I cracked a metatarsal. Same foot, identical circumstances, twice the agony. Once again I came into the line from full-back, took a tackle, stumbled and, under the weight of two or three bodies not my own, felt my right foot give way beneath me. I sensed instinctively that this was even more serious than my previous injury. Sure enough, whereas the previous X-ray had shown the faintest of cracks on my fourth metatarsal, this one showed a much more distinct line. There was ligament damage as well. I'd be out for some time.

My absence coincided with an injury crisis that stripped a very inexperienced squad to its bare bones and an appalling run of results that saw Cambridge thrashed by just about all the teams we played. Cardiff, Bedford and Steele-Bodger's XV racked up huge scores against us while, in quite the worst performance of the season, the Light Blues went down by 50 points to London Scottish at the Richmond Athletic Ground.

The only relief was an extraordinary victory at Grange Road against Gloucester. I still wasn't fit enough to play but, as captain, was summoned to entertain the visiting Vice Chancellor, His Royal Highness the Duke of Edinburgh, introduce him to the players and sit next to him during the match. Another prized photo in my collection shows that I got it as wrong off the pitch as the players got it right on it. I had obviously forgotten about the royal visit. With no jacket and no tie, an Adidas waterproof encasing a V-necked jumper and a shirt that I had forgotten to iron, I look more like a shabby down-and-out than an elected official of the university rugby club. The prince's smile, as I introduce him to some of the Cambridge players, appears to be forced through gritted teeth as if he still can't quite believe that he was going to have to spend the next hour and a half seated next to this scruffy vagabond.

But soon I was fit. Sort of. I could run without excruciating agony as long as I taped my foot in yards of Elastoplast and I had no trouble convincing myself that my team – weak, inexperienced and bedevilled by injury – needed me. I survived a run-out with the LX club – the university second team – and picked myself against Harlequins, knowing that this was the last fixture before the Varsity Match and my last chance of taking part in the big occasion.

Cambridge hammered Quins 31-14, produced their best performance of the season and scored six tries in the process. I converted two of them, kicked a 45-yard penalty and, fortified by a cortisone injection, did enough to convince myself, and coach Ian Robertson, that come the Varsity Match I would be firing on enough cylinders to do some damage. With Cambridge's other two full internationals, All Black Mike O'Callaghan and Ireland's John Robbie, both proving their fitness in the same week, things at last were looking up. Indeed we were spoilt for choice on the left wing with the final decision between two future England cricketers. In the event, Paul Parker failed a late fitness test, and Ian Greig got to play at Twickenham.

Once again we lost. As a team, we got it all wrong on the day. As a captain, I got it all wrong. As a player, I had a nightmare. After landing an early penalty, I missed three more and failed to convert Ian Greig's try before surrendering the responsibility to John Robbie. My lack of real match fitness was ruthlessly exposed by Oxford's future Welsh international outside-half Gareth Davies, while my goal-kicking errors were put into perspective by a near faultless display from Dark Blue centre Tony Watkinson. A 16-10 defeat looked close on the scoreboard but in truth we never got into the game. After three wins from my first three Varsity Matches, the climax of my student rugby career had ended on a bum note. I was the first losing Cambridge skipper since 1971.

And any illusions I may have entertained about at least being on the road to full fitness were shattered less than three weeks later as I pulled a hamstring on my debut for the Barbarians in their Christmas fixture against Leicester. As a result, I missed both the trials and England's first international of the season. But so did my chief rival David Caplan, as he strained a groin muscle just as the team to face France was assembling. Dusty Hare took the field against France in Paris but England were once again hammered and my chances of a recall for the second match of the championship season – against Wales at Twickenham – were good.

All I had to do was prove my fitness, my form and my goal-kicking ability in the Cambridge University match against the RAF on the last weekend in January – incidentally only my seventh match all season. The first two were relatively easy as the *Guardian* confirmed in an article headlined 'Hignell in fine fettle' and full of praise for a 'typically forthright performance, running into the line, tackling with unerring force and giving perfectly timed passes'. I also scored a try, but the goal-kicking was not so straightforward. After missing three penalties in a row at the start of the match, I was swiftly replaced as kicker by new skipper John Robbie. Even so, England picked me against Wales, dropped proven points-scorer Alan Old yet again and relied on me to get my goal-kicking into shape.

Which, of course, was easier said than done. If a goal-kicker wants to practise his craft in the modern era he sticks a bag of balls and a kicking-tee in his car and takes himself down to the stadium, accompanied by at least one assistant and very often a specialist coach as well. Back in January 1978 it was impossible to lay my hands on anything that resembled a match ball – those were shiny, slippery, brand new and kept in their plastic wrapping until just before kick-off – I didn't have a car, and if I could have arranged the time off from teaching practice at the Leys School to traipse down to Twickenham I wouldn't have been allowed onto the pitch. And as for persuading anyone to fetch and carry on a wintry afternoon in the Fens – forget it.

But in true Jonny Wilkinson fashion I still went that extra mile. Every lunchtime on the week of the Wales match I collected a bag of balls from the Leys School groundsman – not all of them leather, not all of them correctly inflated, none of them shaped like a match ball – and trotted down to find a set of posts on an exposed and solitary part of the school playing fields. I would dig the mound for each kick and go to fetch the ball when I'd done. And then I'd get myself back to school and change for the first lesson of the afternoon.

It was a routine that inspired awe in the media. The *Daily Mail*'s Peter Jackson was moved to impress his readers with both the number of hours (nine) and the number of kicks (290) that I had devoted to the task. His headline read, 'Hignell ready to boot out Wales'.

If only. In appalling conditions, Wales contained England's ferocious opening onslaught, seized control of the match through the peerless fiftieth cap-winning Gareth Edwards and hung on to win as Phil Bennett kicked his third penalty and I, after two first-half successes, mangled four more shots at goal, including a late penalty from 45 metres out that missed by inches.

Wales were on course for a Grand Slam and England, only two years after their last whitewash, were on course for the wooden spoon. So too were Scotland, but that didn't stop 70,000 cramming into Murrayfield for the Calcutta Cup match a month later. I was one of them, because I'd felt a tweak in my hamstring during some restart practice on the Friday and before anyone could say Jack Robinson or even suggest a late fitness test, the selectors had whistled David Caplan up from Leeds and stuck him straight in the team. England's third full-back in as many matches had a dream debut and nearly scored in the second minute of the match. Suitably galvanised, England trampled all over Scotland and romped to a comfortable 15-0 victory. Up in the stands, I didn't know whether to cheer or cry. It was a sensation that virtually every top-class sportsman gets to experience at least once in his career. On the one hand, your team is winning and your mates are doing well. On the other, so is the bloke wearing your jersey. It's an exquisite kind of agony and I defy anyone in a similar circumstance not to feel the tiniest bit sorry for himself.

There was little doubt that Caplan would keep his place for the season's finale against Ireland at Twickenham a fortnight later – even though I was back in action in a College Cup match within two days of missing out at Murrayfield. There was still plenty of rugby to be played and most of it as captain. I skippered a British Universities side to victory over our counterparts in France, led Cambridge on their third consecutive Easter tour to that country and was then, despite the imminence of the cricket season, invited to attend a training weekend as captain of the England Under-23s.

And that was when my experience let me down – and scuppered any chance Phil Boulding had of gaining a foot on the international ladder. Phil, now a High Court judge, had been a teammate in the dim distant days of Cambridgeshire Colts and had won a couple of Blues as a committed and courageous member of an often overpowered university front row. Now playing club rugby in London he'd been summoned for his first ever England Under-23 squad weekend and, as he was driving down from his parents' home in Cambridge, had offered to give me a lift. And I had offered to mark his card.

'What we need to do, Phil, is to stock up on food on the Friday night because once the weekend starts, there'll be practice on the Saturday morning, a couple of trial matches on the Saturday afternoon and another session on Sunday. You won't have time to eat, and you certainly won't feel like it. The same goes for drinking. Have a pint on the Friday night, 'cos you won't get another one all weekend.'

Before that day, I'd only ever gone to Bisham Abbey by train, and I hideously overestimated the time it would take by car. The place wasn't even open and we still had a couple of hours to kill.

'You know what you said, Higgy, about that last pint,' ventured Phil. 'I couldn't help noticing the Bull was open in the village... '

Having got our rehydration in early, we didn't need much of an invitation to stock up on protein at the squad supper when we eventually got back to the centre. Second helpings of steak and kidney pie, lashings of vegetables, suet pudding and custard (the whole concept of diet was still a long way away from the collective consciousness at the RFU) had passed our lips when Technical Director Don Rutherford dropped his bombshell. After welcoming us all to the set-up and explaining that all this weekend's efforts were to be directed towards a match against the county champions at Leicester at the end of the month, he proceeded to explain a new method of fitness testing. By keeping a record of the performance of each and every player in the national and age-group set-ups, over timed runs of 100, 600 and 3,000 metres, the RFU hoped to learn some valuable information about their players and ultimately devise ways that England could become more competitive. The Under-23s, he assured us, were at the forefront of this new initiative and had been specially chosen to be the first to undertake the tests which, considering we had so much to get through over the weekend, would start within the hour, with the 100-metre run.

Leadership! As the senior international in the squad, as the appointed captain of the Under-23s, I had a duty to speak out. I was also full to bursting with food and ale and I was already worried that my hamstring might not stand up to three days of continuous stress.

'How,' I asked, 'would it be possible for us to see where we were going? It's almost dark already, difficult to see 100 metres, never mind run it.'

'Easy,' said Don, 'the 100 metres is actually five 20-metre shuttles, and I and the other coaches will drive our cars onto the playing-field and use our headlamps to illuminate the course. And, before, you even mention the dew making it difficult underfoot, wear your rugby boots!'

There was no escape. Under the full glare of the car headlamps, every single one of the 56-man squad was set off to shuttle the 20-metre distance between two flags posted on a barely discernible patch of grass and the time taken by every single member of the squad was recorded for posterity. Guess who was the slowest back? Guess who was the slowest forward? Sorry, Phil!

The 600-metre test – two laps of half a rugby pitch – was slotted in after a punishing morning session and before an extended period of match play. Neither of us pushed our way up the rankings. The final test, ten laps of the previously marked out course, was scheduled as the very last activity of the weekend. Once again I attempted to exert some authority.

'Listen, lads,' I said to the backs as we waited our turn for the test. 'We're all completely knackered. We've given it our best shot. They've already picked the team so all we're doing now is setting ourselves a target which we'll have to beat next time to show we're making progress. But we'll never be as knackered as this so we're bound to post a better time, whatever we do now. So, why don't we take it easy and stick together so that no one gets shown up for being too unfit, or too keen. The best way to make it look as if we're all giving it our best is to take it in turns to lead the group. I'll take the first lap just to set the pace and then someone else can take over, and then just slow it down to manageable speed. OK?'

If I thought my team were as one with their captain, I was swiftly disabused at the end of the first lap. A whole gang of three-quarters, led by future England coach and knight of the realm Clive Woodward, swept past me at considerable speed. By the time I'd completed the course, I'd already been lapped by Clive and was comfortably trailing the slowest of the other plodders.

I was knackered. If I'd stopped to think about it, I would, I hope, have reached the conclusion that I'd never been properly fit all season, and I'd made things a whole lot worse for myself by continually trying to rush my recovery from injury. But I kidded myself that I didn't even have the time for that. I'd got this far by volunteering for everything, never taking a backward step and never entertaining the idea that anything was impossible. As long as there were enough hours in the day, and as long as I could cram everything into them, I was up for anything. Sometimes things got a little frayed at the edges, literally so in the case of my appearance next to the Duke of Edinburgh, but I could still kid myself that I had the important things under control. I was determined to grab every opportunity with both hands, and I was convinced that the result would be fun, or memorable, or both.

And what was not to enjoy? The rugby season may have ended with a whimper but the next challenge – the new cricket season – had already begun. During it I was due to qualify as a teacher and bid farewell to the place that had been home for four fantastic years. Before it ended I was due to enter the world of work.

'F-me, Cyril! It's like Come f-ing Dancing!'

'Cyril' was Graham Roope, the England batsman and Surrey slip fielder. The speaker was Robin Jackman, the England fast bowler on his way to taking five for 26 in 14 overs on a damp grey day at Fenner's in late May 1978. The object of his anger was me. The reason for his reference to one of the BBC's most popular programmes was my new batting technique.

During pre-season training Cyril Coote, who as well as being head grounds-man was also a fine judge of cricket in general and batting in particular, had noticed that I had developed a weakness outside off-stump. He suggested that I concentrate on moving into line as the bowler delivered and, safe in the knowledge that my off-stump was covered, resist all temptation to reach for any ball that was leaving the bat.

And it was working. I had already hit a century in a non-first class match against the MCC and now, as Jackman was running through the Cambridge top-order batting I was, as the cricket idiom has it, blazing it to all parts. As Cambridge were dismissed for 213, I was seventh out for 108, scored in just under three hours. And when Cambridge batted again in response to a rather dismissive Surrey total of 319 for 1, I was again in commanding form. At the end of day two, I was on 78 not out and within sight of becoming the first Cambridge batsman since Roger Prideaux in 1960 to score a century in each innings. On the third and final morning of the match I galloped past that landmark with what *The Times* described as 'workmanlike drives and thumps, short arm blows, drives without too much movement of the feet and clipped strokes off his legs'. The *Telegraph* likened me to a comic-strip hero and reckoned the story of the match was like a script out of the *Eagle* comic, especially when, against all odds, we threatened to win the match. By reaching 298 in our second innings, Cambridge had left Surrey 193 to win in three hours but the county made a mess of it, losing seven wickets for 116. At that point our one strike bowler Mark Allbrook, having taken four for 43 off 16 overs, had to leave the field with just over half an hour left to play. The reason? He had to collect a hire car from a local garage. He was the only driver among the five of us due to play a Benson and Hedges Cup match at Taunton the following day. A car had been hired in his name, the garage was due to close for the weekend and, not to put too fine a point on it, couldn't give a flying fig about the state of the match.

Still, my batting feats inspired sponsors Croft to award me a magnum of port – which didn't last long in a student household – and prompted one or two newspaper calls for my promotion to the England team – which also didn't last long and were never to be repeated.

Not that I knew at the time that I would never find batting as easy again. I smacked another three centuries for Fitzwilliam as we reached the final of the College Cuppers Competition and deployed the same appetite in squeezing every last ounce – or should that be every last drop – out of my last few weeks at Cambridge. Once the exams were out of the way and I'd handed in my dissertation I was free to do the rounds. Cocktail parties on sunlit lawns, booze-ups in back street pubs, five-course dinners in baronial dining-halls, an all-night May Ball followed by punting on the river and breakfast in Grantchester – I embraced them all. This was what it was like to be young and free and healthy and happy – and, of course, privileged. I knew I was experiencing something magical, and that I was incredibly lucky to have been given the opportunity both to study and to socialise at a place like Cambridge. I had no intention of squandering either gift.

Back in the real world, however... quite suddenly and quite inexplicably, I lost all semblance of form. The Varsity Match itself was a washout – each team bowled the other out on a poor pitch on day one and then twiddled their thumbs for the rest of the match. I scored just eight in total of 92 all out – the first time I had failed to reach at least one half-century in the fixture. The nearest I got to a fifty for the rest of the season was a 44 against Somerset in September. In between times I bashed a few good 30s and 40s but was dropped by Gloucestershire before the end of July.

I did occasionally get a call to fill in for a temporarily injured first-teamer but it was incredibly difficult not to feel like an outsider. My recollections of that season are enveloped in gloom. Gloucestershire had had a miserable season – 12th in the County Championship, third from bottom in the Sunday League – and, come the last match of the season, had little to play for. When the rain hammered down throughout our long journey up to Scarborough to play Yorkshire, very few of us were praying for a sudden break in the weather. Most of us were looking forward to being able to enjoy our traditional end-of-season celebration – when all the money collected as fines throughout the campaign had to be spent on a party – without having to worry too much about playing any cricket either side of it. The first day was such a washout that it did not look as though we would play at all on any of the three days. While some of us kicked our heels in the dressing room playing cards, doing crossword puzzles, walking endlessly around the ground, Jimmy Foat took himself off to the local joke shop and came back with a bag full of goodies. Brian Brain cadged a cigarette and took off like a startled rabbit when it exploded. David Graveney stirred a sugar lump into his tea and several seconds later saw a plastic spider floating on the surface. The Lord Mayor of Scarborough was a little bit put out when Jimmy marched into the sponsors' marquee in full Groucho Marx disguise kit, waving a plastic cigar and demanding, 'Is that a pistol in your pocket or are you pleased to see me?'

Umpire Dickie Bird turned red with embarrassment when Jimmy interrupted one of his favourite stories to embrace him warmly and affectionately, and though initially flattered at the suddenly increased size of his audience took a wonderfully long time to realise that we were finding his story far more hilarious than he was. We knew, but he didn't, that Foaty had managed to smear some itching powder just behind his ear.

'Ah was just sayin' to Wayne Daniel... ' Dickie's broad Yorkshire boomed louder to take his enlarged audience into account. 'I said, "Die mund..."' He stopped and scratched the back of his neck. We sniggered. 'That were his nickname, see – "the Black Die-mund".' The itch grew more aggravating, the scratching more urgent, our giggles more pronounced. 'You're a Test bowler Die-mund ...' Another scratch, and other snort of laughter. 'You've got to be able to pitch it... ' Prolonged rubbing, helpless giggling. 'You cannot be bawling beamers!' Dickie by now was unable to keep his finger from rubbing the back of his neck, and we were unable to keep from crying with laughter. By now word has gone around the whole room and Dickie realised that everyone was laughing at him. He also realised that it all started when Jimmy Foat had cuddled up to him a few moments before.

'Fawty – were that you? Were it? You booger – I'll 'ave you!'

And he did. By the end of day two the rain had stopped and the captains had agreed to keep the huge holiday crowd happy with a single innings match. We lost quick wickets and it was soon Jim's turn to bat. Left-arm spinner Phil Carrick greeted him with a loosener, which wouldn't have hit the stumps but did strike Jimmy on the pads and did elicit a disgusted grunt from the bowler. Umpire Dickie Bird grinned from ear to ear and immediately pointed his finger to the sky.

'That were never aht, Fawty, Ah knew that. And ah knew t'bawler 'adn't really appealed,' explained Dickie at the end of play. 'But ah 'ad this turrible itch at back o' t'neck and ah were just raisin' t'finger to scratch it... but next thing ah knew, you were walking off... Sorry Jim!'

CHAPTER TWENTY

KICKING ON (1978–79)

'I don't think rugby should be professional. It would never work and I don't think it will ever be tested.'

Oops. Hindsight is a wonderful thing, but in the middle of 1978 there was more chance of hell freezing over than of rugby going professional. Teaching was what I did for a living, and as far as rugby was concerned, all I wanted to do was play and practise, stay fit and keep in the selectors' good books. When it came to cricket, I was equally short-sighted. I ventured that while the Kerry Packer-inspired revolution 'could lead to some kind of bumper warfare, I can't see it changing the present format'. I was on much safer ground discussing my own sporting philosophy and my own ambitions. 'I play these games because I enjoy playing them and I want to play at the highest level in both. All I can do is try like hell...'

The big difference, as the rugby season started in 1978, was that while I was still hell-bent on making it to the top in both rugby and cricket, I also had a living to earn. There was no money in top-class rugby and precious little in first-class cricket. Although I was guaranteed somewhere relatively cheap to live – my parents' new house in Bristol – I still needed my first-year teacher's salary to pay the bills.

As well as a career, I was also embarking on a first full season of club rugby. At Cambridge we had trained most afternoons. At Bristol, sessions had to be squeezed in at the end of a day's work on two evenings per week. Initially I found it incredibly difficult to deal with the mental and physical tiredness of a day at work and then push myself through an inevitably combative, physically demanding and concentrated couple of hours that were often uncomfortable as well. But, after the traumas of the previous season, I was determined to give myself every chance of getting back into the England team. I'd even taken advantage of my absence from the Gloucestershire cricket team to attend pre-season training at Bristol during August. As a result, I was able to play a full part in Bristol's punishing early matches: a Saturday match against Northampton followed by the triple Welsh whammy of Newport, Cardiff and Swansea inside eight days. The All Blacks were due to play autumn fixtures against the South West counties in Bristol and against England at Twickenham and, as the regional selectors sat down to pick their team, I produced the most timely of reminders that I was not only back to fitness but also in great form. Two weeks before the visit of the All Blacks, I scored two tries and kicked seven conversions in a man-of-the-match performance against Exeter University at the Memorial Ground. Three days later I tore medial ligaments in my right knee during training.

The autumn injury jinx had struck again. This time it was even more excruciating because I knew that I had done everything in my power to prevent it. I was lighter, fitter and more rugby-hardened than I'd ever been. I was eating well – thanks to my mum's home cooking – I was keeping sensible hours – getting to grips with a full-time and demanding job worked wonders on my sleep patterns – and, no longer the carefree student, I was hardly socialising at all. I deserved a decent run of matches but I didn't get it.

The All Blacks came and went, and my knee took its own time to get right. My target now was the final trial at the end of January. It was England's turn to sit out the opening round of matches in the Five Nations Championship, which meant that I had an extra two weeks to prove my fitness. Even though the torn ligaments in my knee had limited the amount of goal-kicking I had been able to do, I was in pretty good shape as I prepared to compete for a place against the incumbent England full-back David Caplan and perpetual rival Dusty Hare. So was Neil Bennett. The former Bedford outside-half was now playing with trademark insouciance for London Welsh. More importantly, he was kicking goals. I did earn my place in the England side to face Scotland at Twickenham, as a full-back pure and simple.

As such, I had a dream start and a near perfect ending. With my first touch of the ball, I burst into the line, drew last line of defence Andy Irvine, and put left-wing Mike Slemen in for a try. At the end of the match, with the sides locked at 7-7, I exchanged passes with right-wing Peter Squires and wriggled my way over the line for what could have been my first-ever international try. I was convinced that I had managed to touch the ball down before being dragged back, but this was well before the days of fourth officials, slow-mos and instant replays. Referee Clive Norling had to make the decision on his own. No try. Match drawn.

Still, England's championship campaign was up and running, and my international career was back on track. Bizarrely, the game against Ireland at Lansdowne Road in Dublin began in similar circumstances to the match at Twickenham. England attacked; I came bursting into the line and flicked out an inch-perfect scoring pass – to Freddie McLennan. The Irish left-wing had read the situation, gambled on the interception and raced away to score under the England posts. We lost the match 12-7, but again I played well and the reports

I preferred to read after the game all said things like 'Hignell marshalled his defence with aplomb'. The report I chose to ignore came below a two-inch headline screaming 'I was to blame – Hignell'.

The home game against championship favourites France was my favourite in an England shirt. We had been given next to no chance against a team that had already beaten the previous year's Grand Slammers Wales, but for once we played to our potential and withstood a ferocious barrage to hold on for a 7-6 victory. A last-ditch tackle on flying wing Frederic Costes was a personal highlight but what will really keep me warm for ever is the memory of the unity, solidarity and camaraderie displayed by the whole team in those last desperate minutes. It was priceless.

So England headed for the final game in Wales having scored seven points in a match for the third successive time. Even more remarkably we were still in with a shout of the championship. All we had to do was to beat Wales in Cardiff for the first time since 1963 and the first time anywhere since 1974, while hoping that Scotland would beat France in Paris for the first time in a decade. Nevertheless, buoyed by the manner of our win over France and by injuries to Wales, we fancied our chances of an upset.

We were upset all right. Wales hammered us. Just 9-3 down at half-time, we folded completely in the latter stages of the match with Wales scoring 18 points in the last 20 minutes. Worse still, they didn't need any of the usual suspects to complete our humiliation. Gareth Edwards wasn't even playing, nor was Phil Bennett, while JPR Williams – in what was supposed to be his last international before retiring – actually left the field injured after an hour. The stars on the day were men like JPR's replacement Clive Griffiths, London Welsh lock Mike Roberts and Neath wing Elgan Rees. They all scored tries – so did JJ Williams and Paul Ringer – and the 27-3 scoreline was a record victory for Wales. England's dejection was complete.

It was an awful way to end the championship, which had promised so much more. But a new coach had been appointed – all-conquering England schools coach Mike Davis – and there was a genuine belief that provided we could remove the mental block that Wales had become, we had the players to do great things. And a tour to the Far East that summer – with non-cap internationals against Japan (twice), Fiji and Tonga – would provide the ideal environment for players and coach to gel before the next Five Nations Championship. England leant on me to make the trip, and wrote a letter to Gloucestershire indicating how important it was for senior players to declare their availability. Gloucestershire agreed to let me go – and declined to pay me if I went. This was the dilemma that I had always feared. When I had gone on England's tour to Australia in 1975, I had been a student with no salary to give up, and precious few financial commitments to meet. Things were slightly different in 1979 – but not irretrievably so. I was not married, didn't run a car and, if I could persuade my mum to waive the rent for a month, the tour wouldn't cost me too much. The chances of recapturing the cricket form that I had lost so disastrously at the end of 1978 would be compromised but on the other hand my status as a senior player in an England rugby team that we all believed was on the verge of great things would be cemented. Rugby careers in the amateur era were necessarily short and sweet. I would be playing cricket long after I had hung up my rugby boots. I was only 23. What I lost in the short term on the cricket field, I could still retrieve. Even though my cricket form had nose-dived in 1978, I still believed I could become a double international. England rugby needed me in summer 1979. England cricket could wait.

There was another reason why I was keen to extend my rugby season. I had finally learned how to kick. I didn't know it at the time but I was the first part of a process that would lead, via Jonathan Webb, Rob Andrew and Stuart Barnes, to World Cup glory for Jonny Wilkinson. What we all had in common was kicking guru Dave Alred. I was his first guinea pig.

I first met Dave on the back training pitch at Bristol's Memorial Ground. I'd stayed behind to practise some kicking from hand and was more than grateful when a stocky dark-haired stranger volunteered to kick the balls back. Gratitude turned to surprise when his returns tested my fielding abilities to the full. Dave kicked the ball so hard and so high that I was dazzled not once, but twice, as it passed through the brightest glare of the floodlights both on the way up and on the way down. Every kick was struck with unerring accuracy and unwavering power. I'd never witnessed anything like it.

We chatted on the way back to the dressing room. Dave was no threat to my position – he didn't think his left knee would stand up to too many match situations – but he might be a threat to my status. He had been a kicker for American football outfit the Minnesota Vikings and that, in the eyes of the RFU, made him a professional. I, on the other hand, was an amateur – even though I played professional cricket six months of the year. As the regulations stood, I was not allowed to be coached by David, even on a voluntary basis.

But Dave clearly had an encyclopaedic knowledge of the mechanical and mental processes of kicking and he promised to pass some of that on to me, on the quiet, in our own time, far away from rugby officials and prying eyes. I'd meet Dave at the Bristol comprehensive school where he taught and belt hundreds of American footballs up into the air from hand or into the shot-putt netting from the floor. Under Dave's guidance, I strengthened the specific kicking muscles with pulleys, measured the hang-times of each punt with a stopwatch, and separately practised both the 'planting' of the non-kicking leg and the follow-through of the kicking foot. The improvement was dramatic. By the time of the Barbarians-Swansea match – when I was successful with nine kicks out of 11 – I was not only striking place-kicks with undreamed-of consistency and accuracy, but I was belting the ball yards further out of hand. I set off on England's tour of the Far East with my kicking confidence sky high and a gut feeling that both the team and I were ready to take our game to another level.

In the decade leading up to England's tour of the Far East in 1979, they had won just 11 matches in the Five Nations Championship. Immediately after it, they won a Grand Slam. The tour had next to nothing to do with it. Grand Slam half-backs Steve Smith and John Horton were not even selected for the tour, nor were props Fran Cotton and Phil Blakeway, flankers Roger Uttley and Tony Neary or centre Clive Woodward. Neither the opposition – lightweight, sophisticated Japan, heavyweight, naive Fiji and Tonga, nor the conditions – baking heat, rock-hard dustbowls and coral-strewn recreation grounds – proved much preparation for the Five Nations. But we had a lot of fun.

It took me a while to enter into the spirit of things. After putting my cricket career on hold, and passing up on a month's salary, I got to Japan to discover that the England selectors had decided that, if they were to win matches on a regular basis, they had to have their best goal-kicker on the pitch, regardless. All the flattery they had used to persuade me to make the trip – that I was vital to England's plans etc – was quickly forgotten. I was to be a dirt tracker, only playing the midweek games, and Dusty Hare was going to play the four internationals. I was livid and initially couldn't care less when, in the opening game of the tour, I felt a twinge in the knee that I had damaged back in the autumn. I handed over the goal-kicking duties to fresh-faced, fly-half Huw Davies, and resigned myself to a month of misery.

But the injury responded to treatment and although Dusty kicked a late penalty to get England out of jail for a very fortunate 21-19 victory in the first match against Japan, Huw's goal-kicking success in the midweek matches – combined with my own form – persuaded manager Budge Rogers and coach Mike Davis to reverse their pre-tour policy. Huw and I were picked for the second match against Japan in Tokyo – which England won 38-18 – and for the other two 'Tests' in Fiji and Tonga.

There was only one thing to mar our departure from Japan. Under the media conditions that operate today, the fact that four members of the England squad were arrested after a scuffle in a Tokyo bar would almost certainly have been splashed across all the front pages of every newspaper in the country. In 1979, it hardly raised a ripple, not just because the half dozen or so journalists accompanying the tour never got to hear about it, but also because the manager remained in almost total ignorance throughout. I take some of the blame, or credit, for that.

'Stop staring at what you can't afford.' The blonde American, shapely, drunk and surrounded by Japanese admirers, was directing her remarks at England No. 8 John Scott.

'You wouldn't catch me paying for that – on a month of Sundays' was the gist of a reply, which prompted the blonde to hurl herself towards the Englishman, with the obvious intention of slapping his face. There was a moment of pure farce as John held her away with one hand while, unable to reach him, she furiously rained blows into thin air. And it was still quite funny when somebody starting lobbing the paper-wrapped toothpicks that were found on every table in her direction. The jostling turned into a good-humoured missile fight with sugar-lumps before one of the Japanese revellers got a bit confused and decided to chuck a cut-glass ashtray as well. This caught England flanker Toby Allchurch a glancing blow on the head. Feeling blood between his fingers, Toby launched himself in the direction of the mêlée. Seeing a bloodied and clearly upset Englishman charging towards them, some of the Japanese lads in the room opted for a pre-emptive strike. Within seconds a major fist-fight had begun. Standing by the bar, I was struck by one more moment of pure comedy. Maurice Colclough, England's giant second row, was clearly itching to get into the action but, sitting at a table intended for much smaller Japanese drinkers, he was trapped. Every time he tried to hoist himself to his feet, he caught his thighs under the table and subsided back into his seat. It all became too much for him. With a roar of rage, he upended the table, glasses and bottles scattering in all directions, and waded in.

My decision to beat a retreat was shared by the captain Bill Beaumont. We arrived back at our hotel to find a very worried and very young receptionist with a phone in her hand. She recognised Bill Beaumont as the captain and presumed that I must be the manager. 'We've got the police on the line for you,' she said handing me the phone. The voice of the other end was quiet and businesslike. 'We are holding four men who say they are from the England rugby squad. Can you confirm that Mister Allchurch, Scott, Davis and Colclough are members of your party? We need to see their passports before we can let them go, and one of them has asked for a Doctor Raphael to attend to his injuries. Can you arrange that?' I assured him I could, and while I left Bill to sort out the passports – thankfully they had all been deposited in the hotel safe – I went to wake the England reserve hooker, who also doubled up as the tour doctor.

'Bugger off, Higgy' was his immediate response. I hammered even harder on the door. 'Come on, Raphs, this is urgent. It is not a wind-up.'

'It better not be,' said Jon Raphael, as he shrugged on his blazer and grabbed his scalpel and stitching kit. As he was going to the police station anyway, it seemed like a good idea that he should take the passports as well. In next to no time, the five of them had returned to the hotel, the passports were back in the safe and we all settled down to grab some sleep ahead of our departure for Fiji.

The accompanying media – all four of them – were due to take the same flight out of Tokyo. John Mason of the *Daily Telegraph* knew that he would have to file his copy before we left Japan and accordingly sought out manager Budge Rogers to get a more considered opinion on the Test match and an update on injuries.

'Absolutely nothing at all to report, John. A few bumps and bruises but the whole team is fit and well.'

'But what about the players outside the match squad?' enquired John.

'Also fit and well,' said Burge. 'They all trained after the match. Everybody's fine.'

'Then how come I just bumped into Toby Allchurch in the lift and he told me he cut his head open during training?' Budge was stumped and he knew it. After spending most of the morning attempting to eavesdrop on any conversations between players he called a meeting.

'I know exactly what happened,' he said, 'and I am going to send those responsible home immediately. They will make it easier for themselves and with the RFU if they come forward now.' Nobody spoke. We were all pretty confident that Budge knew nothing, and was attempting the classic schoolmaster's tactic of pretending knowledge in order to get errant pupils to confess.

'I'm waiting.' Rogers by now was drumming his fingers on the table. 'And I promise you that no one's leaving this room until I have some names.' The drumming resumed. Still no one spoke. 'And I'm quite prepared for us all to miss the flight to Fiji unless I get to the bottom of this.' Silence. 'And if the RFU has to call off the match against Fiji, I'm sure the entire tour party will be judged guilty, and I can't see them allowing us to pick any of you to play for England ever again. But if I get some names I will send the miscreants home and we can get on with the tour.' The only sound was the drumming of his fingers until Mike Davis pulled off a masterful counter bluff.

'Listen Budge, this is a team thing. Something we deal with in-house. Everything that happens to the team, good and bad, we deal with collectively. We are all responsible. But if you're determined to send someone home, you might as well send me.' It was quite obvious that Budge had no idea that Mike had been one of those arrested.

'That, of course, won't be necessary, Mike, but it's a fine gesture.' Turning to the rest of us he declared, 'That is precisely the sort of self-sacrifice, togetherness and team spirit that we're looking for in the England set-up. You should be proud to have such a man as your coach. Let's get ready for Fiji.'

Fiji was wonderful. The guitars were strumming at the airport as we were garlanded with fresh floral leis. The kava was flowing as we took part in the traditional Fijian welcoming drinking ceremony. As memory serves, we had to sit cross-legged in a large circle and pass round a wooden bowl filled with a warm cloudy liquid from which we had to sip until there was no liquid left and our lips were numb. The golf course – designed, so we were told, by Peter Oosterhuis – was spectacular, the weather was idyllic and the palm-fringed stadium enjoyed the most breathtaking setting. Oh, and we won the rugby.

Tonga was a different world. Hens and goats roamed the streets of some of the villages we passed through on our way from the airport to our hotel, where, in our honour, a huge pig was roasting above a giant pit on the beach. On match-day we had to change in what could have been the groundsman's shed under the stand – no electricity, no showers, no light. If you opened the door to see what you were doing and to let the air in, the crowd came too. We spent the first part of the pre-match warm-up clearing shards of razor-sharp coral from a pitch that seemed to have an equal number of bumps and potholes and considerably fewer blades of grass, and the second part being introduced to the King of Tonga. This gentleman was built on the same lines as his mother whose diminutive carriage-companion at the Coronation was famously described by Noel Coward as 'her lunch'. Even so, as I stepped out from blazing sunshine to the gloom of the stand all I could make out was a flashing set of white teeth and a huge pink palm into whose handshake mine completely disappeared. Memories of the match, which we won, are less clear than memories of the after-match function when, because of the inadequacy of the electric lighting and because of an island-wide gender imbalance which encouraged a significant proportion of young males to dress up as women, I was not the only England player to find myself dancing with a bloke!

But as far as the rugby was concerned, it was mission accomplished. England had won every match on the tour including the four non-cap internationals, several younger players have been given an opportunity, several of the senior players had stepped up to the plate as far as leadership was concerned and the new coach Mike Davis had bedded in well with everyone. Now all we had to do was get home – far easier said than done given that Tonga was even more inaccessible in the 1970s than it is now. The itinerary included an 18-hour stopover at a luxury hotel back in Fiji and, with no rugby to distract us for at least three months, we were determined to make the most of it. Those were the days when the media earned far more than the players, and some of us were more than happy to be taken out for an off-the-record dinner by the handful of rugby correspondents covering the tour. This, under the direction of Chris 'Crash' Lander of the *Daily Mirror*, progressed to an all-night drinking session in the swimming pool, under the stars, and then morphed into a Bucks Fizz breakfast with most of the rest of the squad. I was locked in one of those earnest 'meaning of life' discussions with Huw Davies when the 'duty boy' (the player rostered to convey instructions from the tour management to the rest of the squad) came rushing round with the information that the coach was ready to take us to the airport.

'Bloody hell, Higgy,' said Huw, 'Get your skates on. We've still got to pack!'

'What do you mean "we"?' I replied. Apart from taking out my swimming trunks for the drinking session in the pool, I hadn't unpacked at all.

Although Huw was only marginally late, that wasn't the end of our problems. On checking in, we discovered that we were flying by DC-10 aircraft – the very make that had recently been involved in a widely reported crash-landing. We also discovered that we were flying to Los Angeles airport – the very place where the DC-10 had got into trouble. This was too much of a gift for the comedians of the team. As the pilot welcomed us on board, he made the mistake of using aircraft shorthand, 'ETD from Nandi airport is 13:00 hours.' 'What's that?' shouted out

Bristol flanker Nigel Pomphrey, 'Estimated Time of Death?' And when the pilot went through the meal arrangements – 'The cabin crew will be serving supper at 18:00 hours' – Pomphrey demanded to know, 'Is that the Last Supper?' Some of the older passengers were not amused, but it was a very happy tour party that was heading home.

For me, that meant stepping straight into the Gloucestershire team. If my immediate return to the cricket pitch was not particularly covered in glory – I was run out without scoring in my first Sunday League match a few days later – I still was able to wipe out some of the memories of the previous season's misery. According to *Wisden* 'after his return from the England rugby tour, Hignell made such a success of his role at No. 6 that his average zoomed up by better than 25 an innings after his disastrous 1978'. It was by no means all plain sailing. I hit a couple of good fifties for both the second XI and the first XI to re-establish my place in the side but then endured a run of five noughts in six innings. It needed an extraordinary stroke of luck in the match against Yorkshire at Cheltenham to get me back on track.

I knew that if I didn't want the season to peter out for the second successive year, this was my last chance. I was therefore horrified when, still without scoring, I played a defensive shot to left-arm spinner Phil Carrick and saw the ball trickle backwards to rest against the stumps. By some miracle it didn't dislodge the bails. Reprieved, and relieved, I relaxed and started to play shots. I was eventually out for 102. And, when I rounded the season off by equalling my career-best score of 149 not out in Gloucestershire's final match against Northamptonshire at Bristol, I really knew my luck had changed. There were just two hiccups on a day when batting seemed the easiest thing in the world. Chris Broad, who scored his maiden first-class century, and I had put on 228 – just a handful of runs short of an all-time Gloucestershire record for the fifth wicket – when a breakdown in communication led to him being run out. David Partridge, who came in to replace Chris, had all sorts of problems giving me the strike and when the 100 overs was up (all that was allowed in the first innings of a County Championship match in those days) I was still one short of both a new career-best and a special landmark.

Nevertheless, a great finish to the season was made even more special by events off the field. Just a few days earlier, I had met the woman with whom I was going to share the rest of my life.

CHAPTER TWENTY-ONE

A PAIR (1979–82)

We met on a blind date. Jeannie worked at the university alongside the fiancée of my friend and Bristol teammate John Watson. Separately they invited us to a barbecue organised by John's accountancy firm and suggested we meet beforehand at a pub in Clifton. I was instantly attracted to a beautiful, vivacious, red-haired woman with a stunning figure, a brilliant smile and a warm melodious voice. Jeannie was not so enraptured. Her first impression was that I had a self-confidence that bordered on arrogance. Having next to no interest in sport, she was totally unimpressed by my status as a minor celebrity. She watched with detached amusement as the other invitees – particularly, she reckoned, the female ones – seemed to be hanging on my every word. But we chatted and I was delighted to discover a shared sense of humour and flattered beyond words to discover that Jeannie was far more interested in what made me tick than in what made me famous. Emboldened, I invited her to my 24th birthday party the following week. Within a month we were spending all our spare time together.

Not that there was much of it. As a teacher, I was fully stretched. As a rugby player, I was keen to lay down an early marker both for the autumn international – the All Blacks were visiting for the second year running – and the Lions tour to South Africa the following summer. Bristol had their usual hectic start to the season, and I was in the thick of it.

For the fourth time in five seasons I made it safely through September, and not much further. Once again, it was an ankle injury that laid me low. In an away match at London Irish's ground at Sunbury, I burst into the line and, slightly off-balance after getting my pass away, failed to take a double tackle. The agony in my right foot was familiar, and in no way comforting.

Weight bearing was impossible for the rest of Saturday, but by Sunday afternoon I was able to hobble about. A bit. On Monday, I borrowed one of my dad's walking sticks, gritted my teeth and got on the bus as usual. Bristol Cathedral

School, with its steep staircases, narrow passageways and scattered classrooms was a challenge too far. I organised cover for my pre-lunch lessons and took a taxi to the Bristol Royal Infirmary. An hour or so later the junior doctor on duty gave me what I took to be good news. 'Some previous damage here, but nothing much to worry about. It looks like a sprain. Take some painkillers. You'll be all right in a few days.'

What a relief. Nothing broken, no ligament damage. A week or so for the swelling to subside, and I would have every chance of making it in time for England's match against New Zealand in six weeks. The following evening I took myself off to see Les Bardsley, the Bristol City physio who worked with Gloucestershire in the summer, to decide on a plan of campaign.

'If it's a sprain,' he said, 'you should be able to run on it almost immediately. The X-rays show that there is no structural damage, so as long as you can put up with the pain – and that's just caused by the initial trauma – you can run in straight lines. The more you run, the more likely the swelling is to dissipate.'

I had to be playing by 10 November for the Gloucestershire county championship quarter-final against Oxford. I then had an England training session the following day and then two weeks to get match fit for England against New Zealand on 24 November. I had three weeks to go through the pain barrier and come out the other side. But the pain got worse instead of better and although I played against Oxfordshire – at outside-half – it was more in the hope of a miracle than the expectation of a sudden cessation of pain. When I reported for England training at Leicester the next day I was a hobbling wreck. I wasn't going to be fit to face the All Blacks, and the England doctor suggested I get a second opinion on the ankle.

'Why wasn't this leg put in plaster immediately after the injury?' The surgeon holding up my X-rays at the Nuffield Hospital in Clifton was aghast. 'There is an old fracture, sure enough, but there are also three new fractures. From the look of your foot, there is probably ligament damage as well. No wonder you are in pain.'

I'd left the Cathedral School on foot during my lunch break. I returned to it for afternoon lessons on crutches. I had instructions to use them for the next couple of weeks at least and not try to run till Christmas. I had tried and failed to be fit in time for England's match against New Zealand. Now I would have a fight on my hands to be fit for the Five Nations.

Although I got back to playing, I never got back to full fitness. More importantly, I never regained full confidence in my ankles. I played with them heavily strapped in any case, but for the rest of the season I entered every match dreading that they would let me down again. I lost a yard or so of pace and felt more heavy-footed, less agile, less confident as a result. I was still good enough to get back into the Bristol first-team, and I played for Gloucestershire in the county championship final against Lancashire – as a centre – but I was kidding myself that I had a realistic chance of making the Lions tour. I still dreamed the dream right up until the day the tour party was announced, especially as Andy Irvine had declared himself unavailable. The full-backs who were chosen – Scotland's Bruce Hay and Irishman Rodney O'Donnell – had much less international experience than I had, while utility back Peter Morgan was uncapped by Wales, but I wasn't altogether surprised to be omitted. Oh well, I consoled myself; I still had a lot to prove on the cricket field.

Although I had been a professional cricketer for six years, I had yet to play a full season for Gloucestershire. In 1974, my registration had been delayed. Then there had been four years at Cambridge and an England rugby tour to the Far East in successive summers. In 1980, once the Lions selectors had extinguished any faint hopes I had of making the tour to South Africa, I was set for a clear run.

That was the theory. But as soon as we started playing cricket, I smashed my nose. I was fielding at short leg – my specialist position. I wasn't wearing a helmet. I had always argued that they compromised both vision and balance and, in a position where I often only had a split second to react, that was unacceptable. I had become an expert in knowing when to take cover and when to hold my position. A short leg has no chance to watch the ball. He has to concentrate on the batsman and read from the way he shifts his bodyweight or picks up his bat what his intentions are. I enjoyed the challenge and prided myself on my reflexes. I had picked up some very sharp chances and I had avoided serious injury.

Until Gloucestershire fast-bowler Brian Brain bowled a rare full toss at Northamptonshire No. 10 batsman, Tim Lamb. Tim was a fine seam bowler for Oxford University, Middlesex and Northants. He would go on to be a very able sports administrator as chief executive of the ECB. By no stretch of the imagination was he a batsman. And, in this split second, he didn't act like one. Instead of hinting at his intentions with some kind of back-lift or some kind of a shift in bodyweight, he jabbed hard and late at the ankle-high delivery – and from just over a yard away smashed it at full throttle into my face.

The blow knocked me off my feet and stopped the ball stone dead. I could just about see it out of the corner of my eyes as, on all fours, I could sense great gobbets of blood gushing from my nose. I didn't feel any pain but my whole face felt numb and was obviously starting to swell. There was a split second when nobody moved, and then my teammates crowded round. I could tell from their eyes that my face was not a pretty sight. One or two of them waved frantically in the direction of the pavilion. The May Bank Holiday crowd gasped – and then started laughing as a truly comic foot race unfolded in front of them. Gloucestershire physio Les Bardsley, in his sixties and with the bandy-legged gait of an ex-footballer, was hurrying as fast as he could towards the middle. So was the St John Ambulance man, who despite giving Les twenty years in age and a head start, was catching up fast. They reached me about the same time and, having ascertained that I could hold the bloodied towel to my face, escorted me to the dressing room. The duty doctor took one look at my face and asked whether, given that I was a rugby player and could expect further damage, I wanted to go to all the bother of surgery. I took one look at my face – my nose now seemed to be immediately below my right eye – and asked him to get on the case right away.

It took some time to locate the cosmetic surgeon – he'd taken advantage of the bank holiday to go sailing – but he was able to operate on me that night and send me home the next afternoon. Jeannie came to the clinic to pick me up and was shocked at what she saw. Across my forehead and down my nose was a T-shaped plaster of Paris. I had two black eyes, although some parts of the bruising were purple and other parts yellow. Stuffed up each nostril were yards and yards of string-like wadding. But, said the medical staff, the operation had been a success, the bruising would swiftly go and all I had to do was relax and take it easy.

I did try. But I panicked. I found myself gasping for air, even though there was plenty of it about. I couldn't trust myself to eat or drink in case I needed to breathe. Logic told me that I had managed to do both when suffering from a cold in times past, but I was past logic. I had to go back to hospital for another night's observation.

When I got back to my flat – I'd moved out of my parents' house at the start of the summer – I found that local television company HTV were camped outside. Jeannie had already turned down all requests for interviews on the basis that I neither looked nor felt like a million dollars. Precisely, argued my future employers. They were in the picture business and what could be more graphic than a few close-ups of my multi-coloured and mangled face? They would ask a few questions about safety in sport, but it didn't really matter if I didn't make much sense. All they wanted was the gory detail. I declined, with as much grace as I could muster.

The medics were right. The swelling did go down very rapidly and the bruises did disappear without trace. My new nose was a real improvement, and a tribute to the cosmetic surgeon's art. But I decided that from now on I would not only field in a helmet but bat in one as well. I returned to action against Somerset but had no chance to use the helmet in the field as they smashed us for a record 534 for six, the highest ever total since County Championship first innings had been limited to a hundred overs. Ian Botham, coming in at 119 for three, belted a gargantuan 228 and the only consolation was that Viv Richards wasn't even playing. We needed to score 385 in our hundred overs just to avoid the follow-on and Somerset could afford to crowd the bat when I came in, sporting my new visor. I could afford to take my time, and concentrate simply on watching the ball onto the bat. Of course, Somerset tested me with the odd short ball, but the pitch was not particularly hard and, with Botham resting a slight injury, the bowling was not particularly frightening. I battled my way to a top score of 80 and, when we had to follow-on 295 behind, hit an unbeaten century in the second innings. My season was very definitely back on track.

Until, that is, my ankles packed up on me completely. Out of the blue. I'd reported with the rest of the first-team squad for a match against Yorkshire in Sheffield, watched the rain fall down on the first day, fielded for most of the second and then watched as Gloucestershire overtook the Yorkshire total. But on the third morning, I found that I could hardly walk. My right ankle was worse, but both ankles were solid, stiff and painful. When I got to the ground, I forced myself to go for a run. Surely a bit of exercise would break down the stiffness and pain would gradually ease? Absolutely not. The ankles, despite some manipulation and some ultrasound treatment from the Yorkshire physio, remained stiff and sore. I was in no fit state even to act as twelfth man as Yorkshire batted through the rest of the day. I returned to Bristol a very worried man.

The specialist was blunt and, to illustrate my current predicament, referred back to the first problem I had ever encountered with my ankles. Way back when I was 14, and had damaged my ankle skiing, the orthopaedic surgeon had pointed out that I had been born with 'an extra centre of ossification on the medial malleolus'. This, explained the Bristol consultant, was like having a car with no shock absorbers. Over a period of time, the rest of the car is prone to all sorts of damage. Ultimately it seizes up. This is what had happened to my feet. In the short term, he proposed knocking me out with a general anaesthetic and rotating the ankles forcibly in order to free up the joints. In the longer term, he could only predict even more debilitating ankle problems. The only way I might be able to extend my cricketing career for more than a season or two was to give up rugby.

His logic was impeccable. I had had four ankle injuries in the last five rugby seasons. Each had been more painful than the last, and the recovery time had been longer. I had to strap my feet up before every match, and use heavy ankle-length boots just for support. I found it much more difficult to run on hard or uneven ground, and I had started to entertain the suspicion that my ankles were not as reliable as they should be, and that I had lost some pace as well as a lot of agility. Deep in my heart, I knew the surgeon was right. But it did not make the decision any easier. Although cricket had been my first love, rugby had become central to my way of life, my way of being, my sense of myself. There was so much more in the sport that I wanted to achieve. I wanted to be part of a successful and long-lasting England set-up. I wanted to reach my potential with the Lions. At 24, I was too young to call it a day.

But in the middle of the cricket season I didn't have to make an immediate decision about my rugby future. And at least the consultant was confident that, as long as I looked after my ankles, I could continue to play cricket for some years to come. County cricket that is, played over three days – in England. We both knew, though we didn't need to say it, that Test cricket, played over five days on hard baked overseas pitches in gruelling heat, was a whole different ballgame. It was unlikely that my ankles could stand up to international cricket even if I could reach the standard required. The death-knell for my international rugby career would almost certainly be the death-knell to my dreams of international cricket. But that was only hypothetical, and I didn't want to confront it head on.

There was some good news. Jeannie and I had decided to get married. The attraction we had felt at the end of the previous summer had blossomed and grown during the winter. We were both absolutely sure that we wanted to spend the rest of our lives together, and there seemed little point in waiting much longer. Jeannie had already made the supreme sacrifice of giving up her sports car – a mustard-coloured MGB Midget – because there was simply no room for crutches, cricket 'coffin' or any of the sporting and teaching paraphernalia that I dragged around with me. We each had a flat and it made sense to sell them both and buy a home of our own. We set the wedding-date for late December, the only part of the year not taken up with teaching or cricket.

In the end I just didn't go back to the rugby club. I had no trouble finding things to do on Tuesday and Thursday evenings and the school was only too happy for me to spend Saturday afternoons with the first-team. It was well into September before anyone noticed I was missing and the news that I had retired from all rugby leaked out. But there wasn't much of a fuss about it anyway. In the 1970s and early 1980s, rugby was very much a pastime. It was a hobby that you fitted in around your work. It was never a career and you'd be foolish if you let it get in the way of one. Time spent playing rugby, or preparing to play it, was time taken away from your work or your social life. As far as I was concerned, as a newly-wed at the start of a teaching career that was already struggling to get off the ground because of my county cricket commitments, my life was already full to overflowing. It wasn't as if I was making any money from rugby. In fact, in those rigidly amateur times, it was costing me a fair bit to play. If I was going to earn anything from sport, it would have to be from cricket – and that would never make me rich. The heart may have wanted me to continue playing rugby but the head – as well as the ankles – were arguing the opposite.

With the new season well underway, the newspapers dedicated a couple of paragraphs to the event and moved onto other things. The tribute I treasured most came from David Frost of the *Guardian*. In an article headlined 'Injuries end Hignell's career' he wrote 'with his broad vision of a game, an acute sense of timing, a fearless commitment in defence, and a startling pace for one so stockily built, Hignell became one of England's most accomplished all-round full-backs. Without his injury problems, he might have become as vital to England as JPR Williams was for Wales. Certainly the Lions could have done with him last year in South Africa.'

Did I miss playing? Acutely. I could think of nothing I would rather be doing than running out with my mates to test my own skill, courage, speed and mental agility and our collective spirit and cohesion. The butterflies in the stomach, the smell of the changing rooms, the springiness of the turf, the roar of the crowd, the blood pumping through the muscles, the air filling the lungs, the adrenaline, the physicality and the sense of excitement had defined my Saturdays for as long as I could remember. So had the sense of achievement, the teamwork, the camaraderie and the humour at the end of a game. I would miss it all right.

By the start of the 1981 cricket season, Jeannie and I were expecting our first child and we had even more incentive to enjoy our first season as a married couple. By now I had made the necessary mental adjustments. International cricket was an impossible dream. Even if I could transform my batting – I was still only 25 so had plenty of good years ahead of me – the weakness in my ankles would almost certainly rule me out. Still, I could forge a valuable and useful career as a county cricketer, aim towards a benefit in my thirties and provide a reasonable financial base for my growing family. And there were changes afoot at Gloucestershire. Mike Procter's body could no longer put up with the wear and tear of county cricket and the great man was due to retire at the end of the season. The captaincy would be up for grabs and, with my Cambridge University experience, I felt I would be in with a shout. I had already had one chat with Gloucestershire secretary Tony Brown about the job and I knew that the other main candidates, David Graveney, who was to get the job, and Andy Stovold, had been sounded out too.

I started 1981 with a bang, scoring a hundred at the Parks against Oxford University. But then the season turned grey – as rain washed out the entire month of May, reduced the tour match against Australia to a farce and provoked several forfeited innings in attempts to produce results. But, even though that was my only century, I did manage a full season for the first time in seven years and, with 970 runs at just under 35 per innings, finished third in the county averages. Top of the national averages was the astonishing Zaheer, who smashed an incredible 2,306 runs at an average of 88, despite not getting to the crease at all in May.

But this was the end of an era. Mike Procter suffered his last and most serious injury and returned to South Africa before the season was over. With Brian Brain also failing to last the course, the Gloucestershire attack had lost all venom. With no strike bowlers to speak of, we slumped to 14th in the championship and bottom but one in the Sunday League.

Adam was born on 7 September 1981, and I very nearly missed being there. I only took the decision on the day to travel up to Nottingham for our final Sunday League match of the season when Jeannie assured me that there was nothing to worry about.

'First babies never come early, do they?'

As soon as the game was over, I rang again. Nothing to worry about. It was a shock therefore to arrive home and find our car missing and no sign of Jeannie in the house. Her waters had burst shortly after my phone call, and on being told that the ambulance would take some time to arrive she had driven herself to the hospital and checked in to the labour ward. Adam arrived with a mighty wail, and some foetal distress, which at one time necessitated the presence of nine obstetric professionals, just after midnight. He was healthy. Jeannie was exhausted, but otherwise in pretty good shape. I was over the moon and, like a true romantic, determined to mark the arrival – and the end of the season – with a big score. The rest of the team let me down against Lancashire, as I was left high and dry on 80 not out.

The 1982 cricket season began early and with a bang of an entirely different kind. A number of leading England cricketers – including Graham Gooch, Geoff Boycott, Alan Knott and Derek Underwood – signed up for a rebel tour of South Africa in March. They were banned from representing England for three years, just as they had been warned they would be. That, however, did not stop them from demanding, at the professional Cricketers Association annual general meeting in Birmingham that spring, that we should all go on strike in order to force the TCCB to reverse the ban. I felt compelled to speak out against the rebels. It was the first time I'd ever chosen to open my mouth in public, but I had no desire either to be the cause of county cricket matches being cancelled, or to sit around twiddling my thumbs while others played in them. I urged the largest audience I had ever addressed to congratulate the rebels on their good fortune – they had earned more in a couple of months than many of us would in six years – but to remember that we too had a living to earn. I reminded them that we had all been sent a letter warning us that if we went on unauthorised tours we would be banned from playing for England. We should sympathise with Graham Gooch, Geoff Boycott et al but we should remember that if we stood shoulder to shoulder with them on the picket lines, they would not be the ones having difficulty meeting their regular bills. My speech seemed to galvanise others to take a more realistic approach. The motion to take industrial action in support of the rebels was defeated.

If only my bat had been as eloquent as my tongue. I began the 1982 season in the first-team and ended it there, but in the middle of the campaign I lost form so badly that I spent a month or so in the seconds, and missed the Cheltenham Festival completely. For the first time in six seasons I failed to make even one three-figure score. Not only was I failing to establish myself as a good solid reliable county pro, I was actually going backwards.

I found it especially difficult to get out of the rut I found myself in because of the way my batting technique had evolved. I was never the most orthodox of players, but over the years, as I found new ways of getting out, or in response to what I or others identified as weaknesses, I had fiddled, adapted or changed just about everything about my batting style. I no longer walked across in front of my stumps – as Robin Jackman would put it, no more Come f-ing Dancing – but in order to cut out the number of lbw dismissals, I had adopted a very open stance. I was very bottom handed and did not always bring the bat down straight, prompting the Derbyshire spinner, and future chairman of the England selectors

Geoff Miller, to declare very loudly every time I came in to bat 'spread out, lads, here comes Alastair round-bat!' My attempts to work the ball into spaces where there were no fielders were ugly to say the least, and led Lancashire players to enquire whether my other Blue had been for rowing.

In *Another Day, Another Match*, his diary of the 1980 season, Brian Brain had described me best when he said 'he must break a bowler's heart by the way he gets into such awful positions, but he gets everything behind the ball. He gets very square on against the spinners, but he does this so he can focus both eyes on the ball and really watch it come on to the bat. With his crab-like stance he tends to miss the ball by a mile when he makes a misjudgement but then, out of the blue, he'll hit the ball a long way by dint of his natural sportsman's eye.'

The trouble was, I wasn't even managing that in 1982. To make matters worse, the stiffness in my ankles was taking longer to run off each day, and as my form disintegrated on the pitch, the urge to get on with my chosen career in teaching increased. The season before I had decided to hang on in county cricket, be the best I could possibly be for Gloucestershire, and earn myself a benefit. Now, though, I was determined not to play on just for the sake of it. Everywhere on the circuit I'd seen seasoned pros blocking the progress of talented young cricketers by doing just enough to get by, playing more for their own averages than the good of the team, hanging on, time-serving. I didn't want to be like them. I'd rather do another job and, as I packed away my cricket-gear in September, I was very much open to suggestion.

That suggestion came in the form of a job offer from Sherborne public school in Dorset. They wanted me to teach A-level history, run the cricket, coach an age-group rugby team and become a house tutor. The facilities were second to none. Acres and acres of sports fields, small class sizes, all the teaching resources I could possibly wish for, an ethos and a structure with which I was familiar from my own school days, and a large academic staff with whom I was sure I could find plenty in common. The Dorset market town was situated in an idyllic part of the country, accommodation was cheaper than in Bristol, the local primary schools enjoyed excellent reputations and, all in all, it seemed the perfect place to bring up kids. A conversation with Mike Davis, who had been my coach both of England schools and at senior level and who now ran the sports centre at the school, confirmed my impression.

It was the sort of job I'd always aspired to, but did I want it now? It was a part of the country I'd always seen myself settling down in, but did I want to move there yet? In taking up this position, I would be giving up on a dream that I had had since childhood. I had set my heart on becoming a professional cricketer and although I had achieved that, I still felt there was unfinished business. On the other hand, actually playing cricket was getting harder, my ankles would always cause me problems and I knew now that I would never play for England. I'd always known that at some point my career in sport would come to an end and I would have to carve out a new one in a different field. This was earlier than I had envisaged, but was it the right time? Was this the right job?

Jeannie and I thrashed it out for weeks on end. There was no getting away from the fact that Adam was proving a real handful, or from the fact that Jeannie was pregnant again. Our second child was due in the summer of 1983 and we had already acknowledged the fact that professional sport was not kind to young families. Jeannie's retired parents had recently moved to Yeovil, just a few minutes' drive from Sherborne, and they had already been worth their weight in gold as doting, supportive, hands-on grandparents. Jeannie had always been particularly close to her mum, Margaret. Geographical proximity could only cement the bond. A move to Sherborne would be great for us all.

But leaving Bristol would be a wrench. It was a wonderful vibrant city, full of excitement, possibilities and action. Things happened here – in sport, in the arts, in everyday life. It had been our home, separately and together, for the best part of a decade. We knew it and loved it. The Downs, the Docks, the Suspension Bridge, the River Avon; these were the landmarks of our life. We were uplifted by the city's buildings, its monuments, its green open spaces and its leafy suburbs. Could we really turn our backs on all this?

We decided we could. We had a great opportunity to forge a new life for ourselves, in a new part of the world, as a new family. Of course we would have regrets, of course we would always look back fondly on the past, but this was about the future. We decided that it was the best thing for all of us – as a growing family, for my long-term career and as individuals – to move to Sherborne at the start of the next school year, September 1983. In the meantime, we had a baby on the way, a house to sell, a house to buy and some farewells to make.

CHAPTER TWENTY-TWO

OPEN MIKE (1983)

No regrets. Or as Australian captain George Gregan rather more picturesquely put it to me before the 2003 Rugby World Cup final, 'Don't die wondering'. I had made my decision to quit county cricket and take up the offer of a full-time teaching post at Sherborne public school in Dorset, and I wanted to go out on my terms. I was going to savour each and every moment of my final season, and I was damn well going to enjoy it. I would have to report to Sherborne at the beginning of September and would not be available for the last two matches. I was determined to be at Jeannie's side when our second child was born, and therefore might miss a match or two at the end of May. But I was absolutely determined to make the most of the opportunities that came my way. If David Graveney opted to leave me out of the first-team in an effort to build for the future, then so be it. I would just have to fight harder to prove I deserved a swansong.

But it rained for most of May. The last day of the County Championship match against Surrey at Bristol was lost to rain – though I did manage an unbeaten half-century in the time available – and the three-day match against Sussex at Gloucester was abandoned without a ball being bowled. The Sunday League match against Leicestershire at the Waggonworks Ground went the same way.

Dan, as we'd already decided to call our soon-to-be second son, was due anytime from the end of the month and, as I'd only just made it back in time for Adam's arrival, I was determined to take no chances this time. As the Gloucestershire first-team set off on a mini-tour of the Midlands, I opted to stay within hailing distance of both home and hospital – and made the highest score I had ever made in any form of cricket. I went in at No. 4 for the seconds against the Warwickshire second XI at Bristol, scored a hundred before lunch and was dismissed well before tea for 217. On a flat pitch on a rare fine day, I couldn't put a foot wrong. I was seeing the ball early and timing it effortlessly. I was moving instinctively into line, playing comfortably off either foot and hitting the ball much straighter than I had done for several seasons. I had never played better and was as surprised as anyone when I finally made a mistake – against future *Sunday Times* rugby writer Peter O'Reilly, then a coltish and fresh-faced triallist from Ireland.

Dan was born on 3 June 1983 – with none of the drama that had accompanied the arrival of his elder brother – and as I returned to the first-team in the second week of June, I was as relaxed and as contented as I'd ever been. I scored a century against Somerset at Bath in my first game back and another against Hampshire at Bristol a week later. I hit a career-best 70 in the 40-over John Player League at Northampton and, almost without fail, delivered runs when Gloucestershire needed them. Even when we followed-on in the return fixture against Hampshire at Portsmouth, I was in the thick of the rearguard action.

The fixture was a collector's gem in that it perfectly highlighted the bizarre and unforgiving nature of life on the county circuit in the 1980s. After a late, and losing, finish to our three-day championship match against Lancashire at Southport we had to drive on a Friday night all the way down to Portsmouth for the first of three matches in five days – in three different competitions at three different venues – against the same team. It was entirely understandable that a Hampshire top three of West Indian star Gordon Greenidge, England batsman Chris Smith and future television commentator Mark Nicholas should belt our knackered bowlers all round the United Services ground. It was less forgivable that our batsmen should collapse on day two and that, following-on, we should collapse to 13 for three in the second innings with more than eight hours still to play.

When I arrived at the crease, legendary West Indian fast bowler Malcolm Marshall had his tail up. The wicket was fast and bouncy and wicketkeeper Bobby Parks and his slip cordon were in full voice as, with the very real prospect of a two-day victory and therefore a day off, they egged on the Barbadian.

'Bowled, Macca,' they screamed every time he induced a false shot.

'What a Jaffa, Macca,' they chortled every time I played and missed.

'Let him have it,' they encouraged him to bowl at my body.

'World-class!' they pronounced with glee as Marshall raced in ever faster and bowled a mixture of lightning fast outswingers and lethal bumpers, which had me ducking and bobbing and weaving and wafting my bat into thin air as the ball did everything except hit the stumps. I actually did have a plan, which was solely focused on survival. I would simply get my bat in the way of anything that looked as though it was going to hit the wickets and get it out of the way of anything else. I didn't care how late I made the decision or how ugly my desperate attempts to avoid contact with the ball appeared. I began to enjoy the contest. I don't suppose that it helped that I grinned every time I avoided the ball, or that I began to congratulate Malcolm on the aesthetic brilliance of his bowling.

'Far too good for me, Malcolm,' I'd say when the ball speared past the outside of my bat. 'That one went late... I'd have to be really good to get an edge on that!'

I could see, and hear, that he was getting upset.

'Never mind, Malcolm. Look on the bright side. I'm retiring at the end of the season.' I attempted to mollify him as another volley of swear words escaped his lips. Somehow I knew he was going to bowl a bouncer next ball. By some miracle of timing, honed to perfection by a strongly developed survival instinct, I picked the right height, the right angle – and the right shot. The best hook shot of my life sent the ball racing – along the ground, as I'd even managed to roll my wrists – to a point just in front of square on the square leg boundary.

'Great shot, Higgy.' Non-striker John Shepherd was clearly impressed. His fellow Barbadian clearly wasn't. Malcolm Marshall let out a scream of anger, I felt it more advisable to stress how lucky I had been, and how I hadn't really intended to play an aggressive shot at all.

'Absolutely brilliant, Higgy.' John Shepherd was equally determined to keep Marshall's temper at boiling point. 'Wasn't that a great shot, Malcolm?' he inquired. 'Fancy you getting smacked around by someone who's retiring at the end of the season!'

Malcolm Marshall was a phenomenal bowler and more than made up for his lack of height by having a greater array of tricks up his sleeve than most of his contemporaries. It was often said of him that he had the ability to bowl two different types of bouncer – one that reared up towards the batsman's throat and one that skidded through the middle lower and a little faster. His next delivery smacked me in the box before I was halfway through my shot and left me in a crumpled heap on the ground. Gasping for breath, tears in my eyes, a thumping pain in my nether regions I was only vaguely aware of the St John Ambulance team preparing to rush onto the field, the physios grabbing ice buckets from the bar and the Hampshire fielders gathering round in a concerned circle. And I couldn't avoid Malcolm Marshall.

'Never mind, Higgy. You look on the bright side. You won't have to wait till the end of the season to retire, will you?'

But I soldiered on into the final day to make 65, while a century from Andy Stovold enabled us to save the match, and I was still averaging above 35 per innings as my last match approached. Gloucestershire still had two more championship fixtures to play but I had no intention of missing the start of term at my first full-time teaching job. It was agreed therefore that the match against Nottinghamshire at Bristol at the end of August would be my final match for Gloucestershire. It was also the final match for Chris Broad, who had already decided that his England ambitions could be best served at Nottinghamshire. He had made some outspoken and indiscreet criticism of both the club and his playing colleagues in a newspaper interview, and the committee had decided that he should be suspended for the rest of the season.

While Chris made his point with a masterful, career-best 145 in the first innings, I was more concerned with creeping past 1,000 runs for the season for the third time in my career. On 23, I charged down the wicket and smacked England off-spinner Eddie Hemmings over long off for four to reach the landmark in some style. Thirty-one not out in the first innings, another 40 in the second and it was all over. Match drawn. Career ended.

In 170 first-class matches for Gloucestershire and Cambridge University, I had scored 7,459 runs at an average of 29.48. I'd hit 11 centuries and 41 fifties with a highest score of 149 not out. I'd taken three wickets and 150 catches, mostly at short leg or bat-pad. In 138 limited overs matches, I'd batted 124 times for an average of 23.37 with just nine fifties and a highest score of 85 not out.

Could I have done better? Yes. Should I have done better? Yes. I would be very surprised if any professional sportsman – even the Jonny Wilkinsons of this world – could answer those questions in the negative. Could I have done things differently? Of course. I could have chosen to join a county other than Gloucestershire. I could have chosen to concentrate solely on cricket. I could have immersed myself in the sport, served an apprenticeship in overseas winters, and dedicated myself to developing the perfect technique. I could have devoted more time and energy to both mental and physical preparation. I could have been more single-minded about my chosen profession.

But I wasn't, and I didn't. I was lucky enough to have so many opportunities in areas other than cricket, and I was lucky enough to be able to take them. I can't imagine that there will ever be a time when talented youngsters can keep so many options open for as long as I was allowed to do. In the 21st century it seems that you can either be an Oxbridge graduate, a professional cricketer or a top-class rugby player, but not all three. Each sport requires such specialisation so early that it is now impossible to pursue a career in both.

From a purely cricketing point of view, it was quite obvious that rugby didn't help. From a purely rugby point of view it was obvious that cricket was limiting my pre-season training and injuries were preventing me from reaching my potential. If I weren't playing both sports, I would have had time to get my body right between seasons, to polish my skills and develop my technique. But that was never really an issue. Sport – even cricket – was far from being a profession. It wasn't quite the hobby of the gifted amateur, who achieved excellence without being seen to put in too much effort, but it wasn't the ruthless, commercialised, results-driven process that it is now. 'It's better than working for a living,' we'd say whenever we were asked what county cricket was like, but we knew that it wasn't a career. It was either a way of delaying the inevitable entry into the world of work or a means of escaping from it for annual stretches of six months or more.

For the vast majority of the populace, cricket was a recreation, a weekend pastime that provided the light to the shade of their everyday lives. It was a leisure activity, and they played it – or watched it – for fun and enjoyment.

And we weren't much different from the people who supported us. Nobody regarded us as elite athletes. We had no specialist training programmes, fitness regimes or diets to follow. We ate the same, we socialised the same and we were paid the same as our neighbours. We might get our names in the papers a few times and we might see them plastered on the side of a sponsored car, but for the most part we considered ourselves as ordinary guys lucky enough to have been given the chance to play cricket all summer, and to have some fun doing it.

And I'd been lucky enough to play at Gloucestershire in a team that enjoyed its reputation as the happiest and friendliest on the circuit. I had been lucky enough to test my skills, my courage and my temperament against most, if not all, of the greatest cricketers of my time. I had experienced the extraordinary elation that comes from hard-earned victory and I'd experienced the crushing disappointment that comes with defeat. I'd nearly been to the top of the mountain when we just missed out on the County Championship in 1977, and I'd played and lost in semi-finals. I'd been capped – and dropped. I'd hit hundreds and scored ducks. I had taken some amazing catches and dropped some sitters. I'd experienced frustrating injury as well as the sheer exhilaration of being young and fit and active and outside, and paid for doing something I loved. I had been privileged to be a professional cricketer for ten wonderful years. Now I was moving on. First to Sherborne public school in Dorset, and then, only two years later, to the BBC.

I loved teaching but the bright lights were already calling. I'd had a taste of local radio when, during lengthy spells on the injury-list, I'd been spotted hobbling around the Memorial Ground and co-opted onto the Radio Bristol commentary team. I'd displayed enough aptitude for them to ask me back – and I'd been in the right place at the right time when national radio got in touch. *Sport on Two* was short of a summariser for a county match between Gloucestershire and Yorkshire in Bristol. The commentator was my old Cambridge coach Ian Robertson and he was more than happy to have one of his former players sit alongside him not just that afternoon but, as I proved to be reasonably competent, for several other afternoons as well. By the time I had summarised at a county championship final between Gloucestershire and Somerset and a cup final involving most of those same players for Bristol and Bath, I had begun to develop a huge appreciation not just for the medium of radio but also for the skills of those who performed on it. When *Sport on Two* switched to another sport for a reasonable length of time during one of the finals, Robbo's co-commentator Peter West persuaded me to swap roles; he would be the summariser if I would have a go at commentating.

'Why don't you apply for a job at the BBC?' he said at the end of the exercise. Robbo backed him up and pointed out how many teachers, including himself and Nigel Starmer-Smith, had made the transition to broadcasting.

As a final coincidence, the BBC advertised for a Sports Assistant in the *Guardian* a few weeks later and, by chance, I spotted it. I wasn't quite sure what the job entailed – the title seemed more likely to belong to a worker in a department store – but I strung together a CV and sent off my application. Apparently, some 1,500 other people, most of whom had several years' experience working full-time on local radio, did the same. I don't know how many were invited to audition but I think I can safely say that none of them would have been more nervous than I. I had never applied to any job outside teaching before and my only knowledge of sports journalism was from the receiving end. I had been interviewed, written about and commented upon but I hadn't really focused on the other person's job. Now, I was advised, I would have to pass a test on my ability to interview, précis information received from the newswires, write and deliver precisely timed reports and commentate on some rugby action.

I had two big problems. As I hadn't listened to the radio out of choice for the best part of a decade and a half, I had no idea what made good radio. I had no idea what a 40-second report either looked like on paper or sounded like on air. In the weeks leading up to the interview, I locked myself away with a transistor radio and a stopwatch, using up reams of paper as I tried to churn out reports that were neither too long nor too short, and also made sense. When the big day came, I took the train up to London convinced that I would fall apart when put under pressure of writing and delivering a sports report. But the BBC seemed relatively relaxed about my lack of broadcasting experience. They could see that I knew a lot about two sports in particular and a little about other sports in general. They were prepared to take the gamble that they could teach me how to broadcast. When could I start?

Not immediately, was the answer. I was prepared to take a gamble of my own in embarking upon a new career, but I wasn't prepared to throw all caution to the winds. If broadcasting didn't work out, I needed to be able to get back into teaching. My chance of doing that I felt would be limited if I didn't serve out a proper notice. That meant teaching until the end of the summer term 1985. It meant not starting with BBC radio sport until halfway through the cricket season. But it also gave us the chance to pack up home once again, get our heads round the idea of living in commuter-belt London and get used to the idea of working in the big wide world.

The BBC's offer was a relief to HTV. The local television station had been stringing me along for several months, after I had responded to their advertisement for a news reporter. I didn't have the credentials or the experience for such a post, and they didn't have the resources or the time to train me. They would love to have me as a sports reporter but they didn't have any vacancies. They didn't want to reject me outright, nor offer me any false hope, but they were saved from making a decision by the BBC.

PART FIVE

MS (BARGAINING)

CHAPTER TWENTY-THREE

GOING PUBLIC

My MS went public in September 2000 – nearly two years after diagnosis and five months after I had told employers, friends and colleagues. Their reaction had initially been exactly as I had hoped. After the initial shock of the announcement, they had turned their attention to other things, as I had. We had worked our socks off to cover the traditionally frantic end-of-season as Premiership play-offs, European finals, relegation dogfights and awards dinners crowded thick and fast on one another. We'd followed England on a three-week tour of South Africa, and, with one extraordinary exception, had gone to ground for what was left of the summer.

The amazing Ian Robertson not only offered immediate and unqualified support but also instinctively grasped – long before I did – that dealing with a progressive and incurable condition was going to be a long and costly business. Exploiting all his contacts in the world of rugby he set about organising a fund-raising dinner for November, and persuaded Saracens' owner Nigel Wray to advance me the costs of the anti-inflammatory beta interferon drug in the meantime.

While Robbo was mobilising his friends, I was getting to know the enemy. I hadn't consciously refrained from reading about MS but in the early days of denial I hadn't dug too deeply for information. The self-help section at WH Smith had stocked a guide, written by journalist Chris McLaughlin, that promised to be 'positive, comprehensive and authoritative' but that for a long time was my only reference book. I had been recommended *Me and My Shadow* by Carol Mackie, a flight attendant who described her experiences of the condition, but until I'd taken the decision to acknowledge that I had the same health problem, I hadn't made a conscious effort to find out much about MS.

Now I was determined to find out everything I could about it. I trawled the Internet, devoured all the publications I could find and bombarded my neurosurgeon with questions. What I discovered was initially dispiriting. Nobody knew what caused MS, nobody knew how to cure it and nobody had a clear idea of how to treat it. What was worse was that there was absolutely no way of predicting what course the disease was going to take. There was some agreement on the four 'types', although some experts argued that there was no such thing as 'benign' MS – just very long periods of remission between relapses – and there was some argument as to the exact stage when sufferers moved from the secondary into the primary progressive category. My initial feeling though was that these were just labels, maybe useful for the medics but of little practical value for me. The fact that I had appeared to by-pass the relapsing-remitting stage and was officially 'secondary progressive' merely confirmed what my body was telling me. My symptoms – outwardly manifested by a loss of functionality primarily in my right leg and my right arm and inwardly by the onset of a debilitating and all-consuming fatigue – were getting worse. I didn't particularly need a man in a white coat to tell me I was on a downward slope. I could feel that. Everything I read suggested that the earth-levellers weren't going to swing into action any time soon. I was determined not to roll up into a ball and facilitate the descent. I needed to know how to dig my heels in and how to apply the brakes. And I would have the best chance of that, I reckoned, if I got to know the ground first.

I learned for instance that MS is the most common form of neurological disease in the UK, with an estimated 85,000 sufferers – since revised upwards, almost certainly as a result of improved diagnostic techniques, to 100,000. I learned that more women than men had MS, in a proportion of three to two. I learned that the UK was an MS hotspot, for hitherto unexplained reasons, and that the further you lived away from the Equator, the greater your risk of contracting MS. I also learned that, while there was still no sure way of predicting the course of the disease, a ready reckoner was a five-year assessment. Some experts professed to know, by measuring the rate of decline over that period of time, what course the disease would take over the rest of a natural lifespan.

The list of MS symptoms was frighteningly long, the description of them terrifying. Some I was already experiencing – the fatigue, the poor balance, the lack of coordination, the loss of strength. Some I had so far avoided. I wasn't experiencing any significant pain and, mercifully – in view of my career as a commentator – my speech and vision were unaffected. I didn't have difficulties in swallowing, or any sexual problems, although I was as terrified of those developing as I was of my bladder problems getting worse. I was aware of some psychological changes – sharper mood swings, loss of memory and concentration – and I was conscious that others – I had become much more openly emotional, aware of and in touch with my feelings – could be seen as progress. But I was also aware that none of the symptoms were going to go away – or at least not for long – and all of them were likely to worsen. I was determined to do as much as I could to prevent that happening.

But in looking around for ways that I could best help myself, I discovered that many of the difficulties I faced, the obstacles I encountered and the helplessness that I felt at times were shared by the rest of the MS community. I know that there's no easy way to tell someone that they have an incurable disease but I wasn't alone in feeling let down by the doctors at point of diagnosis. I know that everyone reacts to bad news in different ways – and some initially shut down to the point of being unable to take much in – but I felt and still feel – that the neurologists could spend a bit more time spelling out the possibilities and probabilities and make a bit more effort to discuss the pros and cons of possible treatments. All I got was a few vague words of encouragement, the promise of a follow-up appointment in a few weeks and a next-to-useless referral to an already over-subscribed physiotherapy department. The physios may have been exceptionally good at their job but the only regular appointment they could offer was on a Saturday morning – just about the only day of the week when I could guarantee to be working. Although there was a specialist MS nurse with specific responsibilities to act as a conduit between patient and the medical establishment, she too had more work than she could handle. In common with so many more of the newly diagnosed, I had left the hospital very much under the impression that I was on my own.

And it had taken me well over a year to discover that there was some support and help out there. I found out from the Internet that oxygen therapy (the administration of oxygen at higher than normal pressure by the means of a diving bell, or tank) helped alleviate some MS symptoms and that a specialist MS treatment centre in the Somerset village of Nailsea could offer it, as well as provide physiotherapy, acupuncture and a range of so-called alternative treatments. I also got the pretty clear impression that my consultant didn't approve. He was not only instinctively distrustful of alternative therapies but unconvinced that there was any demonstrable scientific proof that oxygen therapy actually worked.

The cynic in me argued that the reason that no one had yet conducted properly evaluated clinical trials into the use of hyperbaric oxygen was that, unlike the new drugs that were constantly coming onto the market, it was not a commercially licensed product. No one company stood to make millions from the widespread use of oxygen therapy – as it would whenever a new drug was approved – and no one company was therefore prepared to bankroll the clinical trials. The optimist in me argued that thousands of MS patients wouldn't choose to be shut into a claustrophobic diving chamber for at least an hour a week unless they were convinced it was doing them some good. I was happy to take their anecdotal evidence that some MS symptoms could be alleviated by the therapy and I was convinced that regular physiotherapy would also help.

But I realised at the same time that if I had been unaware of the therapy centre's existence for so long, then others must be too. If it had taken me over a year to discover *New Pathways*, a bi-monthly magazine aimed specifically at the MS community, then others must still be in the dark. And, if the lack of resources within the NHS had forced so many people with MS to look outside the system for the support they needed, then the least I could do was to use whatever profile I enjoyed to raise awareness both of MS and the charities that were dedicated to making life easier for those of us with the condition.

The brand leader as far as MS charities are concerned is the MS Society. I contacted their PR department to offer my services and, as well as diverting one or two fees for after-dinner speaking engagements in their direction, agreed to be their non-running captain at the next London Marathon. But what really brought the media to my door was when I agreed to be president of the Nerve Centre Appeal, an ambitious plan to create a state-of-the-art, one-stop shop, incorporating clinical research and all the latest treatments for MS under the one roof at Frenchay Hospital in Bristol. A local journalist asked why I was interested in the project and, when I told her of my personal experience of the disease, ran a headline in the *Bristol Evening Post*. Within hours, the nationals had picked up the story. Within days they were beating a path to my door, as anxious to reflect my experiences in the health as well as the sports sections of their publications.

It was weird. I felt as if I was 'coming out' about my MS for a second time, and I was totally unprepared for the level of interest shown in me. It was painful to relive the dark days following my diagnosis but in a way it was also liberating. I was flattered by the interest shown in me and was determined not to let the opportunity slip for banging the drum about the disease and its effects. Even so, being on the other side of the microphone was strange. For the last decade and a half I had been the one asking the questions. Now, here I was, admittedly under the most sympathetic of interrogations, attempting to describe my own innermost feelings, attempting to make sense of what had happened to me in the last couple of years. And I was finding it very difficult.

But if I was flattered by the articles that ensued, I was overwhelmed by the public response to them. Hundreds of letters poured into the *Daily Telegraph* after rugby correspondent Mick Cleary wrote a touching piece referring to our socialising on the rugby circuit. More followed an article by *Observer* cricket correspondent Vic Marks in which he recalled our shared sporting history. There were even a couple of fan letters for our cat Sydney who had seized a photo opportunity when a *Telegraph* feature writer came to do a profile. All of the writers mentioned the exorbitant cost of the beta interferon drug that I was taking and all of them mentioned the fund-raising dinner that Ian Robertson had organised to help me pay for it. Only a couple mentioned the experience that only a couple of weeks previously had brought panic into my life and, thankfully only briefly, had me peering into the black hole of despair.

The day, a Tuesday in September, had begun normally enough. I'd had a cup of tea, showered, dressed, read the papers, and started work on an article I was writing. Within half an hour, however, I was aching from head to foot. I felt the need to lie down but as I moved from my desk, I started shaking uncontrollably. Within minutes I was burning up with a temperature. I had a bout of diarrhoea and by the time the doctor had arrived, I had lost control of my right leg, and all sense of balance. By the time I got to hospital, I couldn't feel my right arm and I was sweating profusely, my stomach was cramping and I still had diarrhoea. I lay in bed and contemplated the abrupt end of any kind of normal life.

I looked at my right arm lying on top of the bedcover and willed it to move. 'Turn your hand over and show me your palm,' said the doctor. I focused on my inert fingers and willed them to move. They wouldn't. My right leg was like a lump of concrete under the sheets. I couldn't move that either. I gritted my teeth and sent the messages screaming from my brain. Absolutely no response from arm or leg. I've caught myself since describing the sensation as 'scary' or a 'bit frightening' in a stiff upper lip, understated, very British sort of way, but it was much worse than that. I was terrified.

Even though by this time I'd read a lot about MS, nothing had prepared me for this. Even though I had read and understood that the damage MS inflicts on the central nervous system affects its ability to carry messages from the brain to different parts of the body, I hadn't expected it to pack up so suddenly and so completely. Although I had read that 'relapses' were a common symptom of MS, I had never consciously experienced one. Although I had read that in some cases relapses could be quite severe, I had never imagined they could be quite so debilitating. Although I had read that relapses were usually followed by remissions, which returned the body to near normal, the logical, thinking part of my brain had gone AWOL through terror. I couldn't think straight but whenever I could marshal my thoughts, all I could contemplate was a nightmare scenario.

If I couldn't move my leg or my arm, how would I ever be able to do anything vaguely normal again? I'd have to give up work, move to a specially adapted house and rely on others to feed me, dress me and ferry me about. I wouldn't be able to walk again and I'd have to spend the rest of my days in a wheelchair. Or bed-ridden... or...

Thankfully, the crisis passed as suddenly as it had arrived. By Tuesday evening some feeling returned to my hand. By Wednesday afternoon I could move my right leg. On Thursday evening I was ready to go home. On Saturday I reported a match for the BBC, and I didn't tell anyone about my stay in hospital. The same instinct that had prevented me from disclosing my MS for 16 months kicked in again, especially as my recovery was so swift and especially as the explanation for my relapse made such sense. According to the hospital doctors, my immune system had been confused by the beta interferon I was taking to treat my MS while a bout of campylobacter food poisoning had sought out the body's weakest links. As with so much to do with MS, no one could be absolutely sure, but it made enough sense for me to accept it, and it meant that I could push the black-hole scenario to the back of my mind.

But I couldn't banish it entirely. Nor, given everything I had read about MS, did I want to. Burying my head in the sand would only mean that a shock to the system, if it came, would be more traumatic. Physical deterioration – either at the rate I was currently experiencing or through a more rapid decline – was almost inevitable and the campylobacter scare had made me – had made us – confront some unpleasant scenarios. We were naturally optimistic and naturally competitive. While we could hope for the best, we also had to be ready for the worst. Unless someone came up with a miracle cure, my MS wasn't going to go away and, even if they did, it wasn't going to be any time soon. I had been given a life sentence, although I preferred to think of it as a life membership of a club I didn't want to join, and it was up to me to come to terms with that. My MS wasn't like cancer. I wasn't in pain, there was even less of a chance of a cure, but it wasn't life threatening. All the evidence suggested, however, that it could be life ruining. I was determined not to let it be so. Until the day I died, MS was always going to be a part of my life. I had tried to deny its existence or its relevance and used up an awful lot of energy and anger in the process. I had taken it head-on and not been able to subdue it. Now, instead of swimming against the current, I was going to go with the flow. Instead of trying to get rid of MS, or suppress it or deny it, I would acknowledge its presence. Instead of trying to battle it, I would deal with it. I would adapt my life to take MS into account but I wouldn't waste precious energy on trying to eradicate it. I would live with it, and concentrate on living with it to the best of my ability. From now on my motto would be: 'I have MS. So what?'

CHAPTER TWENTY-FOUR

DOING THE DRUGS

'Don't worry, I'll get you some great s–t!' The speaker had heard that cannabis alleviated some of the symptoms of MS and was determined to do his bit to make me feel better. 'The best that money can buy, and I'll guarantee you get a good deal!' He was absolutely desperate to help. 'I know just where to go...' The conversation really was going in the wrong direction. 'I can get it any time. Just say the word...'

The word was no. This was my teenage son and not only did I not want to try an illegal substance, I genuinely didn't want to know how Adam could get hold of it.

The truth of the matter was, I was already doing drugs. As the son and grandson of doctors, and as a child of my time, I had been brought up with a near-religious belief in science. The 20th century had seen the invention of aspirin, penicillin and insulin, vaccines against polio and hepatitis and the eradication of smallpox. If there was something wrong with you there was bound to be a pill, an injection or an operation that could cure you, or at least make you better. This was the era of heart transplants, test-tube babies and CAT scanners. The boundaries of the medically possible were being pushed backwards all the time. Surely there was something I could take for MS?

Well, yes and no. While the disease had first been identified in the mid-19th century, it had taken another hundred or so years before scientists could link MS to problems with the immune system. It wasn't until 1993 that scientists came up with a drug that could modify the disease. Even then, beta interferon – the standard drug issued to sufferers – was initially thought only to have some effect in the early stages of the relapsing/remitting form of MS. Although later studies showed that beta interferon could act as a brake on progressive MS such as mine, they also highlighted the side effects and the drawbacks. The commonest problems were listed as flu-like symptoms, inflammation at the injection site and depression, while further research showed that 40 per cent of recipients developed antibodies to the drug, which in turn ceased to be effective.

Nevertheless, as far as I was concerned it was the only drug that offered any hope, and I was determined to access it. That's when I fell foul of the 'post-code lottery'. NICE (the National Institute of Clinical Excellence) ruled that the cost of the treatment (just over £11,000 per year, per patient) far outweighed the benefits, while some surgeons pointed out that the disadvantages, especially as there was some doubt that beta interferon actually slowed the development of disability, were huge. As a result, eligibility for the drug was left to local health authorities and the bottom line was that their decisions were affected by the bottom line. Authorities with overstretched budgets wouldn't fund certain courses of treatment however pressing the medical need. Authorities with more money at their disposal could and did cover the cost. Patients with identical symptoms could get different levels of treatment depending on where they lived.

The system was blatantly unfair, and I found myself under pressure to act as a spokesperson for the disadvantaged. I understood the ways of the media sufficiently well to know that an issue had much more impact if it could be 'personalised' and even wider appeal if the subject of the report was familiar to at least some of the audience. I knew that, in news terms, 'ex-rugby international, ex-cricketer' gave me a certain amount of cachet, while my familiarity with the mechanics of the media made me an easy subject to interview. But now the spotlight was on me, I felt uncomfortable. I wasn't having second thoughts about speaking out, but I still found it difficult to talk about my own experience. The certainties in my old life had been removed at a stroke and I hadn't completely come to terms with my new self. On the surface I was fine, and without doubt the calming, loving, rational support that Jeannie had instinctively extended had allowed me to keep things in some sort of perspective. But I wasn't kidding myself. I may have got over the initial shock of learning that I had an incurable, progressive and debilitating disease, and I may have come through a period of denial, but I knew that I had plenty of grief still to resolve and I knew that I had only just started to scratch the surface of what it meant to be disabled. But I fronted up anyway. The chance to give a face – however ugly – to MS, and a voice – however feeble – to the disabled was too important to turn down.

My local authority was one of the most cash-strapped in the country. Only a few years later it was to declare a £48 million hole in its budget. I shouldn't have been surprised therefore to be informed, in mid-2000, that while it was going to fund beta interferon treatment for a dozen MS patients that year, I didn't meet its criteria. At least, not if the health authority was paying. But I was lucky. The fantastic fund-raising activities of Ian Robertson enabled me to cover the cost of treatment myself, a prescription was immediately available, and so was tuition in the not-so-gentle art of self-injection. This involved loading a spring-operated plastic tube with a pre-filled syringe, choosing a part of the body with a decent layer of fat underneath the skin (not a particular problem in my case), swabbing it clean and releasing the 'trigger'. Three times a week, at least 48 hours apart, at the same time of day on each occasion and in a variety of sites on the body to avoid irritation. I then had to dispose of the used syringes in a supplied 'sharps' box, which needed to be processed by the hospital rather than chucked out with the usual household rubbish.

If the routine was simple enough – even though my right hand and right arm weren't functioning well, I still had sufficient dexterity to administer the interferon myself – I was having difficulty getting used to the pain. However much I rationalised that it was, on the scale of things, neither excruciating nor long-lasting, I was still taken aback by the suddenness and intensity of the experience as the needle slammed into my skin. I was also finding it hard to cope with the side effects. I felt lousy for several hours after each injection and, although I delayed taking the drug until last thing at night so that I would sleep through the worst of it, I was well below par for three mornings a week.

But that was immaterial. The important thing was that I was taking positive, proactive steps to minimise the effects of my MS. I had chosen to take beta interferon because I was convinced that it would do me good. I had fought for the right for all people with MS to at least have the option of trying the only drug that offered some hope. I was convinced that it would delay the progression of my MS and I was convinced that I would soon get used to the side effects. If dealing with MS caused me some discomfort, then so be it. I had, after all, got a disease that had so far baffled some of the best minds in medical research. But I was taking some steps to deal with it, and that, I felt, kept me in control.

So did choosing not to rely on steroids. I had been put on a course of prednisolone tablets immediately after my diagnosis in January 1999 and, over the course of the next 18 months or so, I had accepted the offer of a couple of intravenous steroid top-ups accompanied by a couple of days' bed-rest in hospital. But the stay – in a busy and noisy hospital ward – had been anything but restful, I had felt almost hyperactively fidgety and restless for weeks afterwards, my face had become noticeably redder and I had whacked on the weight. I knew a lot of people with MS who swore by steroids but I just swore at them. They were not for me, and that, as I felt good in reminding myself, was my choice.

And so was a more regular attendance at the MS therapy centre in Nailsea. I needed no convincing of the value of physiotherapy – it had been an essential element in my cricket and rugby careers – and I had discovered that aromatherapy massage worked wonders on the increasingly frequent cramps and stiffness in my legs while oxygen therapy significantly topped up my dwindling energy levels. The only problem was fitting the treatments into my life. My work took up every day of the week and most months of the year. It was impossible to predict with any certainty where I would be from day to day. I had made the decision to get to the treatment centre as often as I could. I just couldn't work out how to get there as often as I would have liked. For the time being, however, it would have to be the thought that counted.

But I wasn't going to be put off when it came to making fundamental changes in other areas. My biggest problem was fatigue. Everything I did, every move I made, every step I took was so much harder than it had been. The chances were it was going to get harder still. As the central nervous system carried increasingly mixed messages around the body, some muscles refused to respond, while other muscles overworked in compensation. Some fibres wouldn't switch off, while some wouldn't fire up. Some straightened when you wanted them to bend and others bent when you wanted them to straighten. My right limbs weren't pulling their weight. The leg at times felt like a lump of concrete and was nearly as flexible. My right arm felt weak and heavy and I struggled to lift it high enough to wash my hair. Moving either for any length of time was a whole-body effort. Standing still was nearly as energy consuming as walking. Climbing a staircase was like climbing a mountain. Walking round a rugby stadium was like running a marathon. Driving a car was a real challenge for an arm that was getting weaker, a leg that was getting less responsive and a brain that, when tired, was increasingly prone to what the books described as cognitive dysfunction.

All of those activities were essential to my job. I could give that up – and I've only recently read a report in which my neurosurgeon predicted I'd retire within the year – or I could lessen their impact. But I had absolutely no intention of retiring and no wish to compromise the job I loved. I had always been bloody-minded. Whenever my teachers or parents or coaches had said something couldn't be done, I had regarded it as a challenge. No matter what it took, I would find a way.

And finding that way, as Jeannie and I discovered over the course of the next few months, would take a lot – of physical effort, mental anguish and emotional heartache. We began by putting our house on the market. We'd fallen in love with our lovely Edwardian home when we'd first set eyes on it, 11 years previously. It was ideally situated in the leafy and sociable suburb of Westbury Park and we had fondly believed it would be our home for life. It was big enough and safe enough for a growing family. It would be small enough and convenient enough for Jeannie and me in our old age. We couldn't imagine any circumstances in which we would want to move. Until I got MS.

I had never been a particularly keen gardener but it was soon painfully clear that I had neither the energy, the balance or the strength to provide the barest minimum upkeep of a garden that was 100 feet or so long and accessed by narrow concrete steps. I had never been remotely competent at anything to do with DIY but it was obvious that I was now lacking the dexterity, agility and co-ordination to attempt the simple maintenance jobs that even the best preserved of Edwardian houses demanded. I was finding the interior staircase just as daunting. Long and steep, it required real effort to negotiate. With the passage of time, it was only going to get more difficult.

So we chose to sell the beautiful but potentially high-maintenance house of our dreams, and buy a brand new city centre apartment with a buildings guarantee, a maintenance contract, a basement garage and no steps to speak of. We'd sacrifice the calm of the suburbs for the clamour of the inner city. We'd give up the known for the unknown, the Downs for the Docks, Waitrose for Asda and peace and quiet for hustle and bustle. But, we reassured ourselves, at least we would be in control. And with a third floor, low ceilinged, efficiently heated, much smaller apartment, we'd be saving energy in more ways than one.

Once I'd made the decision to do everything in my power to hang on to my job, the other decisions made themselves. I bought a walking stick to give my faulty right leg as much help as possible getting about in press conferences and at team hotels, and a four-wheeled electric scooter for getting about in the stadiums. I still had to overcome a deep psychological hurdle to be seen with either. Both were badges of disability, both proclaimed that I was different and both demanded modified behaviour from me and from the people who came into contact with me. But the benefits were obvious, immediate and gratifying. I found that the stick was not only incredibly useful in helping me keep my balance and climb banister-less stairs but also created a sort of exclusion zone in crowds. People who saw the stick kept well clear. When I might have expected to be jostled and lose my balance, I was now given a wide enough berth to reduce the fear of falling. The buggy may not have been a thing of beauty and it may have reduced my field of vision but it was incredibly useful as a beast of burden. Where previously I would have struggled to lug around both an overnight bag and my broadcasting equipment, now I could manage both without working up a sweat.

And once I'd made the decision to enlist all the help I could get to remain a productive member of the workforce it was but a couple of short steps to a Blue Badge and Access to Work. The former made it so much easier to park near the venues at which I would have to work, and significantly reduced the distance I would have to walk before I could start. The latter formalised a three-way partnership with the BBC and the Department of Work and Pensions whereby the latter would fund a support worker to help me perform my duties for the former. Between us we looked at my totally unpredictable work-patterns and calculated how many hours a week I would need assistance and for what. It was then up to me to engage the support worker, or workers, who would drive me to matches and press conferences, load and unload my bags and buggy, and then drive me home in a car provided and insured by the BBC. Although I would lose a fair amount of privacy and a certain degree of spontaneity and autonomy, I would have every chance of being rested and refreshed before I started a job and of recharging my batteries as soon as it finished.

The DWP also completed an assessment of my home office. On its recommendation, I revamped the desk and chair and invested in speech recognition software. By speaking into a microphone, I would make up for any tiredness or weakness I might feel in my right arm as the computer – not always infallibly, especially early on – turned the words I had uttered into sentences on the page.

And then there was the 'MS half-hour'. Neither Jeannie nor I came up with the idea but we were damned glad to borrow it. Every day we aimed to set aside thirty minutes for a free and frank discussion of the problems we faced in living with MS. The idea was that we could unload all our fears and worries, all the niggles and annoyances that were bound to crop up and, by airing them in a way that didn't imply judgement or apportion blame, we could at least try to keep our problems in perspective. If we wanted to, we could have a good old moan about the unfairness of it all. We could have a go at the people or the practices or the attitudes that made our lives that little bit harder and we could have a laugh at the events and words and gestures that had enriched our experience that day. It was all about keeping everything in proportion and once we'd done that, we could get on with the rest of our lives. MS had a part to play, we acknowledged that, but only a bit part. We were absolutely determined that it wasn't going to take a starring role.

PART SIX
MICROPHONES (BEFORE MS)

CHAPTER TWENTY-FIVE
THE RADIO YEARS

'Out of my way, I've got work to do.' Cricket producer Peter Baxter was clearly a force to be reckoned with at the BBC. The pickets outside broadcasting house parted before him. I tagged along behind. Just as we got to the vast, heavy, art deco doors that marked the main entrance, a portly, bearded, bespectacled middle-aged man stepped in front of us.

'Excuse me, sir, I don't think you understand. This is a legally convened strike on behalf of the National Union of Journalists to protest against the government's decision to prevent the BBC from showing the *Real Lives* documentary on Northern Ireland. We respectfully request that you do not cross the picket line.'

'And I don't think you understand,' said Peter Baxter. 'We are working on *Test Match Special*!' As far as he was concerned, that was more than enough reason for us to be entering Broadcasting House that day.

This was the beginning of August 1985, and he had just returned from Manchester where England had drawn the fourth Test against Australia. The series was tied one-all, the Ashes were still up for grabs and the fifth of six Test matches that summer started in just over a week's time. With the Gillette Cup final and the climaxes to the County Championship and the John Player League to cover as well as the two Test matches, Peter had plenty of planning to do and not much time to do it in. I had been detailed to help him.

I don't know what I had expected my first day at the BBC to be like. I certainly hadn't expected to push past a picket line, scurry round a near-deserted building and sort letters. Over the course of the summer, several sacks of mail had arrived for the *Test Match Special* commentators. My job was to open them all, compose replies to the ones that required nothing more than a formal acknowledgement, highlight the ones that could be used as talking points whenever there was a break for rain and put the rest into piles for the individual commentators' attention.

I suppose I should not have been surprised that by far the greatest number of letters were for Johnners. Brian Johnston was the undisputed star of the show. Listeners were captivated as much by his enthusiasm as by his beautiful speaking voice. They shared the delight he took in the sport of cricket, the matches themselves and all the characters involved. Above all, they appreciated Johnners' undisguised sense of fun. Letters to the great man were overwhelmingly appreciative. Letters to Fred Trueman, recipient of the only other large pile of correspondence, were either highly complimentary or scathing. To some, the pipe-smoking former England fast bowler was a true son of Yorkshire, a man who told it like it was, would never dream of calling a spade anything other than a shovel and was nothing less than a breath of fresh air. To the rest he was a biased and reactionary old bigot who lived in the past, had nothing good to say about the modern game and came across as a cantankerous, begrudging and bitter old man.

'How can you bear to offend so many of your listeners?' I asked Peter Baxter as I pointed to the huge pile of critical letters. 'How can Fred bear all that criticism?'

'Easy' was the reply. 'He has a hide like a rhinoceros, and it's great for our audience ratings. We get people who daren't miss *Test Match Special* in case they miss Fred. It gives them something to get upset about.'

It wasn't long before I got to meet the men whose letters I'd sorted. The fifth Test, at Edgbaston, was scheduled to start in just over a week's time and I was to be Assistant Producer. This was considerably less daunting than it sounded to someone who had never worked in radio. As Peter explained, my chief responsibilities in the role would be to fetch and carry, primarily for him but also for the commentary team. My job was to ensure that they had everything they needed to get on the air and stay on it. I might be required to escort a guest into or out of the commentary box, put tickets on the gate, collect refreshments from the caterers and run errands. In fact, I swiftly concluded it was just like being twelfth man on a cricket team, and I'd had plenty of experience of that.

'Higgers, delighted to see you, pull up a chair and tell me all about the Glosters.' Brian Johnston in the flesh conformed absolutely to his on-air image – genial, affable, interested, welcoming. Fred Trueman was also true to form. 'That's my chair you're sitting on' was his opening gambit followed, a few moments later when my presence had been explained, with a peremptory request to 'b-er off to t'kiosk and get me some matches for my pipe!'

By the time of the sixth Test at the Oval, I was an accepted part of the team, especially as I had proved adept during England's innings victory at Edgbaston at opening Brian Johnston's champagne and cutting and doling out the chocolate cake which was delivered to the commentary box by the hundredweight every time he quite shamelessly rhapsodised on air about its qualities. And I fitted in so well that Peter Baxter completely forgot that in radio terms I was a complete rookie. Perhaps he just couldn't believe that he'd been saddled with an Assistant Producer who'd never even wielded a microphone before...

As close of play loomed at the end of the first day of the final Test – England on 376 for three had made virtually certain of batting Australia out of the match and out of the Ashes – Peter Baxter felt he needed an interview with unbeaten centurion Graham Gooch to illustrate the close of play highlights package he was compiling. Shaking his head at my cluelessness, he'd loaded the tape and rigged the machine so that all I would have to do was point the microphone and release the pause button.

'You t-t! I'm not doing an interview with you' were certainly not the words that Peter was expecting to hear, much less to broadcast. 'You spoke against us at the PCA meeting. Why should I speak to you now?' Graham Gooch, one of the rebel cricketers to South Africa a few years before, remembered my contribution at the Cricketers' Association AGM and had no intention of passing up the opportunity to make me pay. While my brain conjured up and rejected any number of explanations for an empty-handed return to the commentary box, my mouth uttered words along the lines of how I had only been saying what I believed in, and surely he would respect anyone who stood up to be counted and anyway that was a long time ago, and then I saw that he was grinning from ear to ear! First hurdle crossed.

Test Match Special proved a gentle introduction to the world of radio. My first shift on *Sunday Sport* was the exact opposite. Somebody had cried off sick that morning. Would I mind filling in and provide the cricket scores? What I said was 'Of course, I wouldn't'. What I should have said was 'What did the job entail?' I'd kind of got the idea that when presenter Stuart Hall had finished getting updates from the grounds where we had reporters, he would ask me for a summary of the other scores. I had a vague idea that I would just read them out from the wires that were constantly spewing information into the sports room. I had no idea that I would be expected to précis the scores, analyse their significance and present a crisp coherent summary to a length decreed – and changed according to circumstance – by the programme producer. 'Forty seconds please' said the voice in my headphones, and I suddenly realised that I was about to broadcast (as opposed to summarise) on national radio for the first time in my life. Then I panicked; I had no stopwatch!

After 75 seconds of car-crash radio my limping, shambling incoherent first ever cricket scoreboard trailed off into a stunned silence. 'Has he finished?' Stuart Hall wondered aloud to the hundreds of thousands of listeners who had endured it. 'I wonder if there's any more... ' Unfortunately there was. Throughout the afternoon I was asked for reports of differing lengths that I could only guess at. 'Is that it?' Stuart could only ask when on one occasion I came up 15 seconds short. The infamous 'It's A Knockout' chuckle was all he could manage on another occasion when I went hideously over time. He – and the producer – may have been relieved when *Sunday Sport* finally came to an end, but they couldn't have been anywhere near as relieved as I was. Except...

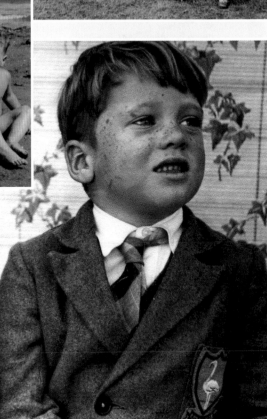

Above On the beach in Devon with Dad and Rob.

Above right Cathy's christening: Pictured with Rob, Mum, Cathy and Dad. Even at 22 months, I couldn't be parted from a ball.

Right First school: Blazered and freckled at Primary School, RAF Akrotiri, Cyprus.

Above Five kids in six years: Rob, Ben, Cathy, Steve and Alastair. Photo taken in 1965, when I was nine.

Left 200 not out: In 93 minutes, 10 sixes, 25 fours. I was 13 and too shy to wave the fly away from my lip.

Opposite Schoolboy batsman: Gallons of runs for Denstone, Ely, Cambridgeshire Colts, England Schools and anyone who would offer a game.

Above Bristol scrum-half: A skinny 18-year-old when Bristol officially became the best club in England by beating Leicester at the Memorial Ground.

Left England full-back: Just over a year later I was England's full-back, though this photo was taken in 1977.

Opposite top Cambridge University batsman: Less than six weeks after my England rugby debut, I was facing Imran Khan in the Varsity cricket match at Lord's and finding a novel way to avoid the bouncer.

Opposite middle and bottom Keeping busy: In 1977 I became the first person ever to captain both rugby and cricket teams, and in the same period gained a degree in history, won my county cap at cricket, played in all of England's Five Nations matches and was a reserve for the Lions tour to New Zealand.

Above Doing the honours: When the Duke of Edinburgh came to watch the Light Blues, I was his scruffy host. Here introducing Joe Davies, Jamie Barron and Ian Greig.

Left Flannelled fool, muddied oaf: *The Sun* came up with a novel way of illustrating my sporting double life.

Opposite In the runs: In full flow for Gloucestershire.

Above The reward for a century against the West Indies: Sponsors Harveys represented by former Gloucestershire and England spinner David Allen made me man of the match against the tourists. Mike Procter and Gloucestershire skipper Tony Brown look on.

Left Welsh hoodoo: I played four years in a row for England against Wales and finished on the losing side each time Clearing under pressure from JPR Williams at the Arms Park, Peter Dixon looking on.

Opposite top The best day of my life was getting married to Jeannie on December 20, 1980.

Opposite Going out with a bang: Pulling Derbyshire's Colin Tunnicliffe for four at Bristol; England players Jackie Hampshire, Geoff Miller and wicketkeeper Bob Taylor look on.

Above top A young family: Dan's christening in the summer of 1983 was our last appearance in Bristol as a family for some time.

Above bottom Presenting the documentary series *Rugby Warriors*.

Above top Coochy: Closer to home, commentating at Kingsholm with Gareth Chilcott.

Above Commentators: When the *Mail on Sunday* wanted a photoshoot with the commentators, it was easy to get excited. I'm standing third from the left in the middle row. Nigel Starmer-Smith, Bob Willis, Ray French, Miles Harrison, Jonathan Pearce, (unknown) (back row, left to right); Stuart Barnes, Barry Davies, Christine Trueman, Jim McGrath and Peter Brackley are alongside me (middle row); and Brian Moore, Peter Bromley, David Vine and Reg Gutteridge (front row).

Above Last day at Twickenham: Sharing a joke near the players' tunnel at my last pre-match interview. Pictured with Dave Rogers, photographer and friend.

Left The last commentary: Just before the match, the Beeb allowed me talk about the MSRC with Lawrence Wood, the man who made me patron. Producer Ed Marriage is pictured in the foreground.

Opposite top The last pint: The Five Live gang – Ed Marriage, Ian Robertson on one side, John Inverdale and Matt Dawson on the other.

Opposite The BBC's Sports Personality of The Year Awards 2008: Expressing my gratitude to Martin Bayfield, Eddie Butler, Ian Robertson, Hugo MacNeill, presenter Sue Barker and a television audience of nine million.

Above top Higgy's Heroes: Enlisting England captain Phil Vickery.

Above Fundraising with friends at the Stroud Farmers' Market.

Above top A sea of green: Over a hundred Higgy's Heroes signed up for the Stroud Half Marathon.

Above With Jeannie, Dan and Adam at the Stroud Half Marathon – I'm so proud of them all.

Left Receiving the CBE from the Queen at Buckingham Palace.

Below The official photographs in the courtyard – flanked again by Jeannie, Dan and Adam.

'Who's doing the cricket round-up?' One of the studio managers poked his head round the door of the sports room, just as the *Sunday Sport* team made their way back from the basement studio. I was just unhooking my jacket from the coat-stand when I realised that everyone was looking at me. 'It's just that the reporters at the ground want to know whether you want them to file reports, or are you going live?' I wasn't thinking about going live. I was only thinking about going home. It hadn't crossed my mind that by agreeing to provide the cricket scores in the afternoon, I'd also undertaken to present a three-minute mini-programme, complete with live inserts and taped clips, that would not only give a concise accurate and to-time summary of all that had happened in the world of cricket that day, but was also due on air in precisely 26 minutes!

May Mark Saggers be blessed for ever. The future Sky Sports presenter and Radio Five Live anchorman had only joined the BBC a few months before I had, but he sensed my utter panic as well as my complete ignorance of what I was supposed to do. 'I'll get CMJ and Pat Murphy to do 40 seconds each, you write ten-second cues to them and decide which of the other live games you want a report from. Then you'll be able to work out how much time you've got left for the other scores. OK?' I scribbled furiously and crossed out savagely. With Mark's help, I formulated a running order and cobbled together some cues. I compiled a script of sorts with seconds to spare. In a complete and utter state of funk, I watched the red on-air light go on and, my throat dry and my voice high-pitched and quavering, I started to read... And, somehow or other, got to the end of the round-up without making too many mistakes. The reporters at the grounds were professional as well as patient, the studio manager was crisply efficient and Mark was calmly encouraging. But as I caught the train home that night I was in no doubt that I had been incredibly lucky not to have made a complete fool of myself. And I was more aware than ever that I had a hell of a lot to learn.

And what a place to learn it. The radio sport department was, especially compared to the size it is today, tiny but it was brimming over with talent. John Inverdale joined the same year as Mark Saggers and I. So did Ian Brown, the Welshman who would go onto become one of the mainstays of Five Live's football commentary. Jeff Stelling, now a cult figure as polymathic presenter of Sky's *Soccer Saturday*, had been there slightly longer. So had Ian Darke, who was to find fame and fortune as a boxing and football commentator on Sky, while Garry Richardson became the longest-serving presenter on Radio 4's *Today* programme.

Mike Ingham, future football correspondent, and Tony Adamson, who was to prove equally authoritative as both tennis and golf correspondent, both operated out of the third-floor sports room at Broadcasting House at that time, as did Rick Blaxill, a man who was to win all sorts of awards in a different field as producer of *Top of the Pops*, and resident sports expert Rob Nothman.

The correspondents – Ian Robertson (rugby), Christopher Martin-Jenkins (cricket) and Bryon Butler (football) – were based on the fourth floor, which was also temporary home to two extraordinary Welsh wordsmiths. Cliff Morgan hosted the beautifully crafted, beautifully written and beautifully presented *Sport on Four* magazine programme on a Saturday morning. Peter Jones, as the main commentator, was equally lyrical – painting extraordinary word pictures at all the events covered by BBC Radio. These men were master broadcasters and I was a complete novice. But they were great people too, generous with their time, open-handed with their encouragement. They were not just my colleagues but also my teachers and my inspiration. I couldn't have started my broadcasting career alongside better people or in a better environment.

There was no question of starting anywhere other than at the bottom. In those days the BBC set such high standards and asked so much of its broadcasters that there was no question of my being officially trusted to go on air – even to read the racing results – until I had completed several shadow shifts. I would be allocated a desk near the main sports bulletin reader, given access to the same news wires and, after he had broadcast to the nation, I would slip into the studio and record my version of the sports news. Then everything would be picked apart – from the words I had chosen and the way I delivered them to the order that I chose to put each item and the weight I gave to it. There was an accepted way of writing – and reading – the racing results, the football scores and the cricket scoreboard. I had to prove that I had mastered these before I could be trusted to broadcast them.

I was sent on courses so that I could get a better understanding of how the BBC worked. A news journalism course taught the basics of getting a story and verifying it from different sources. A writing for radio course instructed us on the best way of condensing for news bulletins and how to deliver it. The pronunciation department not only gave the definitive way of pronouncing foreign names and faraway places but also summoned us for regular seminars to highlight how we stressed – or mumbled – particular words.

During a four-week radio production course we took turns at being presenters, producers, disc jockeys, editors, researchers, production assistants and studio managers. We got to plan and produce our own half-hour magazine programme – and write and deliver our own documentary.

Putting what I learned into practice was not so easy. Rolling news may be a feature of the 21st-century broadcasting experience but back in the late 1980s it wasn't even a pipedream. Radio Five Live, with its stated ambition of providing news and sport 24 hours a day on the BBC, was still only a glint in a visionary's eye. The reality was that the daily commitments of the BBC sports department amounted to hourly and half-hourly bulletins on Radio Two from 11 o'clock in the morning, a 15-minute round-up of the day's sports news at 6.45 in the evening and another shortened version just before the 10 o'clock news. Apart from that, it supplied Radio Four with a sports presenter for the *Today* programme and a half-hour programme on Saturday entitled, imaginatively enough, *Sport on Four*. During the cricket season it was responsible for *Test Match Special* on Radio Three medium wave and a cricket scoreboard at 7.30 every evening. But the department's main focus was *Sport on Two* presented live every Saturday and most Sundays of the year from 1.30 to 6 p.m.

All wannabe broadcasters served time as back-up producers on the show. Fielding calls from reporters in the field, turning round tapes for use in *Sports Report*, feeding information to the presenter, fetching and carrying for the producer or the editor, you got to understand how all the elements in the programme fitted together. At its best, it was fast-paced, constantly changing seat-of-the-pants broadcasting and everyone involved had to be on their toes. And at 5 o'clock, with the start of *Sports Report*, the programme slipped into overdrive. There was no time to ponder, to fine tune, or to get it wrong. Everything had to be slick, fast and to time. Adrenaline pumped around the studio during the programme and euphoria enveloped it as 6 o'clock arrived and the presenter cued James Alexander Gordon's reading of the football results. This was teamwork at its best and, for those of us who wanted to be out and about reporting matches, a valuable insight into what was happening back at base.

But I was still a long way from being sent out into the field. First I had to prove that I could read the racing results. In those days BBC Sport broadcast the results of individual races as soon as possible, while the full round-up would usually be broadcast near the end of the day's sports desk. Partly to give the public a break from the main presenter's voice and partly to give him a chance to receive any last-minute instructions from the producer, this was usually entrusted to the junior broadcasters. And, knowing that nearly all of the editors and producers in BBC sport would be listening, it became a matter of pride to get the stress and the intonation just right.

From reading the racing results, I progressed to the Friday night late bulletin. This was a shift that few wanted. It ate into the weekend, meant you didn't get home before midnight and quite often involved a raft of lower division football matches whose results would not come in until just before the broadcast. Collating these results, deciding which matches merited a report, re-editing some of the tapes that had been used earlier in the evening, and writing and delivering a script to time – and all out of a newly deserted sports room – was a real test of nerve.

So was my first interview. The day finally came when the *Sport on Two* editor felt he could trust me – or perhaps there was no one else available – to go out and interview a young athlete that he wanted to profile in the early part of that weekend's programme. I am ashamed to say that I cannot remember her name, only that she lived at Osterley at the very end of one of the tube lines out of London. I did all that I'd learnt on the course. I checked and rechecked the batteries and microphone on my cumbersome Uher tape-recorder, tested my headphones, loaded and reloaded the tape a few times to be absolutely sure that it wouldn't snag, and lugged the whole lot, plus an exhaustive list of carefully thought out questions, to Osterley. My interviewee was an elfin-like long-distance runner who was as nervous as I was. She sat herself down in an armchair and offered me the sofa. This, if I'd been Martin Bayfield, would have been at arm's length. As God made me a good foot shorter I soon discovered that I would have to perch on the edge of the sofa leaning forward with my arm at full stretch to get the microphone anywhere near my interviewee's mouth. And only then if she'd been leaning forward. But she wasn't, and her normal speaking voice was close to a whisper. I was too polite to ask if we could shift the furniture, or start again, and so for the next half-hour I continued the interview crouching painfully forward, locking my arm at full stretch every time she answered, twisting my head at regular intervals to check that the tape was going round and that the recording-level was registering. It was, but that fact cut no ice with the producer. 'Completely unusable' was his withering assessment. Not one fragment of a half-hour interview was loud enough to be broadcast. As far as interviewing went, I had fallen at the first hurdle.

And I didn't do much better the first time I was sent to cover a rugby match. The good news was I didn't have to take a COOBE (Commentator Operated Outside Broadcast Equipment). The bad news was that BBC Radio Nottingham had trouble providing a link that worked. I spent an hour before the match and most of the first half traipsing between my seat in the stand and their control point in the car park. In the former, I could watch the match. At the latter, I could communicate with Broadcasting House. Nowhere could I do both. Until, well into the second half, the BBC engineer fixed the problem and my headphones were suddenly filled with the sound of *Sport on Two*. And, only a few seconds later, with the ominous words 'live from Beeston, Alastair Hignell... ', I knew what the score was – the scoreboard told me that. I could recognise a few players – I'd even played against a few of them. But I had no idea who had scored the points or how the game had progressed. I hadn't got my stopwatch out of my bag, or my notebook ready. But I made the crucial mistake of believing I could wing it. I embarked on a report that started confidently enough and then took on a life of its own – rambling, repetitive nonsense that I hadn't the wit or the experience to bring to a halt. In just over a minute I died a thousand deaths. 'I've got to congratulate you,' Deputy Head of Sport Mike Lewis stopped in front of my desk on the Monday morning. 'That was a perfect demonstration of how not to do a rugby report!'

It didn't put either of us off too much. Come the international season, Mike felt confident enough to allocate me a first commentary. While *Sport on Two* would be concentrating on Wales against Scotland in Cardiff, BBC Northern Ireland listeners would be offered full commentary from Ireland's match against France in Paris. They needed a second commentator to work alongside Ulsterman Jim Neilly, former Ireland great Fergus Slattery and producer Joy Williams.

The day before that I was scheduled to produce my first Friday night preview package. For the commentary, I needed to watch the players of both teams in training for as long as possible. For the package, I needed to interview the captains of each team and broadcast from the BBC office in the centre of Paris.

'Absolutely nothing to worry about, darling.' Joy was reassurance itself. 'Jim and I have done this for years. I know exactly where both teams are training, and we've got a car and a driver at our disposal all day. He's booked for 9 o'clock. Let's meet at breakfast before that. OK, darling?'

The next morning I was up, showered and shaved at 7.30, breakfasted at 8 and was sitting in the lobby with thrice checked Uher, notebook, spare pen and batteries by 8.45. I wasn't feeling great, although I was confident that I had upheld the honour of England rugby in the previous night's whisky shindig. Still, I was glad that I had set my alarm, and I was ready to go. So was the driver. Joy was fast asleep. 'Oh my God, darling! I feel like death!' she croaked down the telephone, 'Order me some black coffee, get some for the driver and I'll be down in the breakfast room in a few moments.' Half an hour later, after Jim and the driver had each polished off half a dozen croissants and nearly as many cups of coffee, she was just taking her first sip. 'Don't worry, darling. I know exactly where the French are training. It won't take us long. And anyway you know what the French are like – always late!'

But she didn't, and they weren't. At Joy's insistence we had chosen a vantage point – in a café overlooking the only sports field in the village of Rambouillet. But when I used my A-level French to quiz the café owner as to what time the French team usually turned out and to ask him if it was usual – on the Friday before the big international – for there to be not a single photographer or film crew in attendance, he looked at me as if I were mad. He insisted that the French team was never late and that if I wanted to catch any of the French media several of them would be popping into the café on the way back from the session at the team's headquarters on the other side of the village. Chateau Ricard was a magnificent old house set in the forest, with a gravelled drive, well manicured gardens, and its own rugby pitch – from which, as our Mercedes screeched to a halt in front of the main building, the French team were walking back. Jim and I tried desperately to match names and faces, as they trooped past us. I also had to find out which one of them would be able or willing to be interviewed in English. Jean-Baptiste Lafond! Something clicked in the inner recesses of my brain about an article I'd read that praised the Frenchman's bilingualism. He may have been surprised as a short, flustered, out-of-breath Englishman tumbled out of the car in front of him, but the magic letters 'BBC' did the trick. He reeled off a couple of beautifully constructed answers in English and sauntered back to the team hotel. I breathed a huge sigh of relief. Mission accomplished – at least part of it. The Irish were much less unpredictable. Joy and Jim knew them really well. It could only get better from now on.

'Let's have lunch, darling.' We were arriving back at the hotel – and the Ireland team was getting on a bus to leave it. 'Don't worry about that, darling; we've got plenty of time. They'll be training round the corner.'

Except they weren't. Our long and leisurely lunch was followed by a long and complicated journey. By the time we had reached our destination, the Ireland players had finished training and were in a hurry to get back to the hotel. Jim interceded on my behalf and I got a couple of snatched interviews with the coach and Ciaran Fitzgerald, the captain. Now all I had to do was play them back from the BBC office in the centre of Paris. Driver Michel, however, was heading back to the hotel. No one had told him our destination, and he'd been looking forward to dumping us and getting home. The last thing he wanted to do was to work his way into the centre of Paris with the *périphérique* all but gridlocked and the Friday rush-hour about to start with a vengeance. We made the studio with seconds to spare.

Still, with the report now out of the way, I could at last concentrate on my commentary. I'd read that Bill McLaren turned up with playing cards with names and numbers on to help him with his recognition, and I'd bought a brand new pack for the purpose. I also tried writing the numbers down out of sequence before trying to put a name to them. I rehearsed scenarios in which the front-rows (Nos. 1, 2 and 3) would be packing down against each other and made sure I could put a name and a face to them. I knew that the French No. 11 would be lining up against the Irish No. 14 and that if the Irish No. 10 tried an up-and-under the most likely person to be underneath it would be the French No. 15. In my head, I ran through every play I could think of and rattled out the names of the players involved. I spent the night flipping cards and the morning poring over facts and figures. Bill McLaren never went into a game without several hundred statistics to hand. I may not have had as many of those at my fingertips but I was as well prepared as I could be. But I was still as nervous as hell.

'Don't worry, darlings, Auntie Joy has everything under control.' I didn't find that particularly comforting as we staggered out of the ridiculously tiny lift at the Parc des Princes and installed ourselves in a deserted commentary box. 'I'd have thought our engineer would be here by now,' said Joy, 'but you know what these Frenchmen are like. He's probably having one of those long lunches. Still, this is the studio we always broadcast from, we might as well set up shop here.'

With 15 minutes to kick-off, there was still no sign of our engineer. I went in search of a loo and spotted a door marked BBC Radio. Behind it, a bored-looking Frenchman was reading a novel. He explained that he'd rigged the box as best he could and was now waiting for some radio broadcasters from Ireland but, he shrugged his shoulders expressively, 'you know what the Irish are like.' I persuaded him to stay, and raced off to find Joy and Jim. When I slipped on the headphones I discovered that there was no background noise. The windows of the Parc des Princes commentary box were made of thick, soundproof plate-glass and there was no sound of the 50,000 crowd outside. What we needed was something called International Sound to feed crowd noise back to the commentators, but for some reason we weren't getting it. Joy rose magnificently to the challenge and realised she needed to do something about my fast-waning confidence. 'Don't worry, darling. Jim's got some idea of the crowd noise in Paris. He can take the first 20 minutes of the match, and when you take over all you have to do is match his level of intensity. And take it from me, you'll be great.'

Great in theory. Except that when the words ('and now, France have a scrum five metres from the Ireland line, and to take you through to half-time, here's Alastair Hignell') launched my commentary career, I found not only that the action I was expected to describe was on the right-hand touchline, and therefore in the worst possible line of sight from our commentary box, but at a moment of maximum French excitement I felt as if I was commentating from the inside of a confessional box. I felt horribly self-conscious, and exposed and vulnerable. Was I up to the job? Was I conveying the right level of excitement? Was I sharing the excitement of the occasion with the viewers, or my nerves? In the cathedral-like calm of the commentary-box, there was absolutely no way of telling.

But after a while I began to realise I was enjoying myself. Here I was, in one of the best seats in the house, in one of the great rugby stadiums in the world, witnessing an absolutely absorbing encounter between two sets of highly talented and supremely committed athletes, getting paid for putting words to the action that was unfolding in front of me. I got a little buzz whenever I got a name right – offering a silent prayer of thanks to Bill McLaren – and a burst of satisfaction every time I read the play right. I felt a great sense of achievement as the words kept tumbling out of my mouth in roughly the right order and a great sense of wonder that it all seemed to be making sense. The adrenaline rush that I had felt whenever I took the field as a player gripped me now as a commentator. This was exciting, demanding and, in the sense that a single mistake could wreck the whole performance, dangerous. In live commentary there were no rehearsals, no re-takes and no retractions. I was under pressure to come up with the goods, and I was loving it.

I may have discovered what I wanted to do with the rest of my working life, but the BBC was in no hurry to oblige. Radio Two never aspired to the blanket sports coverage to which Five Live listeners have become accustomed. There was a logjam of highly competent and considerably more experienced broadcasters waiting to avail themselves of any opportunities that came their way. I was well down the pecking order. But, while I was increasingly being sent out to report on – and sometimes commentate at – rugby matches, I felt the weight of dead men's shoes when it came to cricket. I was entirely comfortable with the idea of serving my apprenticeship in the studio, providing the cricket scores for the hourly bulletins and delivering the cricket scoreboard – complete with inserts, clips and interviews where appropriate – but I was impatient to get out into the field myself. I started to believe that I was getting too competent at delivering the cricket round-up, and that while I was becoming Mister Reliable at base, all sorts of other broadcasters were being given the chance to report on matches. I could accept that men like Charles Colville, Andy Smith and Ron Jones had been on the staff for a lot longer than I had, but I started to feel more than a little aggrieved when, in presenting the cricket round-ups, I, as a former professional cricketer, had to cue in reports from a Radio One disc jockey (Andy Peebles), a world-famous lyricist (Tim Rice) and a spokesman for the National Farmers Union (Anthony Gibson). I know now there were sound reasons for their preference. I just couldn't see them at the time.

And what progress I did make seemed to make even more of the wrong sort of demands. When the first ever Rugby World Cup was held – in Australia and New Zealand in 1987 – BBC radio sent all of two people to cover it. While Ian Robertson flitted about between the two countries, rugby producer Gordon Turnbull based himself at broadcasting house in Wellington. My role was to act as anchorman back in London and, as most matches kicked off in the afternoon, local time, that meant that for several weeks I would take a middle-of-the-night taxi to Broadcasting House, issue a perfunctory cue and settle down to watch television pictures of the matches, with my own commentary notes handy in case the line from the ground went down. It never did.

And when the Cricket World Cup came from India in the same year, guess who was the anchorman on BBC radio? There may have been slightly more of a preamble to these matches – I occasionally had to cue in some commentary, or an interview clip – and I did on one memorable occasion get to commentate for the best part of two hours on England versus Sri Lanka – but they served only to add to a sense of unsettledness. I was doing well as a broadcaster, but I felt that, however long I stayed at the BBC, I would never get the chance to develop much further. Ian Robertson was the rugby correspondent and would automatically be sent to cover all the big stories, report on all the big tours and commentate on all the big matches. Christopher Martin-Jenkins was the cricket correspondent and would enjoy the same prerogatives in his sport. Both were relatively young men. Both were likely to remain in their posts for at least the next two decades. I couldn't displace either, and I didn't really want to. I was keen on a career in broadcasting, but I didn't want to stay an understudy for the next twenty years. I was determined to check out other options.

I remembered the way I had left it with HTV three years previously. The commercial television company had wanted to offer me a job but didn't think I was equipped to do it. But they had left the door open. Come back, they had said, when you've learnt a bit more about broadcasting and have a little bit of experience under your belt. Nothing ventured, nothing gained. I'd cut my teeth in radio, and I had been thoroughly trained by the BBC. Would HTV be interested in another chat? They would.

CHAPTER TWENTY-SIX
HTV DAYS

I am not taking all the blame for this. The HTV I joined in January 1989 was a reasonably successful independent television company, employing hundreds of people in two huge studio complexes in Bristol and Cardiff. It was vibrant, creative and prolific, producing a raft of programmes for the region and generating significant income for the network. Within months of my departure, HTV had been swallowed up by Granada. Six years later it surrendered its name, rebranded and sub-let its studios. As I write these words, it's as if the company that employed me for seven exhilarating and exhausting years has been airbrushed out of broadcasting history.

To be fair, the gravy train that was ITV was already slowing down. Few in the industry doubted that fact. Channel 4 was flourishing and Sky had just been launched. Advertising revenue would have to be shared more widely but there still seemed plenty to go around. There wasn't the faintest hint of suspicion, as I pulled into the Television Centre's Bath Road car park on 6 January 1989, that HTV was on the skids.

My first impressions were favourable. Whereas before I used to take a bike, two trains and a half-mile walk to get to work, now I could go by car. A journey taking the best part of two hours had been succeeded by one of twenty minutes. Whereas before I had kept my belongings in a metal cabinet and 'hot-desked' around a sprawling sports room, now I had my own desk, my own computer and, in the form of a company blazer and a couple of embroidered sweaters, my own uniform.

And, at last, my salary was heading in the right direction. As a rule, telly pays more than radio and ITV pays more than the BBC. After taking one pay cut when I gave up cricket for teaching, and another to start at the bottom of the pile at the BBC, there was now a real prospect that I might have some money left at the end of the month, instead of the all-too-familiar opposite.

When it came to doing what I was paid for, I experienced a huge culture shock. Having grown accustomed to the lean and mean ways of the BBC, I couldn't quite get my head round how many people it took to get a programme on air. My last sports desk at the BBC had required a presenter, a producer and a studio manager. My first bulletin at HTV required three cameramen and a floor manager in the studio, a director, producer, sound mixer, vision mixer, graphics operator and assistant producer in the gallery, as well as make-up artists and a crew of riggers, whose roles and responsibilities were forcefully impressed on me during the soundcheck.

'I think you'll find that's my job,' said a man in dark blue polo shirt with a brick-sized walkie-talkie strapped to his scruffy grey trousers as he appeared from out of the shadows. My hand froze in mid-air. I had instinctively responded to a voice in my ear, which suggested that the desk microphone in front of me needed to be pointed a little bit to the right. Did the other presenters breathe a sigh of relief that a demarcation dispute had been avoided, or was I just being fanciful? The broadcast unions – particularly in television – had become hugely powerful over the years and management had learned that you crossed them at your peril. It was probably just as well that I let the rigger move the mike.

Although the basic requirements of the job were similar – I asked questions, compiled packages, presented links and delivered reports – there were infinitely more tricks of the trade. For radio the most important thing was getting the microphone in the right place to produce the best possible sound quality. On television, what things looked like was far more important than how they sounded. As an interviewer you had to concentrate not only on delivering sensible questions and getting intelligible answers but also on how you looked, how the interviewee looked and how the piece would stitch together. It wasn't enough to take back an interview to the editing room, you also had to take a plentiful supply of pieces to camera, establishers (to put your package in context), cutaways (over which you could voice a link to the next part of the item), two-shots (just in case you didn't have much obvious or relevant material) and 'noddies' (when, long after the interview, the cameraman filmed the reporter's 'responses' to the answers he had long ago received).

Another huge difference between radio and TV was talkback. As presenter on the 'wireless' you would only hear noise from the studio if the director flicked a switch and spoke to you directly. In a television studio there's open talkback from the gallery. For a rookie presenter it's a nightmare. There are any number of instructions being issued, clarifications being sought and conversations going on in your ear, while you are trying to broadcast. You have to know which voices to listen to, and which ones to block out. You have to learn not to display your reactions to what you hear, how to absorb new information while listening to something completely different and how to react to new instructions when they come. If you're unfamiliar with the workings of television, as I was, it's doubly difficult.

But I'd been chucked into the television deep end and I had no choice but to swim, or sink. Apart from researching, reporting and presenting sports stories for the daily news bulletins, I was also required to co-present a half-hour sports magazine programme on a Friday and be part of a two-handed, extended sports round-up on a Monday. With three professional football clubs in our region (Bristol City, Bristol Rovers and Swindon Town) as well as three first-class rugby outfits (Bristol, Bath and Gloucester), two county cricket sides (Gloucestershire and Somerset) and countless other top class performers in a whole variety of sports, it was a six-day week just keeping pace.

In those pre-Sky days, the BBC was the only broadcaster of club rugby and the corporation had little interest in exclusivity. As long as rival broadcasters didn't attempt to broadcast the same match as *Rugby Special*, they were at liberty to go where they wanted. That meant that, at the very worst, HTV could get news access to the weekend's big matches – and show good chunks on the Monday round-up and any preview shows – and at the very best could mount an outside broadcast. Before I arrived, John Pullin had been the summariser at these games, but he was a farmer and had very little time to watch any matches when he wasn't summarising. Although John and I worked pretty well together, I felt the need, especially for our Monday round-ups, to tap into some more contemporary viewpoints. I invited different current players to come into the studio on a Monday night and it didn't take long to discover that Bath and England prop Gareth Chilcott was a natural. 'Cooch' possessed if not the most recognisable face in rugby, at least the most recognisable shape. He had a rich deep voice, distinguished still further by an unmistakable Bristol burr, he knew the sport inside out – even back play – he had a great sense of humour, and, crucially amid all the dramas and crises of daily television, he was absolutely dependable.

When ITV broadcast the next two Rugby World Cups, he made a seamless transition to network television. When Radio Five Live needed a summariser on England and Lions tours in the late 1990s and early 2000s, they turned to 'Coochie'. In between times, he appeared in panto at the Theatre Royal in Bath and in John Godber's play *Up and Under* at the Old Vic in Bristol, he advertised beer on billboards all over the West Country and became a star turn on the after-dinner speaking circuit. Little did we know it in 1989, but a media star had been born – with the baby weighing in at 18 and a half stone!

Gareth became such a key part of our rugby coverage in the next season or so that even when a shoulder injury should have prevented him from climbing a ladder to the commentary position at Bristol's Memorial Stadium, the company hired a crane to deposit him on the platform alongside me. With the crowd roaring their approval, and Coochie waving regally with his undamaged arm, the crane made stately progress down the walkway in front of the stand, and ever so sedately and carefully swung the platform into position alongside the scaffolding, spectacularly misjudging the top rail and dumping Coochie in an undignified and painful heap at our feet! That was just one of many treasured experiences working alongside a man who has become a true friend.

'Cooch' – so called after children's comic book character 'Coochie Bear' – was a shining light in a whole galaxy of stars at Bath. The best team in the land had already won the rugby knockout cup four times by the time I started at HTV. They were to win it in five of the seven seasons I worked in the West Country – and pick up four Premiership titles along the way. This was the era of Stuart Barnes, Richard Hill, Andy Robinson, John Hall, Gareth Chilcott and, of course, of a local boy who, with the advent of professionalism, was to become the sport's first pin-up, Jerry Guscott.

Guscott's explosion onto the international scene took us all by surprise. Ever present as Bath won the Premiership and Cup double in 1989, he was a late call-up to the England side for a hastily arranged late-May fixture against Romania in Bucharest. In blazing sunshine, England put 50 points past the hapless Romanians and the hat-trick hero of a quite scintillating display by England was Jerry Guscott. Watching at home on TV, I had no doubt that my Monday mission would be to track down the young prodigy and get him to talk the viewers through an astonishing debut.

But how? We knew he worked at a building site but had no idea which one. There was never any question that he would take the day off – whatever they got up to at the weekend, rugby players wouldn't dream of not turning up for work. Some frantic phone bashing provided the information that he was working on a new housing estate in Calne. His employers graciously gave us permission to film him as long as we agreed not to take up too much of his time, and that we swung by their offices to pick up a clean set of company-issue overalls for him to wear during the interview. At the building-site Jerry was welcoming enough, fairly tongue-tied for what was probably the first proper television interview of his life, and a little embarrassed by all the attention. But not as embarrassed as his foreman, who quietly pulled me to one side as we were packing up: 'You're not going to broadcast those shots of Jerry building the wall, are you?' I tried to explain that we were cutaways and might be used to get from one part of the item to another. 'Don't show too many close-ups,' he said, 'that's a crap wall he's just built. We'll have to knock it down when you're gone!'

The fact that rugby players had real jobs as well was manna from heaven for a TV journalist. Stuart Barnes could be found in a series of building society offices, while Gloucester's Mike Teague was invariably building a house somewhere. Jerry Guscott soon swapped his builders' overalls for an office – without a phone, we noticed – at the headquarters of British Gas in Keynsham, while Gloucester's Dave Sims worked in a fruit wholesale warehouse run by former England selector Peter Ford. We filmed future England captain Martin Corry painting the gates at Bristol's Memorial Ground and Jon Webb doing his rounds at one of the region's hospitals. We caught up with Andy Robinson teaching at Colston's and Jon

Callard at Downside, while towards the end of my time we filmed Bath's 'Three Degrees' – Victor Ubogu, Adedayo Adebayo and Steve Ojomoh – pitching up for training in a flashy white stretch limo they'd hired to ferry them from their jobs in the City to Thursday night training in Bath. Even more bizarre than that, we tracked Bristol outside-half Neil Matthews back to Gloucester where he worked in a business selling and demonstrating trick cycles. All made great pictures. All made the interviews fun. All made my job easier.

Which was probably just as well because it was starting to seem as if the more I did, the more I was asked to do. Before long our four-handed Friday night leisure programme became a sports only show, with co-presenter Roger Malone and I doing all the writing, research, and packages, all the fixing, planning and presenting. On top of that HTV had its own live *Sports Review of the Year* show, and, just to block off any spare time I might have had, I was sending a weekly column to the Plymouth-based *Sunday Independent* newspaper and contributing regularly to the new Allied Dunbar Premiership match-day programmes.

I was revelling in the creative freedom that television was giving me. I was starting to add frills to my pieces to camera – ducking under the surface in perfect timing with a synchronised swimming team, donning a cricket helmet to face Somerset fast bowler Andre van Troost, hurtling round the Bristol Docks in a feature on powerboat racing – and I was starting to plunder the music library for cheesy but appropriate tracks – 'It Takes Two' for a feature on twins in Taunton, 'Feet's Too Big' for a piece on an outsize Bristol basketball player and 'Hello, Goodbye' to mark Gareth Chilcott's retirement from rugby. I was getting the opportunity not only to present documentary programmes, but to research them, write them and edit them as well. Of course, they were sports oriented, but I got a real buzz out of contributing to the HTV series *The Great Westerners* with profiles of England full-back-cum-violin-playing surgeon Jon Webb and the all-conquering Bath club. And I leapt at the opportunity to get away from rugby altogether with a one-off documentary charting cricketer David Lawrence's desperate struggle to recover from devastating injury.

I was beginning to develop some stand-alone television skills. When the Inner City cycling series came to Bristol, I presented an HTV special from College Green and, though I had next to no knowledge of the sport, I co-commentated alongside the extraordinarily knowledgeable and enthusiastic Channel Four Tour de France commentator, Phil Liggett. I filmed equestrian features with Ginny Leng and, whenever HTV produced a soccer special, I acted as highlights editor for the matches on the undercard. I even got to commentate on football one season, but I don't think I enlightened HTV viewers very much with my constant references to touch-judges, line-outs and the 'blind side'!

But the real proof that I had made it as a television presenter in my own right came with *Let's Go*. This was a series designed to inform HTV viewers about all the wonderful tourist attractions, historic locations, beauty spots and leisure facilities in the region and persuade them to participate in any or all of the activities on offer. With producer Terry Miller, I'd choose a town or village a week or so in advance, spend a day on-site, checking out camera angles, locations and backdrops, and the next few days lining up venues, activities and guests before returning to film the links with Terry, a camera crew and co-presenter Gill Impey. The whole process ticked just about all the boxes. I was getting involved with a project from start to finish. I was coming up with ideas, researching, planning, shaping and delivering. I was polishing up my presenting skills and at the same time getting a valuable insight into how to make programmes. I was thoroughly immersed in the media, and I had created a niche for myself. I would have continued building a reputation as a good solid regional TV all-rounder and would have been more than happy to do so until, in autumn 1990, ITV dropped a bombshell. Against all odds, in complete defiance of their own history and other people's expectations, they'd snatched the exclusive rights to broadcast the Rugby World Cup.

CHAPTER TWENTY-SEVEN
ITV (1991)

'That's the trouble with this lot. They're a bunch of f-ing cheats!'

Clive Woodward and I stared at each other in alarm. Our commentary box was perched high up in the stands of Beziers' magnificent Stade de la Mediterranee. The second match of Rugby World Cup 1991 was about to begin. The day before, the first competition to be held in the northern hemisphere had got off to a rousing start as reigning champions New Zealand had crushed England at Twickenham. Now it was the turn of beaten 1987 finalists France to take on Romania. Down below us the teams were lined up for the anthems.

'Higgy! Clive! Give us a wave!' the voice insisted.

The French players led by peerless full-back Serge Blanco engaged in discreet callisthenics while their Romanian counterparts, chests puffed out and tears in their eyes, belted out the interminable 'Desteapta-te Romane' national anthem. To our left a handful of yellow-shirted travelling supporters waved their flags enthusiastically. Everywhere else there were tricolours. As far as we knew, we were the only English speakers in the entire stadium. So where was the voice coming from, and what did it mean?

'I'm catching my f-ing death waiting for these anthems to end. And that's the last f-ing swearword you'll hear from me this evening!'

Referee Les Peard, a police inspector from south Wales, had a novel way of testing new technology. For the first time ever in international rugby, referees at the 1991 Rugby World Cup were required to wear a microphone and Les was keen that the only people who would hear him during the match – the commentators – should miss nothing. A minute or so later, he whistled for kick-off and *Coronation Street* fans knew for sure that, for almost the first time since it aired in 1960, their favourite soap had been shunted around the schedules.

It was as clear an indication as any that ITV knew what they were doing when they'd scooped the television rights to the tournament. The BBC had covered the first World Cup from Australia and New Zealand in 1987 and even though miniscule crowds had turned up to watch the live action, and afternoon kick-offs had deterred all but the most dedicated European fans from getting up in the small hours, the competition had been deemed a success. Now, with the tournament due to take place in prime European time, the potential for some serious money-making was huge and ITV had blown the BBC out of the water by bidding three times as much for the rights. Rugby was about to take a giant leap in the public consciousness, and I was ideally placed to witness it.

And the England rugby team was ideally placed to cash in. Not literally. Not yet. The laws didn't allow the golden generation that had developed under the management of Geoff Cooke and the captaincy of Will Carling to be paid, but those players who had read the signs were happy to dedicate themselves to the pursuit of excellence, keen to surf the sport's burgeoning popularity and anxious to discover where it might lead them.

The first steps, that took place early in 1991, were farcical.

'Nothing personal, Higgy, we're just not speaking to you.' The England players had scurried tight-lipped from the Cardiff Arms Park changing room after beating Wales in Cardiff for the first time in 28 years and Brian Moore was keen to explain that he had nothing against me personally. 'In fact, we're not speaking to anyone.' Gloucester No. 8 Mike Teague had scored England's only try and I knew that my Monday mission for HTV would be to track him down and interview him. I also knew that as a self-employed builder he got up early and that the houses he was building would be unlikely to have a phone installed. I thought I would kill three birds with one stone; wait for the pressure to ease at Cardiff railway station, personally congratulate the West country players involved, and find out where Mike Teague would be on the Monday.

When the message came back to my post at the dressing room door that the normally affable Mike Teague was not only not able to talk to me, now, he was also unable to tell me where he would be on Monday and, even if he could, he wasn't sure whether he would be able to talk to me then, I was intrigued rather than angry. I decided to wait and check personally, only to be told that, rather than leaving by the dressing room door, the players were going back out onto the pitch in a bid to evade us. The train home wasn't due for an hour so I decided to follow them back across the pitch to their post-match headquarters at the Cardiff Centre Hotel. I was part way across when Brian Moore caught up with me and issued his cryptic explanation.

Inside the hotel, I discovered a posse of journalists in various stages of bewilderment. It transpired that since the final whistle had blown on one of the most significant victories in English rugby history, not one of the England players had uttered a single word to any of the media. A female journalist was briefed by one of the hacks to go up to the front desk, and pretend not only that she had lost the key to her room but that she was also Mrs Carling. Most of those in the vicinity seemed surprised when the ruse didn't work. Personally, I thought it was all going really well till she opened her mouth. 'Right, but,' she began. 'I'm Mrs Khyaer-ling, see...' Under some circumstances – if, for instance, the receptionist had only just arrived in Wales and never spoken to another human being – she might have got away with the extraordinary pronunciation of the first syllable that only true inhabitants of 'Khyare-diff' can manage, but I doubt it.

Next we heard that, instead of coming back down through reception on their way to the post-match dinner at the Angel Hotel, the England players had availed themselves of a first-floor fire exit. Half the journalist rat pack raced off like Keystone Cops. The rest stayed put, in case it was a diversionary tactic. None of us got more than a glimpse of Richard Hill and a guarded apology from Rob Andrew.

It transpired that the England players had been badly advised by the very people brought in to guide them through as yet uncharted waters. This company, WHJ Promotions, had apparently interpreted the new guidelines as a licence to demand payment for any recorded interviews given by the players, on the assumption that these interviews would almost certainly be aired in general sports and news programmes, which could therefore, at a pinch, be construed as non-rugby related. What they failed to understand was that a *Saturday Grandstand* on an England-Wales weekend in January, while containing references to other sports, was almost entirely rugby-related and that a Sunday afternoon's *Rugby Special*, while admittedly a recorded show broadcast well after the match, could only be described as a rugby-related programme. They argued therefore that as any interviews given by the players immediately after the match would almost certainly be used in the following day's *Rugby Special* and in subsequent recorded programmes, they were entitled to some payment. When the BBC refused to be blackmailed into paying for what they considered to be live interviews, the players felt they had no alternative but to boycott all post-match interviews.

But the Cardiff fiasco was but a minor dent to rugby's image. Geoff Cooke was leaned on by the RFU to make a fairly grovelling apology on the following week's *Rugby Special*, England marched onwards towards their first Grand Slam in over a decade and the media needed little encouragement to rekindle their love affair with the sport.

ITV did their very best to fan the flames and I was perfectly placed to wield the bellows. In their desperation to establish themselves as a credible force in rugby, they snatched up any broadcast rights that were available, staffed them on an ad hoc basis and only then worked out when they could actually broadcast the matches. Only HTV Wales, and to a lesser extent HTV West, had any experience of broadcasting live rugby matches, and only those two would be likely to devote significant airtime to any internationals that ITV might acquire. Certainly, to begin with, only those two could divert any of their staff from regional soccer programmes. But ITV were desperate to get some rugby footage in the bank, desperate to check out the credentials of those who might be working for them at the World Cup and desperate to establish some sort of foothold in the rugby world. John Taylor, the former Wales and Lions flanker and then rugby correspondent for the *Mail on Sunday*, had been involved in the rights negotiations, had cut his teeth with ITV as a gymnastics commentator and was set to head up the World Cup commentary team. Bob Simmons was a vastly experienced commentator for HTV Wales. I, as I stressed in the letter I wrote to ITV Head of Sport Bob Burrows the instant I heard that ITV had the World Cup rights, was a reporter and presenter, as well as a commentator.

As an all-rounder, I was much in demand. In autumn 1990, for the France-New Zealand Test matches in Nantes and Paris, I joined the HTV Wales commentary team – Bob Simmons, resident summariser Gerald Davies and producer John Roberts – as presenter-reporter. Unfortunately my luggage didn't make the same flight. The trip to Paris was even worse. An accident on the M4 meant we missed our scheduled Friday afternoon flight, while fog at Heathrow delayed our take-off next morning. I had to write the script for the opening links in the back of the taxi on a frantic dash from Charles de Gaulle airport and when I did get to deliver them pitch-side at the Parc des Princes I fell victim to the Chainsaw Theorem. This, as any television reporter will know, is a law of mathematical probability that states that no matter how secluded the spot, no matter how tranquil the setting, the moment you choose to deliver a piece to camera is almost certainly the moment when an invisible and totally unexpected chainsaw will roar into life. Only this time it was a brass band, belting out French marching tunes as soon as I opened my mouth and showing absolutely no sign of letting up till well after our satellite link was due to expire.

A trip to Romania to watch the French again was a golden opportunity for ITV to see how I shaped up as a commentator, it gave them a chance to assess Gareth Chilcott as a pundit and it gave their newly appointed rugby editor John D Taylor a chance to meet some of the key figures in European rugby. One of these was John Reason, the legendary rugby correspondent first of the *Daily Telegraph* and then the *Sunday Telegraph*. I knew John of old – he'd interviewed me many times in my playing days and we'd travelled to several matches together. I was therefore quite prepared for the usual exotic cocktail of rugby sagacity, self-aggrandisement and vitriol that enlivened every conversation with the great man. John D Taylor and Gareth were not. Both were accordingly a little bit upset when 'Treason', after offering a masterful analysis of the French team's strengths and weaknesses and discoursing expansively on his favourite subjects – how he devised the format for the Hong Kong Sevens, practically invented the World Cup and was largely instrumental in ending the miners' strike – moved on to a less than friendly dismissal of ITV's forthcoming rugby coverage.

According to John, ITV were barking mad to even think of using former players as commentators, wanted their heads read if they felt that prop forwards could make good summarisers and had missed a huge trick in not employing a decent journalist to oversee their output. In just a few minutes, in what was a quite brilliant piece of oratory, John Reason had managed to insult the three people he was sitting with, who also happened to be the only other English speakers at the post-match banquet. While Coochie, with some difficulty, managed to restrain himself from punching Reason on the nose, John D Taylor spluttered out a defence of his own journalistic credentials and then demanded to know what made the pressman believe that he, alone of all the other highly respected rugby writers, had the right credentials to edit ITV'S World Cup coverage. 'Quite simple,' he drawled. 'When it comes to rugby, I'm the only shark in the pool!'

ITV sent another of their head honchos with me to New Zealand in August 1991. Phil King was a football man, with an unfathomable fondness for Derby County, but he was to be the network's senior rugby producer for the next five years. Apart from supervising our coverage of the Bledisloe Cup match against Australia, his mission was to extend the hand of friendship to the TVNZ and ABC television executives who would be using ITV facilities at the World Cup in a couple of months' time, and to produce a network-commissioned feature with opera singer Dame Kiri te Kanawa, who was going to record ITV's incredibly powerful theme tune, 'World in Union'. Everything went really well, except the rugby.

If it beggared belief that, on a perfect playing surface on a bright autumnal day, two attack-orientated sides boasting the likes of Tim Horan, Jason Little and David Campese (Australia), John Kirwan, Michael Jones and John Timu (New Zealand) should fail to score a single try between them, it bankrupted comprehension that the two best goal-kickers in world rugby, Michael Lynagh and Grant Fox, should between them miss nearly a dozen penalty kicks in a desultory 6-3 win for the All Blacks. And if that wasn't surreal enough, Mikhail Gorbachev, leader of the second most powerful nation on earth, was overthrown in a political coup while we were away and had got his job back without a drop of blood being spilled by the time we got home. You just couldn't make it up.

Nor could ITV graft rugby experience onto camera operators, sound technicians, videotape editors, vision mixers and all the other technicians who had developed their expertise in football. The ITV crew assembling at Teddington in the autumn of 1991 wasn't just encountering a whole new ball game, it was experiencing a seismic culture shift. The skill-sets required to follow the two sports were similar yet wildly different. Where one required a close-up to explain the action, the other demanded a long shot. Where the golden rule in one was to follow the ball, in the other it was to linger a little longer on the kicker. A slow-motion in one sport would replay all the pertinent action if the tape was spun back ten seconds. In the other it might require half a minute. The key figures in one sport could be found in a different place in the other, and they would be doing different things. The rhythm of the two sports was completely different.

It was just as well then that ITV not only stepped up to the plate in the 1991 Rugby World Cup but also helped to rewrite the rules of how the sport was broadcast and how it was portrayed. Determined to get the technical side right, they employed more match cameras than the BBC had done and, in a move that appeared fly in the face of broadcasting convention, placed one of them on the far side of the pitch to provide a reverse angle. More subtly, they used many more close-ups than the BBC had done, and many more slow-motion replays. The reasoning was simple. They wanted to use the increasingly sophisticated technology at their disposal to highlight the physical, often brutal, nature of the sport. They set out to emphasise the big hits in the tackle, the collisions in the set scrum and the athleticism in the line-out. They were keen to depict rugby players as rough, tough and powerful, as well as agile, athletic and courageous. They weren't afraid to dwell on the physical attributes of the players, they made no attempts to play down the ferocity of their approach and they weren't at all surprised when the surveys showed that television viewers were lapping it up and that the number of female rugby fans had increased exponentially. If the BBC had represented the broadsheets in their rather studious, clubby approach to the sport, ITV were unashamedly tabloid. Whereas rugby players had, by and large, been shadowy figures, hidden behind a cloak of anonymity and carefully guarded privacy, they were now, if ITV got their way, to be superstars. ITV wanted to tell the stories behind the World Cup, to show the players not just as extremely skilful athletes but also as real people. They wanted to show how the players trained and what they did in their spare time. They wanted to show what made the players tick and what made them laugh.

This emphasis on personalities was revolutionary at the time and demanded unprecedented behind-the-scenes access. Although the players were still amateurs and therefore entirely within their rights to demand to go about their preparations in privacy, they were much more alert to the spin-off benefits from a heightened media profile than the administrators, and a number of the major teams readily agreed to camera crews being 'embedded' with them. The only, very muted, protest came surprisingly enough from New Zealand. Although the World Champions were far more accustomed to the celebrity treatment than their European counterparts, they took some convincing that Alison Holloway, the ITV reporter assigned to them, was actually a bona fide journalist with an impressive track record, and not the 'honey trap' of their paranoid imaginings. All the other teams happily accepted the presence of an ITV crew at their hotels and willingly contributed to the 'bulletins from the camp' which were used to illustrate the almost-nightly magazine programmes that the network put on to augment their match-day coverage.

The only sticking-point came on the very last day of the tournament, when

Dudley Wood, the Chief Executive but going under the title of Secretary of the RFU, suddenly baulked at the idea of a cameraman inside Twickenham's sacred changing rooms. No matter that Ian O'Donohue had been attached to the England team since the tournament got underway, and no matter that in six weeks he had never abused his position and filmed anything that might cause offence to anyone in the RFU hierarchy, no matter that the players liked him, trusted him and wanted him to be with them for the whole day of their World Cup final against Australia. The RFU, despite a desperate appeal from ITV Head of Sport Bob Burrows, wanted to exclude him from the dressing room. He went anyway. The England baggage man loaned him a tracksuit to wear and a kitbag to conceal his camera, while the England players formed a muscular guard of honour round him as they left the bus and marched into the stadium. The security man on the door may have looked askance at a tall, skinny forty-something with thinning ginger hair and a shambling gait but can only have assumed that Ian was a new physio brought in specially for the occasion. Ian filmed merrily away before the game, though, as he wasn't supposed to be there, he couldn't send any tapes out to the broadcast truck. After it, he captured some extraordinarily moving pictures from the losing dressing room. Dudley Wood, it appeared, forgot his objections to the presence of the cameraman, especially, apparently, when the edited sequence for the highlights programme showed him hobnobbing with Prime Minister John Major!

England's run to the final – after losing their opening match to New Zealand, Will Carling's men had to do it the hard way by winning a quarter-final in France and a semi-final in Scotland – was undoubtedly good for ITV – viewing figures on several occasions peaking above ten million – while ITV's coverage was undoubtedly good for England. Jim Rosenthal's reporting and Ian O'Donohue's camerawork chimed perfectly with the celebrity cult that was just beginning to take root in Britain. And the players were not just winners on the field – they went into the tournament, don't forget, on the back of a Five Nations Grand Slam – they were natural and hugely engaging personalities whose individual characteristics were tailor-made for ITV'S broad-brush, tabloid approach. While Carling was the stereotype of a dashing captain and Guscott was the pin-up glamour boy, aggressive little hooker Moore was the 'pit-bull' and gangling line-out expert Wade Dooley was 'the Blackpool Tower', while outside-half Rob Andrew was 'Mr Reliable' and big-tackling back-rower Mick Skinner was 'Mick the Munch'. And so on. At the start of the tournament rugby was by and large back-page and broadsheet news. By the end of the tournament it seemed highly appropriate that the *Sun* should carry a front-page photo of Will Carling draped in the cross of St George.

And ITV's determination to promote personalities extended to the 'talent'. Rugby had a reputation for tall tales, good humour, ready banter and larger-than-life characters but, beyond the after-dinner circuit and *The Art of Coarse Rugby*-

style books, lacked much of a stage. ITV's 1991 World Cup coverage changed all that. With a commitment to hundreds of hours of programming to fulfil, the network set out to populate their programmes not just with rugby worthies, but with rugby 'characters' as well. Almost by definition, however, none of their experts would have had much experience of working on television and there was no telling which of them would struggle and which would flourish under the spotlight. Rather than back the wrong horse, therefore, ITV opted to back all of them. At least a dozen summarisers were hired for the pool matches with, in a move that wouldn't have sat too well with Bill McLaren, two of them allocated to each commentator, while at least the same number would appear as studio guests at the ground or in the highlights programme. And, just to keep everyone on their toes, the ITV bosses stressed that the list of experts would be culled at the knockout stages, with the implication that only the best would be kept on. Which was the equivalent of dangling a red rag in front of some very competitive bulls. As the tournament progressed, it became clear that the ITV decision makers were going to be swayed less by rugby reputations and more by rugby banter. For instance, based purely on their performances in front of the camera, Gareth Chilcott was deemed more of a success than Fran Cotton, Steve Smith was preferred to Clive Woodward, and former international referee Clive Norling was kept on in place of Gerald Davies. If there had been any doubt before, it became glaringly obvious that entertainment value was paramount when a camera crew was taken to Twickenham to film Gordon Brown performing a Morris dance and Clive Norling was asked to provide a disco version of the referee's signals.

Despite their rumbustiousness and their lack of television experience, not one of the summarisers was remotely bad value for ITV and every single one of them was good value for morale both in the studio and on the road. For those of us on commentary duty, it was like being on tour, without having to do the training, or risk injury by taking to the field. The schedule was punishing – I commentated on six pool matches inside nine days, involving two trips to France, two matches at Twickenham and one each at Murrayfield and Lansdowne Road – but the downtime was a delight. It was a privilege not just to chew the fat with some of rugby's most engaging characters, but also to work alongside them in the commentary box and, just occasionally, share some memorable journeys.

To ITV's hyper-efficient transport manager Pauline Hamilton, dawn was a time of day when traffic would be minimal and flights cheap, which would leave plenty of room for error in the form of inclement weather, delayed flights and missed connections. To us it was for sleeping, especially after the late nights of socialising that inevitably followed evening kick-offs.

A 6 a.m. flight out of Toulouse after the France v Canada game in Agen was always going to be a tester, especially as L'Hotel Portakabin – our name for the soulless, no-expense-considered, kit-form box that I and the two summarisers, one of whom was future director of rugby at Wasps, Gloucester and the USA,

Nigel Melville, had been checked into – was a long taxi ride from Toulouse airport. It became even more of a problem when we discovered that while Monsieur le patron, a lumpy, grumpy fifty-something, had begrudgingly set his own alarm clock to make sure we settled our bills, he'd quite forgotten to book the taxi we'd requested. Agen's cabbies were where they should be at 4 o'clock in the morning – in bed – and none responded to le patron's increasingly desperate dialling. With a massive shrug, and with what seemed more of a threat than a courtesy, he volunteered to drive us to the airport himself. The fact that he was still dressed in his pyjamas, slippers and dressing gown was of no concern. Pausing only to change his slippers for some black leather lace-ups, and apply a lighter to his first Gauloise of the day, he loaded us into his beaten-up Peugeot and hurtled in the direction of Toulouse airport. We caught the flight with minutes to spare.

Though we had been told that we were playing for our places in the commentary box for the knockout stages and though both Bob Simmons and I knew that there wasn't the slightest chance of being preferred to John Taylor for the final, we both fed off the competitive zeal of the summarisers and the increasingly confident performances of the match-day production teams, very few of whom had been anywhere near a rugby match before the tournament started. By its end, no one would have known. And I like to think that, just as the match-day directors, cameramen, sound engineers and videotape operators upped their game, so did I. Most of the pool matches I commentated on were one-sided affairs – convincing wins for France over Canada and Romania, for England over Italy and the United States and fifty-pointers for Scotland and Ireland over Zimbabwe – but I was getting the names right, coping well with the concept of two summarisers and, where appropriate, letting the pictures tell the story. I felt I was at the top of my game and was delighted to be told that as well as being trusted with the second semi-final, I was to stay with the ITV team for the final – as emergency back-up in the event of anything disastrous happening to John Taylor.

First, though, was the Murrayfield quarter-final between Scotland and Western Samoa, whose pool defeat of Wales had been the shock of the tournament. Fortunately for Scotland there was no repeat performance – the home side running out comfortable winners 28-6 – and while they could prepare for a home semi-final against the Auld Enemy, I was able to concentrate on the first ever meeting on neutral soil of equally inimical opponents from the southern hemisphere, Australia and New Zealand.

New Zealand were the holders and short-odds favourites to retain the title but they were nobody's favourite team. They may have been clinical and efficient all tournament, but they'd also been sullen and suspicious. By contrast, the Wallabies had been open and engaging and, even though they had dumped Ireland out of the tournament, were firm favourites with the Lansdowne Road crowd. They also had David Campese. The arch-showman was the undoubted star of the tournament. He'd already scored five tries, two of them in the pool match against Wales and another two in the quarter-final against Ireland. He was on fire.

Two sublime pieces of Campo magic did for the All Blacks. With just seven minutes on the board he bamboozled the entire New Zealand defence to score in the left-hand corner. The match was less than half an hour old when he appeared on the right and delivered a sublimely audacious over the shoulder reverse pass for Tim Horan to score. Aussie fans were jubilant, and so was I. I felt I had nailed the commentary on those key moments – just as well, given that the tries have been replayed at least ten times a tournament in subsequent World Cups – and that I had done myself justice not just on the biggest occasion of my broadcasting career but in the tournament as a whole. ITV still wanted me to do various voice-overs for inserts into the build-up and review programmes for the final, and I did go through the motions of preparing for a late call-up to the commentary box, but to all other intents and purposes I was free to sit back and enjoy the last few days of an absolutely exhilarating adventure.

Off the field, motormouth Campese stoked the fires with personal digs at Will Carling and carefully chosen insults about England's boring and safety-first style of play. On it, England appeared to have taken 'old rent-a-quote's' comments to heart, playing up with an uncharacteristic abandon that, even thirty years on, the players are at a loss to explain. Ask lock-turned *Sunday Telegraph* columnist Paul Ackford or hooker-turned BBC pundit Brian Moore to justify such a fundamental change of approach, and they shake their heads and mutter darkly about backs. Ask Rob Andrew, fly-half-turned Director of Elite Rugby in England, and he'll talk passionately about playing what's in front of you and deny vehemently any suggestion that England were suckered. Ask David Campese and he'll chortle.

England's defeat was the only thing that could possibly take the edge off what was, in purely broadcasting terms, an outstanding success for ITV. The 15 individual regional companies had sent their very best operators up to the London Weekend headquarters at Teddington and seen them combine in exhilarating and undreamt-of harmony. Director John Watts and his team had set new standards in match-day coverage, while the behind-the-scenes reporting from the various camps and the pairing of veteran presenter Frank Bough with a bunch of effervescent, extrovert and highly entertaining rugby characters had received rapturous acclaim. Rugby World Cup 1991 had been an unprecedented success for the IRB and the RFU, who both made mouth-watering profits. It had been an outstanding triumph for Australia and ITV, both of whose reputations were considerably enhanced. It had been a watershed in the development of rugby union and of my career, both of which were about to take off. And, waiting in the wings, was South Africa...

CHAPTER TWENTY-EIGHT

BOKS AND LIONS (1992–93)

'*Uit die blou van onse hemel, uit die diepte van ons see,*'
It was the moment all South African rugby fans had been waiting for. I was a neutral observer but the hairs on the back of my neck were rigid.
'*Oor ons ewige gebergtes waar die kranse antwoord gee.*'
It was August 1992. After eight years in the rugby wilderness the Springboks were playing New Zealand in an officially recognised Test match.
'*Deur ons ver-verlate vlaktes met die kreun van ossewa.*'
Standing tall, chests puffed out, eyes shining, they belted out their battle cry into the Johannesburg sky.
'*Ruis die stem van ons geliefde, van ons land Suid-Afrika.*'

But hang on a minute; it was the wrong song. Or rather a song that the ruling ANC government had asked supporters not to sing. 'Die Stem', they reckoned, was associated with the old apartheid South Africa. Nelson Mandela had been released and a new constitution was being drafted. The country's first truly democratic, multiracial elections would be held in 1994 and the ANC had high hopes that the change in mood among the white ruling class would be reflected by the supporters of a sport that had come to be identified with the Afrikaner and white supremacy.

But the call for Springbok supporters to put away their old flags and refrain from singing their old songs went unheard. South African rugby fans, at the best of times neither malleable nor meek, had no time for anyone else's sensibilities. Test matches, especially against their fiercest rivals New Zealand, demanded they wore the green and gold, demanded they had their *braais* and their beer before the game, demanded they snacked on their biltong during it and demanded that they waved their flags and sung 'Die Stem'. That was what Springbok supporters had always done.

The world's rugby media, including ITV who were to broadcast the match live, had descended on South Africa for this historic match and the following week's Cape Town encounter with Australia. The result, a narrow 27-24 victory for the All Blacks, was completely overshadowed by the 'Die Stem' controversy and the next few days were filled with frantic speculation about the ANC's response. For several days, there was some doubt as to whether the fixture with Australia would go ahead. Not for the last time, the ANC showed remarkable tolerance, and South Africa's rugby rehabilitation could continue.

Truth be told, the International Rugby Board was desperate to welcome South Africa back into the fold. In fact, so keen were they to gain access to the bewitching numbers boasted by the Republic, from players to stadiums to sponsors, that, not long after the Boks had lost 26-3 to the Wallabies in Cape Town, the IRB invited South Africa to host the 1995 World Cup.

In so doing, they made the advent of professionalism even more inevitable. It was an open secret that during their years of sporting isolation, the South African rugby authorities had used money to attract touring teams and so make their time in the wilderness more bearable. Even the arch-conservative RFU could sense the way the wind was blowing and from 1992 suggested that contrary to previous interpretations, rugby players, while still not being paid for playing, could now be financially rewarded for 'rugby-related' activities.

This opened up a potential goldmine for the likes of the telegenic Jerry Guscott. Before long he was in huge demand as a male model and was desperately trying to get the best possible return from this brave new world. He was as intrigued as I was to find out what he would really be worth now the market had been opened up. 'Hundreds of thousands of pounds' was the guesstimate from London-based lawyer Mel Stern whom I had interviewed for HTV in his role as Paul Gascoigne's agent. The Spurs and England footballer was reckoned to be the most marketable player in football at the time and it was a fascinating exercise exploring Jerry's earning power with his agent. Apparently one of the key things to establish was, no oxymoron intended, Jerry's 'intellectual property rights'!

Jerry was a shoo-in for the 1993 Lions. And I got the gig as well, the last-ever Lions of the amateur era, and the only one ever covered by ITV. It may have been less than twenty years ago but few of the New Zealand provincial grounds had floodlights and no consideration at all was given to the evening kick-offs that might possibly engage a northern hemisphere audience. Possibly for this reason, the BBC showed little interest in televising the tour while ITV – already in possession of the broadcasting rights for the next two World Cups – seized the opportunity to develop their rugby presence. Reasoning quite astutely that early morning audiences for midweek matches would be minuscule, they decided that only the three Test matches would be broadcast live while the other ten games would be presented as edited highlights packages, decorated with player profiles from the camp and travelogue-style features from different parts of New Zealand.

That's where I came in. My job was to provide a piece to camera from each of the towns the Lions stopped at and voice-over a piece of film which dwelt lovingly on its tourist attractions, as well as all the usual match-related interviews and previews. On match days, I would record an introduction from the venue itself and provide pre- and post-match interviews. All of these, together with tapes of the match itself, would be sent to TV Centre in Wellington where editors specially flown in by ITV would cut everything to the right length for broadcast.

The rest of us took to the road, travelling most of the length and a little bit of the breadth of the Land of the Long White Cloud by minivan, and if there's a better way of learning about a country and its people, I have yet to find it. I was absolutely enthralled by New Zealand.

In North Island's Whangarei, the venue for the Lions' first match, I was invited, along with Eddie Butler, to take part in a rugby ritual that has no northern hemisphere equivalent. 'A Noggin and a Natter' were the words used to describe what amounted to a cross between a quiz, a social get-together and an after-dinner speech without the dinner. After plying Eddie and me with weak beer, wilted salad and stale sandwiches, the locals invited us first of all to take part in a fiendishly difficult rugby quiz (we both, I remember, felt badly exposed by our lack of familiarity with All Black and Lions touring parties of the 1950s and 1960s), then tell a few rugby stories of our own, before taking part in an open-ended chat about rugby that lasted well past midnight.

At Dunedin I was handed a hospital pass by ITV commentator John Taylor. 'Would that be the former England full-back and Gloucestershire cricketer, Alastair Hignell?' said the voice on the end of the phone. I should have realised that he'd never heard of me until John, in his desperation to get out of a speaking engagement the night before the Otago match, had volunteered me as a replacement.

'We'd really be honoured if you could speak at our annual Otago sports dinner on Friday night' the smooth talking continued. 'Nothing fancy, just a simple black-tie do with a chamber orchestra and about 350 guests, including the Governor General of New Zealand.'

I tried several variations of the 'love to, but don't know whether we'll get to Dunedin in time/whether the producer needs me for a pre-match briefing/how can I get from my hotel to the function?' excuses, reasoning that at least one of them might drop the subtle hint that attending the dinner was not very high on my list of priorities, while delivering a speech to the great and the good of the South Island was even lower. But New Zealanders don't do subtle, and this one, with a little help from a Welshman, had every angle covered.

'John Taylor's told me that you'll be in Dunedin in plenty of time, that you're not required at the producer's briefing, and I know that your hotel is just round the corner. And, just to reassure you, I can promise we'll make it worth your while.' The prospect of reward still didn't make it a great way of spending a Friday night.

Cornered as I was, I produced what I thought was the clinching argument. 'And anyway, we're travelling light round New Zealand, and I haven't brought my dinner suit with me.'

'Don't worry, we've arranged for the dress hire shop just round the corner from your hotel to stay open late on Friday, and collect the suit on Saturday,' closed the last avenue of escape.

And the dinner was every bit as grand, and formal, as I'd dreaded. There were umpteen courses, a toastmaster, plenty of tiaras and the only guests below fifty were those receiving awards. Not that, from my place among the top-table stuffed shirts, I got much time to talk to any of them. Still, when my turn came, I told a few stories, made a few jokes, and received a standing ovation. And a woolly jumper. Made from pure New Zealand wool, heavily patterned in a style that could charitably be called retro, and in the wrong size. My 'while' was obviously worth less than I'd thought.

It was freezing cold in Hamilton as we checked into a motel that was theoretically closed for winter refurbishment but whose owner couldn't resist the chance to make a bit of extra money from some gullible poms. That he hadn't told his workforce, who had an alarming habit of barging into a room to attend to a call of nature whether or not there was anyone in it, was mildly disconcerting. That he had disconnected the heating was more so. We spent two nights with the cookers in our 'suites' turned up full.

In Auckland, for the final week of the tour, the sun finally shone and we got to play golf, sail in the harbour and extend a bit of hospitality to the Lions players who had assisted at our outside broadcasts. Stuart Barnes had been injured at just the wrong moment before the first Test and his chance of wresting the No. 10 jersey away from Rob Andrew had evaporated. As he was not needed on the bench we had gladly brought him on board as a studio expert. It was clear even then that a career in the media would be his for the taking. In order to show our appreciation for his efforts, ITV offered to take him, and the other summarisers, out for dinner on the night before the deciding third Test. Impressed by his Oxford University pedigree, his growing reputation as a bon viveur and his own claim to be a connoisseur of fine wines, we even let Stuart choose the restaurant. 'The best Vietnamese restaurant in Auckland' was Stuart's proud claim for his choice. The only Vietnamese restaurant in Auckland might have been a better description, or the only restaurant in a crowded city centre on a Friday night before a Test match against the Lions to be completely empty. The rule of thumb that insists that deserted restaurants mean poor food was waived in the face of Stuart's confidence – and reasserted halfway through the first course of what I can safely say, after more than two decades of life on the rugby circuit, is the worst restaurant meal I have ever tasted. Stuart continues to roam the world on the behalf of his Sky and *Sunday Times* employers. I can only hope that his ability to judge a restaurant has improved, and that his colleagues retain the right of veto.

Stuart had started all three of the Saturday matches before the first Test and had been injured in the unluckiest of circumstances, coming on as a replacement for Rob Andrew against Southland and getting his head split open by a stray boot belonging to teammate Robert Jones. The only match the Lions had lost up to that point had been to a brilliant Otago side in Dunedin. In winning five of their first six matches, they'd crushed Canterbury in a midweek fixture at Lancaster Park and had fought back with real character to beat the Maori in Wellington. In the first Test they had conceded a soft early try to Frank Bunce but were leading as the match went into injury time – only for Australian referee Sandy McNeill to award a hotly-disputed penalty against Lions No. 8 Dean Richards, and Grant Fox to land a nerveless penalty. The Lions had gained their revenge with a scintillating second Test win in Wellington only to be taken to the cleaners in the third and deciding Test in Auckland the following week. The midweek side had begun well, but faded badly. If the win over Canterbury was the high point, defeat by Hawkes Bay in Napier was demoralising and a 38-10 thrashing by Waikato in Hamilton was downright embarrassing.

If the events of the last week suggested that the players just wanted to get home, the same was true for the ITV team covering the tour. The last of the old-fashioned tours had demanded a change of venue every three or four days, and countless criss-crossing of the country. The tour had started and ended in Auckland and we'd returned to it twice in between. We'd also had two separate visits to Christchurch, and two to Wellington, as well as single stops in six other towns. It had been exhausting, exhilarating and fun. I had enjoyed the pieces to camera ('This is One Tree Hill, so called because... ') and the live studio work before the Test matches (where the most memorable quote was Tony Underwood's description of his brother Rory skinning John Kirwan to score the Lions first try, 'like a Porsche going past a Lada'). I'd even enjoyed the voice-overs, especially the one to describe a Scotland win in Samoa when I had to describe the edit with no notes to guide me, squatting on the floor of a motel room with all the cushions we could find stacked up to form some kind of soundproofing.

And I'd obviously acquitted myself well enough for the ITV head honchos to pencil me in as anchorman for the next World Cup. Their hand may have been forced by a Sunday tabloid exposure of Frank Bough in 1992, and they may not exactly have been spoilt for choice, but, in what I interpreted as a sign of confidence in me, they put me on a retainer (a relatively modest topping-up of my HTV salary) and they sent me round the world as part of their campaign to break the monopoly of the BBC.

It had already started by picking off the rights to any international rugby not already nailed down by the corporation. The 1993 World Sevens tournament at Murrayfield should have been a natural fit for the BBC but it was the IRB who owned the rights and not the Home Unions. The fact that England won – with a boyish Lawrence Dallaglio and an almost child-like Matt Dawson giving a glimpse of the prodigious rugby ability that, ten years later, was to take them to the biggest prize of all – was yet another feather in ITV's cap, while the tournament itself produced one of my most memorable pieces of commentating.

With 20 teams in the finals, each with ten-man squads, there were a lot of names to learn. With teams from Japan, Hong Kong and Taiwan as well as the usual suspects from Tonga, Samoa and Fiji, there were a lot more tongue-twisters than usual. During 'homework' that was more intense than normal I couldn't help noticing that the names of most of the Taiwanese began with the same two letters. There was a Choi, a Cha and a Chen in their starting line-up, as well as a Cheung and a Chan. The following afternoon one of them kicked ahead and my commentary, which provoked hysterical laughter at the time and brings a smile to my face even now, went ... 'Choi... to Cha... the loop around from Chen, then Cheung... the chip and chase...!'

ITV may have been able to boast big audiences whenever it showed rugby, it may have gained friends and allies on the IRB and it may have convinced regional television companies – even those without a significant rugby following in their area – of the commercial viability of its coverage, but it was still making no headway against the game's entrenched old guard. In the early 1990s, the network launched an all-out assault in an attempt to win the broadcast rights not just to the Five Nations but to all domestic rugby as well, and they asked me to present their case to the Home Unions' broadcast committee. ITV, I was proud to point out, promised in-depth coverage of overseas tours, and had demonstrated, in their revolutionary approach to the recently completed tour of New Zealand, just what could be achieved. I pointed out some impressive audience figures; apparently more people had got up in the middle of the night in Britain to watch the Test matches on ITV than had watched them live on a mid-afternoon in New Zealand. ITV, so I argued, had shown its commitment to the international game by offering to broadcast not just the World Sevens, and the whole of the qualifying tournament, but England's 1994 tour to South Africa as well. It would show its commitment to the domestic game by getting all 15 regional companies to sign up for a weekly rugby highlights programme at which they were prepared to throw both money and resources as long as they gained the rights to the Five Nations. I presented a pilot programme which ITV had filmed especially to show the Home Unions committee, and introduced a galaxy of rugby greats who were prepared to add their expertise to a show which would make the BBC's *Rugby Special* appear not just cheap and nasty, but outdated, unimaginative and dull. But the Home Unions would not be swayed either by money – it was an open secret that ITV had bid considerably more than the BBC – or by the prospect of a revolutionary approach to the coverage of the sport. They were inclined to stay loyal to the BBC. ITV, congenitally incapable of understanding such wilful obstinacy, were inclined to wash their hands of the sport.

At least they still had the World Cup and, thanks to the cunning of their original negotiators, they had it for the next two tournaments, in South Africa and Wales. Both of these would be played in prime advertising time as far as the major European markets were concerned and ITV executives were already licking their lips in anticipation of some more big pay days. And in order to whet the viewers' appetite as well, they commissioned a documentary series called *Rugby Warriors* from HTV.

CHAPTER TWENTY-NINE

WARRIORS (1994–95)

In terms of creativity, *Rugby Warriors* represented the finest hour of my broadcasting career. Or two hours, to be precise because, by the time all the horse-trading was done, the series had been whittled down to four programmes of half an hour each. The first was to focus on the Five Nations, participants in the oldest international competition in the game, while the second would spotlight New Zealand and Australia, the two winners to date of rugby's newest trophy, the World Cup. The third would be devoted to the outsiders, nations like Italy, Samoa and the Ivory Coast, for whom reaching the World Cup finals was the overriding goal, while the final programme would showcase 1995 hosts – and competition newcomers – South Africa.

Time was tight. By the time ITV gave us the green light for the series it was late autumn 1994. The World Cup was due to kick-off in Cape Town the following May. *Rugby Warriors* was scheduled for a Wednesday night showing in the four weeks leading up to the tournament. We had a month to organise a filming schedule, three months to film in 12 different countries, and less than a month to put the programmes together. We would have our work cut out, especially after HTV entered into a deal with an independent production company who were looking to signpost the beginning of RWC 95 by making and marketing a series of profiles on the world's greatest players. Why not, they argued, knock off an in-depth interview with some of the game's superstars, especially when you'll be in their part of the world anyway and what they have to say may well be useful for your series?

It seemed like a good idea at the time. What we'd lose in terms of time by having to add extra filming to our schedule we'd more than make up in content. There's not a rugby player alive who, though he might find himself too busy to contribute to a wide-ranging documentary series, won't clear his diary to feature in a series entitled *The World's Greatest Rugby Players*! Once they agreed to that they could hardly refuse to answer questions more relevant to the requirements of *Rugby Warriors*.

For the series opener – about the Five Nations – we decided to focus on history, tradition and ritual. In England we poked around Rugby School to evoke both the origins of the game and the up-to-date public school version of it, before heading off to Twickenham and the Varsity Match and bringing the whole thing up to date with a sell-out local derby and a tour of the battle-lines between amateurism and professionalism. In Scotland we looked at an alternative claim to the invention of rugby, the birth of Sevens and the extraordinary concentration of rugby clubs among the farming communities of the Borders. In Wales we focused on Pontypridd, the links between rugby and mining, the Grogg shop with its ugly pottery caricatures of rugby heroes, and the extraordinary working-class passion for the game. We followed a bus-load of Wales supporters all the way to Paris for the international against France, accompanied the staff of France's weekly rugby newspaper *Midi Olympique* back to the game's heartland in the south-west and took in a third division club game near Agen in the company of the legendary – and charming – multi-capped French centre Philippe Sella. The game stopped as Sella took his seat in the stands, stopped again when an almighty punch-up between both sets of forwards ended with a player from each side being sent off, and stopped for a third time as they continued trading punches on the touchline. In the end, play could only continue after the referee – in a creative interpretation of IRB regulations – ruled that for the remainder of the match the culprits should stand next to the corner-flags at opposite ends of the pitch.

If our snapshot of the French game conformed to stereotype, so did our first glimpse of the game in Ireland. In our attempt to define the 'craic' which is so much a part and parcel of the game in Ireland we had made a conscious decision to avoid the obvious clichés of Dublin and Guinness – but as we ended up instead at the Murphy's brewery in Cork it didn't make much difference. Wherever you go in Ireland, it seems, rugby folk don't need much of an excuse to party.

Our schedule demanded that we arrive at the brewery late on a Thursday afternoon to get some shots of stout production before making tracks to a local pub to film some Irish music and hopefully a little bit of impromptu dancing. But the plane from Bristol was delayed and by the time we got to the brewery, production had closed down for the day, the workforce had gone home and there was just a single security light to illuminate the complex. An icy rain lashed down onto the windscreen of the van we'd hired and there didn't seem much else to do but head for our hotel. 'Come along anyway,' said our contact, whose day job was PR manager for Murphy's, 'I'll get some lights on and open up the tasting-room. At least you can film the stuff being poured.' By the time we'd found the entrance and unloaded the camera, our host had found not only the light-switch but half a dozen colleagues anxious to demonstrate the delights of Irish stout to their English guests, as well as a table full of food, and one of the best Irish folk-bands in the area (or did he say world?) which was going to play that very night at a nearby pub which (did he happen to mention?) was also owned by Murphy's!

On the same long weekend in Ireland we also filmed a segment on road bowling – a sport which sees contestants hurling cannon-ball sized stones down winding country lanes – took in an All-Ireland league match at Cork Constitution, kissed the Blarney stone, picked up 'colour' shots at Kinsale, interviewed Irish rugby legends Tom Kiernan, Noel Murphy and the current Ireland captain Michael Bradley, and chatted to a Catholic bishop who was also an ardent rugby fan. Oh, and on our way to the airport on the Monday morning we picked up the brewery production line shots we'd missed. Given that the segment on Ireland was only going to take up one fifth of a half-hour programme, it was quite clear that *Rugby Warriors* would never be short of things to film. It was also hugely reassuring; our filming schedule had little room for error and, although we could conceivably have nipped back to Ireland – or to any of the Five Nations – in search of the 'must-have' shot, that wouldn't be an option on the next trip we had planned. We were going to film the bulk of the series in one hit, over a three-week period. Our next expedition was going to take in New Zealand, Samoa, Australia and South Africa.

The southern hemisphere was to provide all of the material for part two of *Rugby Warriors* (on winners New Zealand and Australia), all of the material for part four (on hosts South Africa) and a third of the material for part three (on one of the outsiders – Samoa). In Australia we wanted to show just what was meant by a sporting culture. The country enjoyed huge natural advantages – a climate that encouraged a healthy outdoor lifestyle, space that allowed the creation and maintenance of huge numbers of sports facilities – as well as some entirely man-made ones – a press that lionised winners, a government that recognised the political value of sporting success and a trail-blazing Institute of Sport that was specifically designed to maximise the country's sporting potential. We interviewed the Prime Minister, Bob Hawke, visited the New South Wales Rugby Academy – and spent time with the most charismatic player in the game, David Campese. We also interviewed George Gregan, a young man at the start of his career who, a decade or so later, was to become the most capped rugby international in history. George had a very part-time job with national airline Qantas but spent several hours a week working on both the technical and mental sides of his game at the Institute of Sport. We filmed him getting in and out of a floatation tank where he would watch repeated showings of the greatest moment of his rugby career so far – a match-saving tackle on All Black winger Jeff Wilson that secured the Bledisloe Cup for Australia. Nowadays each international team has both a technological department and the technology to create any number of motivational, affirmational, instructional and highly personalised videos almost at the drop of a hat. Back in early spring 1995 George

Gregan and Australia were at the cutting-edge of the new technology and the rest of the world was miles behind.

In trying to show the role played in Australian life by sport in general and rugby in particular, we decided to focus on a town called Gunnedah in up-country New South Wales. Our eagle-eyed researcher had spotted a story on the Internet which described how, because of the drought, kangaroos had come in from the bush in search of food and had been spotted chomping away at the grass of one of Gunnedah's rugby pitches. The temptation to get rugby and kangaroos into the same story was too great. The drought – and the rugby season for that matter – may have been officially over and the kangaroos long returned to the bush but nobody in Gunnedah was going to let a little detail get in the way of an appearance on British television. 'There will be kangaroos,' promised the rugby club, 'even if we have to truck them in from the local animal sanctuary for sick animals. We will organise a rugby training session that the 'roos can interrupt, even if we've got to mark out the lines and put the posts back up. The town mayor's going to fly back from his holiday in Fiji, we've fixed up a visit to a local sheep-station, organised a sports festival to make sure all our best young athletes are available to talk to you, and we're having a barbie at the rugby club. Apart from that, is there anything you'd like us to do?'

We had the same sort of welcome in King Country in New Zealand – the self-styled sheep-shearing capital of the world. We wanted to show that even though New Zealand had a tiny population – less than four million at the time – rugby had acquired a status, importance and identity within society that was unmatched by a single sport in any other nation in the world. We filmed four-year-olds playing barefoot at primary school and talked to some of the game's grizzled elder statesmen like Colin Meads. Jeff Wilson, a first-class cricketer as well as an All Black rugby player, talked of the rugged competitiveness that underpins the New Zealand approach to sport, while the boys at the Bombay boarding school just south of Auckland emphasised just what rugby meant to the average Maori.

We had arrived at the school to a *powhiri*, a ritual greeting ceremony involving an incredibly passionate, powerful – and complicated – haka performed in perfect rhythm by some 250 boys, and after filming part of a history lesson I asked some of the teenagers about what it meant to be a Maori and a New Zealander. All of them seemed much more patriotic than their counterparts in Britain. All of them were concerned about New Zealand's standing in the world, and knew exactly what it depended on. 'To the rest of the world, New Zealand only means two things,' explained one of the students. 'Sheep and rugby. Lots of other countries have sheep... ' As far as he was concerned, no more needed to be said, just as there was only one answer to my question about what sport the school played in the summer term. 'Rugby, of course.' The way he looked at me suggested he felt the question was as superfluous as the last two words of his answer.

Perhaps the only country in the world that is even more fanatical about rugby than New Zealand is Samoa – as we discovered within minutes of landing at Apia. On every patch of roadside ground between airport and hotel, we saw youngsters playing rugby. It didn't seem to matter whether there were boulders underfoot or trees in the way. It didn't seem all that important for the pitch to be rectangular – or flat. It didn't seem necessary even to have a rugby ball. In one of the games we glimpsed, they were playing with a plimsoll, in another a plastic lemonade bottle. All of the kids – whose ages seemed to range from maybe four or five to late teens – were playing barefoot. Many of them displayed a quite astonishing natural talent – for handling, running, dodging and, above all, tackling. Touch rugby wasn't an option. The big hit was everywhere. And so was the joy.

And such staggering talent. As I write this chapter Samoa has just won the IRB World Sevens Series, Samoan players are plentiful in the Aviva Premiership and the French Championnat and it seems a production line that has already delivered the likes of Michael Jones, Inga Tuigemala, Tana Umaga and Jerry Collins will continue to churn out world-class rugby players for some time to come.

But why were Samoans so good at rugby in the first place? Our attempts to find out included attending the national trial: a seemingly haphazard and cheap-as-chips affair with players stripping off mid-pitch and handing sweaty jerseys to each other as the teams were constantly jigged and rejigged – a meeting of village elders, at which even minor misdemeanours were discussed and adjudicated upon – and a visit to one of the largest schools in Apia, where the pupils were smilingly courteous, deeply religious and passionately knowledgeable about rugby. Our conclusions suggested that the social structure, with its emphasis on the village community, promotes both leadership and a sense of responsibility while a warrior tradition – 'the advantage of rugby' explained one of the village elders 'is that we can indulge our natural aggression and play out ancient tribal rivalries without having to kill each other' – explained the Samoans' affinity for the physical side of the game. The fusion of national and sporting culture – outwardly manifested in the body tattoos proudly worn by just about every single Samoan rugby player – helped, we hoped, to explain the phenomenon.

Wherever we went in South Africa we came across an incredible spirit of optimism – that somehow or other the transfer of political power would work, that the economy would survive and prosper and that society would be reconfigured fairly – and all without widespread violence. There was also an overwhelming belief that the forthcoming World Cup would be a force for good. For rugby die-hards, it was all about showing the rest of the world what it had been missing. South Africa was one of the great powerhouses of rugby; a global tournament without them was a World Cup in name only. For most ordinary South Africans it was, after the miserable isolation of apartheid, a chance to showcase their beautiful homeland. For the nation's entrepreneurs, excited by the imminent arrival of tens of thousands of well-heeled visitors from overseas, it was a chance to make money. Even the minibus operators offering tours to Soweto were upbeat – 'things are so much better now that the most popular car in the township is a BMW, which as you know stands for Break My Windows!'

Rugby men like Jake White, the future World Cup-winning coach who was then running a talent-spotting programme at one of the universities, Francois Pienaar, captain of a team that used to be known as Transvaal, was then known as Gauteng and would come to be known as the Golden Lions, and Errol Tobias, the first-ever coloured Springbok, assured us that the game in the Republic was in fine fettle. Louis Luyt, President of the South African Rugby Union, assured us that this would be the biggest, best-organised, most profitable World Cup ever. Dr Luyt was a ruthless businessman with a reputation for being a bit of a bully. He obviously didn't feel it necessary to add the words 'or else'.

The Cote D'Ivoire came from nowhere to qualify for the 1995 Rugby World Cup. In the spring of 1995 there were still only ten clubs in the entire country, and eight of those were based in the largest city, Abidjan. Following so soon after our visit to South Africa, the comparison between the haves and the have-nots of world rugby could not have been greater. The Ivorians had bags of natural ability, boundless enthusiasm and that was about it. They had been well coached by a succession of French educationalists but they had neither the physique nor the fitness to compete at the highest level. They knew they were heading for the World Cup on a hiding to nothing and yet they displayed nothing but excitement. They saw themselves as the standard-bearers for black Africa and they were determined to do their continent, as well as their country, proud.

Italy was a land where *calcio* (soccer) was king, and rugby had struggled to establish itself until a change in the tax laws encouraged multi-national sponsors, like clothing firm Benetton, to invest in the game. To the consternation of the IRB, this had led to the influx not just of foreign internationals of Italian descent – like Frano Botica and David Campese – but also of superstars with no obvious connections, men like Naas Botha, John Kirwan and Michael Lynagh. Although there had been no obvious or immediate improvements in the fortunes of the national team, the seeds had been sown and, on the back of their exposure in the 1987 and 1991 Rugby World Cups, the 'Azzurri' were starting to press for admittance to the Five Nations Championship.

We had already picked David Campese's brains in Sydney. Now we wanted to hear how Treviso boy-made-good Luciano Benetton had set about a multi-sports empire in his home town and how rugby star Michael Lynagh fitted into his plans. We also wanted to examine how, in a country where no rugby was played in schools and where soccer cast such an enormous shadow, the game could create a robust enough infrastructure and we wanted to find out what motivated Italians to play and support rugby.

Maybe we were getting good at it. Maybe the assistance of Chris Thau, a genial Romanian who worked for the IRB and possessed the fattest contacts book in world rugby, did the trick. Whichever, the whole expedition went like clockwork, and my abiding memories are of the downtime in general and two meals in particular. Italian players Diego Dominguez and twins Massimo and Marcello Cuttitta not only took Chris and myself to their favourite restaurant outside Milan but spent hours with us in fascinating rugby conversation and then insisted – even though they were amateurs and we were 'on expenses' – on picking up the bill. And, at a restaurant in Treviso Michael Lynagh told us how he was introduced to the Treviso club president over dinner. Michael, as bright and polite as he was congenial, had mugged up on a few Italian words and phrases to help proceedings along. What he hadn't mastered was pronunciation. So, when he proffered the bread-basket to the man who was almost certainly going to foot the bill for dinner and enquired in his best Italian, 'Excuse me, Mr President, would you like a little penis?' how was he to know?

Lynagh was just one of the superstars I interviewed for the *World's Greatest Rugby Players* series and like the others – men like Colin Meads and John Kirwan in New Zealand, David Campese in Sydney, Morne du Plessis in South Africa, Philippe Sella in France – he was an absolute pleasure both to research and to interview. My only regret was that, because the production company concerned hadn't been able to sell the programmes to any of the television channels I watched, I was unable to see them. To be honest, I didn't really get a chance to watch *Rugby Warriors* either. As soon as filming had finished I spent 12-hour days first of all going through the footage – we had approximately an hour on tape for every minute that would be broadcast – and then turning it into the required programmes with VT editor Lyndon Matthews, a Welshman who was as extraordinarily patient as he was extraordinarily talented. The programmes were broadcast on successive weeks in May 1995, and I'm told they were tolerably well received. I didn't have time to mind. I was on my way once again to South Africa – as ITV's main presenter for Rugby World Cup 1995.

CHAPTER THIRTY
LOMU (1995)

'Watch out, world!' New Zealand commentator Keith Quinn could not have been more prescient. The warning came at the end of the All Blacks' final trial before the squad for the 1995 Rugby World Cup was to be announced, and he'd just seen a 19-year-old giant by the name of Jonah Lomu bulldoze his way through, past and over some of the best players in the land.

It didn't take long for the world to notice. In New Zealand's opening match – against Ireland at Ellis Park – Lomu trampled all over the hapless Richard Wallace for his first try. In the second-half, in quite the most chilling exhibition of raw power ever seen in top-class rugby, he swatted aside a succession of opponents as if they were so many irritating flies and, 80 yards later, put Josh Kronfeld over for a try. The scoreboard says that Lomu scored two tries. Most match reports indicate that he made two more. None of them do justice to the impact made by the 6-foot-5-inch, 18-stone winger.

This was only Lomu's third game in an All Black jersey. He'd performed badly in fitness tests undergone by the players in pre-season training and had only just made the cut for the trial matches. Not a single New Zealand pundit had predicted he'd make the squad for South Africa. Yet in the space of 80 minutes – in which he'd demonstrated not just phenomenal power but also pace, balance and the deftest of ball-handling skills – he'd made himself the most talked-about rugby player on the planet and New Zealand odds-on favourites to lift the trophy. And all this even before his four-try semi-final against England.

Mind you, I'd have put up with being trampled ten times by Lomu if I could have avoided the nightmare that I had during our coverage of the opening match of the tournament. 'That was awful.' I mouthed the words when I thought the cameras were off me. They weren't, and in actual fact the experience was far, far worse than awful. At the most fluid part of the programme, when the match was over and the need for flexibility – in switching between live contributors, linking to taped packages, chatting to studio guests – was at its greatest, the talkback between our studio at the Newlands ground in Cape Town and the producers at ITV headquarters in Johannesburg had 'gone down'. It was up to me to improvise, to think on my feet and keep the programme moving smoothly along. Above all, it was my job to stay calm, paper over any cracks that might be showing and guide the viewers through to the time we went off air. I got it wrong. I got flustered at not being able to hear any instructions or any timings. I started to stumble over my words and as successive live links failed to materialise, I started to panic that I might not be able to close the programme properly. Once self-doubt creeps in you're in trouble, whatever you're doing. When you're live on air in front of 14 million people at the biggest moment of your broadcasting career, it's a thousand times worse. Believe me.

Somehow or other, we got through to the end of the programme. Somehow or other, we got off air, and somehow or other, producer Pete Barraclough managed to find me, wandering about, unseeing amid the 60,000 odd fans leaving the stadium, deep in my own world of despair. Somehow or other, too, he got me to the airport on to the plane and back to ITV headquarters in Johannesburg.

The debrief was painful – I felt I'd let down the whole operation and was finding it difficult to look my colleagues in the eye. Sure there were mitigating circumstances – we should, for instance, have had a better back-up talkback system, we might perhaps have been better to let the on-site Cape Town director take over instead of persevering with a faulty line to Jo'burg – but I still felt I could have done better. I was inconsolable – until I remembered that we had another live broadcast to do the next day, and maybe a couple of dozen more to do before the end of the tournament. And nobody had died. The show must go on.

Up to that point it had all gone so well. ITV had hired an apartment building in the Wanderers suburb of Johannesburg, which was to serve as our base throughout the tournament, and organised a fleet of cars to take us to and from the South African Broadcasting Centre and the airport. In the week or so we'd been out there the new team had bonded well. There were plenty of familiar faces from ITV's 1991 World Cup team – summarisers Gordon Brown, Clive Norling and Steve Smith, commentators John Taylor and Bob Simmons, producers Phil King and Dave Wood – but there were also plenty of newcomers who either were already or would shortly become household names. Future ITV *News at Ten* anchors Mark Austin and Mary Nightingale went into partnership for the first time on the Rugby World Cup highlights programme, while future Sky commentator, the effervescent, zany and at times completely bonkers Mark Robson, was a roving commentator/reporter. In a different category altogether, legendary newscaster Trevor McDonald joined us for the opening and closing programmes.

Trevor was as urbane, charming and easy-going in real life as he was on the screen. He was also the consummate professional, as I discovered when we recorded the links to the opening programme at a succession of locations in Cape Town. Whereas I found it difficult to do my pieces to camera without frequent recourse to notes and not a few re-takes, Trevor was entirely comfortable in front of the camera, rarely consulted his script and, even if he ad-libbed the odd line, always made perfect and compelling sense. I could only watch and admire, and hopefully learn.

Trevor's presence on ITV almost certainly gained us the interview that turned our opening programme into solid gold. While it's doubtful that Nelson Mandela's staff would have even considered an interview request from Alastair Hignell, they needed only a little persuasion to put the great man forward for a chat with Trevor McDonald. I was lucky enough to be allowed to sit in on the interview, shake the hand of the most famous man in the world and gain first-hand experience of the extraordinary aura that surrounded Nelson Mandela. The South African President was much taller, and frailer, than I'd imagined and his voice was thinner and less authoritative. But his whole demeanour oozed charisma. He had grace, charm, dignity and a way of holding himself that commanded instant and absolute respect. When he spoke everyone hung on his every word, and you could have heard a pin drop when he'd finished talking. All of us who were lucky enough to be there came away from the interview absolutely convinced that we'd just spent time in the presence of greatness.

The Nelson Mandela interview guaranteed that the preview programme was a triumph. Although not in the same league as Trevor McDonald, I had done my bit well. I was rested, relaxed and I'd done my homework for the first match of the tournament – between holders and pre-tournament favourites Australia, and hosts South Africa. I'd written a script and rehearsed the links in my head. I was nervous but so determined to be in the best possible shape that I'd laid off the alcohol, grabbed an early night in Cape Town, got myself to the ground in plenty of time and, in terms of preparation, had left as little as possible to chance. And I'd fallen at the first hurdle.

I didn't sleep much after the Cape Town debacle. Mind you, there wasn't an awful lot of time after the Jo'burg debriefing before we had to be up and on the road to Rustenburg for our next live programme, from Scotland's opening match of the tournament against the Ivory Coast. I could only guess at the press reaction to the previous day's horror-show but I got an understanding of the palpitations that were afflicting the ITV top brass when I received a call from one of them mid-journey. The caller, future Sky Sport executive Trevor East, ostensibly wanted to talk about the weather on the high veld and Scotland's chances that afternoon but I was under no illusions that he was really ringing to reassure himself that I hadn't been completely traumatised by the cock-ups of the previous day. The other travellers in the Rustenburg minibus obviously felt the need to bolster my spirits as well and what had begun as a quiet, introspective sober-sided journey soon became loud, animated and filled with nervous laughter.

Great human being that he was, even Gordon Brown would not have deliberately left his kilt behind just to make me feel better. Nevertheless, the anguish he displayed and the lengths he went to get a replacement were comical enough to dispel all gloomy thoughts. After trawling the nearby bars – which were now rapidly filling up with his countrymen – Gordon announced that he'd persuaded one of the travelling supporters to relinquish his own kilt for the afternoon.

'I hope nobody will look too closely, because it's the wrong tartan,' said Gordon as he entered our makeshift studio. The rest of us were hoping nobody would look too closely because not only was it the wrong tartan, it was very definitely the wrong size – an impression confirmed by the sight of a skinny 5-foot-6-inch man in the crowd trying desperately not to draw attention to the enormous shorts he was wearing and the glimpse, whenever he shifted in his seat, of Gordon's pink printed boxers.

Rustenburg, translated in the media guide as 'the restful village', was the perfect restorative – a romp in the park for Scotland, whose 89 points was the highest they'd ever managed in an international, a world record for Gavin Hastings, whose 44 points included four tries, and a nice, clean, glitch-free transmission for me to restore a bit of confidence in time for England's first match in Durban the following day.

The King's Park Stadium was to become a sort of home from home for ITV. It was certainly the stadium at which we spent the most time. All of England's pool matches – against Argentina, Italy and Western Samoa – were played there, and so was the extraordinary semi-final between South Africa and France.

'It never rains in Durban,' said the locals. As England played their matches under clear blue skies, it was easy to believe them. But the heavens opened on the morning of the semi-final and, as monsoon-like rain lashed down from the angry sky, showed no signs of shutting. King's Park was totally unable to cope. As kick-off approached, the pitch resembled a lake and there was a very real chance that the match would have to be put back at least 24 hours, even though tournament organisers were all too well aware that that would cause more logistical problems than it would solve. The meteorology office predicted that the rain would ease at 4 o'clock. Kick-off was scheduled for 3 o'clock, and ITV were on air at 2.30. As the credits rolled, the organisers were still in a huddle with Welsh referee Derek Bevan and there was no official word as to whether the game would go ahead at all.

'Keep talking,' said the voice in my ear, 'chat to the studio guests, and we'll try to find out what's happening.' Fifteen minutes later, the same voice told me that kick-off had been delayed.

'Keep talking, we'll try to find some more studio guests, and we'll try to get some more information.' The next time the earpiece crackled into life, it informed me that the organisers were putting all their faith in the weathermen.

'Kick-off's at 4.30. Keep talking to your studio guests, and we'll try to find you some tapes to play in, and some reporters to throw to. We'll let you know when to cue to an ad-break. Oh, and good luck!'

Never, in my whole life, had 90 minutes dragged so slowly. Never had I felt so isolated, exposed and uncomfortably in the spotlight. In front of an audience of ten million, not all of whom would have forgotten the horlicks I had made of a much simpler assignment on day one of the tournament. Fortunately for me I had no time to dwell on anything except the demands of the moment, keeping the chat moving, throwing to hastily summoned reporters, introducing newly edited packages, looking as if everything was under control. Even so, it was hard not to be transfixed by a set of images that would inevitably be beamed around the world, and would inevitably reflect badly on South Africa. At one point, when one of the last hopes of staging the game at all rested on the removal of surface water from the pitch, the task was given to a squad of black women, equipped only with brooms. There was not a single white person, not even one man, involved. With the television cameras of the world trained on King's Park, and with nothing else of remotely visual interest to divert them, they had no choice but to highlight the supreme political incorrectness of the situation and invite speculation as to how far the rainbow nation had really come.

Fortunately for South Africa, the final, only a week later, produced an image that was even more iconic, infinitely more flattering to the new regime and, according to World Cup historian Gerald Davies, 'one of those instances which may help to define the 20th century'. He was talking of course about the presentation of the Webb Ellis Trophy by Nelson Mandela to Francois Pienaar. The symbolism of the moment could not be underestimated: blond, blue-eyed and beefy, Pienaar could have been a pictorial stereotype of the apartheid regime that had kept Mandela in prison for over a quarter of a century. Yet not only was the thin, frail black man showing off one of the biggest smiles in Ellis Park, not only was he finding it difficult to keep from jigging with delight at an unexpected victory, but he was also wearing the green and gold jersey of South Africa with the leaping Springbok on his breast and Pienaar's own No. 6 on his back. Thousands of words could not have painted a picture more eloquent. Nelson Mandela, the absolute epitome of magnanimity and reconciliation, was giving his seal of approval to the millions of his countrymen whose desperation to support the nation's rugby team had hitherto been muted by the memories of that sport's association with apartheid. And Pienaar was quite obviously of the same mind as Mandela. His post-match comment on the Ellis Park crowd – 'we didn't have the support of 63,000 South Africans today, we had the support of 42 million South Africans' – could not have been more apt. The post-match celebrations around the stadium, with South Africans of all shapes, sizes and colours sounding car-horns, trumpets and vuvuzelas long into the night, could not have been more riotous.

The match itself was much less memorable than what followed, or indeed preceded, the action. ITV were on the air half an hour before kick-off but, because no British teams were involved, had taken the decision to use the time to look back at the tournament from a Scottish, Irish, Welsh and, particularly, an English perspective. As this would involve lots of videotape, and lots of comment from extra guests like Will Carling and Gavin Hastings, the focus would have to be on what was happening in the studio rather than outside it. Which was rather difficult when, behind our backs, the cameras could pick out wellington-booted Zulu dancers cavorting about the pitch and our pitch-side microphones could, even with the volume turned down, report the persistent efforts of a blaring PA system to get a highly excited crowd to join in with the singing of 'Nkosi Sikileli Africa'. Still, I thought we were coping pretty well until...

Everybody in the studio ducked instinctively as a Boeing 747 roared over the stadium so close to the upper stands that no one had the slightest difficulty in reading the 'Good Luck Bokke' message painted on its undercarriage. The room was still shaking when I decided to go off-script. Thankfully, one of our roving cameramen grabbed a magnificent shot of the airplane climbing away from Johannesburg, and the ITV audience at least had a clue what was going on.

As to the match itself, South Africa gang-tackled Jonah Lomu into oblivion while New Zealand – in stark contrast to the sublime rugby they had displayed in the semi-final against England – were frantic, imprecise and at times directionless. With neither side scoring a try – though perhaps South Africa came closest – the match was settled by a Joel Stransky drop-goal seven minutes from time.

Our coverage went well. We may have underplayed the pre-match extravaganza but other than that we'd done justice to the occasion and its significance. We'd had an imposing array of guests – David Campese and Gareth Edwards also making an appearance – and I felt I'd handled them well, asked good questions at the right times and struck the right note in opening and closing the programme. I still had one more programme to present – looking back at the tournament as a whole – but that was scheduled for lunchtime the next day. In the meantime I'd been invited to the official post-match banquet and, the editor wanted to know, if he sent a cameraman along with me, could I get some more considered post-match reactions from the victors and vanquished?

The All Blacks were both dignified and gracious. Even though they'd just lost a World Cup final they had been widely expected to win, not one of them refused to speak to me. Manager Colin Meads may have had tears in his eyes and the players may still have been in shock at seeing the greatest prize in world rugby slip from their grasp, but to a man they were polite, respectful and generous. Even though some of the team had been ill on the morning of the match – in circumstances that would later lead to allegations of food poisoning by a waitress named 'Susie' – none of them offered that up as an excuse. They gave credit where it was due in public and prepared to suffer their pain in private.

And then Louis Luyt waded in with his hobnail boots. While the South African players had managed to cloak their jubilation in a certain amount of modesty, their president took gloating to entirely new levels. In a speech that was as rambling as it was ill conceived, Dr Luyt managed to offend just about everyone else in the room. His boorish claims that the first two tournaments should never have been called World Cups because South Africa had not taken part sparked a walkout by New Zealand, and some England players. His decision to award a gold watch to Derek Bevan as referee of the tournament was not just going to embarrass World Cup final referee Ed Morrison and his supporters, but was also quite needlessly going to cast doubts over the reasons for the Welshman Bevan's decision both to allow play to go ahead on the waterlogged Durban pitch and, when it did, to rule against a potentially match-winning score by the French. As speeches go, it remains quite the most arrogant and inappropriate that I've ever heard, and it could so easily have tarnished for ever a wonderful achievement by the Springbok rugby team and the rainbow nation. That it didn't is no thanks at all to Louis Luyt.

Luyt's comments, of course, gave extra spice to ITV's closing programme the following lunchtime as did the eve-of-final announcement of a massive television deal struck between the newly formed SANZAR (South Africa, New Zealand and Australia Rugby) and Rupert Murdoch's News Corporation. The latter had been persuaded to stump up a mind-boggling US $555 million in return for the rights to broadcast rugby in the southern hemisphere for the next ten years. What all this meant, it was far too early to tell. What only a few people knew was that this announcement was a precursor to a savage multi-million dollar battle for the heart and the soul of the sport. What we all suspected was that rugby would never be the same again. And what I didn't know was that, once all the dust had settled, my broadcasting career would also head off in a totally different direction.

CHAPTER THIRTY-ONE

BACK AMONG
THE CHRISTIANS

Just about the only thing Kerry Packer and John Birt had in common was that neither of them had heard of me. Yet, separately, the big extrovert Aussie and the slim buttoned-down Englishman made decisions that were to change my life. Packer launched the 'Rugby War', which catapulted the sport into the professional era and, much to his own chagrin, sent it straight into the arms of Rupert Murdoch's Sky. Birt launched rolling news on the BBC, which led to the formation of Radio Five Live and the massive expansion of BBC Sport.

Sky's US $555 million deal with the SANZAR countries gave them a ten-year monopoly on the broadcasting of southern hemisphere rugby. ITV – continually rebuffed in their assault on the domestic market – weren't going to be allowed even a sniff of international rugby outside of the quadrennial World Cup. If I stayed in independent television, I would have a long wait between rugby assignments. BSkyB's takeover of domestic rugby coverage – in an altogether more possessive way than the BBC had done – meant that the chances of HTV broadcasting West Country rugby in the way we had been able to were minimal. HTV itself was also in the process of retrenchment. The chances of my making any more documentary programmes were almost non-existent. My career – apart from one final fling presenting the last bit of rugby left to ITV, the inaugural Heineken Cup competition – had entered a cul-de-sac.

But Birt's decision to revamp Radio Five as a service of rolling news, talk programmes and sport – dubbed 'Radio Bloke' because of the way the station swiftly became popular among male listeners in general and football fans in particular – created all sorts of openings. Two things immeasurably helped the new station, which came into being in April 1974. The determination of BSkyB to get full value for the mind-blowing £304 million deal it had brokered with the Premier League in 1992 dramatically increased the number of matches that were to be televised live. In turn this ensured that kick-offs were spread not just across the weekend but into the week as well. The strategy was manna from heaven for Radio Five Live bosses desperate to keep the new schedules filled. In a separate development, the adoption and refinement of ISDN (the Integrated Services Digital Network) enabled broadcast-quality reports to be transmitted over the normal telephone network. Reporters no longer needed to head to the nearest BBC studio before they could transmit their material. They could even appear live on the BBC from the comfort of their own homes. Provided they had the right equipment, they could broadcast at any time of day or night, from anywhere.

To cope with the newly imposed 24/7 culture, the newish station needed considerably more staff. To deal with the advent of professionalism in rugby union and the inevitable media interest that would follow in its wake, Five Live was in the market for broadcasters with an intimate knowledge of the sport. They were more than happy to welcome me back into the fold. I was not quite so happy to take a pay cut, but was easily swayed by the promise of a company car and the assurance that, thanks to the developments in ISDN, I would not have to move house. Of much more importance than that, however, was the knowledge that I would be back among friends.

Head of Sport Bob Shennan had been a very junior producer during my previous incarnation at the BBC. The department's senior sports editor, Gordon Turnbull, had been my first rugby producer while Charles Runcie, the man now responsible for *Sunday Sport*, had been my second. Another editor, Graeme Reid-Davies, had loaned me his flat for a few weeks as we relocated to Bristol, and the number of colleagues who had stayed put and worked their way up the corporation ladder while I was at HTV ran into dozens. And, of course, there was my friend, my mentor and my former coach Ian Robertson.

'You're back among the Christians, now.' His remark illustrated not only his loyalty to the corporation – he had already completed two decades as the BBC's rugby correspondent – but was also a perceptive analysis of my natural predisposition. The BBC I had left had been highly professional and also highly enthusiastic. It had a reputation for getting the job done, for not taking itself too seriously, for priding itself on teamwork and for having a bit of fun along the way. And the BBC I rejoined had hardly changed. I was glad to be back.

The fact of my return to the BBC was, I think, more important to both of us than the definition of my new responsibilities. It was accepted that I would come up from Bristol to Broadcasting House at least once a week to read *Sports Desk*, while I had already been lined up as holiday cover for Gary Lineker on *Five Live Sunday Sport*. As for the rest, I would commentate on the Five Nations, report from at least one rugby match per weekend for the rest of the season, deputise for Ian Robertson where applicable and cover all the rugby stories during the week that the rota would allow. I would also be expected to cover cricket.

That was the theory. The practice proved slightly different. Rugby stories by and large failed to comply with the BBC rota. In the early months of 1996,

I increasingly found myself tied to the office while reporters with a sketchy knowledge of rugby were sent to cover stories that I felt were crying out for my expertise and personal contacts. Part of me acknowledged that it was important that I 'pay my dues' and that some of my frustration was caused by the inconvenience of driving all the way up from Bristol to sit in a London studio at least once a week. But I recognised that the reason why there were so many rugby stories was that, no longer wholly amateur, and not yet fully professional, the sport was in complete turmoil. I felt I would be in the perfect position to explain what was happening to the game I loved if only I didn't have to keep serving time at Broadcasting House.

This was silly season for the game of rugby in England. Although the RFU had accepted that the game was no longer amateur they had imposed a moratorium on the implementation of professionalism. All that had done was to create a power-vacuum at the top end of the game and, as the entrepreneurs had come pouring in, the rumour mills had gone into overdrive. There was speculation about which player had signed for whom and for how much and, of course, there was no smoke without fire. Sir John Hall at Newcastle was the first to jump the gun, luring Rob Andrew from Wasps to be his director of rugby and choosing Tony Underwood as his 'marquee' signing. Neither came cheap. Most of England's top players did not have to do anything except sit and wait for the good times to roll. They had already been tapped up by Ross Turnbull, agent for Kerry Packer's World Rugby Corporation. They had gained some idea of their value when salaries of £150,000 a year were mentioned. Now they were being wooed from all quarters. And paid. In Martin Johnson's autobiography he recalls receiving a completely unexpected cheque from England for £20,000 and another for the same amount from Leicester for 'image rights'. He reckoned that both were trying to keep the players sweet until a new order could be finalised.

Some clubs flashed the cash. Third Division Richmond snapped up Ben Clarke of England, Agustin Pichot of Argentina and Scott Quinnell of Wales, while Saracens signed Australian Michael Lynagh and Frenchman Philippe Sella. Other clubs couldn't cope. My own club, Bristol, made a complete pig's ear of the move to professionalism, while Coventry also had to sell their ground to pay off debts and Moseley were forced into administration.

These were momentous times for rugby and I argued that Radio Five Live would neither be able to fulfil its own objectives of providing up-to-the-minute coverage of every news story that mattered nor be able to give rugby the attention it merited, unless it took me off the rota and put me on rugby full-time. It was agreed, therefore, that from the start of the 1996-97 season I would go on the rugby 'beat', attend as many as possible of the ever-multiplying media briefings that the world of professional rugby deemed essential, and produce a regular weekly round-up for local radio. I would also cover at least one rugby tour every summer, starting that very June with the Wales tour of Australia and Scotland's trip to New Zealand.

That first tour experience was all pretty surreal. Joining the Welsh tour late and having to leave it prematurely, I didn't really get to know either the players or the coaches. Arriving halfway through the Scottish tour, I also had plenty of ground to make up.

It was a tour of firsts. It was the first time I had returned to Brisbane since making my debut for England in the infamous Battle of Ballymore in 1975. By some extraordinary coincidence, the Australian team of that era were holding a 21st anniversary celebration at the ground. Out of curiosity, I invited myself along, and could only marvel that this unremarkable group of middle-aged men – all in their best suits and blazers, some gone to seed, some gone to fat – could have been that rough, tough, almost psychopathic bunch of yellow-shirted athletes that had belted the living daylights out of England 21 years before. Or that this gentle, mild-mannered, softly spoken old gent was the same David Brockhoff whose fire-breathing, tub-thumping, expletive-filled outbursts had put them up to it.

It was the first time I had operated as a one-man band overseas, and it was the first time I realised the importance of having a back-up link to the studio back at base. In broadcast terms, the Australia-Wales match at Brisbane had gone smoothly enough – though Wales were not particularly happy with a 56-25 defeat – but, less than halfway through a 62-31 thrashing of Scotland by New Zealand in Dunedin and completely unbeknown to me, the commentary line went dead. I carried on commentating to the very end, bringing in former Scottish full-back Peter Dodds for some pithy observations from time to time, and it was only when I returned from the dressing rooms ready to play back an interview with Scottish coach Jim Telfer, that I realised that the link to London had been broken. It was only when I re-dialled that I was able to find out just how long we had been off the air.

'How come you didn't notice that the light on the ISDN box had gone out?' was the totally reasonable question from the studio manager in London. The answer was that I didn't see it. The commentary position was so crowded at Carisbrook that I had been switched to an overflow press box into which so many other pressmen had been crammed that there was no room on the work surface for the ISDN box. I had tucked it away on the floor and an unsuspecting journalist had obviously dislodged the connection with his feet.

It was also the first time I witnessed a volcano at anything like first-hand. Scotland were in Rotorua and were just about to start a morning training session in the week leading up to the second Test. Those were the days when journalists were welcome to attend training sessions and, with nothing much better to do on a beautiful, crisp autumn morning, most of the rest of the Scottish press pack and I had decided to walk from our hotel to the training ground to watch them. As we walked, it gradually got darker overhead and before long it seemed to be snowing. Except this wasn't snow that was drifting slowly to the ground and settling, it was lava. Nearby Mount Ruapehu had exploded the day before and volcanic ash was on its way back down to earth. Before we reached the training ground we saw the Scottish players coming back. Grit kept blowing into their eyes and mouths and even the legendary tough man Jim Telfer agreed that to continue was hazardous. The lava continued to settle throughout the rest of the day, and by the next morning it lay inches thick on the cars outside the hotel.

This spelled double embarrassment for photographer Dave Rogers. Dave began taking rugby photographs on the Lions tour to South Africa in 1974 and has almost certainly attended more international rugby matches since then than any journalist in any country. He is also one of the most congenitally cheerful men I have ever met, and warm-hearted and generous to boot. So generous in fact that he had promised to let the Scotland players have copies of some of the photographs he had taken during the tour. He chose that morning to take the negatives to the developers and for the first time missed a Scotland training session. Now, to make up for missing the once-in-a-lifetime photo opportunity afforded by the falling lava, he had written 'Please clean me' on the lava-covered bonnets in the hotel car park. That, as the locals were at pains to point out, was harmless enough when done with snow, which melts. Lava might look the same, but was actually much grittier. His words had, to all intents and purposes, been engraved on the cars.

The volcano almost certainly had an effect on the weather – the Test in Auckland was played in torrential rain – and that almost certainly prevented the phenomenal 20-year-old All Black full-back Christian Cullen from adding to the seven tries he had already scored in his first two Tests and restricted the margin of defeat to an acceptable level. The deluge continued for the next 24 hours and there were calls for Auckland airport to be closed because of the ash cloud still swirling about the stratosphere. In the end, though, we got away and, as the plane battled its way through the thunderstorms on its way first to Los Angeles and then to London, I could reflect on a pretty satisfying first few months back at the BBC. I had got my feet under the table as a rugby journalist and would be raring to go when the new season started in September. It would be the first season proper of professional rugby in England, the first season of English involvement in the Heineken Cup and it would be the first time ever that the British and Irish Lions had taken on the world champions in their own backyard. And I would have a ringside seat.

CHAPTER THIRTY-TWO

LIONS GO PRO (1996–97)

What did professionalism mean? Ever since the first World Cup in 1987 it had seemed inevitable that rugby union players would eventually be paid. The stakes were too high, public expectation too great and media interest too intense for the game to remain a part-time hobby. The only questions that remained to be settled were how much should they earn and how it would affect the way they played the game and we viewed it. For the last hundred years the central plank of the game had been amateurism. Now that was gone, what was left?

In truth, nobody really had much of a clue. They could draw parallels with football and the obscene wealth it generated for the top performers. They could draw parallels with rugby league, which had gone professional exactly a hundred years earlier but, despite attracting huge following in certain states in Australia, had still not penetrated large parts of the British Isles. And, perhaps, they could draw the closest parallels with cricket, which had until very recently cherished its amateurs, paid its professionals an absolute pittance and was still totally reliant on international gate receipts to keep its head above water.

The new paymasters had very little to go on whatsoever. The players – certainly those who had been tapped up by Kerry Packer's World Rugby Corporation – had gained a rough idea of what they were worth, but most couldn't quite believe their luck as they were now going to be paid for playing a game which they loved but which until only a few months ago had been little more than a time-consuming leisure activity. Some of the senior players had for some time received small amounts of money from sports goods companies for wearing a certain type of boot, or endorsing a certain range of sports gear, while Brian Moore and Rob Andrew had secured several sponsorship deals for the England rugby team. But, until the IRB meeting in Paris in April 1995, nobody could afford to give up the day job. Now, not only could they afford to, but also they were expected to become full-time rugby players. They had enjoyed one type of relationship with their club, their country, the media and the rugby-watching public. Now they would have to forge another. Mistrust between all the parties were entirely understandable and almost certain to be played out in public.

I felt I had a perspective on the matter because, admittedly getting on for two decades earlier, I had been both an amateur and a professional sportsman. As an England rugby international in the 1970s I didn't feel particularly valued or valuable. I never expected to get any reward from the game and though I had heard rumours of under-the-counter sponsorship deals, I was more than happy with a free pair of boots and the odd piece of leisure gear. I was well aware that the international side played in matches that brought huge revenue to the RFU, but I didn't particularly feel I was entitled to any of it. My hold on an England place was always going to be tenuous and I was determined to enjoy every moment of the experience in the certain knowledge that it could well be my last. My teammates were the same. We never regarded ourselves as elite, or even athletes come to that. We knew our international careers could come to an end at any time and, while we would summon up an extraordinary competitive intensity for each big match, we would treat it as a one-off, enjoy it while it lasted – and then go back to real life.

When asked to compare the two sports I played I always used to say that rugby – particularly at the level I played for Bristol and England – was the most 'professional' of amateur sports, while cricket – certainly the way Gloucestershire played in the 1970s – was the most amateur of professional sports. Salaries were small – pitiful even, when compared to other professional sports – and old attitudes – from the days when professionals were hired hands brought in to make up the numbers – had not entirely disappeared. County cricket clubs, it seemed, existed for the benefit of the members and not as businesses in their own right. Players were expected to do their best for the team and for themselves, but ultimately they owed their livelihood to an unqualified bunch of worthies for whom cricket was nothing more than a pleasant form of relaxation. And, possibly because the County Championship had evolved out of a need to keep the members satisfied, professional cricketers had precious little time to work on either their skills or their fitness. We were always either actually playing matches, or travelling. We were professional in the sense that we were paid and, of course, we knew that if we failed to perform, then we would lose our jobs – but that was about it.

I was concerned, therefore, that while we, as seven-days-a-week cricketers, had too little time to practise or prepare, newly professionalised rugby players – with only one match a week – would have too much time on their hands. I had observed, from the days I spent having physiotherapy at Bristol City Football Club, how young well-paid sportsmen with bags of energy, loads of free time and plenty of cash could fall into bad habits. I had seen from my time in county cricket how some talented young players had been unable to cope with a lack of structure and fallen by the wayside. I was not at all sure that the current generation of rugby players would be able to handle either the extra money that was now coming their way or the extra free time that they now had to fill.

I wasn't at all sure, either, how the clubs would cope. Most of them had progressed from being gentlemen's drinking clubs putting on a bit of 'rugger' for the benefit of their members, to become businesses in their own right. But they had never had to do much more than break even. If they took enough through the gate and at the bar to cover the upkeep of the ground, and paid the very few salaries necessary to keep the club functioning, they were happy. If they made a profit, they could maybe send the team on tour, or afford to buy a scrummaging machine, or do a bit of redecorating and refurbishment, but it wasn't absolutely essential. Now, at a stroke, they would become employers, responsible for salaries, contracts, insurance, health and safety and so on. They would have to balance the books, or go under. I feared that many would do the latter.

And how would the governing bodies, the media and the fans cope with the change in the status quo? For the unions, there would be a subtle change in the relationship with their players; where it had been master-servant it would now be employer-employee. For the media there would in one sense be a complete revolution. Before professionalism, journalists had enjoyed superior economic status. As a player I remember feeling flattered whenever a journalist offered to buy me a drink but I sensed also that it was a mark of his greater economic power. After professionalism, there was every chance that the journalist would be earning far less than the player he was interviewing. I wondered how that would change the relationship.

As far as the fans were concerned, I had few worries. They might be more envious, less tolerant of mistakes and they might moan about the increased cost of tickets. But most of them would be more than compensated by an improvement in creature comforts at the venues and, if the evidence from football was anything to go by, they would be no less passionate about the sport they followed and the team they supported. If any had been wedded to the idea – frequently spouted by traditionalists – that rugby union's real strength was that it was 'seamless' with no real divide between the elite few and the grassroots many, they quickly settled for an amicable divorce.

If the fans saw nothing but good in the new arrangements, the same could also be said of the media. Professionalism was a much easier concept to explain to the public and there was a sense that now everything was out in the open. In the sad old, bad old days of 'shamateurism', it had been easy to be cynical and suspicious. It was a widely held belief that people in rugby did not necessarily divulge everything about their affairs to the media because they had something to hide, something to be ashamed of, and that almost certainly coloured the attitude of the media. Now, theoretically, everything was open and above board, and everybody was accountable. Money, of course, made good copy; who was earning what, how much sponsors and broadcasters were prepared to pay, how much clubs and unions were taking through the gate. With the advent of professionalism, coaches and players were unable to hide behind the excuse that they were too busy at their day jobs to be able to talk about rugby, while the clubs and unions were conscious that, as newly signed up members of the entertainment business, they had obligations to both their partners and their consumers. Soon the media couldn't move for PR professionals and media liaison officers but soon too we were never short of something to write – or broadcast – about.

Rugby, for almost the first time in its history, was becoming big news. Radio Five Live was determined to establish itself as the provider of 'news and sports 24 hours a day'. From a career point of view, I could hardly have been in a better place at a better time. And what was happening on the pitch wasn't bad either.

If proof were needed that the RFU were caught napping by the advent of professionalism, it could be found in the fixture list for the autumn internationals of 1996. England's visitors at Twickenham that year were Italy (a comfortable win), Argentina (a narrow victory) and the New Zealand Barbarians (a narrow defeat). As was the custom, all the matches had been set up several years previously – long before the game went professional, long before the need to keep the cash tills ringing became imperative. In the Five Nations, England had big wins at home to Scotland and away to Ireland, but tripped up at home against France before winning their final match in Wales. It was obviously a team in transition with Will Carling bowing out at the end of the season in a match which also marked the end for Rob Andrew – brought back as a replacement in a sentimental gesture by England coach Jack Rowell – and, on the other side, Jonathan Davies. Up front, Jason Leonard may already have got past 50 caps and Martin Johnson more than 30, but Richard Hill was just starting his international career and his back-row colleagues, Lawrence Dallaglio and Neil Back, had less than 20 caps between them. Behind the scrum, Carling was playing for the 72nd time while replacements Jeremy Guscott and Rob Andrew had over a hundred caps between them, but the scrum-half rivalry between Kyran Bracken and Matt Dawson had not yet begun – Andy Gomarsall and Austin Healey shared the duties in 1997 – while Will Greenwood had not yet been capped. Jason Robinson was still playing rugby league and Jonny Wilkinson and Mike Tindall were still at school.

Wasps won the last ever Courage League – Allied Dunbar would take over the sponsorship the following season – while, as English clubs entered Europe for the first time, Leicester reached the final of the Heineken Cup. Their opponents, Brive, produced quite the most electrifying club performance I had yet seen. At the time, Radio Five Live were not the converts to European rugby that they later became, and I can remember screaming with frustration down the talkback as the Saturday afternoon sports programme meandered around the standard football matches and quite failed to do justice to not only an extraordinary display of rugby by the French team but a quite thrilling occasion. It was colourful, passionate, noisy and mesmeric – and I was desperate to convey the exhilarating scenes to the Five Live audience. All I heard in my headphones was 'we'll be with you for a score update when we've been round the football grounds'! To be fair, I wasn't the first reporter to feel so marginalised by what I considered to be a blind obsession with the round-ball game. It wasn't even the first time I'd been so upset by what seemed to me to be faulty editorial judgement – and it sure as hell wasn't going to be the last. It would take the best part of a decade – and the onset of an incurable condition – to realise that, although my convictions remained unshaken, some things were just not worth getting angry about.

Leicester were quite obviously the dominant club this side of the Channel and it was no surprise when, at a live extravaganza stage-managed by new broadcasters Sky, it was announced that the Tigers would supply five players to the Lions, including a surprise choice as captain. Martin Johnson, who had already played two Test matches on the previous Lions tour, was a near certainty as a player. Coach Ian McGeechan explained his selection of Johnson as skipper on the grounds that when it came to the pre-match toss-up he wanted the South Africans to look up at the Lions captain – a statement of intent from the Lions management that they fully intended to win all the important mind games, as well as the series. And the appointment of Fran Cotton – like McGeechan a member of the victorious Lions side in South Africa in 1974 – was also an inspired choice. The hard-nosed Lancastrian is a big man in every way and his willingness to act as a buffer between his squad and the outside world, while at the same time reminding them of the history and tradition of the Lions, set exactly the right tone. So did the deliberate selection of a number of rugby league players. Alan Tait of Scotland, John Bentley of England and the Welsh trio of Scott Gibbs, Scott Quinnell and Allan Bateman were not automatic selections for their countries yet McGeechan, Cotton and co. took a calculated punt that these players' rugby league-inculcated attitudes to preparation, practice and training would rub off on teammates who had never yet been on tour as professional rugby players.

Sky's acquisition of the broadcast rights meant that the first Lions tour of the professional era was also going to have the most extensive television coverage. South Africa occupies a similar time zone to the UK, and the satellite broadcasting company was hoping to collar a big audience and drive up dish sales. A fly-on-the-wall camera crew would also garner unprecedented behind-the-scenes footage, while some of the players were to be issued with camcorders to augment the finished product. Advances in camera technology, and the desire on the part of assiduously courted and newly acquired sponsors to get value for money on their investment, would guarantee the presence of a record number of photographers, while a showdown between the world champions and the most famous touring team in rugby history would guarantee the largest travelling press corps in living memory.

And I was going to be part of that media 'rat-pack' – from start to finish. While Ian Robertson would jet out to cover the tour when the games started getting serious, Five Live wanted to have a reporter in South Africa from the outset. I was to travel with the team, attend every press conference they gave and report on every movement they made. When I wasn't conducting interviews with the newsmakers among the Lions and their opponents, or reporting and commentating on the matches, I would be compiling features about South African sport and sending weekly audio postcards back to the network. I would be on my own for the first few weeks before Ian Robertson and the producer joined me at the 'business end' of the tour. I would be expected to hire a car at every stop and, whenever it was impossible to install an ISDN line at the hotel, I would be responsible for finding my way to the nearest South African Broadcasting Company station to transmit my material.

Those were the days when Radio Five Live was in the market for features – little clips of interview material topped, tailed and linked by a reporter in the field – and those were the days when the station's sports news editors felt that South Africa was still – to most Britons at least – a closed book. Perhaps it was a quiet summer in the UK as well, for they seemed keen to take any and every feature idea I suggested.

I was indebted to a new invention – the minidisc recorder. When I first joined the BBC the portable tape recorders were incredibly heavy. They used bulky and old-fashioned spools of reel-to-reel tape and if you wanted to record any material, you needed a hefty microphone and a pair of padded headphones. If you wanted to edit it, you needed a wax crayon, a razor blade and various colours of sticky tape. When I rejoined the corporation, I was issued with an audio cassette tape recorder – much lighter to lug around and less prone to operator-clumsiness but next to useless when it came to editing. Just before the Lions tour, however, I was instructed in the mysteries of the minidisc. As small and as light as a pack of cards, with discreet in-ear headphones, the player was far smaller than the microphone that was issued with it. But I could record, mark, move, edit and play back tracks at the push of a button. If I had material to play out from one of the local radio stations, I could save myself time and the BBC money by marking the relevant material and moving it to the front of the disc. If I was compiling a feature, I could identify and mark the relevant tracks and even perform a rough edit before sending them back to Broadcasting House in the correct order. It was close to magic, and enabled me to produce an absolute flood of material.

It wasn't difficult to come up with ideas. Even though the Lions hadn't visited South Africa for nearly two decades, they were mobbed everywhere they went. Thousands of fans turned up to greet them at Jan Smuts airport on their arrival in Johannesburg and I remember getting some great NATSOT (natural sound on tape, i.e. general background noise) from the arrivals hall, as well as a snatched interview with Sports Minister, rugby nut and former Robben Island inmate, Steve Tshwete.

Although some of the euphoria engendered by World Cup success only two years previously had dissipated, I was still able to get some great material from young black players in the Transvaal, development officers in Natal and a coaching clinic in Soweto. And it wasn't just the Lions that hogged the headlines in a sports-mad country. I talked to Shaun Pollock about cricket in Durban, listened to Thabo Mbeki address a rally in Cape Town about South Africa's bid for the Olympics and talked to several competitors in South Africa's annual long-distance running event, the Comrades Marathon from Pietermaritzburg to Durban.

The first Lions tour of the professional era produced fascinating stories of its own. I was part of the largest-ever media contingent to follow a rugby tour, while an extraordinary army of travelling fans also made it the best supported – and the Lions' determination to get absolutely everything right led to huge logistical problems. There was no question, for instance, that the Lions would be caught short when it came to equipment. Kit sponsors Adidas were determined that no member of the 47-strong tour party should ever be seen in anything other than branded gear, while Doctor James Robson insisted on bringing with him every piece of medical equipment that he or any of his assistants might need throughout the eight weeks of the tour. The Lions determination never to be without a scrummaging machine meant that Nigel Horton, my former England teammate, had to trundle a machine across the republic by road, while baggage master Stan Bagshaw had to pack up and oversee the safe transportation of several tons of gear – as well as all the players, coaches and support staff – by air. Because it was an old-fashioned tour, with the Lions never staying in one place for very long, he had to do it twice a week for seven weeks.

If the length of the tour – 13 matches in just over eight weeks – was a nod in the direction of tours past, everything else about the Lions tours of Africa in 1997 was set to break new ground. Sponsors who had been persuaded to part with huge sums of money to bankroll the tour were determined not only to get their money's worth but to make sure that the world knew all about their investment. Their representatives attached themselves to the tour with specific instructions to maximise the photo opportunities. Training sessions were enlivened by the bizarre sight of invariably very young, often unathletic and usually inappropriately dressed, PR people rushing around pitches whose markings they clearly didn't understand in a desperate bid to get sponsors' banners they could barely carry into the background of any shot that the photographers might be contemplating. These same earnest individuals often interrupted interviews, so that sponsors' logos could be clearly visible on the subject in front of the camera. It reached the height of surrealism in only the second match of the tour when the Lions had squelched to a hard-fought 18-14 win against the Border Bulldogs in East London. The winning captain Rob Wainwright presented himself to the television interviewers immediately after the game; his face streaked with mud and his shirt and shorts a uniform brown.

Even though he were starting to shiver with the cold and wet, he took the time to speak intelligently about the Lions' shortcomings and generously about their opponents' qualities and then, as I was next in line waiting to do an interview for the BBC, he turned patiently towards me. At this point the PR whiz kids stepped in – not with a tracksuit to keep him warm, but with a baseball cap for his head. His shirt was still a filthy, dirty brown, but on the top of his head was now a spanking new piece of headgear with the sponsor's logo proudly, vibrantly proclaiming its message – on radio.

Fran Cotton was the ideal Lions manager. He'd played on two tours and had huge respect for the concept, traditions and ethos of the Lions. He'd been to South Africa many times and had earned the unqualified respect of both the Springbok fans and the rugby establishment. A very successful businessman, he had a keen analytical mind, a mile-wide competitive streak and a winner's mentality. He also understood that his public role was to be a figurehead for the tour party, to deflect the pressure from both the players and the coaches, while his private role was to impose and enforce the highest behavioural and playing standards. He was also great fun to interview.

So too were coaches Ian McGeechan and Jim Telfer. There isn't a more knowledgeable coach in world rugby than Ian McGeechan, nor one capable of getting their knowledge across as articulately or as enthusiastically to both players and media. Jim Telfer knows everything there is to know about forward-play, and in 1997 delighted in living up to his image as the dour Scot, the bad cop to Geech's good 'un. And when it came to his relationship with the media, Jim gave as good as he got. By the end of the tour, when perhaps we were all a little demob happy, I joined the other journos in a pick-up game of touch rugby while the Lions were going through some set moves on an adjoining pitch. Jim was spotted at various times looking in our direction. As we all packed up and headed back to our hotel one of the journalists asked him what he thought of our rugby playing efforts. 'I've always thought,' said Jim, 'that I'm a pretty good judge of rugby. I can look at players and can immediately tell the good ones. It's the same with coaches. I can tell who's got it and who hasn't. All I can say after watching you rugby writers play rugby, I can immediately tell why you write such crap!'

And as far as the relationship between players and media was concerned, this was the golden crossover period between the unstructured, slightly shambolic amateur period when players and journalists breathed the same air but were not compelled either by their editors or their sponsors to speak to one another, and the choreographed, slightly paranoid present when the two interact much more but communicate much less. In 1997, we more often than not shared the same hotel as the tour party and could socialise with them in the same way as our predecessors had done. No doubt influenced by the positive open nature of Cotton, McGeechan and Telfer, they were happy to embrace their responsibilities to the media. As a result we had almost unfettered access to the players and I, as an enthusiastic reporter looking to make his mark with relatively new employers, was able to build up a wonderful working relationship with men who, though we didn't necessarily know it at the time, would figure hugely in my broadcasting career.

There were 17 English players on the tour. Most, if not all, of them would feature in Grand Slams and Grand Slam attempts in the near future. Nine of them would win World Cup-winners' medals in 2003. All of them would spend hours of their lives in front of my microphone. If old-school rugby men like Lawrence Dallaglio and Jason Leonard were absolute naturals, new kids on the block Austin Healey and Will Greenwood had a wit and a sparkle about them that almost invariably ensured a memorable interview. Matt Dawson – a treasured colleague in the latter days of my career and now a consummate broadcaster in his own right – won't mind me saying that in the early days at least he came over as chippy and maybe a little too full of himself. Martin Johnson has likewise transformed himself. As tour captain in 1997, he was the player I interviewed most, but even at the end of the tour I wasn't sure that familiarity had bred anything other than discomfort. I had first interviewed the Leicester lock when he flew out as a replacement on the 1993 tour. It was clear then that, while he might acknowledge the media as a necessary evil, he couldn't quite see why an adjective should be used at all. In 1997, he still acted as though he would rather stick pins in his eyes than answer our questions. He had a habit of avoiding eye contact in one-to-one interviews and he rarely went out of his way either to make an interviewer comfortable or to offer more than was strictly asked for. I look at him now, in his role as England manager, and marvel at how far he has come.

And the media, too, were a joy to be around. The hard-core of us were there for the full eight weeks – touching down at Johannesburg airport at the same time as the Lions in the third week of May, acclimatising with them at Umhlanga Rocks in Durban and criss-crossing the Republic in their wake before leaving the way we'd arrived on 5 July. Of necessity, we were in each other's pockets – sharing the same hotels, attending the same media briefings and working, by and large, to the same rhythms. I'd heard plenty of tales of previous tours when relationships – even between journalists in the same organisation – had broken down irretrievably. I was fully expecting squabbles between, for instance, the red tops and the broadsheets, or the television crews and the print media. I had envisaged us all jealously guarding our stories, protecting our sources and sharing nothing. I could not have been more wrong.

An extraordinary solidarity was in evidence right from the beginning. I was delighted to be part of a group that met to select a 'Question of the Tour'; the winner came after a training ground spat which had seen rival hookers Mark Regan and Barry Williams trading punches, and is best delivered in the broad Ulster brogue of the then *Guardian* rugby correspondent Robert Armstrong: 'Would you say, Fran, that encouraging your players to beat each other up in practice is a key plank in your strategy to beat the Springboks?'

I was delighted to be elected judge in the journalists' court. We reckoned that if the players could have their own court to sit in judgment over perceived breaches of tour etiquette, then we could too. Sporting a dressing gown and a wig, I sat on a throne consisting of a hotel armchair perched precariously atop a table. Insisting that at all times I should be referred to as 'M'lud', I dispensed even-handed justice to all miscreants brought before me. These included the *Daily Telegraph*'s Brendan Gallagher who had been accused of wasting good wine when he had, quite inadvertently, spilled a bottle of red into my lap at dinner one evening. In a masterful defence strategy, Chris Hewitt of the *Independent* summoned the Lions tour doctor James Robson. James gave his professional opinion that – as I was due a hip replacement operation at the end of the summer – I was quite obviously suffering from osteoarthritis. He also admitted that recent medical research which proved that the antioxidants to be found in red wine had a beneficial effect on conditions such as arthritis. Hewitt's argument – that Gallagher had merely been a little overzealous in applying the alcohol directly to the affected area – was too ingenious to refute. Case dismissed.

I was delighted, too, to inaugurate Higgy's Tours. I was acutely aware that – although there was no getting away from the fact that we were in South Africa to do a job – we also happened to be spending eight weeks in one of the most beautiful and intriguing countries on the planet. I was also acutely aware that if we were to do our jobs properly, we could never stray too far away from the Lions and that there was hardly a day when we would not either be travelling or attending media briefings. The chances of looking around were few and far between. Which is why, when we had a rare day off in Cape Town, I tracked down a minibus driver with an encyclopedic knowledge of both the history and geography of the Cape Peninsula and persuaded him to give a guided tour of the area to me and any of the other journalists who wanted to come along. It was a magic experience, which I was determined to repeat, if I got the chance, on future tours.

Of course, the icing on the cake was that the Lions won the series. It tasted even sweeter because they weren't the better side. Underdogs going into the first Test in Cape Town, they snatched an extraordinary win after Matt Dawson sold an outrageous dummy at the start of the second half to score the decisive try. Outplayed in the second Test in Durban, they relied on nerveless goal-kicking from Neil Jenkins just to stay in touch, and a cheeky drop goal from Jerry Guscott to nick the result – and steal the series. Outscored by five tries to two in the first two matches, they conceded another four in the 'dead rubber' at Ellis Park.

Not that the Lions were too bothered. The last week may have been a bit of an anticlimax and that final Test, which the Springboks won emphatically, 35-16, may have been a more accurate reflection of the strength of South African rugby, but as players and media celebrated in a traditional all-night party in Johannesburg, most of us were beyond caring.

CHAPTER THIRTY-THREE

JUDGE ME ON THE WORLD CUP (1997–99)

It was hardly the finest moment of my journalistic career.

'Hey, Higgy, look at this. He's had his ear bitten!'

The speaker was the future chief executive of the RFU, John Steele, then director of rugby at London Scottish. 'He' was the Exiles' flanker Simon Fenn. The three of us were in the crowded dressing room area at the Recreation Ground, home of Bath Rugby Club. I had a microphone and minidisc recorder in my hand. Instead of switching them on to get the rugby scoop of the year, I asked two entirely inappropriate questions: 'Don't they wear gum shields anymore?' and 'Have you seen Jon Callard?'

In my defence, I wasn't thinking straight. The *Sport on Five* editor had asked me to get an interview from the Bath camp to explain why the club that had dominated the English game for the last decade and a half – the first team to do the double, they had won the cup ten times in 14 seasons and the premiership six times in eight – should have had such a struggle in beating second division London Scottish in a Tetley Bitter Cup tie. I had clambered down the iron ladder which was the only way in and out of the press box at the Rec, fought my way through the crowds that were heading across the pitch and milling around the clubhouse and traded on my long acquaintance with the dressing room attendant to secure a place just inside the door. I had to play back the interview before the end of the programme, and time was likely to be tight. No one had made any fuss about the injury to Simon Fenn during the game – in the press box you can usually tell when players or match officials believe anything untoward has happened – and, call me naïve if you like, I couldn't contemplate any situation where one rugby player would take a bite out of the face of another. Actually I had no defence.

The fallout from the Fenn affair was bitter and protracted. The Australian-born player had to have surgery on his ear while Bath prop Kevin Yates, the man accused of the biting, was suspended for six months – despite protesting his innocence. In the weeks to come, I took a fair amount of ribbing from my colleagues but was relieved to discover that journalists at the post-match press conference were unable to secure any direct quotes. Once the accusations had been made – and immediately refuted – neither club felt able to make any further comment. And, while some commentators tried to argue that such violence was an inevitable consequence of the game going professional, others were quick to point out – citing the Ollie Waldron-Ross Cullen incident in the match between Oxford University and Australia in 1966 – that ear-biting was not unknown in rugby.

Bath were damned by association. They were also squirming with embarrassment as a fly-on-the wall documentary charted their implosion the previous season. But they still managed to win the Heineken Cup final on the last day of January 1998 in what was one of the most extraordinary club matches I have ever seen. Most of the 37,000 fans at Bordeaux's Stade Lescure had been convinced that holders Brive were strolling towards a second successive title. The French players obviously thought they had the game in the bag as, at 15-6 ahead in the second half, they won a series of penalties inside the Bath 22. Rather than take three points by kicking a penalty, they sensed that a try would kill off any faint hope left to Bath, and opted for a series of set scrums. Six times they locked horns on the Bath line – and six times Bath held them out. On the seventh, they won a penalty. Not that I'm an expert, but as an act of scrummaging bravery it has only ever been equalled in my experience by a six-man England pack against the All Blacks in Wellington in 2003. Bath went on to win and, at the same time, pulled both their season and the Heineken Cup out of the fire. The relief on the face of Bath coach Andy Robinson as I conducted the live post-match interview for *Sport on Five* was as palpable as the joy of the fans, whose exuberance all but drowned out our words.

There was absolutely no doubt that in three short years the competition had taken root in the hearts of the rugby public. The great and the good in the game were also captivated. I remember getting up early on the morning of the final to interview England coach Clive Woodward at his hotel on the other side of Bordeaux – the most convenient time and place for me to pick his brains for a radio documentary on the latest developments in the row between clubs and country.

Woodward was caught in the middle of the dispute, but he also had his own axe to grind. His employers, the RFU, wanted to put the players on short-term contracts and lease them back to the clubs. The clubs asserted they had primacy of contract, and flexed their muscles by threatening to withdraw players from England's summer internationals. Clive knew that if he was to have any chance of hauling England up to the level of the SANZAR countries he would need the clubs and the union as well as the players to buy into the dream. He was horror-struck at the idea of going on tour without his big guns.

Although we both came from RAF families, had been born only four months apart in the same county, and both went on to play for England, Clive and I had rarely appeared on the same rugby field – although he had rather embarrassingly shown me up at an under-23 training weekend at Bisham Abbey. When I'd been sent to interview him for the BBC when he was appointed to succeed Jack Rowell in the summer of 1997, I'd found him both highly articulate and hugely likeable, scarcely able to contain his enthusiasm for the job and full of theories about how it could be done. And he'd launched himself into it like a human tornado.

Which was probably just as well because his first four games in charge were against Australia, New Zealand, South Africa and New Zealand again in the space of four weeks. If it was the sort of itinerary demanded by the harsh new world of professional rugby, it was also the sort of workload that would make even an experienced, seen-it-all before Tri-Nations coach go white around the gills. For an international ingénue such as Clive it was Mission Impossible.

By the time I got to talk to him in Bordeaux, England had picked up the Triple Crown, scoring an average of more than 40 points a match, and now, for a tour that could only have been devised by a sadist with a very poor idea of geography, Woodward was having to prepare a team to face all three southern hemisphere nations again. And it was almost certain that – partly through injury and partly because of the war between clubs and country – he would have to do it without most of his senior players.

In the end, 15 key players, including Johnson, Dallaglio, Richard Hill and Mike Catt, stayed at home as England embarked on the 'Tour to Hell' – with Tests against Australia, New Zealand (twice) and South Africa. They were hammered 76-0 by the Wallabies in Brisbane, before going down 64-22 and 40-10 to New Zealand and, at a rain-drenched Cape Town, losing 18-0 to the Springboks. It was the harshest of lessons, though perversely – with future World Cup-winners Jonny Wilkinson and Josh Lewsey making their debuts on that tour and Phil Vickery earning his stripes in the utmost adversity – the tour itself may well have accelerated England's progress.

I missed England's first Test in Dunedin – joining the tour party just in time to catch the fallout from Danny Grewcock's sending-off – because the BBC required me to stay in Australia to cover Scotland's two-Test tour. I missed the trip to South Africa as well, not because the BBC no longer wished to intrude on private grief but because the summer schedule was too tightly packed to warrant commentary from Cape Town. Scotland lost 45-3 in Sydney and 33-11 in Brisbane, which meant that in four weeks I had seen four humiliating defeats for British teams with an average scoreline of 48-8. With the next World Cup just over a year away, there were very few reasons to be cheerful.

But 76-0 was too much to stomach. The clubs realised that it was in nobody's interests for England to be the laughing-stock of the rugby world and softened their stance. The RFU members concluded that England's reputation would plummet still further if the clubs' threat of a 'Premier League' style breakaway became a reality and sued for peace with the clubs.

If the Mayfair agreement was meant to bring 'peace in our time' the appointment of Francis Baron as Chief Executive of the RFU was meant to bring prosperity. It did. When Baron joined, after a highly successful career at WH Smith and First Choice Holidays, the RFU was saddled with a huge debt from redevelopment of Twickenham's West Stand and, in his words, 'teetering on the verge of going bust'. He was tasked with turning things round financially and commercially. And there was no doubt that, despite criticisms that he was ruthless, abrasive and had little understanding of – or feel for – rugby, that's precisely what he did. When he left his post in 2010, the RFU was a flourishing multi-million pound business worth £150m with a turnover of £119m and annual profits of £9m. Twickenham had been completely rebuilt and an international match at the state-of-the-art 80,000 capacity stadium – complete with hotel, health club and conference facilities – was by then worth £10m to the RFU in terms of sponsorship, television revenue, ticket sales and corporate spin-offs. Back in 1998, when he was appointed, it was less than £4m.

Whatever he said subsequently – the parting of the ways was vitriolic and Baron was famously likened to the captain of the *Titanic* – Clive Woodward owed a huge debt to his chief executive. From the outside it seemed at times that no matter how madcap a scheme, and no matter how much it cost, all Clive had to do was to argue some benefit for the England team and Baron would find a way of delivering it. An extra coach? No problem. A visual awareness specialist? Consider it done. A lawyer to travel with the team? The same. From the proliferation of support staff to the provision of extra large beds for the larger players, to the cosseting of their wives and girlfriends, nothing was too much trouble for Woodward. Hardly anything was too expensive for Baron.

The immediate concern of both men was the World Cup. The good news – for Baron – was that even though Wales was the host nation, England would stage nine money-spinning matches, including both semi-finals. The bad news – for Woodward – was that England would have to qualify. Woodward had already made himself a hostage to fortune by demanding he be judged on England's performance in the World Cup. To get there, they would now have to negotiate two extra and potentially tricky fixtures – against the Netherlands and Italy.

It wasn't that difficult to beat the Netherlands – England romped to a 110-0 victory at the McAlpine Stadium in Huddersfield – but Italy almost upset the applecart at the same venue a week later. This was only the fifth win of Woodward's 14-match reign. With Australia – still crowing from that 76-0 victory in the summer – and South Africa – on course for a world record run of consecutive victories – due at Twickenham before the end of the year, the odds against him improving that ratio were small. By the same token, the odds against him even being in a position to be judged on the World Cup should have been large.

But Woodward was a great communicator: to Baron, who by and large funded his schemes, to the media, who hung on his every word, and more importantly to the players, who were beginning to get his drift. There were signs that the message was starting to get through when England put in an astonishingly committed defensive display against the Wallabies, scored the only try of the match and only lost out when John Eales stroked over a late penalty from the touchline. When England went toe-to-toe with the world champions a week later – and held their nerve for a 13-7 win – it wasn't difficult to buy into the idea that a corner had been turned, that England and Woodward were on their way.

And there was no turning back for me, either. While Woodward was using that first big victory to demand even more from his players, I was using the diagnosis of MS – at the start of 1999 – to demand even more from myself. As detailed elsewhere, it was more important than ever to put myself about in the world of rugby journalism. On top of my job at the BBC, I was already doing some voice-overs in London for an independent production company and writing a weekly online column. Now, I was at the stage of subconsciously seeking out the most demanding assignments just to prove I could manage them. In the spring of 1999 that meant immersing myself in the Heineken Cup – the boycott by English clubs and Ulster's stirring charge to the title meant that there was even more travelling to do than normal – attending innumerable club media briefings in pursuit of quotes for my weekly package for regional radio and packing in as many Premiership and knockout matches as I could.

In the week of an international, I would quite often find myself travelling in two different directions on the same day. My first priority was England, and Tuesdays more often than not saw me flogging eastwards up the M4 when it was still dark. Clive Woodward was a stickler for punctuality and quite obviously a morning person. With his minute attention to detail, he clearly had a lot to pack into international match preparation and his fondness for getting the team announcement – and the media briefing it entailed – out of the way as early as possible had us scurrying from our homes in the early hours of the morning in order to get to the Pennyhill Park hotel in Bagshot, Surrey, in time for a 10 a.m. start. In those early days he would announce the team on a Tuesday and preview the match on a Friday, while his players would be available to the media on a Wednesday, and his captain would hold a separate briefing on the Thursday. Then, of course, there was the match on Saturday.

England were increasingly worth the effort. The team that would ultimately taste World Cup glory in 2003 was starting to take shape. The Hill-Back-Dallaglio combination had taken root in the back row, while Martin Johnson and Jason Leonard were inked in to the front five. Matt Dawson and Will Greenwood were firmly established behind the scrum while Mike Catt and Austin Healey had picked up a stack of caps in different positions. And fresh into the mix in 1999 came Jonny Wilkinson.

The precociously gifted Newcastle player had gained one cap as an 18-year-old replacement wing against Ireland in 1998 – and, of course, he'd featured in the 76-0 thrashing in Brisbane and the 64-22 reverse in Dunedin – but now, in the last season of the old century, the last season of the Five Nations Championship, and while still a teenager, he emerged as a fully-fledged match-winner and a vital cog in the England machine.

Even though Wilkinson kicked a record 60 points in his first full season, England missed out on a Grand Slam when they were mugged at Wembley. But they weren't the only ones guilty of counting chickens. As I left the commentary box with five minutes to go, I was busy formulating questions that would give avid soccer fans Clive Woodward and captain Lawrence Dallaglio a chance to refer to great days at the stadium for England's footballers. By the time I reached the players' tunnel, Scott Gibbs had scored a try, Neil Jenkins had converted it and Wales had won the match. While I had to completely rephrase my questions, arch-patriot Ian Robertson was in no doubt how he should start his summary of one of the most extraordinary matches in the history of the Five Nations' tournament. No mention of England's heartbreak, or Wales' jubilation. Instead, live on the World Service, to a potential audience of hundreds of millions, he began his match report with a reference to a team that hadn't even taken part. 'So Scotland are the Five Nations' champions...!'

Apart from extending the number of participants in the Rugby World Cup 1999 to 20, and insisting that all but four of them play their way into the tournament, the IRB also decreed that it, and all future World Cups, should be played in the northern hemisphere autumn. The rugby season – every four years at least – was now officially endless. European teams – and the journalists who followed them – would have to snatch their summer holidays when they could; there would be precious little time between a summer tour and the World Cup warm-up matches and, when the World Cup was over, the next season would be in full swing.

In 1999, England had a short tour to Australia for the Centenary Test, two warm-up matches against scratch teams made up of players from the Premiership, two Twickenham internationals against the USA and Canada and several weeks with the Marines to get themselves ready for the tournament. The BBC excused me from the England tour but only so they could use me to commentate on some of the group matches in the Cricket World Cup that was being staged in England that May and June, and only so that I would be available to commentate on the Wales-South Africa match that was slated to mark the official opening of the Millennium Stadium. Somewhere in the midst of all that, Lawrence Dallaglio resigned as England captain after allegations of drug-taking and drug-dealing surfaced in the *News of the World* and – with Ian Robertson on his way to Australia – I found myself being hauled into a breakfast TV studio to comment on the case. I felt desperately sorry for Lawrence. I'd always found him to be hugely likeable, outgoing and open as a human being and a joy to interview as England captain. If ever there was a man to embody rugby's core values, it was Lawrence. I was personally relieved when the drug-taking charges against him were dropped, though I was professionally livid when Five Live chose to send a news reporter to cover the story instead of me. I was confident that I was a good enough journalist to ask all the tough questions and I believed that my long acquaintance with the key rugby people involved would give me – and therefore the BBC – an invaluable inside track. Looking back now at the brittle and prickly character I was then, I can only wonder. Was I so determined to prove that I wasn't affected by MS that I had to take on and prove myself at everything? Was it a resurrection of the arch-competitor I once had been? Or was it the angry flailing about of a man who'd lost a lot of the certainty in his life and didn't know how to deal with the loss or tell anyone about it?

And when the World Cup finally kicked off I was just as tightly wound. Although I was technically the third commentator after the matchless Bill McLaren had been seconded from television, I felt that it was not only right but also necessary that I should end up covering more matches than anyone else. I was at the Millennium Stadium as a commentator for the opening match on 1 October and at the same venue, as a pitch-side reporter, for the final on 6 November. In between I commentated on ten matches and was pitch-side reporter for that extraordinary semi-final at Twickenham when France came back from the dead to beat New Zealand. I scooted about between media briefings, training sessions and matches in England, Scotland and Wales and, of course, was there in Paris when South Africa's Jannie de Beer fired over five quarter-final drop goals to boot England out of the competition.

England may have been found wanting in the World Cup – although, to be fair, after being bludgeoned by Jonah Lomu and New Zealand in the opening match, they were always going to have to endure an energy-sapping quarter-final play-off just days before their last-eight match – but I hadn't. The public jury might still have been out on Clive Woodward's demand to be judged on the World Cup but my private jury was satisfied. I had taken the stresses and strains in my stride. No one could tell that I had MS, and I still clung to the belief that there was no need for them to find out. I hadn't got MS licked, but I was definitely ahead on points. Perhaps I could keep it that way for ever?

PART SEVEN
MS
(UNDERSTANDING)

CHAPTER THIRTY-FOUR
THE LOCUS(T) OF CONTROL

I couldn't resign, but I could re-negotiate. I was stuck with life membership of a club I never wanted to join and unless a cure could be found for MS – still unlikely to be any time soon – I was locked in for the duration.

But I could alter the terms and conditions. I didn't want to conform to anybody's expectation of how a man with MS should behave, and I didn't want to fit into any neat pigeonhole. After going through a period of denial, I now acknowledged that I had a condition that was incurable, progressive and increasingly debilitating, but I wanted to have it on my terms. How I reacted to the difficulties thrown up by MS was down to me and no one else. I could choose the methods to counteract its effects and I could choose how I lived my daily life in the knowledge that from now on MS was going to be my constant companion. And in being proactive rather than reactive, in making positive decisions about what I did – and also how and why I did it – I was empowering myself in a way which felt good. In the jargon of some of the MS publications, I was buying into the 'efficacy of self-management'. In the words of psychologist Julius Rotter, who invented the concept, I was regaining the 'locus of control'. It felt good.

What this actually meant was that I gave myself permission to make informed choices about what was good for me. By empowering myself in this way, I found that not only was I helping to boost a sense of self that had taken a battering with the initial diagnosis but also that I was taking ownership of my life – MS and all. It was a win-win situation.

And the first proactive choice I made was to come off beta interferon. I had campaigned long and hard to win the right to take the drug. I had clung onto all the positive evidence that suggested that, although it was never trumpeted as a cure, beta interferon had proven success as a disease-modifying drug. But I also discovered that, for me, the side effects were horrendous, and, after nearly two years, showed no sign of getting any easier to tolerate. And I was beginning to suspect that I was investing too much emotionally and psychologically – as well as financially – in the drug. A little part of me was arguing that because it cost a lot, was difficult to administer and came with awful side effects, the drug must be doing me some good. For the same reasons there seemed little incentive – or energy, or resources – to do anything else about my MS. I was falling into the trap of relying on the drug to make my life better, while at the same time abrogating my own responsibility.

It was about this time that I came across a book entitled *The Art of Getting Well*. It was written by David Spero, an American nurse who himself had MS, and promised a way of 'maximising health when you have a chronic illness'. It struck a chord, particularly with its insistence on five key principles: put your life before your illness, listen to your body, conserve your energy for healing, change the things that harm you and get the help you need. The book reminded me of the credo I'd signed up to and was in danger of forgetting: 'I've got MS, it hasn't got me'. Here was encouragement to live that as well as spout it.

England's tour to Argentina in 2002 was the catalyst for ditching the beta interferon. I'd lugged an insulated pouch – containing syringes, 'trigger', ice blocks and 'sharps' box – all around Australia on the Lions tour the preceding summer and felt some relief, when explaining the kit to conscientious customs officers, that at least we spoke the same language. My Spanish, however, was non-existent and Argentinian police had a reputation for asking questions afterwards rather than before. I had no intention of falling foul of the law. I had already been toying with the idea of taking a holiday from the drug. The trip to Argentina made up my mind for me. I decided to leave the drug kit at home.

And instantly felt better. I was no longer covered in bruises. My right arm – the easiest part of my body to get at with the syringe – had taken the brunt of a thrice-weekly injection which invariably caused irritation and was often accompanied by bruising – while my thighs and occasionally stomach had also doubled up as pin-cushions. They all started to look and feel normal again. Far more importantly, I got to savour Monday, Wednesday and Friday mornings. Previously the mornings-after-the-jab-before had been miserable as I emerged from the deep flu-like symptoms engendered by each injection. Now, I was waking up with a clear(er) head, light(er) limbs and at least a modicum of energy. It was wonderful, and when I got home, I had no hesitation in prolonging my drugs holiday indefinitely.

The same philosophy informed a revised attitude towards therapy. I'd started going to the MS therapy centre in Nailsea fairly often for hyperbaric oxygen treatment, some physiotherapy and the odd aromatherapy massage. But I'd always tried to fit my treatment in around my work and frequently, particularly at the height of the rugby season when matches and media briefings came thick and fast, had done without it for weeks on end. Now inspired by *The Art of Getting*

Well, I made a resolution to put myself first for at least one day a week. Monday became Me-day. I informed the BBC that from now on I was going to ring-fence that one day of the week and I was going to devote it to treatment. Although it was a perfectly reasonable request, although Monday was generally a light news day as far as rugby was concerned and although the BBC were more than happy to oblige, I still felt as if I was letting them down. I had somehow deluded myself into thinking that I was the only BBC radio reporter capable of covering a rugby story properly and that if I wasn't available to cover it, it wouldn't get reported at all. More alarmingly, I had deluded myself that it mattered far more that I was out there reporting every rugby story in the country than that I took a regular day off, or attended to my MS. It was a thoroughly unhealthy attitude to take and it took real ill health to shake me out of it.

And, of course, it did me the power of good. The taking of affirmative action gave huge psychological benefits to me as a person, while the carving-out and protection of a fixed period of off-duty time was invaluable to us as a family, and to Jeannie and me as a couple. By focusing on Monday as a day both to recover from energy-consuming weekends that often featured matches on both days, and to recharge the batteries for the challenges ahead, I derived immediate and lasting benefits. I was in control or, more importantly, I felt I was. And I was taking steps to remain there.

Self-management also involved taking a long, hard look at my diet. I'm ashamed to admit that I didn't do an awful lot more than look at it. The rugby media circuit inevitably involves early starts and late finishes, snatched coffees and meals on the run. It's as difficult to stay in control of what you eat as when you eat it. I was aware that every nutritionist who had ever conducted research into MS at the very least recommended a low-fat diet and the avoidance of red meat, alcohol and refined sugars. But I had neither the desire to draw attention to myself by making demands about what I would or wouldn't eat, nor the time or discipline to search out alternative food. I wasn't the only journalist to find that the bacon butties served at RFU press conferences were irresistible but at least I was feeling guilty about eating them. I was certainly more aware of what I was putting in my mouth and I was moving, albeit slowly, towards a better diet.

Exercise was easier to fix. The big problem with MS is a lack of energy. In the past I had attempted to train with only a fraction of the intensity of my sport-playing youth, and wiped myself out for days. Now though I was going to follow David Spero's advice and listen to my body. I wasn't going to even attempt to follow the routines of my pre-MS existence. I was going to find exercises more suited to my new reality.

One of the first things I tried was horse riding, reputedly good for developing and retaining strength in the core muscles, good for balance and recommended for posture. These were all areas that I felt needed work on, and I duly took myself off to a riding school deep in the Somerset countryside. I stuck it for four weeks before deciding that I wasn't, never had been, and never would be a horse-lover. Not that I had anything against any of my mounts or any of the other stable occupants. It was just that I didn't have anything for them. While others had cooed, stroked, offered sugar lumps and talked of the horses as individuals with near human characteristics, I had failed to see where they were coming from. When they talked of the rapport between man and beast and the bond that rapidly builds up between horse and rider, I nodded my head and willed myself to believe. But I never felt anything less than uncomfortable when I was anywhere near the horse chosen for me, and never anything less than vulnerable when I sat on his back. Not only did that leave me a long way from the ground at the mercy of a beast with whom I had failed to bond but also, as my right leg was so unresponsive and inflexible, quite unable to fling myself clear in the face of any problem. I would either have to ride side-saddle, or quit. I quit.

Pilates was also aimed at the core muscles and for a few months I had an instructor come round to our apartment to guide me through the intricacies. The first thing to say about Pilates is that it is a lot more demanding than it looks. The second is that it's so far removed from conventional sports training that if you've got used to the one, you'll probably find it incredibly different to adapt to the other. I knew how to do repetitive rhythmic exercises and I thought I knew when and how they were doing me good. If I needed any convincing I had the sweat and the aches to prove it. The dictum 'no pain, no gain' doesn't apply to Pilates, and I just couldn't get into the right mindset.

There might, however, have been some sort of psychological barrier that prevented me from exercising at home. Perhaps it felt like cheating. It certainly didn't feel right.

What did feel right, however, was the mixture of Pilates and personal training provided by Kinetic Fitness, a gym that had recently set up under some railway arches at the back of Temple Meads railway station. Under the supervision of an encouraging and incredibly knowledgeable physio by the name of James Ross I could have an hour-long session with just the right combination of stamina work – on stationary bike or rowing-machine, strength – using the weights machines, balance – on the kinetic table and co-ordination – using a combination of medicine balls, Swiss balls and footballs. We'd even, if the weather was half decent, work on walking, making sure that my reluctant right leg re-learned the correct techniques and didn't compromise the other muscles in the body by operating incorrectly. It was demanding, interesting and fun. And it was another way of hanging onto what inevitably became known as the locust of control.

Getting the muscles to perform better was one thing. Getting them to respond correctly was quite another. My right leg and my right arm both had a tendency to spasm in direct and seemingly wilful contradiction of the messages my brain was sending. My arm would lock rigid as I was reaching for a plate or a cup on a high shelf. My leg would jerk straight as I was attempting to go down steps. The first put the crockery at risk. The second compromised my balance. After threatening to pitch headlong downstairs several times, I only felt safe if there was a banister to hold onto. When there wasn't – most noticeably down to the commentary boxes at Twickenham and at the Millennium Stadium – I would abandon all semblance of dignity and 'crab' my way down by grabbing onto the backs of seats. At other times I risked coming a cropper if I didn't concentrate on what my right leg was doing. Before MS I could have second thoughts halfway through an action – as in suddenly remembering my keys were on the side table and turning round to pick them up before the front door closed on me – but now my balance would go completely. Once, when trying to complete that very action, I took a real tumble, cannoned off the table and in falling put my shoulder through a plasterboard wall to the airing-cupboard. The mistakes, when I got it wrong, were undignified, painful and costly, but I was determined to do everything in my power to get it right.

I was, however, fighting a losing battle with sleep, or lack of it. To put it bluntly, I wasn't getting much in the way of quality shut-eye. Often I got into a good sleeping position only for my right arm to tighten up painfully underneath me. When I changed position my right leg had a tendency to shoot out violently in an involuntary action that at times left me with a painful cramp in the calf or the hamstring. I tried various drugs, including baclofen, but found that although the side effects were nowhere near as powerful as I'd experienced with beta interferon, it still took a long time for them to wear off. If I took baclofen or an equivalent at night I was what I could only describe as 'zombified' the next morning. My brain functioned, but only slowly. I felt as if I was in a thick fog where reality was slightly blurred and all thought and concentration required huge effort. I came to the conclusion that I would rather have the physical discomfort than the mental confusion.

According to anecdote, cannabis was the answer. A lot of people with MS swore that a regular joint kept their muscles relaxed and spasm- and tremor-free. It also helped them to sleep. And, so they wrote in the MS forums and magazines, it had no adverse side effects.

My instinctive reaction had been to reject the idea. I'd read all the arguments for and against legalising the drug and as much as I could be persuaded of the merits of decriminalising it, I also felt that it must have been prohibited for a reason. As a parent I was a natural target for all the horror stories but I also knew two couples personally whose lives had been turned upside down by their sons' addiction. I knew both Adam and Dan had tried cannabis and, desperate not to give them even the slightest hint of an excuse for indulging any further, I'd rejected their well-meaning offers to get me some cannabis to try.

But the spasms and the tremors were continuing to deprive me of sleep and, if there was a way I could do it legally, I resolved to see for myself why so many in the MS community were so enthusiastic about cannabis. I opted for

Canna-choc, which was advertised in the MS magazines as a bar of chocolate infused with cannabis resin. The firm supplying the stuff stipulated that they could only supply one bar per order, which seemed reasonable enough, and also insisted that although they weren't allowed to charge for the product, they were allowed to accept 'donations', which seemed both naively optimistic and open to abuse. As it turned out, it was also open to prosecution, although not before I had sent for and sampled a couple of bars – with no obvious beneficial effects.

But Jeannie's sleep was also being affected and she was determined to give cannabis another chance. In her work at the Picture Business, an art consultancy firm in Bristol, she came into contact with a lot of artists. From one of them she acquired some 'weed', infused it in some hot water and, describing it as a camomile-based herb tea, persuaded me to drink it before bedtime. No effect. She made it stronger, and then stronger again, but we still didn't get any better sleep.

But the important thing was I was taking positive steps to make my life better. That some of them didn't work was to some extent immaterial. I was deriving immense psychological benefit from taking control of my own life and I'm positive that helped in dealing with the downsides of MS. I wasn't walking very well and my right arm wasn't functioning very efficiently but I was doing my best to keep them working. My balance wasn't always reliable, my sleep-patterns were all over the shop and I was perpetually at the mercy of an extraordinary fatigue. But I was actively exploring ways of minimising my problems and maximising my resources.

For the first time in my life I had enrolled in counselling, and benefited hugely. I had originally seen a leaflet at the doctor's surgery offering one-to-one sessions for people affected by a terminal illness and been shocked to read in the small print that MS was included in that category. On reflection I supposed that in a sense that, barring a miracle cure, I am going to die with MS. I was also curious to see if talking over my fears, frustrations and anxieties with an impartial dispassionate observer might help me get a handle on my life as it now was and put my past as it had been into some kind of perspective. Over the course of nearly a year, all my rather macho assumptions about counselling were swept aside. Under the gentle guidance of the Haven counsellor, I was able to understand so much better what had made me the person I had been. More importantly, I was able to re-examine my relationships – with my wife, my sons, my family and my work – in the light of the person I had become. I was encouraged to take ownership of my emotions and not feel afraid or embarrassed to display them. And I was inspired to aim at living a life that, while acknowledging an emphatically able-bodied past and facing up to a fearfully uncertain future, was nevertheless focused on making the most of the present. And with that sort of impetus, and the support that continued to flow in my direction from family as well as colleagues, friends as well as strangers, there was little wonder that I was in can-do mode and my glass was always half-full. My condition may have been incurable but so was my optimism. If there was a way to make things easier and safeguard precious energy, I was committed to finding it and feeling better for doing so.

Little things were as important as the big ones. Because my right arm didn't always perform as precisely as I wanted it to, and because the fingers of my right hand had lost a lot of their sensitivity, I began to find it really difficult to put things into my right trouser pocket and even more frustrating trying to pull things out. I couldn't feel in my pocket for a specific item and I couldn't fish it out with any certainty. For the best part of two decades this had been the pocket where I kept things I would need every day, things like keys and coins and tickets. Now that I couldn't use it with any degree of reliability, I had to embrace a fashion accessory that was as far removed from my own self-image as it was possible to be – a man-bag. Blessed as I was with rounded shoulders, I had no choice but to wear it strapped across my body, and not answer to the predictable 'bus-conductor' taunts. But, whatever embarrassment I may have felt at wearing the thing more than compensated for the embarrassment I had felt whenever I fumbled in my pocket and came up with a handful of fresh air, or sent coins and keys and tickets tumbling to the floor. What's more, it saved time – and energy.

And once I'd decided on positive action to improve all areas of my life, there was no stopping me. I had started to worry that MS-related symptoms such as bladder urgency and difficulties in swallowing were starting to affect my commentary. Getting caught short in the commentary box is no joke even for able-bodied commentators. To wait until half-time before prising yourself out of your seat, fighting your way through the crowds and elbowing your way into the toilets is a test of the strongest bladder. I had already discovered with MS that once the brain has declared the intention to void the bladder, the message cannot be changed and the execution cannot be delayed – by even a few seconds. To calm my fears – and avoid accidents – I got the doctor to prescribe a drug that worked in the opposite way to a diuretic – only to discover that one of its side effects was to dry up the mouth.

Which was already causing problems. I found that I was losing my voice too easily during an exciting piece of commentary and I began to worry that as my MS progressed the tools of my trade would be the first to wear out. It appeared that difficulties I sometimes experienced while swallowing – caused by the involuntary contraction or relaxation of muscles in my throat – were also affecting my breathing. My vocal chords seemed to tire too easily and whenever I was tired or under stress, my voice seemed to me to be weak, thin and strained. I'd read plenty of articles about how MS affected speech and I'd met plenty of people with MS who had real difficulty in making themselves heard. I dreaded that happening to me, but I wasn't prepared to accept that sort of deterioration as inevitable and booked in for sessions both with a private voice coach and an NHS-funded speech therapist.

While the former was more concerned with finding out whether I could sing – and lost a certain amount of interest after reaching the conclusion that I couldn't

– the latter was a mine of information regarding exercises I could do to improve my breathing and precautions I could take to protect my voice. I made a mental note to keep my neck warm from then on, do a series of vocal exercises before every commentary and to eat at every opportunity before and during the match. The saliva produced by mastication would keep the vocal chords as lubricated as any drink – and wouldn't necessitate frequent trips to the toilet. Seven years later – muesli bars, wine gums and chocolate biscuits on the table in front of me – I began the commentary on the World Cup final in Paris, confident that my voice would last the course. Would it have carried me through a couple of Lions tours, two World Cups and dozens of equally important commentaries if I hadn't taken the steps I took? Possibly. Would I have been absolutely confident that it could do so if I hadn't taken such affirmative action? Probably not.

In my determination to do something positive about my walking difficulties – I was finding it increasingly difficult to lift and bend my right knee while my foot-drop had got worse – I volunteered to be a guinea-pig in a control-study on gait conducted by Leicester University and run out of the Bristol General Hospital. More importantly I went down to Odstock Hospital in Shaftesbury and got myself a prototype FES. The Functional Electronic Stimulator was basically a battery, which clipped on your belt, a couple of electrodes stuck to the front of your lower leg and a switch attached to an inner sole. Linking them all were electric wires, which you concealed inside your trousers. It was all very unobtrusive and initially all very successful. Every time I lifted my heel off the ground the pulse would kick in, sending an electric current between the electrodes, and the 'foot-lifting' muscle would be stimulated until the heel was next placed on the ground. When wearing the FES I saved a lot of energy and never felt in danger of tripping, but I was never entirely happy with either the wires which, unless I kept very still, had a tendency to get tangled up with each other and work loose from the terminals, or the electrodes which were difficult to site correctly and lost their adhesiveness whenever I became hot. Worst of all though, I was trialling the FES at a time when I was passing through a lot of airports and anti-terrorist security was at its highest. I didn't fancy my chances of explaining why I was attempting to pass through a scanner with a gadget that may have been entirely innocuous but looked incredibly sinister. I decided to wait until they'd invented a wireless version. In the meantime I would have to rely on my stick to help me negotiate short distances, my electric scooter to get around the stadiums and my car for anything else. The locus of control demanded I make informed choices about all of them.

CHAPTER THIRTY-FIVE
STICKS, BUGGIES AND THE SIX NATIONS

Think teenage children at their worst. Silent and unresponsive, they're never about when you want them and always under your feet when you do. On social occasions they lean awkwardly against the wall and, if you don't keep your eye on them, choose the worst possible moment to slide gracelessly, noisily and embarrassingly to the floor. That's Michael. Michael is my walking stick.

It wasn't always the case, but I now treat Michael (named after the German tennis-player Michael Stich) as one of the family. Wherever I go, he goes too. I have to know where he is at all times of the day and whenever I have to walk any sort of distance, I lean heavily on Michael.

It hasn't always been the same Michael. My first walking stick was a steel-tipped hiking pole which first saw the light of day two years after my diagnosis on the Lions tour of Australia in 2001 – and was banished to a charity shop after the tip got stuck in a pavement crack on Sydney's Circular Quay and sent me sprawling. I have a 'best' Michael for posh occasions, while an early Michael was bent out of shape after being caught between burly ex-Wales international Emyr Lewis and a tip-up commentary seat at Kingsholm.

I resisted the idea of a stick for some time. Life on the road as a rugby reporter often entailed lugging around an ISDN kit (headphones, microphones, mixer box and connecting cables) as well as the usual tools of the trade (notebook and minidisc recorder). At times I needed to take an overnight bag too. I didn't have enough hands for a stick as well. But, after scraping most of the leather off the right toe of a new pair of shoes during a long and painful stumble to and from the Municipal Stadium in Toulouse, I knew that I had to make room in my life for a stick.

As with so many MS decisions, once I'd made it, I kicked myself for not doing it sooner. It was not just that a stick helped me save energy and therefore walk much further; I had also found it useful in making other people aware that I needed space, especially in crowds. Before people might have nudged into me and knocked me off balance, now they keep their distance – and I feel safer. Though that didn't help the waitress who tripped over Michael in a Scottish hotel and crashed to the floor with a tray full of drinks. Nor did it help a bunch of French journalists at the Stade de France. The commentary boxes are banked particularly steeply at the stadium while the law of gravity is the same all over the world. It only took an inadvertent nudge to launch Michael like a high-velocity spear straight towards the oblivious *écrivains*.

But Michael really came into his own at the greatest sporting occasion of my life – the Rugby World Cup final between Australia and England in Sydney on 22 November 2003. For all matches leading up to the final, I had been able to conduct my post-match interviews for Radio Five Live in the dressing rooms – easily accessible by lift and buggy. For the World Cup final itself, however, it was decreed that the interviews should take place on the pitch.

'No drama' was the confident assurance of the stadium authorities: they would allow me to drive the buggy onto the playing surface at the end of the game. But it rained, and the marching bands had turned the approaches from the stand to pitch into a mudbath.

So my buggy was denied its moment of glory in front of 80,000 spectators and tens of million television viewers as, heavily supported by Michael, and all the time broadcasting live on Radio Five Live, I lurched, microphones and minidisc recorder in hand, headphones on head, from hero to hero. The whole process lasted maybe half an hour but it was 30 minutes of intense mental concentration (to make sure I responded to the cues from John Inverdale up in the stands and the producers back in the studio in London, while all the time asking the right questions) and intense physical pressure (to maintain my balance, wielding two microphones, and stumble back and forth into the throng of players in search of new interviewees). When I got back onto the buggy I was totally knackered and my right leg went into spectacular and uncontrollable tremor. But when it mattered most, Michael had come up trumps.

The 2003 World Cup was the first time I took a buggy overseas. It wasn't my first electric scooter. I'd decided early on that one of the best ways of saving energy was to ride wherever possible. The bustle of my youth, when I thought nothing of walking a mile or two between assignments, had long since evaporated, to be replaced by foot-drop, fatigue and loss of balance. But the life of a rugby reporter inevitably demands plenty of foot slog and it hadn't taken long to realise that I needed some battery-operated assistance.

I chose a buggy rather than an electric wheelchair for two reasons. I found wheelchairs incredibly fiddly, and was not at all confident of my ability to manoeuvre the chair with any degree of dexterity. Of far greater importance, however, was a highly personal antipathy. I just did not see myself as a wheelchair person. For some completely illogical reason I felt a wheelchair would mark me out as being disabled in a way that a scooter would not. I suppose I associated electric wheelchairs with the likes of Superman actor Christopher Reeve. I tried. Believe me I tried. I tried to like a state-of-the art model, with three computers on board that could hoist me up to eye-level, could go up and down stairs like a giant high-tech slinky and cost something like £25,000. Nearer the other end of the scale, I did try a Power Trike – an ordinary wheelchair with the option of attaching a power-pack and steering column at the front – but it was stolen from the underground garage below our apartment block. When the insurance refused to pay up on the grounds that the communal garage wasn't secure enough, I went with my gut-instinct. Wheelchairs were for profoundly disabled people. It was vital for my sense of self-worth to draw a line between them and me. My buggy had to be an aid to getting about and doing my job. It wasn't a replacement for my legs. I knew that down the line I might lose control of those limbs but I didn't (wouldn't? couldn't?) go anywhere near that particular black hole. Not then. Not yet. Please God, not ever.

I soon discovered that there was no such thing as a perfect buggy. My first electric scooter was small enough – when dismantled – to fit into the back of the Peugeot hatchback that came with the job. But it wasn't powerful enough for the workload I imposed on it. Its range was limited and it struggled with anything above a gentle slope. It was an unattractive colour – at that time makers of disabled equipment had an unhealthy fixation with an unappealing shade of maroon – and it suffered heavily from owner incompetence. Although I sat down on it and held onto handlebars, I still approached getting about as if I was on foot. Stepping on and off pavements is easy and natural if you're on Shanks's pony. If you're on a buggy with wheel clearance of only a few inches it's clumsy, awkward and plays havoc with the undercarriage. In the early days of buggy-driving I often got it wrong, ramming into pavements that were just too steep for the wheels, dropping off kerbs straight onto the metal chassis, crunching the fibreglass trim on boulders, bollards and shop doorways.

Plan ahead. That's the golden rule for operating an electric scooter. Anticipate the bumps in the road, the height of the kerb and the steepness of the slope. Avoid muddy puddles and thick grass. Sounds simple enough, doesn't it? It wasn't for me. In my able-bodied past, I had scurried from A to B in the shortest possible time by the most direct route and never gave more than a moment's thought to the process. I had utter confidence that however difficult the journey I could complete it, however daunting the obstacles I could overcome them. Whatever happened I would have the physical resources to deal with it. It was sensible and logical to plan the perfect outcome but it was more important to be able to react and adapt when the plans came unstuck. I learnt the hard way that when you're disabled it's the other way round. It's next to impossible to improvise your way out of trouble. If you don't pay attention to the three Ps – planning, preparation and precaution – you're likely to end up completely four X-ed.

Sometimes even the best-laid plans went wrong. Reasoning that if we got there early enough, we'd find plenty of free parking near the new Stade de France we pitched up in plenty of time for the France-England match of 2004 only to be directed in ever-widening circles away from the ground. We hadn't reckoned on the surrounding neighbourhood being quite so dodgy – it seemed highly likely that when we returned at the end of the match, we'd find the car resting on four piles of bricks – and we hadn't planned on leaving the car at least two kilometres from the stadium. The extra distance – coupled with my own stupidity in not re-charging the buggy overnight – left me badly short of juice.

Ever the optimist, I reckoned that there might just be enough power left if I went at a snail's pace. But I wasted precious energy in finding out that my chosen exit from the stadium was locked, and by the time I had travelled 400 metres from the stadium, the battery had given out. Fortunately, several of my press colleagues were heading in the same direction. They pushed for a while, and so did a drunken English fan. (God bless you, Sir, I would have asked you your name, but I wasn't sure that you knew the answer!) I still did not quite make it to the car, but by then my BBC Radio colleagues had overtaken me, and could bring the car to me.

In Cardiff it wasn't the parking that was the problem, but the lifts. Before the game, the main lift from car park to media centre was, for some reason, shut down. The next closest lift was on the other side of the ground – a journey of some 600 metres each way. To avoid that, a colleague shinned up the stairs, found an official, brought him down in the lift to collect us and extracted the promise that assistance would be forthcoming for the rest of the evening.

Which it was, until five minutes after the final whistle. At that point I discovered that while every lift at the Millennium Stadium was operated by a steward with a key, the stewards rarely hung around at the end of the match. Broadcasters, with summaries, wrap-ups, interviews and de-rigging to do, rarely finished work until an hour after the final whistle. When the latter got to the lift – on the sixth floor – the stewards were halfway down their first pint. Again, a colleague had to go downstairs to fetch a stadium official, before the final descent could begin.

It was even worse when I was required to do the post-match interviews. One season, leaving the commentary box just before the end of the match, I was able to persuade a man with a key to let me descend to the dressing room level. A 600-metre buggy ride there and a 600-metre buggy ride back left me needing simply to get the minidisc on which the non-live interviews had been recorded back to the commentary box on the sixth floor. Guess what? No steward, no key, escalators set to only go down, and 12 flights of stairs to climb!

Fortunately, those troubles at the Millennium Stadium were only temporary. In subsequent seasons the lines of communication with friendly, helpful officials became ever more refined and, save for the clamber down concrete steps and into the commentary box, the whole experience became as painless as possible.

Murrayfield was a doddle for a disabled commentator. Parking was never an issue, and I could take my buggy up in the lift and park it within feet of the commentary box. The distance from lift to players' tunnel was equally short and it was never obstructed by either home or visiting fans. In terms of energy expended Murrayfield was the best of all the Six Nations' stadiums.

Twickenham wasn't bad either – ramp access to pitch-side, tarmac pathway to the tunnel area for pre- and post-match interviews, and lifts to the broadcasting area. The only downside for me was an absence of a handrail on the 12 or so steps down to the commentary box, although cheerful stewards offered any number of shoulders to lean on.

But I had a pass to the West Car Park and everywhere else I needed to go. The Radio Truck, the Media Centre, the players' tunnel, the Good Health Bar (venue for the post-match press conference) and the ERIC room (bar for former internationals) were on the level, or accessible by lift. My seat in the commentary box was adapted to allow easy access, while a special clamp was fitted to hold my microphone and the windshield directly in front of my position was removed so that I could open up my laptop in comfort.

Lansdowne Road was a different matter altogether. The thought of covering a match in Ireland used to make me go weak at the knees. Once the MS took hold, it just made me go weak. The craic was still the same. I'd always found Dublin warm, welcoming and lively. On international weekends it was ten times more convivial. But it was hell for buggy-users. I admit straight away that I was to blame for not charging up the battery before the episode that turned producer Ed Marriage into a latter-day Molly Malone, as he had to push my buggy through the streets broad and narrow in the early hours of the morning after a convivial outing with fellow journalists. But I didn't invent the difficulties for the disabled at the old Lansdowne Road.

Mercifully, the old stadium has now been rebuilt. I hope the new one is easier for those with any kind of infirmity. I accept that there may not be too many disabled commentators in the future but even those with all their faculties and all their energies deserve better than we experienced at the old Lansdowne Road. The commentary box itself was cramped and tatty and there was no way to access it except by climbing a staircase of 40-odd steps. To get any post-match interviews meant leaving the box even earlier than usual, or the steps would be packed with departing spectators. Working my way back against the flow was an ordeal to which I never looked forward. It was a question of fighting to get a hand on the banister and hoping that I didn't meet an outsize Irishman coming down.

Rome also lived down to its reputation – at least for buggy-users. Narrow pavements, cobblestones, endless steps, few ramps, lunatic motorists and crazy scooter riders combined to make life difficult, if not downright dangerous, for those of us trying to get around on four little wheels. The Stadio Flaminio also makes no concessions to disabled journalists. The commentary box is up steep banister-less steps, the dressing rooms down a narrow staircase.

Getting to Rome had its own problems. For the first match of the Six Nations championship in 2004, the powers-that-be at the BBC decided that, because I live in Bristol, it would be easier for me to travel to Rome from my local airport, even if that meant changing planes in Paris. Bad idea.

Experience told me that I should forewarn the relevant airlines, Air France and Alitalia. Alitalia was fine, Air France impenetrable. They claimed that, because I asked for wheelchair assistance at Charles De Gaulle airport, it would be impossible for me to make my connecting flight (an hour and 15 minutes later). I would have to buy another ticket on a later departure from Paris to Rome. I asked why, if, according to them there would be enough time for me to walk between the relevant arrival and departure gates, there would not be enough time in a wheelchair.

'Because we need more warning,' they said.

'I am phoning seven days in advance of my flight,' I replied. 'That gives you well over 150 hours to get a wheelchair in position. How much more warning do you want?'

It cut no ice. Air France refused to acknowledge that they were discriminating against me because I had asked for wheelchair assistance and, in a comic 30-minute interlude, refused to let the words disabled or discrimination pass their lips.

The actual transfer was impeccable. A smiling Frenchman in a van with a specially converted hydraulic lifting platform met me from the plane, drove me what seemed like several kilometres around the airport and waited with me at the terminal entrance, before handing me on to a wheelchair attendant who pushed me to the correct departure gate.

They were even more efficient on the way back. My plane was late leaving Rome and, especially in view of my telephone conversation with Air France, I was resigned to missing my connection. But the 40-minute gap that was left acted as a challenge to the ground staff at Charles de Gaulle airport. They pushed me through the terminal at breakneck speed, fast-tracked me through passport control and raced me to the departure gate – only to discover that the flight was cancelled due to an air traffic controllers' strike. Abandoned at the departure-gate, I was left with a six-hour wait, and only Michael to help me get around.

I did a test run for the 2007 competition by taking my buggy and some ramps to Marseille for one of England's warm-up matches. Ignorance was bliss. In my excitement at getting a good deal on the train, I failed to factor in either the complication of getting from Gare du Nord, where the Eurostar arrives in Paris, to the Gare de Lyon, whence the TGV leaves for Marseille, or the possibility that there wouldn't be a big enough taxi at the station in Aix-en-Provence, our base for the weekend. To solve the first problem I decided to drive the buggy. After all, I reasoned, it was a beautiful August afternoon, the distance between the stations wasn't that big, and anyway I spoke French and could ask directions. How difficult could it be? Extremely difficult was the answer, especially if you're also taking broadcasting equipment, suitcase and a couple of ramps.

With my suitcase over my shoulder, the ISDN kit in a trolley-bag, which I dragged along one-handed behind the buggy, and the ramps strapped either side of my seat, I must have counted as one of the more bizarre sights seen in Paris that summer. But I made it to Gare de Lyon with minutes to spare, enjoyed a breathtaking trip through the French countryside and got to Aix only to discover that the station was deserted and the only taxi-driver left that evening had room in his car for neither the ramps nor the buggy.

But the whole point of the exercise was to get a clearer picture of just how things would work with my buggy as an integral part of Radio Five Live's broadcasting operation. Could we travel comfortably with as many as four people – we'd have to take a summariser as well as correspondent Ian Robertson, producer Ed Marriage and myself – and all our gear, and the buggy and the ramps, between airports, hotels and stadiums? The answer was no. There wasn't a people-carrier large enough to carry absolutely everything, all the time. On the other hand the occasions when we would need to would be relatively few and far between. We would only have all our gear and all our suitcases on journeys to and from airports. We didn't all need to arrive at every stadium at the same time. There were taxis to be hired and lifts to be begged. We could get round the 'buggy problem'.

We may have been confident that we could cope on the World Cup journey round Australia – and subsequent trips to New Zealand, South Africa, Italy and France – but individual airports were often found wanting. Careless baggage handlers left the buggy badly damaged – needing costly and time-consuming repairs – both at Auckland and Johannesburg, while thoughtless airline staff left it 'airside' at Brisbane Airport and disappeared for the night. Rarely did the process of labelling, loading and retrieving the buggy go smoothly. Rarely was wheelchair assistance regarded as anything more than an unwanted chore. The number of times I would arrive early, check-in and surrender my buggy to the baggage handlers only to be left stranded on a bench in the check-in hall for anything up to an hour while a wheelchair attendant was found, was matched only by the number of times the wheelchair assistant would, while friends and colleagues on the same flight were enjoying a coffee or an amble round the shops, rush me through to the departure gate and dump me like a sack of unwanted spuds. Once, I got off the plane at Hong Kong to find that a pre-arranged wheelchair had been commandeered by an inebriated fellow-passenger who, sensing that his legs were too rubbery to get him into the arrivals hall, declared that yesh, he was Alashtair Hignell. He'd promptly collapsed into the wheelchair and demanded to be taken to the nearest bar! On another occasion, I descended the aircraft steps to find that the promised wheelchair was unavailable and that what the stewardess described as an 'easy 15-metre walk' in the terminal was closer to ten times that distance.

Control the controllable. The favourite mantra of Clive Woodward's England doesn't apply to airline flights. It applies even less if you're disabled. I was finding that I was helpless if just one airport official got something wrong. I was bitterly frustrated when rules replaced common sense and lack of imagination precluded progress. But I couldn't do much about it. I had chosen to continue working and I had chosen to take my buggy with me and rely on wheelchair assistance. I would have to take the rough with the smooth.

CHAPTER THIRTY-SIX

CARS, TRAINS AND CHARITIES

Planks catapulted into the air as the car smashed through a wooden picket fence, ploughed into a very full car park, ricocheted from car to car and smashed into the back of a very solid Range Rover. The Range Rover lurched forward and crunched into a brick wall. Then silence.

It was a shortcut I had taken hundreds of times, a right-left dogleg across a Redcliffe side street before joining the ever-heavy traffic out of the city. I had looked left, towards the city, and right from which direction a fierce winter morning sun was poking between the office buildings giving every indication that this would be a good day for the filming I had promised to do at Gloucester in addition to my interviews for Radio Five Live.

I'd heard screeching brakes to my left and, realising that I had pulled out straight in front of an oncoming car, I'd accelerated and swerved in a desperate attempt to avoid the collision. But the other car clipped mine and shunted it across the pavement, narrowly avoiding a street sign and a startled pedestrian, straight into the fence.

I got out of the car and surveyed the wreckage all around me. The driver of the other car and the pedestrian approached rather nervously through the huge hole in the fence. At least, thank God, they were all right. I was a little unsteady on my feet, but whether that was from the shock or the MS was difficult to tell. As we exchanged details, office workers from the building in front of us poured out to inspect their cars and to offer assistance. One of them brought me a cup of tea, and was reprimanded by her supervisor. He felt that tea would somehow compromise the results of the breathalyser test that he assumed I would have to undergo as soon as the police arrived.

That thought had honestly never occurred to me but when it did I offered up a silent prayer that I hadn't touched a single drop of alcohol the night before. Even so, I found it really difficult to blow into the breathalyser with sufficient strength to satisfy the police officers, who by this time had arrived and were taking statements. I was further spooked when one of them assured me that failure to give a proper sample would be construed as a refusal. I tried again. Still not enough puff to register. I started to panic and wondered aloud whether the MS was in some way inhibiting a large enough intake of breath to register on the machine. A second policeman concluded that there was something wrong with the brand-new breathalyser, rather than with me. He produced another one. I blew – and was demonstrably below the limit.

That was a huge relief, but it did not satisfactorily explain how I had made such a mistake in the first place and had caused so much damage – apart from the fence which would need replacing, I had hit six other cars while my own was a write-off. I was pretty sure I had been momentarily blinded by the sun, but there was a gnawing doubt at the back of my mind that I had not been able to react quickly enough once I had got into trouble. At the best of times my right leg and my right arm did not respond either with sufficient speed or enough strength to the messages sent by my brain. Maybe the MS had dulled my reactions to a dangerous level? Maybe, if there was a next time, I would not be so lucky. More importantly, others might not be so lucky. I felt that it would be almost unbearable if I had even the vaguest suspicion that I had caused injury, or worse, because my reflexes, and my ability to react, had been compromised by MS. I didn't make the decision there and then, but that day was the last time I sat in the driving seat of a car. It was 13 January 2005.

But driving was a huge part of the job. As a rugby journalist, I was on the road four, sometimes five, times a week. I would drive the length and breadth of the country to training sessions, media briefings and matches. Most of the days were long, starting early and finishing well after dark. I was never a natural driver – I failed my test first time and didn't gain my licence until the age of 24 – but had grown to look upon time at the wheel as a necessary evil, a small price to pay for doing a job I loved. In the early years of my return to the BBC, I had barrelled up to Broadcasting House at least once a week for shifts at the office. As the job evolved I had struck up an agreement with Chris Hewitt, rugby correspondent for the *Independent* newspaper, to share the driving whenever our respective employers demanded we attend the same matches or press conferences. It was an agreement that worked well – Chris has a great sense of humour, an abiding love of rugby and is never anything less than good company – even after he rang me one day to renegotiate the terms. 'You know we agreed to share the driving fifty-fifty,' he began, 'I'm happy to stick with that, but only if you're happy to do the next three years!' It transpired that he had lost his licence for that length of time after himself falling foul of a breathalyser test.

The arrangement had continued during the 'MS phoney war' – the 16-month period from early 1999 when I knew I had an illness but was determined that no one else should even begin to guess. I had driven thousands of extra miles, particularly during the 1999 World Cup, when I had taken on all sorts of extra journeys in my stubborn determination to prove that I could defeat the incurable. But when I finally decided to be honest with the world about my MS, I also decided to be honest with myself about its effects.

Once I had identified fatigue as the number one enemy, it was a logical and, thankfully, simple step to come up with a way of reducing its effect. An occupational therapist from Access to Work got together with my BBC employers to work out just how much time I was spending behind the wheel and between them they concluded that the best way of helping me to do my job was to provide me with a support worker. We all recognised that there was no set pattern to my work, and that some working days were infinitely longer than others and that there would be a lot of waiting around at rugby matches and press conferences. We needed someone who could put up with my company during long hours of travel, wasn't totally turned off by rugby, didn't mind getting cold when the matches were on and was flexible enough to cope with early starts and late finishes. I was incredible lucky to find three absolute diamonds in Tony Paddon, an old friend from our early days in Bristol, Ron Hooper, who lived in North Devon but still never flinched when the working day started at the crack of dawn or finished after midnight, and Mike Worsley. Initially it was quite tricky for all of us. Other journalists didn't quite know what to make of the sudden appearance of a stranger in their midst. I felt an extra burden of responsibility in making sure that there was an extra pass at rugby matches, and extra coffee at press conferences. Tony, Ron and Mike didn't know what they could and couldn't do, or what they were expected to do. On the whole, however, the arrangement worked well. What I lost in spontaneity, I more than made up for in productivity. Without a support worker to drive me to matches and press conferences and, increasingly, to load, unload and even plug-in broadcasting equipment, I am in absolutely no doubt that I would not have been able to do the job as long as I did, or to the standard that I set myself.

In order to cart my buggy around more easily, I had persuaded the BBC to upgrade my company car, a Peugeot hatchback, to an 807 people-carrier. To begin with we used ramps to get the buggy in and out of the car before progressing to a hoist, which, with a special bracket attached to the buggy, did all the hard work for us. Initially, too, I had driven the shorter journeys myself after learning of, and having installed, a left-foot accelerator. This, of course, only worked with an automatic car and basically provided the option of swapping the position of the accelerator and brake. When I drove the car, the accelerator was on the left. A flick of the lever and it was restored to the normal position for Tony, Ron or Mike.

To get used to the new pedal arrangement, I had to report to the Disabled Living Centre in Bristol, take a series of lessons and pass a test. To begin with, it was extraordinarily difficult to override what, after dozens of lessons and years of driving, had become natural instincts. I had got used to jabbing my left foot down whenever I needed to brake. Now, with the pedals transposed, such an action would send the car screeching forward. I had got used to pushing hard with my right foot to accelerate out of trouble. Now, that would only bring me to a grinding halt. I needed to learn to keep my right foot well away from the pedals and trust my unnatural left foot to work the controls, while at the same time doing everything else as normal. The lessons were demanding and the test was intense but it was still, to my way of thinking, a small price to pay if I could retain some independence, some freedom of choice as to where I went and how. That is, until the crash, and my decision to give up driving.

But that was my choice. I wasn't forced to give up driving, I chose to. The distinction was hugely important to me. It meant that, however limiting the MS was, I was still in charge. As long as I still retained the locus of control, I retained the optimism that I could deal with anything that the disease threw at me, and I felt good about myself. Until I got to Paddington Station.

'You can't take that on the train,' said a woman in a cream-coloured woollen coat as she pointed at my buggy. The queue of passengers edging slowly past the ticket-inspector ground to a halt.

'You can't take that on the train,' she repeated. I smiled pleasantly, and explained that not only could I take my buggy on the train but that I had done so that morning on my way up from Bristol.

'You couldn't have done.' She motioned me out of the queue and directed me to her office. 'It's not allowed.'

When I pointed out that I had made the journey on a regular basis – she refused to believe me. When I insisted that all I wanted to do was catch the train home, she shrugged. I was perfectly at liberty to use the return ticket I had already bought, she said, but only if I left my buggy behind. Paddington Station wouldn't be responsible for it and she had no idea where it might be safely stored until I came to pick it up by car. I was also perfectly at liberty to put my buggy in a taxi and take it back to Bristol that way, but the rail company had no intention of reimbursing me. That, as far as she was concerned, was that. It was only when one of her colleagues recognised me from previous journeys and another remembered me from the train that morning that she shifted at all. In the circumstances she felt that the train company could bend their policy so I could get home. Just this once.

Faced with the prospect of never being allowed to use the train again, I spent the graciously conceded journey composing a letter of complaint to the train company and fired it off by e-mail when I got home. And became embroiled in a farcical dispute which has still not been satisfactorily resolved.

Getting the train company to respond to my e-mail was a triumph in itself; at one point I received a communication saying that just because they had acknowledged receipt of my e-mail that didn't necessarily mean they'd read it.

The rest of their logic was – and is – totally impenetrable. It boils down to this: the law demands they carry wheelchair passengers, but it does not specifically demand they carry electric scooters. It's easier for them to impose a blanket ban than it is either to use discretion or to apply the same criteria they use for wheelchairs. The largest wheelchair they will carry is 120cm long. My buggy is shorter. It's also lower, narrower and more manoeuvrable than the standard electric wheelchair. Yet it's banned just because it's an electric scooter. The only way I am permitted to take an electric scooter on board a train in the West Country is if I dismantle it first and stow the pieces in the luggage rack. My argument – that because of my MS my energy, strength and balance are all compromised – cuts no ice. I have had several dialogues with the train company but the policy-makers refuse to budge.

By pleasant contrast, the railway staff are almost invariably pleasant, cheerful and helpful. One of the huge ironies of the whole story was that when the *Bristol Evening Post* picked up on it and wanted to set up a few photos at Temple Meads, the platform attendants rushed to the ramps at our approach and had to be dissuaded from putting me on a train for which I had neither a ticket nor a desire to catch!

Despite these ridiculous and unhelpful setbacks, I still felt incredibly lucky. Lucky to be doing a job I loved, lucky to have the support of caring employers and lucky to have the assistance of sterling support workers. I was also lucky to be able to use my standing to fly the flag for other disabled people. If I hadn't been disabled, for instance, I would not have been approached to help compile a disability audit of all the Premiership clubs on behalf of sponsors Zurich.

This was a great example of benevolent sponsorship, an indication that the sponsors were as keen to make a solid and lasting contribution to the game as a whole as they were to be seen in the shop window, splashing their cash amongst the elite, getting their name on television and in print. Zurich had commissioned the report in the realisation that the 1995 Disability Discrimination Act would acquire extra teeth in 2005, and with the awareness that most Premiership grounds had been built with little concern for the comfort of ordinary spectators and no understanding whatsoever of the needs of the disabled. To make sure that the needs of the latter were fully represented, they'd asked wheelchair-user David Thomas, a fast bowler for Surrey and Gloucestershire before being diagnosed with MS, to join me in inspecting the facilities at each of the clubs, and they asked report-writing expert Sarah Weston to present our findings.

Our visits served only to confirm our suspicions. There was not a club in the Premiership that was not sympathetic to the needs of disabled spectators. There was not a club in the Premiership that did not promise to do everything in its power to help fans in wheelchairs, with hearing difficulties, with impaired vision, with limited mobility. They were all aware of their obligations and of how and where improvements could be made. Many of them were proud of the relationships they enjoyed with their disabled fans, and were only too eager to help when requested to do so. But there was not a single club in the Premiership that tried to solve problems before they arose. Not one of them was proactive. Not one of them set out to attract disabled fans by promising a match-day experience to treasure. Not one of them felt the need to make changes, unless they were asked to. All of them were reactive, waiting for a complaint or a request to be made before deciding to take action.

Though they were prepared to make life as tolerable as they could for disabled fans, they were all reluctant to go the extra mile. I couldn't help feeling that they missed a trick. As a group the disabled in this country have enormous spending power. It seemed to me that it made sharp business sense as well as being the right thing to do to make a play for their custom. Perhaps, as the population as a whole gets older and the number of disabled inevitably increases, the penny will drop. I hope it will drop soon. In any case, the report was shelved. I never found out why.

I hope that my efforts on behalf of other people with MS will reap more obvious rewards than my efforts on behalf of disabled rugby supporters. Right from the earliest days of my diagnosis, I had resolved to use whatever profile, contacts and communication skills I had to work on behalf of MS charities. I had immediately volunteered my services to the MS Society and one of my first public appearances for them was as their non-running captain at the London Marathon in 2001. An interview with Kate Battersby produced a double-page spread in the *Evening Standard* and a live race-day interview with Sue Barker on BBC1.

I had also accepted an invitation to become president of the appeal for the Nerve Centre, a new MS facility in Bristol. The local health trust had agreed to make an old stable block at Frenchay Hospital available to house the facility, and would both maintain it and help to staff it with doctors, specialist nurses and therapists where necessary as long as the charity raised the money to renovate and re-equip the building. The Nerve Centre appeal was launched with great fanfare. Fundraiser John Nichols worked tirelessly to open up sources of finance. I, and others, donated speaking fees, addressed Round Tables, and persuaded Rotary clubs and golf clubs to adopt us as their annual charity. Gloucestershire's cricketers pledged their support, and so did footballers from Bristol Rovers and Bristol City. I even cajoled the organisers of the satellite tennis tournament at Redland to allow me to address the finals day crowd and take a bucket collection. And all the guests at my parents golden wedding celebrations were invited to make a donation to the Nerve Centre instead of a gift to the couple.

It looked as though we had reached our £1.25 million target through a series of interlinked promises from charitable foundations such as the John James Trust but it all went belly-up when the health trust found a gaping multi-million pound hole in their budget. As a result, they could not give any assurances that they would be able to guarantee the future of any sort of hospital on the Frenchay site. In fact, they hastened to inform us, any promises they might have made were null and void.

The trustees saw no alternative but to close down the charity and try to recoup some of the expenses we had already incurred in drawing up architects' plans and making the old stable block safe. But that meant taking the trust to court and risked a further depletion of the funds we had so enthusiastically raised. We had to offer to give donors back their money.

The climbdown was humiliating and personally embarrassing. I had banged the drum loud and hard for the Nerve Centre, used up a lot of energy and called in a lot of favours. I had believed fervently in the concept and done everything in my power to make it happen. But I had nothing to show for my efforts and felt that I had let down the MS community in Bristol.

But that didn't stop me, much later on, from agreeing to be the figurehead for another appeal to the people of Bristol – to build a new MS therapy centre at Bradley Stoke to the north of the city – and it didn't stop me at the time from agreeing to become the patron of the MS Resource Centre.

The MSRC is a small national charity with an unashamedly positive approach to the problems of life with MS. It offers a 24-hour-a-day, seven-days-a-week, telephone counselling service to anyone affected by anything to do with multiple sclerosis. Its mission, through the mouthpiece of both its website and its bi-monthly magazine *New Pathways*, is to provide people with all the information they need to make up their own minds about what to do or what not to do. The charity is determinedly non-judgemental and seeks to present all the latest information about drugs and diets, treatments and therapies, gadgets and gizmos, benefits and horror stories, as well as government policy and the latest scientific research in a fair, well-informed and easily digested way. Above all it tries to accentuate the positive, to emphasise that although dealing with the disease is no picnic, life must go on.

It's a philosophy with which I wholeheartedly agree with and I continue to bless the day I came into contact with the remarkable people at the MSRC. Jeannie and I had been invited up to London for a fundraising lunch for the charity, organised by David Thomas and his wife Louise. They had been exploiting their contacts in the corporate hospitality world for some time now and wondered if we would like to attend the lunch as guests of the charity? We were instantly bowled over by the warmth of the welcome extended to us not just by 'Teddy' and Louise, but also by the officers at the charity.

The charity's CEO at the time was Lawrence Wood. He is, and I can believe always has been, larger than life. At 6 foot 4, he has the build of a heavyweight boxer and the bearing of an army officer, both of which he was. He also has a warmth, openness and a heart-warming sense of compassion that made him such an outstanding CEO of a charity that, although obviously made in his image, had, and has, so much more to offer. He and his partner, soon-to-be wife Rachel, made an instant impression on Jeannie and myself. Here was a couple with the same sort of values, similar experiences and above all an outstanding sense of humour. Here were people who had been through a lot but were still optimistic and full of joy. Here were people we could relate to.

Thankfully, they felt the same because within months Lawrence had invited me to become a patron of the charity. I was delighted to accept, although initially I was concerned about distance. The charity is based in Colchester and I didn't have the time or the energy to flog across the other side of the country.

'No worry,' said Lawrence, 'the role we had in mind for you was that of figurehead. We would like it if you could turn up to some of our events – we have for instance a big presence at the London Marathon – but we are not going to insist on anything. We just think you are a perfect fit for our charity.'

So did I, but I didn't want to be entirely passive. I volunteered immediately to write something for *New Pathways* magazine – whose brilliant editor Judy Graham had, I discovered, been a BBC radio producer in another life – and promised to do all I could to keep my diary free for the London Marathon.

It felt good. The MSRC was to be a great fit. I had made new friends and branched out in a brand new direction. I still had MS and I still suffered from the most dreadful fatigue, but I'd found a way to keep doing the job I loved. I had had to make some concessions to the MS but equally I had been able to change the way in which I did things – to my advantage. I may not quite have wrested back the locust of control, but I hadn't completely surrendered it either. Things could have been a whole lot worse – but they weren't. I could settle for that.

MICROPHONES
(AFTER MS)

CHAPTER THIRTY-SEVEN
NEARLY THERE (1999–2001)

In the space of 12 hours, the most extraordinary day of my broadcasting career became the most breathtaking night of my life.

This Tuesday morning in November 2000 should have been like the previous one, in that Clive Woodward was due to announce an England team to the media. The previous Saturday, England had beaten Australia with a last-gasp try from Dan Luger and we didn't expect there to be any changes to the team for the encounter with Argentina.

But we arrived at the Pennyhill Park to discover that Clive didn't even have a team. The players had gone on strike and most of them had checked out of the hotel. Clive was fuming, but restricted himself to the bare facts. As a result of an ongoing dispute with the RFU, the players had refused to play against Argentina. He was hoping that they'd see sense after another meeting with their employers but if they didn't, he couldn't see how any of them could be picked for England again. Not if he had anything to do with it.

Clive took it personally. How else could he take it? This was his team for whom he had repeatedly gone out on a limb. They had benefited hugely from his insistence on excellence off the pitch as well as on it. The luxury training base at Pennyhill Park had been his idea, while the occasion on which he had used his own credit card to get the team upgraded from what he considered was a sub-standard hotel in South Africa was the stuff of legend. He had fought the mandarins at the RFU to get what he felt his players deserved and now they had walked out.

Andy Robinson – by now coach to England's forwards – typified the attitude of all proud Englishmen. He just couldn't get his head round the idea that any rugby player could even think about turning down the chance of playing for his country. True, he had played for England – as I had – in an amateur era when you knew what you were getting into and you knew what you were getting out of the experience. Playing for England was its own reward, being selected made all the sacrifices along the way worthwhile. Even though the game was professional, even though it had become a livelihood, he couldn't see how that had changed. To be honest, I couldn't either.

The players' spokesmen – Lawrence Dallaglio, Matt Dawson and Martin Johnson – were therefore at pains to stress just how much playing for England meant to them and to emphasise that they had not taken their decision lightly. But the bottom line was that the dispute was all about money.

In part it was about performance-related pay. Francis Baron hailed from a business world where such practices were the norm and he knew that the RFU as a business would only succeed if the England team were successful. He wanted the players to be on huge win bonuses but a low basic match fee. The players argued that the size of the win bonus would make no difference to the way they approached the game and the recent match against Australia would have perfectly illustrated their point. If the kick-ahead from which Dan Luger scored his injury-time try had bounced the other way, England would have lost the match rather than won it, yet they would have put in no less effort. How therefore could there be such a disparity between the rewards on offer?

And in part it was to do with intellectual property rights. Not so long ago rugby players would not have known what these were, and they would have cared even less. But their agents had pointed out that every time the RFU used a picture of an England player to promote an international, and every time they got the team to sign shirts for a sponsor, they were exploiting the commercial value of the England team. And the only people not gaining from this arrangement were the players themselves. They felt entitled to a payment that would reflect their part in the process and, after being fobbed off repeatedly by the RFU, had finally run out of patience. They had, so they'd informed us, refused to sign merchandise the previous week, refused to attend the sponsors' pre-match dinner and worn sponsored tracksuits inside out at training in an attempt to get the RFU to the negotiating table. But talks had broken down again, and they saw no option but to go on strike.

The cynical could argue – and did – that it was highly convenient that the players should choose to jeopardise a match against Argentina rather than the Australia and South Africa matches on either side of it, and they could nod knowingly when the players went out of their way to say that they had no gripe with the sponsors but only with the RFU. But there was no doubt the matter was serious. On Tuesday afternoon, the England players made it clear that they were not going to turn up to face Argentina at Twickenham on Saturday.

But, as I filed piece after piece for the understandably frenzied news networks, and as I raced across London to appear live in the Television Centre studio, I had a much more pressing concern. Would they turn up at the Café Royal that night? Ian Robertson's wonderful and instinctive reaction to the news that I had

MS was about to bear fruit. He had organised a fundraising dinner at the Café Royal and worked his magic on the great, the good and the wealthy. He had conjured stunning auction prizes out of every conceivable hat and persuaded just about everybody in the world of rugby to take a table. And he'd even got Clive Woodward to promise that he and the England team would attend. But would they? After their walkout from the hotel that morning, the players had ostensibly gone home. If Clive was going to have to find another team by the weekend, he had other things to be doing. The RFU might also deem it advisable to absent themselves from an event that was bound to attract all my friends and colleagues in the media, while the latter would make their excuses and leave if another twist in the story demanded their presence elsewhere.

But they all turned up, and I will bow to no one in my admiration for the way all the protagonists managed to put aside their differences and all the media managed to stifle their instincts long enough to turn the dinner into a runaway success. It's true that dozens of paparazzi and TV crews were camped outside the Café Royal to catch the arrival of the players and nearly as many stayed to see them go. It's true also that at the dinner there was constant movement between tables, huddles were constantly formed and reformed and there was a fair number of mobile phone calls. But, huge credit to all concerned, not one of them appeared to let the crisis detract from their participation at the dinner – or other people's enjoyment of the occasion.

Robbo was in overdrive – magnetic, effusive, persuasive – while World Cup-winning captain Francois Pienaar did an extraordinary turn as a guest auctioneer. Writing about the event some ten years on still brings tears to my eyes. At the time I was an emotional wreck, almost speechless with joy and gratitude and appreciation of the extraordinary warmth and goodwill of the rugby world. It was an amazing example of the compassion, generosity and love of which human beings are capable and I felt incredibly lucky, privileged and humble to have been the recipient. But I'd still rather have not had MS.

And when people asked me how I was – hundreds did on the night and even more in the weeks that followed – I was at pains to assure them that I was all right. I was in full denial mode at the time, convinced that acknowledging I had MS was enough to be going on with. Acknowledging that it had any power over me was, I felt, giving in to it. I was fine as long as I kept insisting that I was. Mentioning fatigue, walking difficulties or problems with my balance or my right arm would give them an importance that I felt they didn't deserve. If pressed, I would hide behind the phrase 'could be worse' partly because it was true – I was very aware that many people with MS were in a far worse state than I was – partly because I felt that even the most well-meaning of acquaintances would swiftly get bored if I relayed every little symptom, and partly because I believed that spending any time examining my physical problems would somehow make them worse. I contented myself by pointing out to well-wishers that, because of the progressive nature of my MS, I was on a slope but that I had every intention of keeping the slope as gentle as possible and digging in my heels, toes, fingernails and anything else to prevent myself rolling down it.

Dwelling any further on the subject would, I was convinced, turn a gentle slope into a slippery one. In public, therefore, I dismissed all talk of early retirement. In private, I had adopted the philosophy of Jeannie's widowed mum. She was in her late eighties and still as sunny, bright and optimistic as ever. When asked whether she was concerned about what the future might bring, she replied that she only ever looked forward two years at a time. She had a good idea what she was going to do next year and the year after. The rest was unknowable and would take care of itself. In her case, old age was advancing inexorably. In my case it was MS. There was little point in looking too far ahead. And thinking in terms of two-year chunks chimed perfectly with the rugby calendar. Every two years there was a major event – a Lions tour or a World Cup. I would set my sights on each of those in turn and, I believed wholeheartedly, I would reach BBC retirement age at the World Cup of 2015.

It was even easier to be upbeat about my job. Rugby had captured the public imagination and it was pretty clear that something special was happening to Clive Woodward's England team, especially after they'd resolved the pay dispute in time to play Argentina. They had become the first-ever Six Nations champions when they had lifted the trophy in the spring, they had beaten the Springboks in South Africa in the summer and now, in the autumn, they had beaten the World Champions at Twickenham. I was charting their every move and recording their every reaction for BBC Radio.

And there were still enough bumps on the road to make the journey interesting. England had, for the second year in a row, gone into the last match of the championship with a Grand Slam in their sights. A year earlier they had mixed poor decisions and unforced errors in the Wembley sunshine against Wales, in April 2000 they committed the same errors in a Murrayfield monsoon. But you can't be a poor side if you get to within a whisker of a Grand Slam two years in a row. Questions might inevitably be raised about England's mental toughness, but few about their playing ability. Victory over South Africa at Bloemfontein in the summer's second Test – they had lost the first in controversial circumstances when a marginal video referee decision had gone against them – confirmed the progress that Woodward and his team were making. In fact, although there was more Grand Slam heartache to come, they weren't to lose to another southern hemisphere side, home or away, until after they had won the World Cup.

There was still some fine-tuning to be done, both on and off the field. Although players and media alike were starting to catch Clive Woodward's drift, some of his decisions still looked daft. His belief that only by providing world-class facilities for his players could he expect world-class performances from them, led to some slightly surreal choices. England's Test matches on that summer tour of South Africa in 2000 were in Pretoria and Bloemfontein. They based themselves for the whole tour in Johannesburg, then saddled with the reputation as the 'murder capital of the world'. His insistence on staying in one place – making brief forays to Potchefstroom and Kimberley for midweek matches – ripped up the rulebooks of touring, while his insistence on returning to Jo'burg as soon as the Bloemfontein Test was over almost ended badly when the chartered plane made a hairy landing in thick fog.

But more pieces of the jigsaw were starting to fall into place. Mike Tindall and Ben Cohen made their debuts in 2000, bringing bulk and power to a backline that already boasted Matt Dawson, Jonny Wilkinson and Will Greenwood. Six of the forward pack could already be inked in – props Jason Leonard and Phil Vickery, the back-row of Richard Hill, Neil Back and Lawrence Dallaglio, and the captain Martin Johnson. By the end of England's tour to Canada and the USA in the summer of 2001, Josh Lewsey was to have reinvented himself as a ferociously committed back-three player, while Ben Kay was to have staked his claim to partner Johnson in England's second row.

Then there was Jason Robinson. The former rugby league star made his England debut as a replacement in the 2001 Six Nations. His performances for Sale – and before that in a previous rugby union incarnation for Bath – had already indicated that, above everything else, Robinson was a game-breaker. He may have been tiny for a rugby union player – match programmes listed him rather generously at 5 foot 8 inches and 13-and-a-half stone – and he may have lacked some basic skills – his kicking was poor and he lacked game awareness – but he had magic feet. Robinson's ability to beat opponents in an enclosed space may never have been matched in either code, ever. His arrival was to give England a cutting edge that the rest of the world could only envy.

But first came the Lions. For a third year in a row, England had got to within a whisker of a Grand Slam. In 1999 and 2000 their own inadequacies had prevented them securing a clean sweep. In 2001 it was foot and mouth. As a result of the outbreak, England's match against Ireland had been cancelled – and rescheduled for the autumn. Clive Woodward's men were streets ahead of the rest of Europe – scoring more than 40 points against Scotland, Wales and France and a championship record 80 against Italy – and it was no surprise they provided the bulk of the Lions touring party.

There was a surprise, however, in the choice of coach. New Zealander Graham Henry was the first foreigner appointed to the job and – two tours later – he's still the last. Hailed as the Great Redeemer in Wales for the way he turned round the national team's fortunes – in his first season in charge Wales had won in France for the first time in 20 years, while that famous win over England at Wembley was part of a ten-match winning run – Henry was at the time an obvious choice. Ian McGeechan had already been head coach on three Lions tours and, when the appointment was made, had only just returned to the top job in Scotland. Warren Gatland, also a New Zealander and a future coach of Wales, was under pressure in Ireland, while Clive Woodward was deemed too English. The future knight had never been overly-diplomatic in his remarks about England's Six Nations' opponents and, with England expecting to provide the bulk of the tour party as well as several of the assistant coaches, conventional wisdom suggested that Clive's presence would not only make the whole expedition too Anglo-centric but might also compromise squad unity.

In the end, the 2003 Lions managed to do that all on their own. Henry – shrewd, intelligent, sardonic and likeable – had the manner and bearing of the senior schoolmaster that he once had been. He was immensely knowledgeable about rugby and, more often than not, a good communicator. But he wasn't British or Irish, which meant that, although he could pay lip service to the Lions concept, it wasn't part of his rugby DNA. By too obviously dividing the party into Test team and 'dirt-trackers', he unnecessarily alienated some of his players. By overworking them all – training sessions were long, repetitive and made no concession to the fact that the players, especially the English ones, were coming off the back of a long and punishing season – he created further dissension. By the time of the first Test – and Matt Dawson's ghosted newspaper column detailing player dissatisfaction – it was clear that there were deep problems within the squad. By the time of the third Test – and Austin Healey's ghosted diatribe against Australia and the Australian players – it was clear that most of the Lions just wanted to go home.

And yet the Lions came within a stolen line-out of winning the series. An extraordinary number of travelling supporters had turned the Gabba red for the first Test and had been rewarded by a scintillating opening try from Jason Robinson, wrong-footing Wallaby full-back Matt Burke in the tightest of spaces, a stunning second-half effort from Brian 'Waltzing' O'Driscoll, and a convincing victory. The Australian Rugby Union had resorted to a 'Go for the Gold' policy for the second Test in Melbourne – urging home supporters to attend the match in Australia colours and handing out thousands of Wallaby scarves and baseball caps to get the message across – and seen the home side canter home after a disgraceful late tackle on Richard Hill and a second-half collapse by the Lions. The lead changed hands repeatedly in the third Test with Australia hanging on at 29-23 when Justin Harrison – the very man labelled a 'plank', a 'plod' and an 'ape' in Healey's misguided column – stole a line-out on the Lions throw five metres from the Australian line. The Wallabies hung on to win the match and the series.

The Lions' disappointment at losing a series that, for all the internal problems, they should have won was matched by my relief at successfully negotiating the first big hurdle since admitting to the world that I had MS. Of course, I had been diagnosed before the last big event of the rugby calendar, the 1999 World

Cup, but the condition was then in its infancy. I had been fired up by anger at the injustice of it all, driven by a determination to prove that I could manage and hoping against hope that it had all been one big mistake. And I had been operating on home soil, with the safety net of retreating to my own house, taking to my own bed if the going got tough.

But Australia was a long way from home and I was on duty, if not 'on parade', for just over seven weeks. I was operating at the wrong end of the day too, in that Britain would be waking up just as Australia was closing down for the night, with every chance therefore of a 16-hour shift. I wasn't sleeping in my own bed – much more important given the way that the MS was affecting my sleep patterns – and, with a flight and a new hotel every three or four days, I was living out of a suitcase. But I had survived. I was absolutely shattered, partly because of the debilitating side effects of the beta interferon that I had lugged around the continent and injected into myself three times a week. I knew it would take several weeks to shake off the effects – but I had done everything that was asked of me and had a trip to remember for all the right reasons.

It helped immeasurably that Five Live chose to send producer Ed Marriage out from the beginning – and that Robbo joined us shortly before the first match. On the 1997 tour I had been a one-man band for the first three weeks at least, driving to and from SABC studios to play out material as well as conducting all the early interviews and providing all the early commentaries. In Australia, however, the BBC had managed to get ISDN points installed in most of our hotels, while Ed was a godsend in terms of taking off some of the workload and doing all the driving. Apart from being a highly congenial companion, Ed was also practical, organised and patient – all of which I'm not – and, although this was his first major tour, fitted in so well that Robbo and I could only marvel at how we'd managed to do without him. Ed was to be the rugby producer for the rest of my time at the BBC and, as I write this, he still is. Without his support and encouragement it's inconceivable that I would have been able to carry on as long as I did.

But Ed couldn't fix everything. Graham Henry – even though the Welsh press had not yet turned on him – had a deep suspicion of the media and even before the ghosted columns exploded the touring party's fragile equilibrium, he had almost deliberately, it seemed, made our lives difficult. He was rarely on time for scheduled media briefings and quite often declined to submit to any one-to-one interviews. While that was just about acceptable to the newspaper writers whose pooled questions usually provoked some usable quotes, it was of little value to radio or TV journalists. It was even more frustrating if Henry announced his refusal to do one-to-ones at the end of the conference. If he made the announcement beforehand, it might just be possible to get usable material by perching a minidisc and microphone on the top table in front of him.

Too often, though, Henry treated the travelling media corps as an irritating irrelevance. Of course he was absolutely right in stressing that what happened on the field was far more important than what happened off it. Of course he was right to give his coaches all the time they wanted with the players. And, of course, if the Lions had won the series then his cavalier attitude towards the media could well have been excused. But by failing to acknowledge what the media had to do, he made a rod for his own back.

It only took until the second match of the tour to realise that the Lions coach had only the scantest regard for the men and women who, if he had stopped to think about it, could have been the Lions' biggest cheerleaders. The first big match of the tour was a Saturday fixture against Queensland and the make-up of that team would give some indication of his thinking ahead of the first Test. It would also give the media a first chance to interview some of the likely stars – captain Martin Johnson, for instance, hadn't played in either of the first two fixtures. The team announcement and players' interviews were scheduled for a Thursday morning in Brisbane. But after the Tuesday match against a Queensland President's XV in Townsville, Henry decided to bring forward the press conference to the Wednesday afternoon, immediately after training and immediately before the flight to Brisbane. The media had been booked on an earlier flight and now had a dilemma – miss the first big team announcement of the tour and take the consequences from your editor back home, or re-book your flight to Brisbane, stay an extra night in Townsville and hope you could justify the extra expense to the company's accounts department. Henry refused to go back to the original schedule and he let training overrun. When the players did show up to the media briefing they could spare only the briefest of moments. It was rushed, chaotic and totally unsatisfactory. I ended up interviewing Brian O'Driscoll as he lugged his kitbag towards the coach that was to ferry the Lions to the airport, only flicking the off switch on the minidisc recorder as he disappeared up the stairs.

Townsville was also memorable for a trip taken by most of the media to the Great Barrier Reef. I wasn't able to join in the snorkelling and scuba-diving – it was the morning after a beta interferon injection – but I went along for the ride, which on the way out, on a calm sea and under blue skies, was absolutely heavenly. On the way back, with storm clouds gathering overhead and the sea decidedly choppy underneath, it was the very opposite. Not since the days of Captain Cook was a bunch of Brits so relieved to set foot on 'Godzone'!

But the day's drama didn't end there. My hotel room had a deep, square bath and a sign that promised a 'jacuzzi experience'. Thinking to soak away the aches and pains of the day, I turned on the taps, pressed the right buttons and settled down for a long, relaxing soak. Pretty soon I could feel all the tension leaving my muscles. But when I tried to get out, I couldn't. The sides of the bath were above head height and, while I just about had the energy to lift my arms up to get a purchase on the edge of the bath, I certainly didn't have the strength in my right arm to haul myself into an upright position. The bath itself was too small for me to get my legs underneath me to help with the hoisting process, while the water was proving more than enough resistance for muscles that seemed to have lost all strength. The only solution was to empty the bath while I was still in it, turn round so I was on my knees and use my hands to push up from the floor of the bath until I could get my feet directly underneath me before straightening from the knees. I got out of the bath more exhausted than I got in – and more mindful of a motto that all the disabled get to know by heart, 'never get into anything – a plane, a train or any new environment – unless you have a pretty good idea how you're going to get out'. As an able-bodied person, I'd always been confident that I had the resources, both mental and physical, to get out of just about any situation I might find myself in. I was beginning to realise that for the disabled, most, if not all, bets were off.

I didn't organise the Great Barrier Reef trip, so it didn't really count as one of Higgy's Tours, but I did organise a quiz that also sailed into choppy waters. All tour, I had been keen to lay on a sports quiz for my fellow-journalists, partly to entertain them, partly to raise money for the MS Resource Centre and partly to test the PowerPoint skills I had acquired on a computer course in Bristol. But the time had never been quite right, the journalists had not all been available at the same time, and it got to the last week of the tour before I could find a suitable opportunity to lay it on. Only for Austin Healey to throw the whole thing into chaos. When he went down with a back spasm in the week of the third Test, the Lions were suddenly without scrum-half cover. Rob Howley had played in the first two Tests but had been injured in Melbourne. Matt Dawson was now the only fit scrum-half in the squad and the only possible option for a place on the bench was Andy Nicol, the former Scotland captain coincidentally leading a supporters' tour to Sydney. Not surprisingly, the media were far more interested in Andy Nicol than in my quiz. Not surprisingly, when it came to the match itself the Lions management were more than happy to keep Dawson on the field for the whole match even though the Lions lost the match and the series.

For my part, I'd just completed my third Lions tour and although I'd not spent any time on the pitch, I had followed each of them from start to finish. I'd been with the Lions on trips round New Zealand, South Africa and now Australia and, as I packed my bags at the Manly Pacific Hotel in Sydney, I was bullish about the chances of repeating those experiences before reaching BBC retirement age. But, in keeping with my new MS-imposed resolution, I wasn't banking on anything that far ahead. I was thinking in two-year cycles – and the biennial big events in the rugby calendar. In two years' time the Rugby World Cup was going to be held in Australia. I was determined to be back.

CHAPTER THIRTY-EIGHT
ON TOP OF THE WORLD
(2001–03)

'Thirty five seconds to go... This is the one... It's coming back for Jonny Wilkinson... he drops for World Cup glory... It's up... It's over... He's done it... Jonny Wilkinson is England's hero yet again... And there's no time for Australia to come back...'

Ian Robertson's iconic commentary is all but drowned out by the roar of more than 30,000 England fans in Sydney's Telstra Stadium. Beside him, Five Live summariser Rob Andrew is on his feet, screaming with delight. Behind him, I strap a backpack containing a radio mike and noise-cancelling headphones across one shoulder, and a bag containing my minidisc recorder, its microphone and a roll of gaffer tape across the other. I'm going to need that to bind the two mikes together before I do the interviews and use the minidisc recorder as a back-up in case the radio mike goes down. I climb aboard my buggy, stow Michael the stick beside the seat, and head for the lift that will take me pitch-side.

I am delighted for England, but petrified for myself. I am being escorted down to the area on the pitch that has been set aside for the live 'flash' interviews, and while we've tested the equipment as best we could, there's no guarantee that it's all going to work. I will need to listen out both to Ed Marriage in the commentary box and the producer in London, ready to do a live interview whenever John Inverdale cues me in. But first I have to get hold of players to talk to.

Out on the pitch, it's blindingly bright. The stadium floodlights, the television arc lights, the popping of thousands of flashbulbs from the crowd make it seem like Bonfire Night. It is also incredibly noisy. At the end of a pulsating, dramatic white-knuckle ride into extra-time, no one has even tried to leave the stadium. Anyone who had lost their voice has found it again. The roars that greet the announcement of each player's name as the teams are perfunctorily and gracelessly handed their medals by Australian Prime Minister John Howard are deafening. When England's captain Martin Johnson hoists the Webb Ellis trophy into the Sydney night sky, the stadium erupts.

But at least I can hear London... and Ed up in the commentary box. I breathe a silent prayer of thanks for whatever instinct it was that made me keep a previously unidentified piece of equipment at the bottom of the bag containing my ISDN. It was some sort of 'splitter' and exactly what we needed to guarantee the three-way link that I am now enjoying and which my counterpart on Australian radio is not.

I manoeuvre myself into a position at the front of our roped-off interview area so I can get a good line of sight on England's media manager Richard Prescott. More importantly, I need him to see me and bring players across when the formalities are over.

There's a hierarchy that has to be obeyed. Host broadcasters Channel Nine have priority, then ITV. The rest of us have to wait our turn and then it's a free-for-all. I'm lucky that I've been wielding my microphone in so many tunnels after so many England matches over the last couple of decades that I've built up a good relationship both with Richard and the players.

And, of course, on the greatest day of their rugby lives, they are happy to talk. As each player approaches, I alert the producers. Within seconds I hear John Inverdale's voice in my ear, telling Five Live listeners that I'm pitch-side with another player. I try to vary the questions and let them tell it in their own words. Martin Johnson is brought over, and Jonny Wilkinson. Others follow. Ben Kay is relieved enough to joke about the scoring pass he dropped at the end of the first half, 'I thought I was going to be in pizza ads for the rest of my life,' a reference to the 1995 World Cup when footage of Jonah Lomu ploughing through the England team had been turned into a witty pizza ad featuring Tony Underwood.

There's only one person missing. Win or lose, Clive Woodward has never failed to front up to Five Live. In the bitterness of defeat in France, after all those Grand Slam heartaches, he has never turned down a request for an interview. Now, at the moment of his greatest triumph, he is nowhere to be seen. Richard Prescott claps his hand to his head. He knows I have asked for a word with Clive but in the excitement of the moment it has slipped both men's minds. Clive believes his media obligations are fulfilled and has gone back into the dressing rooms to celebrate with his players. I'm disappointed, mildly annoyed even, but shrug my shoulders. If I'd just won the World Cup, I know where I'd rather be.

But, to the eternal credit of both men, Richard Prescott re-emerges from the dressing room area with England's head coach. Clive had been sitting down in the dressing room, beer in hand. Richard had approached with some trepidation, fearing that Clive would not want to give up any more time with his team, but the latter had returned like a shot. Richard has been kind enough to say that it was the phrase 'Higgy is still waiting' that did the trick. Whatever, I am eternally grateful to both men. It had been a perfect day for England, with perfect commentary from Ian Robertson and now a perfect end to my part of the radio coverage. Time, at last, to celebrate.

The road to Sydney glory had begun with a defeat. For the third year in a row England had cocked up a Grand Slam. They only had to beat Ireland in Dublin in a match postponed from spring to autumn 2001 to lift the mythical prize, but with some key players missing and others off-form, England once again came a poor second in a match they were expected to win. They would be labelled as 'chokers' yet again when losing to France in the 2002 championship but by that time they had beaten Australia and South Africa at Twickenham and were on course for the Triple Crown. After it, they were unstoppable. In a 12-month period between 2002 and 2003 they beat all the eight other major nations in world rugby. Not content with beating Australia, New Zealand and South Africa in the autumn of 2002, they had finally achieved a Six Nations Grand Slam and then, for good measure, gone on to defeat New Zealand and Australia in their own backyards in the summer of 2003. Going into the World Cup of 2003, they were top of the world rankings – and got what they deserved.

And I was commentating – and interviewing – at every single one of those matches, as well as their warm-up matches against France (twice) and Wales in the summer of 2003 and the tour to Argentina. The latter was a stark reminder of where rugby, despite its England-led upsurge in public interest, really sat with the daily sports producers at Five Live.

'Don't you know there's a World Cup on?' was the withering response when I attempted to get the sports desk interested in some interviews I had done in Buenos Aires. Clive Woodward had just been awarded a CBE and Phil Vickery had just been made England captain for the first time. Both had been bright and engaging in interview. Both, I thought, deserved a bit of airtime at some point in a schedule boasting news and sport 24 hours a day. 'Don't even bother sending them,' was the response from base. 'They probably won't get on.' The football World Cup was being staged in South Korea and Japan. All other sports, as far as Five Live was concerned, were incidental.

Which meant that I experienced not the slightest pang of conscience when it came to getting the most out of my first-ever trip to South America. Robbo and I were scheduled to commentate on the international at the weekend. Other than that, Five Live wasn't particularly bothered. We became avid tourists, dining at a tango spectacular, riding horses at a gaucho ranch, taking in a Mozart opera at the impressive opera house in Colon. I was taking a 'holiday' from beta interferon and finding to my delight that I had the energy as well as the desire to get out and about in a stunning city. In my determination to get the most out of the experience – it could be several years before England came this way again and when they did I might not be able to enjoy it – I also signed up for a personalised guided tour of the city and spent some time at La Recoleta, the celebrated and hugely atmospheric mausoleum-filled cemetery, which contains the grave of Eva

Peron. And when the chance came to visit the spectacular Iguazu Falls on the border between Brazil and Argentina, I jumped at the chance – even if it meant another internal flight and a tiring cross-country journey by car.

And even in that remote outpost it was impossible to escape the football World Cup. It was the week when England was due to face Brazil in the quarter-final and a local Brazilian TV station was delighted to discover that a handful of English tourists had just booked into a hotel at the falls. I was on my own in the lobby – there were several hundred yards of steps to negotiate to get to one of the main viewing points and, after waving the others off, I'd settled down beside the hotel's open fire with a glass of red wine and a book.

'No, there won't be that many watching the match on television in England,' I assured the Brazilian camera crew, 'there's nothing particularly exciting about a match between England and Brazil. In fact, I know a lot of people back home who are much more excited about the idea of England playing Argentina at rugby in Buenos Aires this weekend!' With each sentence I uttered the TV reporter grew more and more agitated. This was emphatically not what she wanted to hear and was in danger of killing her story stone dead. I took pity; assuring her that I was being mischievous and recommended she interviewed one of the genuine English tourists when they got back from the falls.

On the way back from Argentina, where a very inexperienced England side pulled off a stunning victory against the Pumas, Robbo and I continued our sightseeing, stopping off in Atlanta to take in the CNN building, the house where Margaret Mitchell wrote *Gone with the Wind*, the Coca Cola Museum and a nondescript blues' bar, where a man named Bob Paige churned out some amazing honky-tonk piano. In the process I learnt a valuable lesson. Atlanta Airport is huge and, even by American standards, sprawling. The distance passengers are expected to walk is vast and, even for the able-bodied, exhausting. As I had been all but wiped out on the way in, I opted to borrow a wheelchair when we checked in to departures – and Robbo offered to push it. By the time we got to the departure gate he was sweating like a pig, though whether this was as a result of his general lack of fitness or the fact that I had inadvertently left the brake on, we agreed to differ. The whole experience served as a reminder that my lack of mobility could become a real problem unless I accepted that from now on I would not only need wheelchair assistance at airports but would have to find a way of taking my buggy on future trips.

A year later, therefore, I turned up in Australia with my latest buggy, nicknamed the Silver Dream Machine, and the set of ramps we would need for loading it on and off the people-carriers we would have to hire. Ed Marriage was with me from the outset, as we settled down for a 19-day stay in Perth, venue for England's first two pool matches against Georgia and South Africa. It was a long time to be in one place – even a city as beautiful and welcoming as the capital of Western Australia. There were plenty of distractions in the downtime between press conferences – and I am still kicking myself for turning down the opportunity of a day at the Test match between Australia and Zimbabwe in which Matthew Hayden scored 380 to break Brian Lara's world record for the number of runs in a single Test innings. I took a wine cruise with Ed up the spectacular Margaret River and when Robbo arrived we went out to dinner with Nigel Breakey, who had played alongside me in a couple of Varsity Matches under Robbo's coaching and had emigrated to Perth as a hospital doctor. But, like England, we were men on a mission, and couldn't wait for the matches to begin.

Rob Andrew was far too busy as Director of Rugby at Newcastle to be our summariser in the pool matches and we were delighted to welcome my old friend Gareth Chilcott back onto the commentary team. Since retiring from playing, and in between starring in panto, theatre, on ITV and on the after-dinner circuit, 'Cooch' had teamed up with John Hall at Gullivers Travel to provide supporters' tours to all the major rugby events. As rugby events go, they didn't come any bigger than a World Cup in Australia and Cooch – like us – was there for the duration, playing mine host to thousands of fans over the six weeks of the tournament. The majority of England fans may not have arrived in time for England's first match but there were still several hundred more than there had been on the previous year's trip to Argentina.

Cooch was bubbling – until he got to look at the names on the Georgian teamsheet. Eleven of the names ended 'dze', while the other four ended 'vili'. None of them were fewer than three syllables long and two-thirds of them had more than ten letters. One of them – belonging to one of the forwards – was on its sixth letter before a vowel appeared. For a bloke who sometimes had difficulty with the name of England's No. 8 – at moments of high excitement Cooch would call him 'Lawrence Dall-adge-leo' – it was the stuff of nightmare. To me it was a challenge. I studied a video of the victory over Russia, which had earned Georgia their first ever appearance in a World Cup finals, and I went along to the Georgian team hotel, asked each player how he pronounced his surname and spent half an hour with a genial media liaison officer trying to get my tongue round names like Tchkhaidze (No. 8), Mtchedishvili (lock) and Urjukashvili (outside-half and goal-kicker). And, though I blow my own trumpet, I did brilliantly, with my pronunciation nearly as good as my recognition. Robbo had also risen to the challenge and, at the final whistle, with England victors 84-6, we congratulated ourselves on a job well done. Cooch was equally pleased with himself. 'What you didn't notice,' he said in his delightful West Country burr, 'is that I didn't mention a Georgian player's name once! You two were so proud of your pronunciation that all I had to do was refer to the big No. 3, the speedster on the wing or the powerhouse in the second row!'

Cooch was an excellent foil for Robbo and myself in that, while we had been backs with neither the physique nor the inclination to get involved in the rough stuff, Cooch knew all there was to know about the dark arts of scrummage, ruck and maul, and could explain it concisely enthusiastically and in terms the layman could understand. Cooch was also manna from heaven for our producer. Ed Marriage's patience was sorely tested on a daily basis by Ian Robertson's timekeeping, while the need to plan for my buggy presented an added complication. Cooch at least was always on time, always had the right pass and was as adaptable and resourceful as he was reliable. If only he could also do a bit of homework and make an attempt at a few of the names...

Not a problem for the match against South Africa. Most of the names were well known and easy to say. Samoa though was a different proposition. Five of the team had surnames with an apostrophe creating a sort of glottal stop between two consecutive vowels and most had at least five syllables. And then there were the ones whose names were spelt one way and pronounced another. A 'g' for instance is pronounced as if it has an 'n' in front of it, a 'c' is pronounced 'th', while there is a silent 'm' in front of a 'b'. Which made the name of the right wing, who was to go on and star in the Premiership for London Irish, a potential minefield. Tagicakibau should be pronounced 'Tang-ee-thack-im-bau'. Cooch's first attempt – thankfully before we went on air – was 'Take a fucking bow!'

England made heavy weather of beating the Samoans – in a match noted for the few seconds that England had 16 players on the pitch and the words-and-water fight between match official Steve Walsh and England fitness adviser Dave Reddin. Once England's travelling legal expert Richard Smith had warded off the threat of points deduction that would have consigned England to a quarter-final against the All Blacks, a 111-3 thrashing of Uruguay appeared to have got things back on track. But there was enough evidence to suggest that the number one team in the world had left their best form behind them, while the memories of those botched Grand Slams were too vivid to allow any peace of mind among the fans. They were hardly helped by the quarter-final display against Wales. England looked listless and ordinary as they went into half-time 10-3 down, and it took the arrival of Mike Catt to kick-start a revival that eventually took England clear.

If the punters were worried, so were the pundits. Of particular concern was the form of Jonny Wilkinson. Sure, he was kicking his goals but he was starting to look as careworn on the pitch as he looked off it. At one point, his stream-of-consciousness agonising at media briefings prompted Eddie Butler to wonder out loud whether he had become a 'basket-case'. The rest of the team were clearly rattled by the display against Wales and though Clive Woodward continued to make all the right noises, he was clearly worried by the hamstring injury that had kept Richard Hill out of action since the opening match against Georgia.

By contrast, semi-final opponents France seemed to be timing their run to perfection. After putting 50 points past Scotland in their pool match, they'd put another 40 past Ireland in the quarter-final. Although they hadn't really been tested, they looked to be in ominous form and in Frederic Michalak they seemed to have a young fly-half who was everything Wilkinson was not. Certainly the French were by far the more laidback of the two semi-finalists. Ed and I travelled to their hotel in Bondi to find them, almost to a man, happy to lounge about and shoot the breeze with the media for as long as it took. Coach Bernard Laporte was quietly confident.

That was until he drew back his curtains on the morning of the match. The weather for the previous day's semi-final – in which Australia had upset the formbook to defeat New Zealand – had been relatively benign. As kick-off approached for England and France, the rain-clouds advanced on the Telstra Stadium and a sense of foreboding grew among the French players. As the heavens opened, they wilted and were washed away. Whatever doubts that had been growing in English minds – exacerbated by the concession of an early try to Serge Betsen – were eradicated by the same downpour. England finished the match with a swagger with Jonny Wilkinson scoring all 24 points and playing Michalak off the pitch in the process.

An Australia-England final was a scriptwriter's dream. Australia played the part of gutsy snook-cocking outsiders to the manor born, while their media found it child's play to portray England as boring one-trick ponies, still clinging to imperialist notions of effortless superiority. The respective coaches, Eddie Jones and Clive Woodward, were only too happy to fan the flames. Scurrying between the two camps, we rugby journalists were never short of inflammatory sound bites and provocative 'nanny-goats' (quotes).

We had by now been quartered in Star City, a ghastly casino complex whose saving grace was its central Sydney location and, to meet the frenzied demand from every corner of the BBC, had converted one of the rooms into an almost permanent studio. So much use was it getting in that crazy final week that I had to ask for a change of room. Jeannie had flown out to join me for a holiday and had managed to get a ticket for the final but neither of us was going to get much sleep if the next room was going to be used as a studio. In a rare turn-up for the books, however, Star City had an unoccupied disabled room, which was not only quieter than the original but also infinitely better equipped.

Not that we got to spend much time in it that weekend at the end of November 2003. We'd both set off early on the day of the final, and Jeannie, in an England shirt and a see-through rain poncho, was taking one of the hundreds of supporters coaches. I, with my fruit bars, laptop and fully charged buggy, was in a hired people carrier driven by Ed, whose morbid fear of being late was heightened by a natural determination that nothing should go wrong on this of all days.

We'd arrived back well after midnight. Jeannie had blagged a lift on a coach heading vaguely in the right direction, while I, still feeling the strain of standing through all those pitch-side interviews, had gone to the media centre to garner yet more interviews for the BBC, before stowing the buggy back into the people carrier and heading for Star City.

The following day, after escaping early from an all-night party, I had a wrap-up article to write for the *Wooden Spoon Yearbook* before heading off with Ed to the England team hotel in Manly for the absolutely final, definitive interviews of a victorious World Cup campaign.

Like England I had surmounted every obstacle placed in my way. The buggy had stood up well to its first real test, and practice had made the art of loading and unloading it – and stowing people, suitcases and equipment all around it – perfect. I had suffered heavily from fatigue at various times on the trip but nothing more than I could have predicted and nothing more than I could handle. I had gone down with a heavy cold at about the time of England's final pool match but that hadn't affected my work schedule in the slightest. I felt I had been productive, prolific and polished. I was knackered but Jeannie and I were heading off into the wilds of Australia for a three-week holiday. I would recover, and there was no reason to doubt that I would be ready, willing and able for the next big event in the rugby calendar – the 2005 Lions tour to New Zealand.

CHAPTER THIRTY-NINE

A TOUR TOO FAR
(2003–05)

In New Zealand, it all went horribly wrong – for the Lions, for Clive Woodward and for my health.

The Lions had beaten South Africa on their first tour as a professional outfit, and narrowly lost to Australia on their second. There were high hopes that the largest, most expensively assembled and most thoroughly prepared touring side ever would become only the second Lions team ever to win a series in New Zealand. They were hammered 3–0.

Clive Woodward had masterminded England to the Rugby World Cup in 2003 and been knighted for his contribution to the sport. He had left the England post in 2004, which freed him up to devote all his considerable energies to the task of picking, organising and preparing the very best players in Britain and Ireland. He returned from New Zealand with his reputation severely diminished.

I had lived with MS for six years and, with one or two adaptations to the way I did things, had been able to flourish on a rugby circuit that was now punishing in its demands. I had covered two World Cups and returned with health and spirit intact from one Lions tour. Yet in New Zealand I was laid low by illness, dropped out of the tour completely for the best part of a week, and was lucky to see it through to the end.

Hundreds of thousands of supporters had lined the streets of London on 25 November 2003 as Woodward and the England players proudly showed off the Webb Ellis Trophy from an open-top bus. Most of the Royal Family took the opportunity to speak to the squad as they posed for photos with the Queen and her corgis at Buckingham Palace, while the leaders of all three political parties attended a champagne reception at 10 Downing Street. In the weeks to come, as the 'Sweet Chariot' tour made sure that the rest of the country got a chance to see, and be seen with, the trophy, rugby surfed the waves of popularity, with clubs reporting a massive rise in the number of people taking up the game and significant increase in attendances. Jonny Wilkinson was named the BBC's Sports Personality of the Year with Martin Johnson a runner-up, while Clive Woodward was a shoo-in for Coach of the Year and England scooped the team award. The sport enjoyed its highest profile ever with the players – and their agents – under siege. Suddenly, you couldn't open a glossy magazine or watch a chat show without seeing an England rugby player. They were on billboards and advertising hoardings up and down the country. They were writing books, penning newspaper columns, signing modelling contracts and appearing at any number of celebration dinners.

And, of course, the most celebrated of the lot was Jonny Wilkinson. Clean-cut, good-looking, modest, he was the advertiser's dream. Polite, charming and well mannered to boot, he was just about every woman's fantasy figure. Mobbed everywhere he went, he often needed a special security detail just to protect him. Everything he did was news – and seen through a strangely distorted lens. When the car in which he was a passenger skidded off the road one evening, the media conjured up images of a 'horror smash' and a 'near-death' experience and speculated about his injuries. He was unhurt. Even Five Live threw all objectivity to the winds, sending a reporter on an abortive trip all the way up to Newcastle to cover a fairly minor match for the sole reason that they had heard a rumour that he was about to make his return from injury. And, when he was named as a substitute in a midweek match at Northampton, they sent me to Franklin's Gardens on Jonny-watch.

'...Let's get a live update from Northampton where Alastair Hignell is watching England's World Cup hero Jonny Wilkinson in action for Newcastle...' went the cue.

'Not exactly in action,' I explained. 'He's on the bench as one of the substitutes. You join us with the score at...'

'Never mind that,' cut in the presenter. 'What's he doing on the bench?'

Newcastle themselves were not above exploiting Wilkinson's phenomenal popularity. During his numerous injury lay-offs in the years immediately following the World Cup they discovered that whenever they included his name in match-day squads, they got many more bums on seats. When Stade Francais wanted to market their 2005 Heineken Cup quarter-final against Newcastle, they thought nothing of flying the superstar and his entourage across to Paris and hiring a room in the ornate sumptuous and totally splendid Hotel de Ville on the banks of the Seine. 'Our beloved city has witnessed some extraordinary events this century,' began the deputy mayor, while 16 foot-high portraits of kings, cardinals and statesmen gazed down from enormous gilt frames and a giant chandelier weighing several tons and worth hundreds of thousands of pounds glittered and shimmered above him. 'Seven years ago Zinedine Zidane and les Bleus won the football World Cup in our very own Stade de France. Sixty-one years ago Generals de Gaulle and Eisenhower completed the liberation of our city from Nazi occupation. And now, Jonny Wilkinson is coming... '

And I too was guilty of wanting to use the Wilkinson effect for the MSRC. When it was confirmed that he would be the official starter for the London Marathon in 2004, I thought there was nothing to be lost in asking him if he could, at any point in the day, pop into the charity's race headquarters – at the Economist Building in St James – and shake a few hands. Having the idea was one thing. Putting it into practice was a completely different kettle of fish. I conveyed the request messages to his dad, his club and his agent, Tim Buttimore, who eventually phoned me back to say that he couldn't promise anything but Jonny might be able to squeeze in a visit before heading for the airport and a flight back to Newcastle. In any case, I was to keep it secret and, if I kept my mobile phone on all day, he, Tim, might send me a quick message if Jonny was free and willing.

Never has a mobile phone screen been stared at so hard or for so long. Just as we were giving up hope, the news flashed up that Jonny was five minutes away. As he walked towards the building, 200 charity workers, physiotherapists, runners, their families and supporters burst into prolonged cheering and surged towards him. I got an idea then what life must be like for a lad who was basically shy, private and self-contained. 'Help me, Higgy,' he mouthed as I shook his hand and tried to introduce him to some of the key people in the MSRC. We did a quick tour of the runners' area, during which he shook countless hands, signed innumerable autographs, posed for dozens of photographs – and never stopped smiling. Amazing. The effect on those present was incalculable, the boost to the morale of everyone connected with the MSRC immense.

Even Jeannie – normally camera-shy and reticent – couldn't turn down the opportunity of posing for a photo with Jonny and me. As soon as she got home she ran it through Photoshop, completely removed me from the picture, and sent it via mobile phone to all her friends. By return she received dozens of texts containing a single word. None of the words were the same. None of them could have been found in an English dictionary. . All of them were variations of, 'Oooooooooh!' 'Aaaaargh!' and 'Phwoah!'

With Jonny Wilkinson out injured, Martin Johnson retired, and several more World Cup-winners sidelined for one reason or another, England came down to earth with a bump in the 2004 Six Nations. After losing to Ireland at Twickenham they lost the final match of the campaign to France in Paris to finish third. There was more agony on the tour to New Zealand and Australia – as England conceded eight tries to nil in two big defeats by the All Blacks and were humiliated 51-15 by the Wallabies.

From a professional point of view commentating on these games was no harder than describing the matches leading up to England's World Cup success. When you're commentating, it doesn't really matter who's winning and who's losing. The crucial thing is to describe the game as you see it, get player identification right and save your analysis of the bigger picture for another time. Passing judgment on them was far harder, but England's fall from grace was so sudden and so spectacular that it was inevitable. What had gone wrong with English rugby and why had it gone wrong so quickly?

In part it was the 'tall poppy' syndrome. England had hauled themselves above the rest of the world and were there to be cut down. In part, it was historical. For all sorts of traditional and stereotypical reasons, England was always the side that other teams most wanted to beat. In part it was physical. England's players had driven themselves and their bodies relentlessly in pursuit of the greatest prize and they were starting to pay the price. In part it was psychological. They had reached the top of the mountain and didn't find it difficult to convince themselves that they had earned the right to stop awhile and savour the view. And it was mental. The preparation, the tactics and the personnel they had used in the past few years had been good enough to see off the rest of the world. Why change a winning formula?

But when Clive Woodward came to announce his resignation on 1 September 2004 – less than a year after England's greatest triumph – he had another reason to proffer. The RFU weren't giving him the support he needed to take England on to the next stage. He felt he needed more time with the players, not less. He felt that more resources should be thrown at keeping England ahead of the competition and that now wasn't the time for the RFU or the clubs to reward themselves for all the sacrifices they had made in helping England conquer the world. They must be prepared to make greater concessions, not look for a payback.

Unfortunately, in delivering his message in front of a packed media briefing at Twickenham, Clive lost his cool. The man who had always enjoyed the surest of touches with the media got it badly wrong. The man who had always known which buttons to press, and how hard to press them to engineer the desired response, launched into an uncharacteristic and unnecessarily vitriolic attack on his employers. As RFU Chief Executive Francis Baron squirmed in the seat next to Clive, I got the feeing that whatever rapport they had enjoyed had now broken down for good.

And I had to tear up the mental script I'd been preparing for Five Live listeners. I'd got up at crack of dawn to do a live two-way with Nicky Campbell on the breakfast show ahead of the conference. I had been guilty of sarcasm when the presenter asked me what Clive was going to say. 'If I knew that, I wouldn't have got up in the early hours of the morning and flogged my way through the M4 traffic jams to get here' was my rather tetchy initial reply. When encouraged to speculate, I'd predicted back-slapping, hearty congratulations and many best wishes for the future. What we'd got was far juicier, far more newsworthy and of far-reaching consequences. That outburst, as Clive admitted much later on *Desert Island Discs*, was to cost him any chance of getting the job of Director of Elite Rugby at the RFU, a job whose specification he wrote, for which he was ideally qualified and which ultimately went to Rob Andrew.

Apart from immediately revising my assessment of the media briefing and its impact, I had also, in the medium term, to form a relationship with Woodward's successor Andy Robinson. This was no bother at all. I'd first come across Andy Robinson in my HTV days – taking film crews to Writhlington School in Radstock and Colston Collegiate School when he was still a teacher and producing a feature on his dad Ray who, even though he'd lost his sight through MS, had continued to 'watch' Andy's matches with the aid of his own personal commentator. When Bath had won the Heineken Cup I had interviewed Andy as a jubilant head coach and I'd had plenty of dealings with him when he was an assistant coach on the Lions tour to Australia. He was a good man, a rugby enthusiast with a pronounced work ethic, a hard-nosed approach and, even in repose, a deeply furrowed brow. But it had long been obvious to me that his scowl was far worse than his growl and beneath the flinty exterior was a warm, passionate and ambitious patriot. As such he was never going to turn down the chance of coaching England, even if he privately shared some of Clive Woodward's misgivings about his employers and the clubs. Andy was determined to make the system work, whatever the drawbacks, and he certainly deserved more success as England's head coach than he enjoyed.

But he was even more dogged by injury to key players than Woodward was. In his 22 matches in charge – from November 2004 to November 2006 – he never once had Jonny Wilkinson available for selection. Jason Leonard and Neil Back had retired and Will Greenwood and Trevor Woodman weren't to play international rugby beyond Robinson's first autumn international series. And his first Six Nations wasn't any better; in their first three matches, England lost to Grand Slam-winners Wales, France and Ireland. Only Scotland and Italy finished below them. The rumblings of discontent that were first to lead to the sacking of assistant coaches Phil Larder, Joe Lydon and Dave Alred, and ultimately cost Robinson his own job, were already growing louder.

England's poor showing meant that for the first time ever Ian Robertson and I were diverted away from an England match at Twickenham. Wales needed to beat Ireland in their final match to clinch a first Grand Slam for over a quarter of a century while both teams were playing for the Triple Crown. England's Calcutta Cup against Scotland was small beer. No doubt about it, the place to be was the Millennium Stadium in Cardiff.

Whether or not the roof is closed, the magnificent Welsh stadium can be the noisiest place in the world to watch rugby. The towering stands, the sunken playing arena, the singing of a partisan and passionate Welsh crowd and the loudest PA system I've ever experienced makes the Millennium Stadium no place for those with sensitive eardrums. The invasion of tens of thousands of Irish supporters with just as much passion and nearly as many songs was a sure-fire guarantee that, come match-day, decibel levels would soar off the scoreboard.

Cue Health and Safety at the BBC. I had come across this august body of men and women when I'd first been diagnosed with MS. The officer who interviewed me had been concerned about how difficult it would be to fight my way through a rugby crowd to take my place in the commentary box. 'Couldn't you maybe do your commentary on a different day?' she had asked, 'or perhaps from a different place?' Now Health and Safety came up with a recommendation that we wear earplugs or better still a pair of the noise-cancelling headphones used by percussion-drill operators. How, with that lot clamped to our heads, we would then be able to hear ourselves, our fellow-commentators or any of the producers, presenters and other contributors to the programme, they quite failed to explain!

Despite poor Six Nations' campaigns in 2004 and 2005, England still provided 20 players for Woodward's massive 44-strong Lions tour party to New Zealand with another three pencilled in to join them if they could prove their fitness. Of these only Jonny Wilkinson actually made it out there – even though he hadn't played international rugby since the World Cup final and had less than 16 hours of match-play under his belt in more than 18 months – while Mark Cueto replaced the injured Iain Balshaw before the party left these shores.

Perplexity at the size and make-up of the playing squad was nothing compared to the consternation at the size and scope of the back-up team. In all, as Clive Woodward embarked on a revolutionary policy of treating the Lions as two separate teams, 26 support staff were deemed necessary including ten coaches, two doctors, four physios, a chef, a legal expert and a travelling referee. But by far the most controversial appointment was that of former Downing Street spin doctor Alastair Campbell as the Head of Press Relations.

I'll have to take some of the blame for that. I was part of a media advisory panel summoned by Sir Clive to provide a sounding board at the planning-stage of the tour. He outlined his plans to double up on coaches and he impressed us with his determination to leave no stone unturned in terms of preparation. There was only one area where we felt it worth making a point. Lions tours had traditionally provided moments of controversy when a whole country's media would rise up in arms and place a sudden and intense pressure on a touring party. There weren't many of them, but the media in New Zealand were as rabid as any and could, if they even got the merest whiff of a problem, make life extremely difficult for players and management. What was needed, we concluded, was a tough, experienced and respected press officer who, when the going got tough, would know how to keep a recalcitrant media in line and, when all was sweetness and light, would know how to get the best out of the native press. With all due respect we said, that person wasn't Louisa Cheetham, who may have had media experience on previous Lions tours but had never had to face up to a ferocious press pack with the scent of blood in its nostrils. What was needed was a big-hitter.

A few weeks later, when I heard that Alastair Campbell had been given the job, I couldn't help but think it was a vanity appointment – on both sides. Clive's vanity had been tickled by the idea of getting the most famous (infamous?) press officer in the land to work for him and maybe, too, he was sticking two fingers up at those who had dared to criticise his previous choice. Alastair Campbell was flattered to be approached by England's World Cup-winning coach, convinced that sports journos would be pliant poodles in comparison to their Rottweiler political brethren and utterly confident that he could teach them a thing or two, but also that he would have no problem in manipulating the news agenda to suit the Lions.

What neither man realised was that Campbell himself was high up on that news agenda. His reputation went so far ahead of him that everything he tried to do was regarded as suspiciously as his lack of knowledge of how a rugby team functioned and how the rugby media operated. He didn't react very well when the photographers pointed out that the rules which he now wanted them to observe ran counter to both past practice and current editorial requirements. In short, the shots he wanted them to take were not the shots that their editors, and by extension the rugby public, wanted to see. The rules he imposed on both written and broadcast journalists were similarly restrictive and counter-intuitive. We'd all spent years working out what was relevant and how best to report it. We didn't need anyone to tell us what to write or what questions to ask and we resented any attempts to curb established practices. Campbell's determination to have things done his way had already highlighted misgivings among the travelling media and clear-the-air talks were needed with Clive Woodward before the tour was halfway through. But it was the way the O'Driscoll affair was handled that really showed up the folly of Campbell's appointment.

Lions captain Brian O'Driscoll was invalided out of the tour after being subjected to an illegal and highly dangerous 'spear tackle' in the opening minutes of the first Test. Video footage suggested that All Blacks skipper Tana Umaga and hooker Keven Mealamu were the guilty men, but the citing commissioner judged that there was no case to answer. The Lions reacted bitterly and angrily. The sight of Clive Woodward and Alastair Campbell charging through the Christchurch night, trailing managers and media assistants in their wake as they tried to convey their outrage to the two media camps, will live long in the memory. And so will the belief that the New Zealand media mistrusted the message because the messenger was Alastair Campbell. They suspected that Campbell was whipping up British hysteria because he could and because that's what he did – not because there was any validity to his actions. The more vehement the Lions' protests, the more the New Zealand media believed that Campbell was pulling the strings for his own ends – and the more protective they felt towards the All Blacks. The less reaction the Lions got, the louder and longer they shouted. The longer they made a fuss over what had happened – Eddie O'Sullivan, one of the Lions' coaches, was still ranting about the tackle less than two days before the second Test – the less chance the players had of focusing all their attention on the task in front of them.

The Lions lost the series 3-0, the first time in 22 years that they had lost every single Test match of a tour. They only lost one of the midweek matches – against the New Zealand Maori in Hamilton – and, after drawing their pre-tour warm-up against Argentina in Cardiff, escaped with a reasonable success ratio.

But whereas previous Lions tours had stirred the blood with the way that some players flourished unexpectedly to force their way into contention for selection and others formed the unlikeliest of combinations with players of a different nationality and a different playing philosophy, this one had little to commend it. Time after time I found myself, as a guest on New Zealand radio chat shows, assuring listeners that the Lions were much better players than they appeared as individuals and would come together as a team any day now. It never really happened and, as a result, the tour never really took off.

My own tour had to take off twice after a pretty spectacular crash-landing in the middle. It had begun in frustration, with the baggage handlers at Auckland Airport serving up a bashed-up and unworkable control panel on my buggy. Jet-lagged and staggering with fatigue at the end of a 26-hour journey, the very last thing either Ed Marriage or I needed was to push a heavy and useless buggy round the airport in search of the complaints office. And when I got to the hotel and trawled through yellow pages in search of a repair shop, the last thing I needed was for it to be the weekend. Repair wasn't going to be possible till Monday but in the meantime I could have the loan of an electric wheelchair with an over-sensitive joystick and a broken foot-plate. As the Lions were due to be officially welcomed the following day with dancing, singing and all the usual time-honoured rituals, I had little choice but to take up the offer.

Once back on my own buggy, I was determined to make the most of the trip. The presence in the welcoming party of several members of the New Zealand Tourist Board gave Higgy's Tours a kick-start. I was able to gain several journalists free entry to the hot springs in Rotorua, when the Lions were to play their opening match against Bay of Plenty, and lay the groundwork for a wine-tasting trip on our return for the final week in Auckland. I carved out enough time on the morning of the match against Taranaki in New Plymouth to visit the Sir Edmund Hillary Museum on my own and as the tour got underway I was thoroughly enjoying myself.

Only to be whacked by a virus. The weather had turned nasty for the third match of the tour, against the Maori. The commentary box was on the far side of the ground from the dressing rooms and in order to negotiate my buggy through the crowd and along the sloping path that led to and from the flash interview area I had had to allow plenty of time. I'd spent a good half-hour at either end of the game in the freezing cold and had worked flat out in between on commentary and presentation for Five Live Sports Extra. By the time we got to Wellington for the next game I was feeling decidedly groggy. I'd dosed myself up with orange juice, Berocca tablets and the vile-looking spirulina that New Zealand hotels like to serve up for breakfast. But my throat was sore, my head was throbbing and I was quite devoid of energy. By the end of the match I could barely hoist myself out of my chair and into the host broadcaster's radio commentary box next door. I have no memories of the trip to Dunedin. I know I completed the commentary and I know from the record-books that the Lions drew 13-all. As we flew back to our base in Christchurch that night I felt as if I was burning up. I was coughing up phlegm, gallons and gallons of it. I barely slept and by the next morning could hardly stand up. I phoned reception and they organised a doctor to come round later that morning. He took my temperature, prodded and poked and pronounced that I had a severe chest infection, which risked developing into full-blown pneumonia. He ordered me to stay put while he wrote out a prescription and organised the hotel to go and collect it – and gave me an emergency number to ring if I should feel any worse.

For the next four days and four hours I stayed in bed. The Lions tour went on without me – the hotel emptying as the media contingent packed up and headed off to Invercargill – but I was in no state to care. I sneezed and snuffled into yards and yards of toilet paper, which piled up around me on the bed. I cleared the mini bar and restocked it only with water and orange juice, which I ordered in litres from room service. I took the drugs that had been prescribed for me and counted the hours until I could take the next lot. I talked to Ed and Gordon Turnbull on the phone and we all agreed that the crucial thing to concentrate on was being well enough to commentate at the first Test in less than a week's time. They were outwardly calm and reassuring but they were already mulling over contingency plans to fly in a replacement.

I was outwardly calm and matter of fact but I'd been spooked by the word 'pneumonia'. So had Jeannie back in Bristol. So had her sister Paula and brother-in-law John who immediately offered to pay for her to fly out to Christchurch. If I hadn't felt slightly better by the next morning, I'd have agreed. But, as the drugs took hold, the pain in my throat started to ease, the throbbing in my head started to subside and the pile of tissues on the bed stopped growing so fast. I was still as weak as a kitten and hadn't the energy to venture out of the room or even to get dressed. I watched every film in the hotel's movie collection at least twice and by the end of the third day I was starting to remember some of the storylines. The rest of the BBC crew came to visit and cheered me up with tales from Invercargill. Some of my mates from the media popped their heads round the door and offered assistance and support. I started to feel better by the end of the fourth day and, exactly a hundred hours after I'd admitted the doctor to my room in a blind panic, I took a few tentative steps into the public area of the hotel. The first Test was two days away – and the weather was still lousy.

While I had no intention of jeopardising my recovery – the first thing I did when venturing out of the hotel for the first time was to buy long-johns and a thermal vest – I was determined both to make up for lost time and celebrate my lucky escape.

Commentary on the Test went well – although the Lions found themselves at the receiving end both of that controversial spear-tackle and of a Dan Carter masterclass – and I threw myself back into the tour. I organised a sports quiz for the media to raise a bit of cash for the MSRC and I devised another one to entertain some of the thousands of supporters who were being accommodated on board a massive passenger liner in Wellington Harbour. I confirmed the arrangements for a final week wine tour on Waiheke Island followed by a meal in the Mudbrick Restaurant with its incomparable views of Auckland Harbour and – even though the Lions were a beaten and dejected mob – I milked every last ounce of enjoyment from a tour to a country I've always loved.

But the truth was, I was still running scared. I had been determined to put my little flirtation with pneumonia to the back of my mind but I still hadn't quite been able to. I ended the tour with my energy levels at a very low ebb. This had been a year when I had smashed up my car and given up driving, had my buggy broken in an aircraft and had ongoing problems with the trains. Everything was taking that much longer and was that much harder to do. But I wasn't a quitter. This was part of the deal I had made with myself. I had made all sorts of adaptations to my life in order to keep doing the job I loved. I had made all sorts of sacrifices in order to stay in control of my life. I had accepted that I had got MS for the rest of my life and reached an understanding with it. I had expected it to be hard but not perhaps this hard. Still, I had come to the end of another two-year cycle and I was still in there fighting. If I could listen to my body over the next 24 months, if I could pace myself a little better, do only what I was asked to do, not take on quite so much, I'd be all right up to and beyond the Rugby World Cup in France in 2007. Wouldn't I?

CHAPTER FORTY

A FINAL FINAL
(2005–07)

It was the perfect weekend of World Cup rugby. In the sunny South of France England had upset the formbook with a rousing win over Australia. A few hours later France made even more of a nonsense of pre-tournament predictions with a nail-biting victory over New Zealand in claustrophobic Cardiff. The next day the wonderful Fijians gave South Africa the fright of their lives in Marseille, while tournament wildcards Argentina saw off Scotland at the Stade de France. The tournament was boiling up to a final fortnight in Paris.

I should have been bubbling over with excitement, thrilled at England's transformation, exhilarated by the prospects of yet more twists and turns in the tournament, and looking forward to a 14-day stopover in one of the most beautiful cities in the world. But I wasn't. I was knackered, and there was precious little energy left in the tank. I was in a vicious circle of sleep deprivation. A combination of muscle tremor and spasm meant that it was difficult to get off to sleep, while pain in my right leg and shoulder meant it was impossible to stay asleep for long. Awake for long periods of the day, at my best I felt lethargic and listless. For the rest of the time I was in the grip of such bone-wearying fatigue that I had given up hope of doing anything other than eat, sleep and work. I knew it would be a struggle to get through to the end of the tournament.

My worst fears were being realised. Until recently, I had been able to manage fatigue pretty well. Since my diagnosis with MS, fatigue had been the elephant in the room of my life – always there, always looming over me, always threatening to cramp my style without overtly attacking – at least in public. But I was paying the price in private as it was taking longer and longer to recover from periods of the greatest stress at work.

In the past I'd tended to approach everything at 100 mph, taking more and more on, hurtling ever onwards – until I hit the wall. Fortified by the belief that I could pick myself up pretty quickly, dust myself down and race away again at breakneck speed, I'd never really given much thought to changing that approach. With the onset of MS I had had to make a few concessions but part of the deal I had subconsciously struck with myself was that I would accept the periods of 'Dead Stop' as long as I could enjoy the periods of 'Full Steam Ahead'. But the latter were becoming increasingly compromised by a lack of sleep, a lack of energy, or both, and the former were lasting longer and becoming increasingly difficult to recover from.

I reached a tipping-point on England's tour to South Africa that summer of 2007. The moment of revelation came when I realised that I didn't have the energy to go out to dinner with my old Cambridge university teammate John Robbie. Ed Butler, who had played in the same team, and Ian Robertson, who had coached us, were making the short journey from Pretoria to Johannesburg where John lived, and I was too wiped out to join them. Meeting up with old friends in far-flung places had been one of the joys of the job and ever since my first visit to South Africa in 1992 I'd treasured the occasions when I'd been able to catch up with John. But now, I couldn't even make the effort. The 'wow' factor in my job was starting to lose its first w. If it were to lose another consonant it would end up as one tiny, insignificant zero. And I was scared that if the fatigue were to take a greater hold, I would start to duck out of more and more, do my job less and less well and feel more and more frustrated.

All the time Jeannie, my wife, my rock, my shield and my friend, was also lying sleepless in England, trying to keep our life together, knowing that when I got back I would be more a wreck than I had been the time before and that the period of recovery – the brunt of which she always took – would be longer. This wasn't fair on either of us, and I returned from South Africa – England incidentally were hammered 58-10 and 55-22 in the Tests, while my exhaustion was compounded by access problems to commentary boxes and dressing room areas – with the knowledge that the World Cup in France would be make or break.

Looking back, I realise that I hadn't been able to sleep much on the previous tour either. But England had made such a fleeting visit to Australia in the summer of 2006 – playing two Tests in a couple of weeks – that I'd put all my problems down to jet-lag and the weather. I'd hardly left our Manly hotel during the first week in Sydney, but then it had been raining most of the time. In Melbourne I'd taken my buggy on a guided walking tour of the city and enjoyed mooching about Centennial Square. England had been hammered in both Tests – another nail in the coffin for Andy Robinson as England coach – but I hadn't even begun to contemplate calling time on my career.

It was true that in the seasons following the Lions tour to New Zealand, I had been putting myself about a lot less. I no longer felt that I had to attend every single rugby press conference in the country and I had started to factor things like travelling distance and ease of access into deliberations about which games to cover. It was also true that I was spending a lot more time cat-napping on the way to and from media briefings and matches, but I still felt that I was performing at or near the top of my game. I was providing insightful interviews, compiling authoritative regional round-ups and delivering accurate commentaries. With Ed Marriage and Robbo, I was part of a great team – and we continued to hit the heights even as England continued to plumb the depths.

In one way, England's difficulties made the job harder – with a constantly changing team there were always plenty of new names to learn and new players to get to know. In another, they made things easier. There was always something to talk about, always the feeling that things were in a constant state of flux. When Andy Robinson was sacked, less than two years after he was given the top job, he'd already been preceded to the guillotine by three of his lieutenants. When Brian Ashton took over he was England's third head coach in less than three years and he had less than 12 months to go before Rugby World Cup 2007. Three wins and a third-place finish was actually one better than anything England had managed under Robinson, although two 50-point hidings in South Africa told a marginally worse story than the two 30-point reverses England had experienced in Australia the previous summer.

I knew Brian well – we had been England teammates in Australia in 1975 and club opponents in Italy a couple of years later, and I had interviewed him plenty of times when he was coach at Bath, assistant to Clive Woodward and Director of the National Academy. I respected him hugely and felt that his emphasis on intelligence, imagination and space was ideal for the modern game. It was a shame that his players didn't think the same. There were mutterings on the tour to South Africa that some of them felt they needed more guidance about what to do in certain parts of the field – and when to do it.

'I want my players to think for themselves,' he would declare time and time again.

'Yes, but what do you want us to think for ourselves?' they would respond, just as frequently.

If you read their accounts of RWC 2007 – autobiographies from Mike Catt and Lawrence Dallaglio were rushed into print in the immediate aftermath of the tournament – it was only because players took matters into their own hands that England were able to triumph against Australia in the quarter-finals and France in the semis. On the other hand, you could argue that by taking control of the way they played, the players were doing exactly what Brian had been encouraging them to do all along. Whatever, he was a great thinker about the game and had a wonderfully dry sense of humour. For me, England moved him on far too quickly.

Five Live covered England's advance on the final in the manner they'd perfected in World Cups and on Lions tours over the previous decade. I was 'embedded' with the England team from the very beginning, along with Ed Marriage. Between us we attended every media briefing they gave, while Robbo and I provided the commentary – by now accompanied by Matt Dawson – on every match they played. Because France – certainly compared to Australia and South Africa – was a pretty small country, it was sensible to make long journeys on the TGV. But because most of England's early matches – as well as both semis and the final – were scheduled for the northern part of France, we decided to go by car. Because loading and unloading the buggy would be a daily requirement, we decided to take mine – with Ed doing the driving.

And promptly had it stolen. At least, that was the only conclusion we could come to. Our hotel in Versailles, a budget B&B no more than a mile from England's infinitely more opulent headquarters, didn't have a car park of its own but on the other side of the street we had spotted, and regularly made use of, a disabled parking bay. One morning, however, the car had vanished. The local shopkeepers shrugged their shoulders and looked nonplussed, though one vaguely remembered seeing a car like ours on the back of a breakdown lorry. While Ed rushed off on foot to the England media briefing, I buggied round to police headquarters. They assured me that the car had not been stolen, but impounded, and that I would have to pay 120 euros to get it back. I protested that the disabled Blue Badge had been properly displayed and demanded they ring the pound to verify it.

'Yes, indeed,' said the gendarme, 'they can see the Blue Badge but they say it's on the wrong side.'

'Ask them which side the steering-wheel is on,' I demanded. It seemed there was dead silence on the other end of the line, and a red-faced gendarme at my end. Fine cancelled.

The town of Versailles was as quaint as the palace and its surroundings were grand. But even though they welcomed millions of tourists every year, the municipal authorities hadn't quite got their heads round the idea of catering for the disabled. England's opening media briefing was, for instance, held in the extravagantly ornate town hall because the mayor and his town council wanted to celebrate their arrival by combining the welcome ceremony with a cocktail party for the great and the good of the town and the great unwashed of the visiting media. The only lift that served the first-floor reception room was too small even for my tiny buggy.

The zebra-crossing designers had a similar blind spot. Whereas they quite often provided a ramp for a buggy-user, or a pram-pusher to begin their crossing of a busy road, they generally forgot to provide one at the other side. I soon got used to dismounting from my buggy and manhandling it across a four-inch kerb while the lights changed and the traffic thundered past.

And then there were the cobbles. There are millions of them around the entrance to the palace, and millions of them in the surrounding streets. Seasoned buggy-users will know that you only need to travel a hundred yards over cobbles on a buggy without suspension before your body is jarring, your muscles are hurting and your bladder is crying out for relief. I never did summon up the willpower to enter the palace.

It was even worse in Arras where I stayed for England's opening match against the USA in nearby Lens. But the cobbles weren't the biggest problem. For reasons of economy, the BBC had booked rooms in the entirely inappropriately named Hotel Splendide. As I put in an e-mail to Gordon Turnbull that night, it was the sort of hotel that asylum-seekers would have turned down. My room had a threadbare carpet, a bedspread with cigarette burns and no wardrobe. To reach it, I had to cross a wide internal hallway whose only light was provided by a timer on the shortest of settings. I only had to be slightly slow off the mark, or fail to find the lock first-time with my key, and the light would snap off, leaving the hallway so dark that the only alternative was to feel my way back to the light switch and start again. On average I had to cross the hallway six times for every one occasion I got to open the door. And that was when the lift was working. Mine host forgot to mention that he shut it down at 10 o'clock every night. After that time, I had to lug myself up two flights of stairs before attempting the hallway dash. Splendide? I didn't think so.

I wasn't consciously collecting the negatives but when, after parking at the multi-storey car park attached to the Gare Montparnasse, we discovered that every lift that could take us down to the station was either out-of-order or locked, I really started to believe that the first word every Frenchman learns is 'non'. I was more convinced than ever when after parking on consecutive days in the same place at the Stade Velodrome in Marseille, I was nodded through the access gate to the stadium on one day and refused the next – by the same official. I had exactly the same accreditation, I was wearing exactly the same jacket, I was accompanied by exactly the same person and I was yet again the only disabled person in the entire day attempting to use that gate. The word was still 'non'!

How much these difficulties contributed to my general physical malaise I don't know. They certainly sapped my spirits. What I do know is that by the time I got to Paris for the last two weeks of the tournament, I was shattered. I had the energy to do very little. I spent most of the daytime in that last fortnight lying on my bed. Thankfully Ed Marriage had the sensitivity to excuse me from all but the essential briefings, and BBC colleagues Jill Douglas and Alastair Eykyn covered for me. I like to think that my commentaries were still pretty good. The atmosphere in the Stade de France as England notched up another improbable victory by beating France was incredible and when South Africa beat Argentina to set up a re-match it was possible to think that the impossible dream might just come true. England had been humiliated 36-0 when the two sides met in the pool stages. The Australians, the All Blacks and now the French had all been cleared out of the way and it was just conceivable that England might not only complete the most extraordinary comeback in the history of the tournament but also become the first team ever to successfully defend their title.

The build-up to the final was even more intense than four years previously, the speculation more prolonged and Five Live's involvement more enveloping.

But I was so low on energy that I almost welcomed it when a public transport strike in Paris made it impossible to attend some of the media briefings. I was focusing less on how my commentary could enhance a top-drawer rugby occasion than on whether I had the physical resources to get through it. That wasn't fair – to the event, to Five Live listeners or to myself. When Head of Sport Gordon Turnbull arrived for the final, I knew I had to book a meeting.

PART NINE

MS (ACCEPTANCE)

CHAPTER FORTY-ONE
CALLING TIME

I was a failure. When I was diagnosed with MS in 1999, I had declared my intention of working until I reached the BBC retirement age of 60. Yet here I was, preparing to bale out at 52.

I was a success. My original consultant had privately predicted I would be able to keep going 18 months, two years at the most. Nearly seven years later, I had just commentated on a World Cup final.

I was unlucky. I had been forced to retire by an incurable disease, with no known cause and no predictable course, which was both debilitating and progressive.

I was lucky. MS wasn't the big C, and though potentially life ruining was not life threatening. And it wasn't Motor Neurone Disease or something equally scary. Of all the incurable diseases to get, I had the best.

I was a mess. I had been so wrapped up in sport, in my job and in the peculiar lifestyle that it demanded, that I feared I didn't have much of an identity outside it.

I was sorted. I was in control, choosing what to do and when to do it. I was able to dictate the course of my life and I had both a right and a responsibility to live it the best way I could.

As my meeting with my boss approached, I couldn't decide which of these adjectives applied to me, and I couldn't yet accept that it was all of them.

As I saw it I had four options. I could carry on as I had done for the past few years, adapting, ducking and diving during the normal working year so that whenever there was a big event in the rugby calendar I was ready to cover it with all guns blazing, and whenever there wasn't I could crawl under the proverbial rock to recuperate. If I needed to re-load the guns in the middle of an event, or spend longer under the rock after it, then that could be arranged.

But all the evidence suggested that the former would only become more frequent while the latter would only become more prolonged. In the process more and more people would have to pay a heavy price, one they didn't deserve. If I went 'off the roster' during a Lions tour or a World Cup, that would place a huge strain on my colleagues. The more wiped out I was when I arrived home, the more of a burden it would be on Jeannie.

Or I could make a radical change of approach. I could elevate the job to such a level of importance that no sacrifice would be too great to keep it going. I could load up with vitamins, minerals and supplements, I could go wheat-free, dairy-free and even, god forbid, alcohol-free. I could get myself early to bed, I could follow a strict exercise regime and I could put my faith in any or all of the latest wonder-treatments.

But there was no guarantee that any of the new drugs would work. The only things I could be sure of getting from a course of vitamins, minerals and supplements were a hole in my wallet as I tried to pay for them and confusion in my brain as I tried to get my head round both the sheer number of recommended supplements and the sheer variety in the recommended daily doses.

I could go part-time. I could forget the day-to-day stuff, absent myself from run-of-the mill media briefings and miss out on the longer tours. I could just focus on commentating at the bigger matches on this side of the world.

But there's no such thing as being half-pregnant. I couldn't see a way that I could do half – or any fraction – of this particular job. To be done properly, it demanded full-time commitment. I was absolutely sure that I was a better commentator because I attended the media briefings as well. I was convinced that I was a better interviewer because of the added perspective that commentary gave me. And I was as certain as could be that only by repeatedly rubbing shoulders with the rest of the media on the regular rugby 'beat', did I gain the insight and perspective to do both. Of even greater significance, however, were the financial considerations. If I switched to working part-time, there would be a considerable and not very positive knock-on effect on my pension.

Or I could take medical retirement. To do the job as well as I had done it, and as well as I believed it deserved to be done, required more energy than I had. Rugby deserved someone who was ready and willing to fight tooth and nail to preserve its profile on a football-obsessed network, and Five Live needed someone with bags of energy as well as commitment to preserve the BBC's hard-won reputation in the sport. I didn't want that reputation to lose any of its lustre, any more than I wanted people to make excuses for me. I didn't want them to mutter knowingly, however understandingly, that I wasn't doing as well as I had, or could, or should. Using all the old clichés, I could quit while I was ahead, get out while I was still on top of my game and leave them wanting more.

Those were the arguments I rehearsed in the fortnight immediately following the 2007 World Cup. I had deliberately not asked for an early meeting, firstly because I needed to recharge my body's badly-depleted batteries and, secondly, to get my head straight. I hadn't knowingly chosen the Halfway House pub in the

Cotswolds as the venue for our meeting, but as the meeting approached the name seemed fairly significant. I was halfway between my old life, to whose rhythms I had become attuned and to whose peculiarities I had become accustomed, and a new life about which I had no idea at all. Once Gordon had listened to all my carefully rehearsed arguments and realised how much I had agonised over the life-altering choice I had made, it didn't take him long to set the wheels of early retirement in motion. Then it was up to me to make it all make sense.

Of course, Jeannie and I had already done plenty of 'What if?' thinking. One of our early mottoes had been to hope for the best, and plan for the worst. We had felt it important to give some thought to worst-case scenarios without in any way wishing them to happen or even believing that they would. But imagining what it would be like to take early retirement was very different indeed to actually giving up work. To apply for medical retirement was to take a step from which there was no going back and, from constant discussions throughout the summer, we only had a vague idea of what we were letting ourselves in for. Even so, I felt it was vital to get as many things as clear in my head as possible and, as the final few months of my full-time working life unfolded, I ransacked Amazon's bookshelves for advice and information on retirement and took myself off to a counsellor.

It was important for me to get my head round who I was. Because my job was so unusual and so high profile, I had always felt that I was defined by what I did and, within that, by what I had done. I had accumulated a larger than usual number of labels, all prefaced by ex-. I was an ex-rugby international, an ex-county cricketer (as well as an ex-teacher and an ex-television presenter) and now I was to be an ex-commentator as well. I had always had jobs that were more than jobs. They had a strong sense of purpose and they were highly skewed towards job-satisfaction. They were fulfilling, demanding, at times all-consuming and hadn't left room for anything else. Now there was not only room but also a gaping hole and I had to find out pretty quickly how to fill it. What would float my boat from now on?

Apart from finding out how important my job had been to the definition of me as a human being, I also needed to know how important it had been in helping me face up to MS. The job had been so all-enveloping that I had initially submerged myself within it to avoid having to face the fact that I had the condition. Even when I had come round to acknowledging that I had MS, I had used the job to keep MS in its place. I would accept that I had MS and needed to do something about it on Mondays, when I would report for treatment. The rest of the week, when I was at work, I could pretend that I was too busy to give it much thought. Now, however, the rest of the week was going to be empty. Would MS, or my perception of the difficulties it posed, expand to fill that gap? With not much else to occupy my attention, would I end up magnifying those difficulties? My approach to life had always been firmly based on the 'Can-Do'. Now I had admitted one of the biggest 'Can't-Dos' of all, would that open the floodgates for others? Was I in the process of turning from a positive to a negative? By admitting that some things were too much hard work was I taking the first step onto the slippery slope where every thing was too much trouble? Had I stopped being a doer, a contributor, an active person? Had I become a taker, a passenger, a passive person? What would make me want to get up in the morning? What was going to replace work?

At some time or other, everybody wishes they didn't have to work any more. We all, I believe, fantasise about a life without the strain of having to do something, be somewhere at a certain time, perform to someone else's criteria, march to someone else's drum. Even though I had enjoyed a fantastic job, I hadn't been entirely impervious to that impulse. But that was only in my dreams. Now it was actually going to happen, how would I cope with the reality?

And how would I cope with being at home all the time? Most of us also fantasise about spending more time with our life-partners, dream of all the things we could do together and anticipate a special relationship getting even stronger. I was now coming face-to-face with the realisation that our relationship had been forged when we were both members of the workforce and refined, re-defined and strengthened while at least one of us had been tied to full-time employment, and all it entailed. The new reality was scary. How would we react to being in each other's pockets all day, every day? We both acknowledged that we had suffered at the other extreme. I had been away from home far too often and, especially since rejoining the BBC, for far too long. The big events – Lions tours and World Cups – had taken me away for the best part of two months every other year. Every year in the last decade I had spent the entire month of June out of the country – indeed I couldn't remember the last time I'd seen my son Dan on his 3 June birthday. Every period of prolonged absence had been followed by a prolonged period of readjustment to each other and, especially since the onset of MS, a prolonged period of recovery. How would we cope when our year had a completely different rhythm?

And how would we cope with weekends? In 27 years of married life, we had never really had one. Ever since I was a teenager, the weekend had not meant two days of rest but two days of activity. I had always played sport on a Saturday or a Sunday, or usually both, and then coached or commentated on it. I didn't really understand the concept. Jeannie had grown up in an environment where people worked 9 to 5 Monday to Friday, and then relaxed at the weekend. More importantly, they got together with their friends, went on outings with their neighbours and visited their families. Throughout the whole of our married life we had been unable to rely on the weekend for that purpose and it had played havoc with our social life. Now we not only had weekends, but weekdays as well, how would we fill them? The difficulties of hooking up with friends and loved ones on a regular basis had, in my absence, forced Jeannie to rely on a network of female friends and, when I was home, thrown us more and more on each other's company. Nearly all my friends had been made through work. Now that was about to go, how would we cope? How difficult would it be to relate to people outside the sporting environment? How much would potential friends be put off by the labels that had attached themselves to me? How much had I hidden behind those labels to avoid the hard work and emotional investment of making friends, and how much was I able to change? How much would my inability to drive alter the new dynamic of our social life? To be fair, Jeannie had always done the lion's share of the driving but now there was not even a chance of my getting behind the wheel. In employment, the burden of ferrying me around had been shared by others. Now it was to rest squarely on Jeannie's shoulders. That was bound to have an effect, but what?

As well as facing up to the future, I also had to face up to the past. Just about everybody has to draw a line at some stage in their life between a working present and a retired future, whatever either of those phrases might mean. But they usually get to do that when their contemporaries are doing the same thing and they often get to walk away when they've had enough. But I was only 52. I had loved my job and because of that I had been able to accept the enforced absences, the unpredictability and the lack of either a structure or a social life. Now, in saying good riddance to the bad bits, I also had to bid goodbye to the good bits. I wanted to do it right. I couldn't do the job part-time, and I didn't want to be a hanger-on, a spectre at the feast. I didn't want to feel bitter, or regretful, or be a frustrated outsider looking in. I felt it was important to acknowledge the passing of a crucial part of my life, to honour its importance and to acknowledge the grief I felt at its going.

And then I would be free to begin again, to start a new, if inevitably circumscribed, life with Jeannie. I would be free to concentrate on the things that mattered most and to enjoy them for what they actually were and not what they were in relation to my career. I was determined to look on my new status not as 'retirement' but as 'no longer in regular paid employment'. I wanted it to be an opportunity, not a punishment. I had been granted an unexpected opportunity to do something different with my life, and I was determined to take it. And there were plenty of things I fancied doing.

I wanted to devote more energy and time to the MSRC. I wanted to see if there was any mileage in a return to teaching, if only part-time. I knew that the history curriculum had changed hugely in the quarter of a century since I'd been in the classroom but I'd heard of the new subject of Media Studies and thought that my two decades of practical experience might count for something. I wanted to write, for myself and my family as well as a wider public. I would never have had a chance to pen this autobiography if I hadn't taken medical retirement when I did, and I'm already planning some books based on research I've been doing into some of my more colourful ancestors and relations.

But, as I crossed the t's and dotted the i's of my departure from the BBC, those were very much items for the future. The present involved saying goodbye – and I will always be grateful to Gordon Turnbull for allowing me to go on to the end of the season before drawing the curtain down. I was going to enjoy a prolonged Farewell Tour.

PART TEN
FAREWELL TOUR

CHAPTER FORTY-TWO
SAYING GOODBYE
(2007–08)

'London Wasps 23... Leicester Tigers 11... Leicester on the attack, five metres from the Wasps line...'

The first few words of the handover...

It was 31 May 2008 and Wasps were on their way to victory in the Guinness Premiership final in front of a packed house at Twickenham. The last few seconds of my broadcasting career...

How many times had I said that? Far too many to count, that was for sure. In over two decades I had commentated on the first 20 minutes of each half in the Premiership, the knockout cup, the Heineken Cup, on Lions tours and in nearly two hundred Test matches. My last international commentary a couple of months earlier had been a comparative rarity in that it wasn't at Twickenham and didn't feature England.

Despite reaching the World Cup final the previous autumn, England had again disappointed in the Six Nations. Defeats by Wales and Scotland were to cost Brian Ashton his job before the summer was out and they also meant that England's final match of the tournament – at home to Ireland – was a 'dead rubber'. For the second time in four years, Robbo and I were switched to Cardiff where Wales were once again on course for a Grand Slam. The fact that they were up against France provided all sorts of symmetry for me. Just over 22 years previously my first international commentary had featured France. Exactly 20 years ago at this very fixture, I had commentated on my first Grand Slam match, when France had spoiled the Welsh party. And it was in Cardiff that I had bowed out as an England player – at the wrong end of a record defeat in 1979.

This time though there was only joy. The Welsh Rugby Union made me a special presentation before the game – and the Welsh team did the decent thing by completing the Grand Slam. To make a memorable day even more special, I was at the mike when Shane Williams scored what turned out to be the decisive try.

It was coming up for 33 years since I had first become involved in international rugby. As a nervous 19-year-old I'd made my debut in front of a few thousand at Brisbane's quaint old Ballymore Stadium. The Millennium Stadium in 2008 could hold a crowd four times the size, and so could every other Six Nations' stadium except Italy's. The game I had played had changed out of all recognition, and most of the major changes had coincided with my journalistic career. I had just begun at the BBC when leagues were introduced into England and the first World Cup was held in Australia and New Zealand. I was cutting my teeth in regional television when the rules on amateurism were first relaxed and I rejoined the BBC as the game went professional and English clubs signed up for the Heineken Cup. I had covered the last amateur Lions tour and the first three professional ones and I had been commentating on England's finest rugby hour.

I had a feast of memories to draw on. England's finest performance? The first half of the Melbourne international against the Wallabies in the summer of 2003. England's bravest performance? The match against New Zealand a week earlier when, with two players in the sin-bin, England's six-man pack held out against an All Black team that had set itself up for the kill. England's worst performance? The 76-0 thrashing by Australia in Brisbane on the infamous 'Tour to Hell' of 1998.

Best World Cup matches? Australia's 1991 semi-final victory over New Zealand in Ireland, France's extraordinary comeback against the All Blacks at Twickenham eight years later, Jonah Lomu's four-try demolition of England in 1995 and Fiji's exhilarating quarter-final against the Springboks in 2007.

In the Six Nations, England's Grand Slam win over Ireland in Dublin, Wales' Wembley win, Ireland's first win in Paris for 28 years in 2000, and, in 1991, England's first victory in Cardiff for the same length of time.

On four Lions tours there had been nothing to match those extraordinary first Test wins in Cape Town in 1997 and in Brisbane four years later.

Some matches on which I had commentated were inevitably more special than others, and some were harder work. But I hope I never lost the joy; I had travelled the world watching top-class rugby from the best seats in the house, and been paid for the privilege. What's not to like?

'... we're entering the last quarter of the match... '

The Millennium Stadium also provided the setting for my last Heineken Cup match as Munster beat Toulouse in the final. Again, I was overwhelmed when the organisers marked the occasion with a presentation and again I was overwhelmed with memories. It was in Cardiff that I had watched my first ever match in the competition – the final in 1996 – and that too had featured Toulouse. Not surprisingly, considering they are the two most successful sides in the history of the competition, most of the epic Heineken Cup trips that I'd undertaken down the years had involved Munster, or Toulouse or both.

Time was frozen and distances were shrunk when the calendar came round to the Heineken Cup. Back in 1998, my second year with Five Live, I thought I was both romantic and daring in attempting to combine a quarter-final in Toulouse (the home side beating Harlequins 51-10) with a next-day dash down the motorway for Pau against Leicester (the Tigers losing 35-18). By 2005, I was so besotted with the tournament that I thought nothing of haring round France and Spain for a Friday night in Toulouse (Northampton lost 37-9), a Saturday afternoon in Paris (Stade Francais 48 Newcastle 8) and a Sunday in San Sebastian (Biarritz 19 Munster 10). Two years previously, there'd been an 'Irish odyssey' at the pool stages; on Friday I had followed Northampton to Ulster's Ravenhill (a home win by 16 points to 13) and on Sunday I had followed Leinster back to Bristol (a home defeat 12-25). In between I'd hiked myself across to Thomond Park for the 'Miracle Match' when Munster beat Gloucester by exactly the required margin to qualify for the knockout stages.

The finale to that match had been so tempestuous and the permutations so tortuous that all available scrap paper had been used up in the calculations of who had won it. As the final whistle sounded, the studio presenter asked me to clarify what it meant. My mind had flashed back immediately to 1998 when the Brive-Toulouse semi-final ended 22-22 and I'd had no idea what was to happen next. At Thomond Park the solution was easy – all I needed to do was hold a microphone up to the crowd. They'd done their sums all right.

The Munster fans are the living proof that the love affair with Europe is not confined to the rugby media. The Bath fans who witnessed their team's daylight robbery of defending champions Brive in the Bordeaux final of 1998 would have run the Munster supporters close that day. So would Ulster's fans as they watched their team beat four French teams, including Colomiers in the Lansdowne Road final, the following year.

And I will always associate the Heineken Cup with 'The Fields of Athenry', while my abiding visual memory will be of the giant screens in Cardiff in 2006 as they broadcast pictures of the massed ranks of Munster supporters in Limerick's main square. The Munster players saw it too. No wonder they were inspired to carry off the trophy for the first time.

There was no doubt in my mind that the Heineken Cup had taken rugby to a bigger stage. English clubs started using football grounds only in response to the extraordinary demand for European Cup tickets. Leicester, for instance, staged big matches at Nottingham Forest's City Ground and Leicester City's Walker's Stadium before deciding to expand their own ground. Reading's Madejski Stadium was a venue for Heineken Cup matches long before London Irish made it their home. Leinster used to play at homely Donnybrook, now they strut their stuff at the Royal Dublin Showground. Munster have transformed Thomond

Park on the back of their Heineken Cup success, while the Ospreys at Swansea and the Scarlets at Llanelli have new grounds to cope with the larger crowds that flock to European matches. Biarritz's solution to the same welcome problem has been not just to switch to a soccer ground but also to switch to a different country.

The Heineken Cup had transformed the rugby landscape during my time as a commentator. The Premiership had transformed itself. Attendances at club matches had more than doubled since I had covered my first match for the BBC back in 1985. Stadiums had been built, rebuilt, borrowed and in some cases abandoned. Some clubs had embraced professionalism while others had been washed away by it. Some of the great clubs of yesteryear had fallen by the wayside while younger, newer, more ambitious outfits had come thrusting forward to take their place.

The advent of professionalism had rendered the English club game multicultural. There had always been a smattering of Scots, Irish and Welsh. The French had come and, almost to a man, gone again. Argentinians, Fijians, Tongans and especially Samoans had settled in for the duration – or at least until they could find a better market for their extraordinary rugby skills. At the same time, the competition had become the destination of choice for those South Africans, Australians and New Zealanders who were either near the beginning of their careers, and couldn't see a future in their own domestic structure, or near the end of them and looking for one or two big pay days to set up their retirement.

The players themselves had changed much less than I had feared. I'd worried that when the sport became less like a game and more like a job of work, the values that I had treasured so much among rugby people – openness, integrity, compassion, generosity, kindness – would become submerged. I feared that rugby players would feel the need to cloak themselves in the characteristics of the business world they now inhabited – and lose some of their humanity in the process. Being professional meant delivering value for money – I got that. Players would have to devote themselves to their game rather than play at it. They would put in the work – on the training ground, in the gym as well as on the pitch – and they would earn their salaries. In this context hard, uncompromising, single-minded and focused were all good adjectives. I feared that dirty, ruthless, obsessive and blinkered were but a hair's breadth away and that while the commercial world in which rugby now found itself was regularly described as 'cut-throat', 'dog-eat-dog' and 'savage', those qualities would be deeply unattractive if embraced by the players.

But I had been pleasantly surprised. The new breed of player was every bit as instinctively generous as his predecessor. It helped that their mentors set the right example. Clive Woodward was hugely important in encouraging England players to take a broader view of the world. Damian Hopley set the right tone as chief executive of the players' union, the PRA (later the RPA). Men like Lawrence Dallaglio, Matt Dawson and Jason Leonard were as compassionate, generous and giving as they were talented, driven and successful, while the sport's first great superstar was the perfect role model.

Jonny Wilkinson was, still is, a decent human being who just happens to be an outstanding rugby player. In my experience, he had never let his extraordinary fame go to his head. He hadn't always been great to interview – that was either because over-protective media minders were desperate to get him in front of the next microphone or because he was so determined not to bad-mouth anyone that he often didn't say anything remotely memorable. He was an outstanding role model and rugby was lucky to have him. The public image of the game that had consumed most of my adult life was in good hands.

And so were its finances. As I gazed round Twickenham on the last day in May 2008, it was easy to see just how far the game had come in my lifetime. Not a single stand remained from the stadium I had first played in just over a quarter of a century previously. The South Stand, away to my right, had actually been replaced twice since my playing days and its new reincarnation was set to take the stadium capacity to over 90,000. Every big match at the stadium was a sell-out at the turnstiles and brought in millions of pounds.

This one was no exception. Leicester were the best supported club in the land and only Wasps could come close to matching their success on the field. Both had won the Heineken Cup twice in the last decade and were past-masters in cup competitions. Neither had won the league since 2002, but Wasps had won the Premiership play-off final three times in the last five seasons, and Leicester once. I wasn't entirely happy with the concept – I didn't feel it quite right that the winner of a league competition should be decided by a knockout competition – but, looking round a packed and raucous Twickenham, I could certainly see the commercial sense. And, although the West Countryman in me would have been satisfied if beaten semi-finalists Gloucester and Bath had got to Twickenham – I was delighted that my last day in the commentary box should be contested by the two clubs who had given most to England in my time as a journalist. I took one last look at Lawrence Dallaglio. The Wasps captain was also retiring that day and, in previous big matches, had been substituted after an hour of play. During the week, I had joked with him that if he followed the same timetable I was going to change my usual hand-over to 'Lawrence Dallaglio, great servant of English rugby, takes his leave of Twickenham... And if he's going, I'm going too.' But Lawrence was clearly enjoying his final fling too much. His coaches were obviously determined he would stay on and finish the job. I shrugged my shoulders mentally, and went back to the old formula...

'... and to take you through to full-time, Ian Robertson...'

Robbo. The single biggest influence on my career. As coach of Cambridge he had turned me from a county cricketer who could play at scrum-half into an international full-back for whom rugby would gradually assume centre stage. As the BBC's rugby correspondent, he'd encouraged me to abandon schoolteaching in 1985 and to quit ITV a decade later. As a commentator he had been an inspiration. As a colleague he had been generous, loyal, witty and fun. And, when it came to timekeeping, exasperating. Down the years, Ed Marriage had lost count of the hours we had spent waiting in hotel lobbies, studio foyers, car parks and commentary-boxes for Ian to show up. To adapt the John Lewis strap-line, he was 'never knowingly on time', and, to adapt Samuel Beckett, 'waiting for Robbo' had become an absurdist ritual at times, the only solution for which was to tell Ian that we were leaving half-an-hour before we actually needed to.

Robbo's driving was as erratic as his timekeeping. A latecomer to the steering wheel, he was far more at home – although only marginally less dangerous – on his motor-scooter, and he never really got the hang of a manual gearbox. Or parking. On one occasion in Edinburgh he switched off the engine and got out of the car in the middle of the street, before handing the keys to a bemused passenger and asking her if she would manoeuvre it into a parking space as it was too difficult for him. His navigation wasn't much better, and he wasn't a great fan of map-reading. On another occasion in Scotland I had driven him out to Livingston where, as part of an exercise to take the game out to the people, the SRU had sent the team for its final training session before playing England the following day. We got hopelessly lost and, after Robbo had sent me round the same roundabout for the fourth time, I had become more than a little frustrated.

'Pull in front of that bus,' commanded Robbo. 'The driver's bound to know where the rugby pitch is.' I wasn't entirely convinced about the logic of this statement and from the length of time Robbo spent in earnest discussion with the bus driver I assumed my suspicions had been correct. But Robbo returned to the car grinning from ear to ear.

'Just follow the bus,' he said. 'He'll take us straight to the ground.'

'If he knows where it is, why did it take him so long to suggest we follow him?' I asked.

'That's because his first words were "You're that Ian Robertson off the radio" and I felt I had to tell him a little story just to get him in the mood to help us.'

I had to admit that it worked. The bus driver led us right into the rugby-ground car park and waved cheerfully on the way out. I wound down my window to thank him and asked him how the passengers had responded to an unsolicited detour of a couple of miles through the streets of Livingston.

'Dinna' worry about them,' he said. 'They'll understand. I told them it was for Ian Robertson of the BBC!'

As a companion, Robbo is world-class. He is one of the funniest men I know and a born raconteur. Although it is possible to grow tired of his shaggy-dog stories – I reckon I've heard the Jimmy McGhee joke upwards of two dozen times – it's impossible not to laugh at them. Robbo is the greatest company – just as well because we've probably had dinner together several hundred times, even though he has an unfathomable preference for Chardonnay over Sauvignon

Blanc – and he has been the truest of friends as his reaction on hearing the news of MS goes to prove.

My friend's voice, as he adjusted his microphone in response to my handover, was a little huskier than normal. 'Thanks, Higgy... a million thanks... best wishes to you on your retirement... Now, Leicester... '

And the surprises didn't stop there. A tap on my shoulder revealed John Inverdale crouched down in the commentary box wanting to conduct a television interview for the BBC. My words came tumbling out – I was still speaking at commentator speed – and I had to admit that the emotion of the day was getting to me. 'I bit the tears back when Rob Andrew made a little presentation on the pitch before the match, and I've been biting them back all week, to be honest. I'm pretty sure that by the end of the day I'll be blubbing.'

John, of course, knew what I was referring to. On hearing that this was to be my last day, the RFU had organised a send-off. They'd put a bar at the disposal of the Rugby Writers Club – I would have been chairman that year if I hadn't taken medical retirement – and invited all the journalists to a farewell drink for me and for Andrew Titheridge, the genial journalist from commercial radio with whom I had waited outside dozens of dressing room doors and who, like me, was hanging up his microphone for health reasons. He didn't know that the Sky cameras had swung in my direction at various junctures in the game or that Lawrence Dallaglio would pay tribute to me when interviewed on television immediately after the match. But he did know what the occasion meant to me.

I had tried to prepare for the day. I had known that saying a formal goodbye to the colleagues and friends of the last two decades was going to be tough. These were the men and women with whom I'd attended a thousand press conferences, with whom I'd shared notes, jokes, lifts, flights and dinners. These were the people with whom I knocked around at work and, because life on tour throws you all together, at play. These were my mates – clever, witty, sympathetic and gregarious. They loved their rugby, they loved their jobs and they loved life. They were cheerful, loyal and instinctively generous. They were my kind of people – and I was going to miss them.

And I was going to miss the job. But even as I bathed in the warmth, the humour and the sheer goodwill of my colleagues on that never-to-be-forgotten last day, I had a reminder of just why and how life is so difficult for the disabled. The day had begun with a man in a yellow jacket attempting to prevent me from accessing the floor from which I had broadcast for more than two decades on the grounds that there was nowhere to put my buggy when the match was on. I shrugged this off as ignorance – I had left it in the commentators' room ever since I had become buggy-dependent. I regretted the fact that I had to waste energy in a needless argument but accepted the fact that the steward was only doing his job.

The day ended with two doormen carrying my buggy down 20 steps from the function room that had been set side for my farewell. The half-floor it was on had no lift access. The RFU could not have been more amenable in laying on the party in the first place and were most apologetic when they realised the problem. It was a genuine mistake and stemmed from the genuine lack of imagination that so often impacts on the disabled in their ordinary lives. I had been inconvenienced on this occasion and, if Ed Marriage hadn't been on hand to get me up the stairs, and if the doormen hadn't been on hand to get me down them, it could have been highly embarrassing all-round.

But if nothing else, the incident served as a confirmation that my instincts were sound. Over the last few years the job had become even more demanding and the practicalities of broadcasting with MS were becoming a nightmare for me. Trying to lever myself into and out of inadequate and dangerous commentary boxes, assembling and disassembling my buggy, lugging broadcasting equipment up flights of awkward stairs and through unforgiving crowds, were not on their own insurmountable problems. Taken as a whole, they created sizeable barriers both to the performance of my job and its enjoyment.

But while these barriers were showing no sign of shrinking, my ability to cope with them was. I knew I had made the right decision to retire. But that didn't stop it hurting.

PART ELEVEN

MS (HOPE)

CHAPTER FORTY-THREE

WHAT NOW?

Spasticity. Chronic fatigue. Bladder urgency. Optic neuritis. Muscular spasms. Vertigo. Tremor. Tics. Cramps. Cognitive dysfunction. Wastage. Weakness.

Those are some of the symptoms of multiple sclerosis. Staggering. Stumbling. Slurring. Inability to see straight. Inability to think straight. Loss of control of your bladder, your balance, your swallowing mechanism. A tendency to fall asleep. Involuntary movement. These are some of the ways multiple sclerosis manifests itself. For some people; for some of the time.

Multiple sclerosis is a disease with no known cause and no known cure. It's impossible to predict who it will affect and how. It won't kill you, but it can ruin your life. A friend described it as 'a bit like going into the bathroom and flicking the light switch. The light might go on now, or it might go on later, or flash indeterminately, or it might not go on at all. The bath might start to run, or the radio might start to play in another room. Every electrical appliance in the house might roar into life, or none of them. Nothing is certain.'

As well as being uncertain, MS can also be progressive, and debilitating, and scary. Scary enough for a beautiful young schoolteacher to take her own life because she couldn't face the loss of control and the loss of dignity that a progressive illness might bring. (Admittedly this teacher was only a character in the BBC's prime-time soap *Waterloo Road*, but it's safe to assume that the writers only took a small amount of artistic licence.) Scary in the light of the case of MS-sufferer Debbie Purdy, who hit the headlines in 2009 when she had to appeal to the Law Lords to ensure that if her husband were to help her to commit suicide some time in the future, he would not be prosecuted. Especially scary in the case of Cari Loder, who had enjoyed several years in the limelight in the 1990s after claiming to have found a cure for her MS but who in 2009 took her own life because she feared being a totally dependent burden on her carers. And scary enough for *Daily Mail* journalist Hilary Freeman, herself an MS sufferer, to wonder whether she might do the same if she couldn't manage her MS symptoms on her own. She painted the bleakest picture: 'end-stage MS is not a pleasant prospect. You become bedridden, paralysed, in pain, incontinent, unable to speak and swallow, blind and deaf, and possibly demented, too. There's no hope of recovery.'

I admit to being scared. I acknowledge that I do display quite a large number of the symptoms described here – and I'm well aware that they affect me at random, and to a greater or lesser degree. I know that physically I am a lot worse now than I was when first diagnosed in 1999. I have sporadic problems with my bladder, my swallowing mechanism and my thought processes. Most significantly, I have the chronic fatigue which is the one symptom that seems common to all MS sufferers – so debilitating on bad days that I have to rest after my morning shower, and moving from one room in the house to another is a real struggle. It's as if I have a faulty rechargeable battery. Before diagnosis, I was always supremely confident that however much energy I used up performing a task, or series of tasks, I could replace it – in full and reasonably quickly. Now, the energy can drain suddenly and inexplicably and there is no certainty that I will ever get it all back. It's become a precious commodity that has to be rationed. For someone who used to pride himself on his ability to take on anything, to keep going longer and to stay up later in order to get things done, this is by far the hardest aspect of MS to take. The spirit is still willing, but the flesh has become incredibly weak.

I don't drive any more, after smashing my car in 2005. I need a stick to walk and an electric buggy to cover any distance of more than 50 metres. I'm bad on stairs, and my balance is poor. I struggle to raise my right arm above my head and my right leg doesn't function very well at all. As a top-class sportsman I could rely on my body to do extraordinary things – catch a high ball, tackle an 18-stone forward, face fast bowling at 90 miles an hour. Now I can't rely on it to do ordinary things like fasten the top button on my shirt, or do up my cufflinks.

And I am as frustrated as hell that even though MS is the most common neurological complaint among young people in the country, there is still a long way to go until a cure is found. It seems that the research establishment is pinning a lot of hope on stem cells and there has been some success in trials carried out on patients with the relapsing-remitting form of the disease. But the cowboys have also spotted an opportunity and have not been slow to offer stem cell treatment in less tightly regulated parts of the world. The same is true of CCSVI (Chronic Cerebro Spinal Venous Insufficiency), a condition discovered in MS patients by an Italian, Doctor Zamboni. He noticed that most of his patients with MS suffered from stenosis, a narrowing of the veins that are primarily used to drain blood from the spine and brain, and he knew that the resulting hypoxia, a lack of oxygen in the brain, has been linked to fatigue in Multiple Sclerosis. When he found he could reverse the symptoms through an angioplasty, or 'liberation' procedure, shockwaves reverberated around the MS community. But the optimistic assumption that here at last was a cure for MS that didn't involve drugs didn't last for long. As more and more research showed that not everyone with CCSVI has MS and not everyone with MS has CCSVI, it seemed increasingly that the optimism was misplaced and that any trials to link cause and effect would take years to complete.

That is for me one of the most frustrating things about MS. If 'they' discovered a cure tomorrow, it would take several years of tests to establish whether it was safe for me to use. In the meantime, the drugs that I can take are disease modifying, don't work for everyone and can have pretty nasty side effects.

I stopped taking beta interferon because it made me feel as if I had heavy flu three times a week. Another drug that is earning rave reviews has also been shown to result in a thyroid complaint for one in four users. That would be my idea of hell: to take tablets for the rest of my life to deal with the thyroid disorder that only happened because I took drugs to modify the course of my MS. No thank you. I'm convinced that I'm better off with the devil I know. There is no cure, but I can live with that. I'll have to.

I can also say I am blessed to have MS. It has enabled me to discover things about myself and other people that I might never have thought possible. It has exposed me to the incredible generosity, goodwill and love that human beings are capable of. I have been amazed and humbled not just at the extraordinary efforts of Ian Robertson in raising funds to help me deal with this implacable disease but also at the incredible and selfless support of my wife Jeannie whose instinctive promise that this is not my MS but hers as well has been central to my life since diagnosis. And I have been lucky enough, through MS, to have been in the presence of some remarkable human beings; not just those with MS whose courage, cheerfulness and can-do approach to life is incredibly inspiring, and not just those who work for those with MS – among whom Lawrence and Rachel Wood and the folk at the MSRC are outstanding human beings – but also people in general. If I hadn't been diagnosed with MS, it's likely that I would have carried on trying to force my way up the greasy career-pole, focusing almost exclusively on my own needs and those of my family. I wouldn't have had the faintest idea of how much goodness there is out there in the world. I wouldn't have learnt a lesson about asking for help that should have been blindingly obvious. I may have always prided myself on being instinctively generous – and usually pleased and honoured to be asked for help – but before I had MS I just couldn't credit anyone else with feeling the same. Maybe it was because of my boarding school, Armed Forces upbringing. Maybe it was the ruthlessness necessary to survive in top-class sport, but I was so fiercely independent, so resolutely self-sufficient that while I would happily help anyone else, I would rather suffer any amount of physical and mental anguish than ask anyone to help me. How stupid. Since my diagnosis, I have learnt to ask for help – and, shamefully, I have been surprised to find just how many wonderful people there are out there prepared to offer it even without asking.

That's how Higgy's Heroes was born. In 2008, the year I called it a day with the BBC, I was overwhelmed to discover that Joe Davies, a friend of mine from university days, was not only going to run the marathon for the MSRC but was also going to raise a team from among those who had played university sport with and against me way back in the mid-1970s. Somebody at the charity asked if he would mind, because of the connection, calling the group of runners Higgy's Heroes. He didn't, and I was deeply honoured and completely gobsmacked at the thought that this intrepid band of fifty-somethings – all of whom were old enough to know better – should not only be undertaking such a physically and mentally demanding challenge but also, sort of, doing it because of me. And when I heard that between them they had raised well over £60,000 for the charity, I was absolutely ecstatic.

That should have been the end of Higgy's Heroes. And it would have been but for a chance encounter with the *Stroud News and Journal*'s sports editor Ashley Loveridge. Ashley had read all about Higgy's Heroes and wondered if by any chance the team could be reformed for the Stroud half-marathon?

'Not a chance,' I replied, my mind still fresh with the anguished expression of most of the Heroes at the end of the race and the heartfelt words of one of them. 'That was my first marathon,' Mal Malik had said that afternoon, just a pale facsimile of the livewire flanker he had been in a couple of Varsity Matches, 'and it will very definitely be my last!'

'But what if we get a team of runners from the Stroud area?' said Ashley. 'I've always wanted to get fit enough to run the race and if I was a member of the team I know I wouldn't be able to pull out.' I was starting to warm to the idea. 'And then there's a couple of people at the *Journal* I could ask, and, maybe if your wife and your sons volunteered to run,' continued Ashley, 'that would give us some momentum.' I could see the double-page story was already forming in his head and promised to ask my family at the earliest opportunity.

Which wasn't early enough. Jeannie opened that week's *Journal* to find that the double-page spread had not only been printed and also carried a picture of her and Adam and Dan, as well as the announcement that they were going to run the Stroud half-marathon as Higgy's Heroes. When she picked herself up off the floor, this amazing woman committed herself wholeheartedly to the challenge and wasted no time in shaming our sons into agreeing to run as well. And then she badgered friends, accosted complete strangers and even talked visiting tradesmen into taking up the challenge. And my brother, my sister, and any number of nephews and nieces all crumbled before the force of nature that was Jeannie. All agreed to gather in Stroud at the end of October as Higgy's Heroes.

We enrolled 35 runners that first year as well as some volunteer physios. More importantly, we had the wholehearted backing of the charity, which under the guidance of new chief executive Helen Yates threw itself behind the project with extraordinary gusto. On race day itself, the team of volunteers, complete with mascot Maximus Bear, rapper-clappers, banners and specially marked out cheering points, contributed such an extraordinary energy to the event that the decision to re-form the following October was a simple one to take.

In 2009 I ran a campaign to 'Help Higgy Hit a Hundred' and exceed the target comfortably. Over 130 Higgy's Heroes formed a sea of green MSRC T-shirts in a giant team photo at the start of the race, the pubs and businesses of Stroud lent their backing again, friends chipped in to help provide tea and support and once again the route was lined with supporters. After doing a deal with the local sweetshop, I set up a Jelly baby station at the 11-mile mark and was pleasantly surprised how many runners – not just Higgy's Heroes – felt the need to get a late glucose fix and took a detour to where I sat on the buggy with a giant bag of sweets in front of me. It was the least I could do to salute those who had chosen to support the MSRC. To think that some of them had chosen to do so because of me was a wonderful and welcome responsibility. It looks like Higgy's Heroes will run and run. And we're always looking for new events to raise awareness of MS – and funds for the MSRC.

It hasn't been difficult to devote more time and energy to the MSRC and I don't regard it as a substitute for anything. I regard it as an opportunity. I can't commentate any more – in fact there are lots of things I can't do any more – but I can do this. I want to continue being useful and productive and if my name, my example, my words or my contacts can help make life a little better for people with MS, then I'll be happy.

I truly believe that MS has taken me on a journey of discovery. It hasn't always been plain sailing and there have been plenty of troughs as well as peaks. But I'm a very different person from the man who discovered he had MS on 8 January 1999. In one way, it seems pretentious to appropriate a model first designed to deal with death and dying by Swiss psychiatrist Elisabeth Kubler-Ross, but in another it makes perfect sense. Kubler-Ross believed that there were five stages in the way people dealt with grief and tragedy and the more I've thought about it the more uncanny seems the coincidence between her model and my experiences. But whereas Doctor Kubler-Ross details the stages as Denial, Anger, Bargaining, Depression and Acceptance, my experience was that the Anger came first, while the Depression was replaced by a longer period of Bargaining – which I have called (reaching an) Understanding – and Acceptance has been followed by Hope.

That's where I believe I am now. I was incredibly angry when I was first diagnosed. What right did MS have to pick on me? I was fit, healthy, sporting and active. I'd hardly had a day's illness in my life. How could someone as strong as me contract a debilitating disease such as this? I had enjoyed a series of successful and high profile jobs. My feet were firmly planted on the pathway to a fulfilling, demanding and thoroughly enjoyable career. How dare this condition attempt to kick my legs away from underneath me? If it was going to be a battle of strength, the competitive animal in me was up for the fight. If it was going to be a battle of wits, I reckoned that I had the intellectual arsenal to win that too.

And, I reasoned, if it was just me against MS, why did anyone else need to know? If I owned up to any weakness, any crack would soon become a gaping chasm. On the other hand, if I denied the disease the slightest chance to get a grip, then it couldn't even begin to take over. If I excluded MS from my mind, then surely it would leave my body alone? All I had to do was pretend it wasn't there, blame the symptoms on any other cause and carry on regardless. Give MS an inch and it would take a mile? Best not give it anything. Best to ignore it altogether.

If that was impossible, do a deal. If I couldn't disguise the fact of my MS, then at least I could control it. I could undertake to deal with it in my own time and in my own way, as long as the MS would allow me to get on with the rest of my life. The Bargaining, I believed, could be pretty straightforward. I would take ownership of MS but our relationship would be that of master-servant. I would call the shots. I would acknowledge I had MS, but bend it to my bidding. I would employ a few strategies to cope with the worst effects, but basically I was in control. This was my MS and I was going to deal with it.

At this point I diverge from the Kubler-Ross model. She felt that Depression was the next stage. But she was talking about death. That was still miles away from my mind. For Kubler-Ross the realisation of the certainty of death would lead the individual to withdraw, to disconnect from things that were precious, to get ready for the finality of the outcome. I may have realised the certainty of the MS progression but my response was to stave it off with a bit more Bargaining and use the breathing space I so gained to come to terms with the finality. I called that stage Understanding in the sense that coming to an understanding was an extension of Bargaining and in the sense that reaching Understanding was all part of the journey towards Acceptance.

For me, Acceptance meant a cessation of hostilities. It meant that what had been a bitter industrial dispute between militant unions (the MS) and the bosses (me, of course) had called in ACAS. The arbitrators – of rationality, recognition and common sense – were going to settle the matter to the mutual benefit of all concerned. In sporting terms it wasn't so much a score draw as match abandoned. By withdrawing from the contest at a time and in a manner of my own choosing, I was leaving with my head held high, my dignity intact and some energy remaining.

And because I have not been completely wrecked in the exchanges I am able to function at a different level and to a different speed. I've been able to honour my past and bid a proper and fond farewell to my career. I've salvaged enough from my experiences and received such support from my family and friends that I feel a huge optimism about the next stage of my life. This isn't what I planned, and there is a scary element to it. But there's also something new and exciting. I've been given an opportunity to branch out in a completely different direction.

I've had the benefit of some wonderful, exciting experiences in my life already. Now I'm getting the chance to have some more.

And, because of the MS, I'm in an even better position to enjoy them. Since I was diagnosed – the event will for ever be seared into my memory – I've learnt a lot about myself. I've learned to be more open with my emotions and to be more tolerant and compassionate. I've been given a golden opportunity to find out what really matters in life – the people, the relationships, the places and the things. I have a wristband from the Multiple Sclerosis Resource Centre, whose patron I am. It simply says, 'Life is for Living', and I couldn't agree more. And, if it's taken the onset of an incurable disease to bring that simple truth home to me, then I've every reason to be grateful for it.

POSTSCRIPT

It's a mild October morning, slightly overcast but thankfully no suggestion of rain. It's only 10 o'clock and yet the tourists are packed three deep against the railings outside Buckingham Palace. They sense something special is happening as the Rolls-Royces, Daimlers and Bentleys glide up to the security gate and, with the slightest crunch of gravel, purr on into the courtyard. We join the queue apologetically in our Mazda.

At least we have a chauffeur. Lawrence Wood has volunteered to take the strain off Jeannie, the only driver in our family. The car is packed to bursting. Apart from the five of us, there are, following a late decision to be safe and not sorry, five overnight bags, the buggy – scrubbed and polished for the occasion – and my top hat and gloves. A surreptitious glance at some of the other guests prompts a sigh of relief that I don't have to take these with me. I'd been fretting for several days over how to carry them and my stick as well as drive the buggy.

We squeeze out of the car and stretch. Jeannie has been squashed between Adam and Dan on the backseat for the best part of an hour. She still looks amazing in a fitted black dress from the 1950s, which she has customised with large purple buttons. Purple gloves and a black hat with an artificial purple flower complete a stunning picture. The boys are in suits and my rented morning suit is surprisingly comfortable. Quite elegant, too, if I say so myself.

We assemble the buggy and utter a silent prayer of thanks when the light on the tiller shows green and the whole thing moves forward at the first pressure on a lever. They've laid on a ramp for wheelchair-users, looking slightly incongruous as it juts out into the immaculately swept courtyard. Once inside, where we are greeted by a young red-and-gold bedecked footman whom Adam rather irreverently addresses as 'mate', there's a slow and irritatingly ponderous stair-lift to take me up a half-level to the lift. As it inches deliberately upward, I can see a bottleneck forming behind me and feel horribly self-conscious.

Once out of the lift, we are separated. Jeannie, Adam and Dan head off to the Ballroom to be entertained by live music from the orchestra of the Welsh Guards while waiting for the ceremony to begin. (I learn afterwards that they amuse themselves with a game of 'Name that Tune' as the repertoire oscillates randomly between classical and popular tunes.) I'm led down an enormous portrait-hung corridor and shown into a side-room that's as big as a flat. I sip on a mineral water and drink in the grandeur of my surroundings: thick pile carpet, wood panelling, rich red velvet, and gold leaf everywhere. I chat to Andrew Motion, the Poet Laureate, who is to receive a knighthood. In the corner of my eye I catch a glimpse of celebrity hairdresser Vidal Sassoon, who is to become a CBE.

The Secretary of the Central Chancery of the Orders of Knighthood, to give him his job title – his full name and rank are only slightly shorter – strides briskly in to instruct us about protocol. He's tall, in an immaculate black and gold uniform, and he's obviously done this before. He rattles through the routine. We're to walk in order through the back of Banqueting Hall where our families will already be seated, and out the other side where a long anteroom will lead us up to another doorway at the top end of the hall. We're to move slowly forward until level with the first of the ushers. At a signal from him we're to move into the hall to stand in front of the second usher. On hearing our surname we are to advance five paces, turn, bow to the Queen and advance to the dais to receive our honour. We're not to advance too close – we're instructed just how far from the edge of the dais the tips of our shoes should be – and we're told how to address the Queen. We're assured that she will have a brief chat with each of us and that she will offer her hand to signal that the interview is over. We're then to step back five paces, bow and head out of the hall through a doorway opposite to the one we'd entered. In another long anteroom we'll collect the box for our medals, be notified if there had been any media requests, and be free to join our families for the rest of the ceremony.

Buckingham Palace is even bigger than I'd imagined, and the corridors are long. I'm glad I've brought my buggy but still slightly apprehensive that between leaving it at one side of the Ballroom and joining Jeannie, Adam and Dan after my investiture I will be a long time on my feet. Quite rightly, the palace officials have judged that the buggy wouldn't get close enough to the dais for the Queen not to be inconvenienced in putting the ribbon round my neck, and the other alternative is not acceptable. I'm told that a footman can push me down the corridors in a special palace wheelchair and I can receive my honour sitting down, but I've still got a thing about wheelchairs. I still regard them as a sort of last resort, and I reason that as I've spent so little time in one, it would be absolutely incongruous to be sitting in one during one of the greatest moments of my life. No, Michael the stick has supported me round the world. He deserves his moment of glory.

We take our place in the anteroom, those receiving knighthoods at the head of the queue, then the CBEs. A fanfare of trumpets announces the arrival of the Queen at precisely 11 o'clock. I catch a glimpse of a tiny figure in a blue dress and a colourful retinue of much larger figures who take their places as if in a tableau. There are Gurkhas in olive green, Yeomen of the Guard in red, gold and black, and uniformed officers from all the Armed Forces. The Master of the Household is an Air Vice Marshal from the RAF, standing by with a velvet cushion from which the Queen will take the relevant insignia. There's an equerry at her shoulder ready to prompt her about the recipients. I am somehow reassured that the Queen is carrying her trademark handbag and presume that there is an official whose sole responsibility is to look after it during the ceremony. Everything is ordered, measured, timeless. The National Anthem rings defiantly out. Everyone in the room stands proudly to attention, chests out, heads high, pride oozing from every pore of their bodies. The rich reds and golds of the furnishings, the majestic proportions of the hall, the uniforms and the soaring music create an occasion of unforgettable pomp and pageantry.

The queue edges slowly forward. The knights have been knighted, inductions have been made to the Royal Victorian Order and the Honourable Order of The Bath and the first CBEs have been invested. In a few seconds it will be my turn. The officer at the doorway tries to allay my nerves with a few cheering words. I'm concentrating on the ceremony in front of me, desperate to pick up any clues about how to behave in front of Her Majesty, and desperate to remember the instructions. How many paces? Do I bow before approaching the Queen, or after? What if I misjudge the distance and step too close to the dais? What will she say? What will I say? This is the most nervous I've ever been in my life.

'To be a Commander of the British Empire, for services to sport and to charity, Alastair Hignell...' I straighten my shoulders and try to look as if I'm not concentrating on my stick or my feet. After five paces, I turn and bow. I judge the distance to the dais perfectly. My toes are just touching the dais as I lean forward and the Queen hangs a medal on a rose-pink ribbon around my neck. As she adjusts it I can see that it is in the shape of a symmetrical light blue cross with both vertical and cross pieces ending in a three-point star and that there's a gold circle with a red rim in the centre of the cross. But I'm concentrating on our conversation.

'And what do you do?' she asked.

'Well. Ma'am, I played rugby for England, and first-class cricket, and then I was commentator for the BBC and now I'm patron of the MSRC charity...' I rattled the words out, anxious not to waste a millisecond of the time allocated.

'And how long have you been doing it?'

'Well, I played my sport for a decade, I was a commentator for 22 years and I've been involved with the charity for seven or eight years now...'

I could sense that her hand was beginning to move. Time for one last question.

'And have you enjoyed it?'
'Oh yes, ma'am, I've had a whale of a time.'
I really am a very lucky man.

ACKNOWLEDGEMENTS

For making this book happen

Andy Ward gave so much of his time, knowledge and expertise – reading, suggesting, correcting and guiding. Steve Friar persuaded the publishers to meet with me and provided invaluable advice. Charlotte Atyeo of Bloomsbury championed the idea and set the ball rolling. Her colleague Kate Wanwimolruk saw the project through. Copy-editor Julian Flanders weeded out the mistakes and misunderstandings. Richard and Leanne Baker retouched photographs that needed help and Rachel Wood supplied a treasured photo from my last day as a commentator.

For making me the man I am

My father, Tony and my mother Pat are wonderful parents – inspirational without being dictatorial, supportive without being smothering, proud without being pushy.

My brothers Rob, Steve and Ben and my sister Cathy have for over half a century been companions and friends as well as siblings. My sons Adam and Dan have for nearly three decades been a delight as well as a challenge. Now I am pleased to say, they have also become my mates as well.

For the good times

To cram all the things that have happened to me inside the covers of one book has meant that some of the key figures in my life have failed to get the credit they deserve. I take this opportunity to thank: housemates in Cambridge, Brian Christian and Phil Brook; England Schools and Cambridge teammate Paul Parker and his wife Tress. Housemasters at Denstone, Linton Stocks and Keith Clarke; John Watson, teammate at Bristol, who introduced me to Jeannie and, in place of her ill father, walked her down the aisle.

For the bad times

The world of sport in general and the world of rugby in particular have been incredibly supportive, generous and encouraging since my diagnosis with MS. It is impossible to do everyone justice and it would take too long to name them. I hope they know how grateful I am.

For all time

No one, I hope, would mind my giving another heartfelt tribute to my fantastic friend Ian Robertson and my wonderful wife Jeannie.

INDEX